POLISH-JEWISH RELATIONS DURING THE SECOND WORLD WAR

EMMANUEL RINGELBLUM

Polish-Jewish Relations
During the Second World War

Edited and with footnotes by

JOSEPH KERMISH
SHMUEL KRAKOWSKI

Translated from the Polish by

Dafna Allon, Danuta Dabrowska,
and Dana Keren

HOWARD FERTIG · NEW YORK · 1976

YAD VASHEM · JERUSALEM

FIRST AMERICAN EDITION

Library of Congress Cataloging in Publication Data
Ringelblum, Emmanuel, 1900-1944.
Polish-Jewish relations during the Second World War.
Includes index.
1.   Jews in Poland—Politics and government.
2.   Holocaust, Jewish (1939-1945)—Poland.   3.   Poland—
Politics and government—1918-1945.   4.   Ringelblum,
Emmanuel, 1900-1944.   I.   Title.
DS135.P6R495   1976   943.8'004'924   76-1394

Printed in the United States of America

CONTENTS

INTRODUCTION

by Joseph Kermish

The work by Dr. Ringelblum, "Polish-Jewish Relations During the Second World War", is beyond question one of the most finished pieces of research written according to the rules of research worked out in the Ghetto Archives *(Oneg Shabbat),* which in fact was not only a documentation centre but also constituted a clandestine Institute with Ringelblum at its head and supported by scores of active workers—researchers, writers, teachers, people in public office, members of the underground, and simple, ordinary Jews.

An outstanding public figure and fearless fighter, Ringelblum became one of the most popular and beloved personalities in the whole Ghetto, but he made an immortal name for himself as the creator of this clandestine archive, *Oneg Shabbat,* an immense undertaking unparalleled in history, which was and remains unique in the annals of the peoples over-run and enslaved during the Second World War.

Emmanuel Ringelblum was born in Buczacz (Eastern Galicia) on 21 November 1900. His mother died when he was 12 years' old. On the outbreak of World War I, he escaped with his family to Kolomyja and later to Nowy Sącz, where he completed his secondary education in 1919. Because his father was poor, he was obliged to work for his living by giving private lessons while he was still a pupil in high school. But poverty did not break his spirit—on the contrary it steeled his character and tempered his energies. Even then, in high school, he differed from the average pupil in his desire to acquire knowledge and spread knowledge among the masses of the people. He stood out in the Poalei-Zion (Zionist Socialist) group in his high school in Nowy Sącz; he devoured books on sociology, economics, Jewish history and literature. At the same time he himself conducted a study group of young workers and took part in the activities of the local Poalei-Zion branch.

In late 1919 he registered in the Faculty of Humanities in Warsaw University and studied history under Professors Jan Kochanowski and Marceli Handelsman, from whom he learnt the technique of historical work, and in particular the critical analysis of historical sources; his mentor in research on Jewish history was the great historian, Yizhak Schiper. Any time Ringelblum left over from his studies and private lessons he devoted to educational work in the Left Poalei-Zion Youth Movement (he was a member of the Central Committee of this youth movement). Together with Yaakov Kener, Josef Rozen, Yaakov Peterseil and Rafael Mahler, he helped to edit the paper of the Left Poalei Zion Youth Movement in Poland, *Freie Yugend.* He signed his articles Munio Heller (the family name of his mother, who died in the prime of life).

Ringelblum was one of the most popular and beloved figures in the Jewish students' movement, thanks to his devoted work in the academic group of Left Poalei–Zion, *Yugend,* and in running the Jewish Academic Club.

In 1927 Ringelblum was awarded a Ph.D. for his thesis on the history of Jews in Warsaw in the Middle Ages. He later spent a year in Vilna teaching history in Jewish secondary schools there. He also took part in the history department of *Yivo,* of which he was an active member from its foundation in 1925. He returned to Warsaw in 1928, and taught until 1938 in Polish-language secondary schools for Jewish girls.

In 1929 Ringelblum was drawn into work at the Mutual Aid Funds Centre (*G'milat Hasidim*) by Yizhak Gitterman, scholar and active *Yivo* member, director of the Joint in Poland. As editor of the monthly organ of the no-interest loan funds, *Volkshilf* (which went on appearing until early in 1944), Ringelblum gave proof of inborn organizing ability and initiative. The idea he strove to promote here was self-help by the Jewish masses as a means towards their becoming productive. He got excited over every beehive and every additional allotment in some remote little Polish town that had been made possible with the help of the Mutual Aid Funds Centre and on them he pinned hopes of making the Jewish communities productive on a large scale.

It was also at this time that his main activity in *Yivo* started. He was not only one of the most active scientific members of the historical department, to which he was elected at the first *Yivo* Convention in Vilna in 1929, but was also pre-eminent as an organizer. He re-organized the history study circle of the Jewish Academic Home, which he had created in 1923, as a hisorians' study group affiliated with *Yivo*. This group comprised the best young Jewish historians in Poland, a group unexampled anywhere else. Thanks to Ringelblum's ever-renewed initiatives, the group did not rest content with holding regular meetings, lectures and debates, but also published collected papers edited by their leading spirits, Rafael Mahler and Emmanuel Ringelblum, under the title *Yunger Historiker* (The Young Historians) in 1926 and 1929 and later as *Bleter far Geschichte* in 1934 and 1938. The researches published in these periodicals made an important contribution to Jewish historiography, being based for the most part on documents from Polish archives, in which were to be found previously unknown details concerning the history of the Jews in the cities of Warsaw, Lublin, Płock and Kutno in the 17th, 18th and 19th centuries.

Ringelblum also helped to found and build up the Warsaw branch of *Yivo*, where he developed an extensive system of science courses. The Historical Commission for Poland that was created by this branch of *Yivo* did important work under Ringelblum's guidance in registering the records of communities and societies throughout the country.

Alongside all his energetic activity in the Joint and in *Yivo*, Ringelblum kept up his cultural activity in the workers' movement. He worked for the press and was the organizer of the Party circle among the students. He helped work out programmes for the study of history in the Jewish school network, *Zisho*. He was also an active member of the executive of the Jewish writers' association, and from 1937 on he was one of the leaders of the *Ykof* movement in Poland.

In the trade union of Jewish secondary school teachers in Poland he was one of the people who helped to manage its affairs, taking the line of unremitting struggle against the anti-Semitic manoeuvres of the education authorities. On Ringelblum's initiative, the Jewish

Exploration Society organized courses and published regional monographs, including some he wrote himself.

From 1938 until the outbreak of World War II, Ringelblum was almost entirely taken up with his work for the Joint and had to leave off teaching in secondary schools. He left Warsaw for a number of weeks in order to organize aid to Jewish refugees from Germany in the Zbąszyń Camp. In the course of a few days, from the 28 October 1938 on, upward of 17,000 Polish Jews were arrested in Germany; they were thrust into special trains and sent off without any possessions and without any stops on the way across the frontier into Poland. Among them were about 5,000 unfortunates whose Polish citizenship the anti-Semitic Polish authorities refused to recognize and who were refused entry into the country; they remained suspended as it were between the frontiers of the two countries, in a closed camp in the vicinity of the town Zbąszyń in utterly desperate straits. On learning of the Zbąszyń tragedy, Ringelblum organized aid to the deportees together with the Director of the Joint, Yizhak Giterman and his fellow-teacher, S. Ginsberg.

With his remarkable organizing ability, Ringelblum set up an entire village with all the necessary economic departments for a settlement of 5,000 souls. Even more remarkable than this achievement itself was the aid system which he organized and the fields of activity it comprised and put into operation. Not philanthropy but self-help and independent action: thus, through a dozen people acting as emissaries of the aid committee Ringelblum succeeded in harnessing to the task some 500 of the refugees themselves, a tenth of the deportees. Ringelblum devoted his energy to organizing members of the youth movements, mainly pioneer youth, most of whom had been in different training centres in Germany and who were scattered in the Zbąszyń camp with their families; he gave these hundreds of youngsters essential work to do in extending aid and managing the various services. Cultural activity was as varied and as lively as the economic and organizational activity: reading rooms were established, a library with about 2,000 books, a school, language courses—including Yiddish and Hebrew, and there were concerts and theatre performances.

The Zbąszyń refugees appreciated Ringelblum as a faithful friend, and the friends he made in the camp kept in touch with him even after he returned to Warsaw.

A member of the historians' circle of the Warsaw *Yivo* branch, Meir Korzen, who helped Ringelblum in his work of aid to the Zbąszyń refugees, relates that in the camp Ringelblum organized and recorded testimony of the deportees relating what they had undergone at the hands of the Nazis in Germany and their suffering in the course of deportation. From Zbąszyń he brought home to Warsaw "crates full of material and quantities of notes" that he intended to work up when he had time. But war soon broke out and Ringelblum dedicated himself to recording the history of the terrible disaster that was befalling the Jews.

There is no question that Zbąszyń was a landmark in Ringelblum's life. He acquired a great deal of experience in public work which was to be of service to him later in his work in the Ghetto.

His first important work, "The History of the Jews of Warsaw up till the Expulsion in 1527", was published in 1932 by the Warsaw branch of the Polish Historical Research Society. It opened up new horizons in the history of the legal status of Jews, Jewish money-lending and in particular Jewish trading in mediaeval Poland and also partly in Lithuania. It also contained new discoveries concerning Jewish craftsmen, Jewish doctors and Jewish estate-owners. The book gave a largely new picture of the Jewish way of life in Poland in the Middle Ages and of the relations between Jews and Christians. Since Mazovia, the province of Warsaw, existed as an independent principality until 1527, the history of the Jews of Warsaw in the Middle Ages reflects the history of the Jews in the whole of Mazovia, a subject which previous to Ringelblum had been veiled in obscurity.

In 1930 Ringelblum, together with Rafael Mahler, issued two booklets in Yiddish and Polish, "Sources for the History of the Jews in Eastern Europe". His next researches into the history of Polish Jewry were concerned with modern times and he made valuable contributions to knowledge of their economic situation, political conditions and culture. His book, "On the history of Hebrew books and printing in Poland in the second half of the 18th Century", constituted an achievement as regards the legal and cultural aspects of Jewish social history. The conclusion reached by the author in this piece of research was that according to the statistics of books sold in the printing press at Nowy Dwór near Warsaw, the book trade was one of the channels through which the "Enlightenment" reached central Poland.

Ringelblum did pioneering work regarding the attitude of the various political trends in Poland towards the Jewish question, in an extensive essay on, "Jews seen through the Polish Press", published in 1932. This represented preparatory work for his brilliant research on, "Plans for the spoliation of the Jewish economic structure and attempts to carry them out in the period of the Kingdom of Stanislaw August" (1934). Here for the first time was a picture of the terrible impoverishment of the Jews of Poland at that time and particularly of the evicted tenant farmers and innkeepers. In this piece of research Ringelblum also traced the beginnings of the process of industrialization among the Jews, which led to the creation of the earliest cadres of Jewish workers in the factories. By an analysis of the way in which Jews became productive through agricultural settlement, in the light of archive records Ringelblum disclosed how widespread agriculture was among Jews in the villages and small towns as an auxiliary means of livelihood.

The history of Jewish craftsmen's societies was illuminated by an article of Ringelblum's on the Register of the Tailors' Society of Płock, also published in 1932 (in Vol. II of *Ekonomische Schriften* of *Yivo*).

In the last years before World War II, Ringelblum began to publish passages from the second part of his work, "The History of Warsaw Jewry" (up to the end of the 18th Century); the most important of these extracts was his research work, "Warsaw Jewry in the 18th Century and their socio-legal position" (published in Vol. II of *Historische Schriften* of *Yivo*), which depicted the illegal Jewish community of Warsaw, described the role and the authority of their spokesmen who interceded for them with the government administration and these people's methods of organization, exploitation and perversion of justice, which in many fields were even worse than the arbitrary rule of the despots in the legal Jewish communities.

Ringelblum's researches into the history of Warsaw Jewry also led to his book, "The Jews of Poland in the Revolt of Kościuszko", (*Yivo*, 1937), in which he described the part played by the Jews in the defence of the capital in the year 1794, as militiamen and guards, trench-diggers, espionage agents and army suppliers. In the social history of Polish Jewry, importance also attaches to the demonstration of the fact that the masses of the poor among Warsaw Jewry participated in the April rising, which saw the beginning of a rapprochement between Jewish and Polish common people, and also in the revelation of the sharp opposition manifested by poor Jews to their rich brethren, the financial magnates of the capital.

After delving deep into the history of Polish Jews at the beginning of the modern era, Ringelblum gradually turned to research on the 19th Century.

A special theme of his researches was the part of Polish Jewry in medicine and hygiene. In a series of articles published in the periodical, *Soziale Medizin,* based on archival and secondary sources, Ringelblum gave an account of Jewish medicine in the 18th and 19th Centuries. His articles on home industries, on apprentice craftsmen, on Jewish wearing apparel, on beggars and the very poor in the 18th Century in the light of court documents revealed a whole field of research that writers on the history of Polish Jewry before him had never touched on.

The vital interest for the present day of these social, political and cultural questions in Jewish life spurred Ringelblum to the most meticulous historical research, following in the footsteps of his teacher, Dr. Yizhak Schiper. The main aim of his work was to uncover the historical roots of contemporary Jewish ways of life in Poland. The stratification of Jewish social classes, the antecedents of the Jewish proletariat, the historical tradition of social struggle among the Jews, the first blossoming of modern thought and enlightenment, the coming into being of a Jewish intelligentsia, the history of rapprochement between Jews and Poles, the ways in which Jews became productive in theory and in practice in bygone times— all these things are known to us today more thoroughly and in fuller detail thanks to the research work done by Ringelblum.

Ringelblum drew from an inexhaustible fount of ideas in his scientific work; he was always bubbling over with new projects, and he never faltered under the burden of his public and professional tasks.

His teacher, guide and mentor in his scientific work was, as we have said, Yizhak Schiper, whom he admired and believed in all his life, but Ringelblum's view of history put more stress on the theme of the contradictions in society. He also differed from Schiper in his greater interest in contemporary life and in his liking for treating various historical questions in separate monographs. He not only relied on concrete phenomena as a way of illustrating a historical process but deliberately used this method as a principle of research.

His tendency to do research work and describe his results in the form of monographs aligns him to a certain extent as a historiographer with Prof. Balaban, in spite of all the contrasts in their historical outlook. These contrasts explain why Ringelblum speaks of him in an essay with gratitude and great appreciation as "the founder of the great structure of Jewish historiography in Poland" but at the same time does not spare criticism of the shortcomings in his writings: "The economic background is lacking. Balaban had no grasp of this, just as he was unable to reach a correct appraisal of the social contradictions prevailing in the Jewish community".

On the outbreak of the world war in September 1939, Ringelblum had not completed his 39th year, but he had already managed to do so much in the field of research that he was no longer seen as a "young historian"; his stature had become equal to that of the most eminent historians of Polish Jewry. Ringelblum's view that it was the duty of the historian to cover all aspects of life in his researches and writings, in full and without leaving anything out, was to bear fruit in the amazing scope of the research work that he organized in *Oneg Shabbat*. [1]

---

[1] Rafael Mahler, *Emmanuel Ringelblum*, published in "Yalkut Moreshet", No. 2/1964, pp. 6–16; Rafael Mahler, *Emmanuel Ringelblum historiker fun poylishe yidn in zeyer unkum un gevure*, published in "Historiker un vegvayzer", Tel Aviv 1967, pp.274–301; Rafael Mahler, *Mihtavey E. Ringelblum mezbonshin weal zbonshin*, published in "Yalkut Moreshet", No. 2/1964, pp.17–28; Rafael Mahler, *Mihtavaw shel Emmanuel Ringelblum megeto Warsha*, published in "Dapim leḥker hashoa wehamered",

In August 1939, on the eve of the war, Ringelblum was present at the Zionist Congress in Geneva as one of the Poalei-Zion delegates from Poland. Together with other members of the delegation, he managed to get back to Warsaw via Italy and Hungary. He returned to his post in the Joint, and together with a few remaining comrades assumed responsibility for the activity of his Party.

From the outbreak of war, Ringelblum was one of the most energetic initiators of Jewish social aid (called "Co-ordination" at the time). During the terrible siege of Warsaw, Ringelblum did not leave his post in the Joint offices for even a single day. Together with a few other public workers, he organized aid for the wounded, regardless of the rain of bombs and mortar-shells. Under the Nazi occupation, the social aid organization set itself the aim of alleviating the unspeakable suffering of the persecuted Jews, stripped and despoiled of absolutely everything, whose numbers steadily increased. Heading the "public department" of the Jewish aid institution, Ringelblum took upon himself the task of organizing tenants' committees in all the Jewish blocks of flats in Warsaw. This was before the Ghetto was set up, and the Jews were scattered all over the city. It should be remarked that as soon as these committees were appointed they turned into the main nuclei of material, moral and organizational self-help. The number of house committees in the Ghetto reached more than two thousand.

Ringelblum was also active as a lecturer at seminars of the clandestine *Hashomer Hatzair* and *Dror* Youth Movements, and in the Jewish Cultural Federation (*Yikor—Yiddische Kultur Organizazie*) which he helped to establish, with the aim of restoring Yiddish culture through the use of the Yiddish language in public life in the Ghetto. *Yikor* organized lectures, anniversary celebrations for Jewish writers, artistic gatherings, etc.

In the war years Ringelblum's stature increased with the ordeal of appalling stress and the weight of the immense burdens he assumed. The special mission which he saw himself called upon to accomplish

Series 2, No. 1, 1970, pp. 224–245; E. Ringelblum, *Miḥtaw le'Arnon Fishman-Tamir*, published in "Yalkut Moreshet", No. 2/1964, pp. 28–29; N.M. Gelber, *Historionim shel Warsha*, published in "Enẓiqlopediya shel galuyot Warsha", Volume II, Jerusalem 1959, pp. 345–346.

was to record for all time the annals of the martyrology of the nation in that epoch of horror.

His work for this undertaking, *Oneg Shabbat,* was the crowning achievement of all his tireless endeavours. He established the undertaking with the most meticulous care on a wide public foundation under the conditions imposed by clandestine activity, so that for over three years it remained concealed from all suspicion and its hiding places were not uncovered. The *Oneg Shabbat* workers managed to camouflage their collection of material while making contact with thousands of refugees in the small towns in the provinces. Only a few people who were in the secret knew that the material gathered for *Oneg Shabbat* was being used as the first-hand source for news-sheets that the archives personnel closest to Ringelblum were duplicating and distributing to public men and editors of underground papers, both Jewish and Polish. These weekly news-sheets, edited by the Archives secretary A. Gutkowski and H. Wasser, with their reliable information on the condition of the Jews and their liquidation, started appearing at the beginning of 1942, a time when the aim of the German murderers regarding the Jewish population of occupied territories was already sufficiently clear and must necessarily alert public opinion as to the intentions of the genocides. The material also served as a source of news for outside the country on the appalling things that were being done to the Jewish population.

The first comprehensive reports sent abroad in order to raise the alarm in world Jewry over the destruction of Polish Jewry were written by the heads of *Oneg Shabbat.* In March 1942 a memorandum was sent out on the Chelmno extermination camp, in April 1942 on the Lublin *Aktion,* in July 1942 on the condition of the Jewish population under the Nazi occupation, and after that, in November 1942, the first comprehensive, overall account of the first stage of the extermination of the Jews of Warsaw. This material was edited by Ringelblum, Gutkowski and Wasser.

"We sounded the alarm in the ears of the world with our accurate information on the greatest crime in history", wrote Ringelblum in a letter which he and Dr. Berman sent abroad.

Ringelblum himself had laid the first stones in the structure of the clandestine Archives as early as October 1939. As head of Jewish

Social Self-Help, Ringelblum maintained daily contact with emissaries from the provinces who came to the Joint to recount the trials and tribulations of the Jewish population. He recorded everything he was told, adding his comments later. Comrades who worked at his side at this time (Natan Eck, Meir Korzeń) extol his extraordinary degree of vigilance, his constant thirst for news and information, the fever that beset him to record the events taking place before his eyes. With the passage of time these daily notes became a work of hundreds of crowded pages covering the entirety of the problems and events that were the lot of the Jews of Poland in this period. The author of these notes made lavish use of camouflaged hints and shorthand terms because he was in fact preparing to use them himself for historical research on the life and death of the Jews in Poland.

In the course of time, when the team collaborating in *Oneg Shabbat* had become fairly numerous, Ringelblum changed over to weekly surveys and later to more comprehensive monthly ones and to essays or brief accounts such as the one on the wiping out of the Jewish intelligentsia, or on the Jewish police, or about "German war strategy with regard to the Jews", or on the bunkers. These essays were already attempts to evaluate and synthesise events and processes. The fact that he was one of the active leaders of the Jewish underground, whose contacts and emissaries reached everywhere in German-occupied territory, gave Ringelblum a wide field for observation and for gathering the evidence for his notes, surveys and essays. In these writings, the brilliant historian transmitted not only the experience of the individual Jew, mercilessly persecuted by the Germans and their accomplices, but traced happenings and personalities in Jewish community life in the underground.

To our great misfortune, a large historical and sociological monograph of Ringelblum's on Trawniki was burnt in the Polish rising in Warsaw in August 1944. However, many other valuable works of Ringelblum's have survived, those which he wrote in the Ghetto before April 1943 and afterwards, on the Aryan side in the bunker at 81 Grójecka Street, in the second half of 1943 and the beginning of 1944, such as biographical notes on Jewish scholars, writers, journalists, educators, lawyers, painters and musicians who were killed by the oppressor; there is also his essay on *Oneg Shabbat,* and his here published monograph on "Polish-Jewish Relations during the Second World War".

The documentary treasure of *Oneg Shabbat* was hidden in two places, at 68 Nowolipki Street and 34 Swiętojerska Street. While the first cache, the one at Nowolipki Street, was uncovered after many efforts in two stages, in the autumn of 1946 and in December 1950, the documents hidden in Swiętojerska Street are apparently irretrievably lost.

It is imposible to detail all the fields covered by the work of *Oneg Shabbat*: "They are as numerous and varied as our lives, with all their personages", said Ringelblum. What can be stated is that there was not a single important phenomenon of Jewish life during the war that was not reflected in the material garnered by Ringelblum and his colleagues, for *Oneg Shabbat* was not only a centre for documentation but also an institution conducting extensive clandestine research activity, and there is not a single area or aspect of Jewish life specifically in Poland that was not subject matter for *Oneg Shabbat.*

The most important wealth of material is represented by hundreds of monographs on towns and villages, written according to subject headings worked out by Ringelblum, and the system of recording documents and testimony which he devised, organized and developed. These monographs, whose existence was made possible by the daily contact between the Archives secretary, H. Wasser, and hundreds of fugitives and exiles from every corner of the country, covered every sphere of life: the most important events in local life in the period between the outbreak of the war and the deportation or liquidation of the community—such as, the entry of the German Army, pogroms, expulsions, atrocities committed on Jewish holidays, the community and its activities, social aid and economic life, the attitude of Germans and Poles to the Jewish population, religious life, labour questions and problems (labour camps, labour levies, hunting down people for forced labour, the *Judenrat* labour department, attitude of Germans to Jews in working hours), etc. There are other monographs written according to different patterns, but from them all emerged the same tragic picture of Jewish suffering in all the different places. A number of places had several monographs devoted to them, and some even had dozens each.

Beside comprehensive monographs, the Archives endeavoured to collect accounts of the more important separate events in the different towns from people who had been directly or indirectly involved, as participants or as witnesses or otherwise. The aim was to give every event the mark of immediacy of a real experience. For this reason the material of *Oneg Shabbat* is packed with subjective detail in accounts of the most dramatic experiences.

Oneg Shabbat was rich in diaries, in whose pages tragic events were recorded in the light of personal experiences. There were many people who wrote mainly diaries. Some of them kept complete diaries, others were content with short notes which they intended to write up fully after the war. Most of these diaries were destroyed when their writers were deported to their deaths in Treblinka and the writings they left behind them were wiped out with everything else that was theirs.

The daily notes of Ringelblum, and the later weekly and monthly ones, were preserved. They are particularly valuable for the first year of the war, when other people had not yet started keeping diaries. These notes not only contain material concerning the most important events of that period but evaluate what was happening. Given his work as a public servant, Ringelblum's evaluations constitute important testimony insofar as they express what Jewish public men thought about current questions of Ghetto life.

Research material of a special type was recorded in questionnaires prepared by Ringelblum and his assistants on social, economic, cultural and demographic questions; they used them frequently in order to enrich their collection of facts and to "catch"—in Ringelblum's expression—every phenomenon in Jewish life while still "live and fresh". Thus, for example, in the second half of 1941, a survey was conducted among the tenants of 92 houses, which produced important details concerning the economic situation of the Jewish population. At about the same time a second survey was carried out on food consumption, the main purpose of which was to study the level and the character of consumption among different strata of the population and to draw conclusions regarding the average consumption of every component of the Ghetto population. A study was made along with this of the value of the belongings that the Jews in the Ghetto had sold in order to supply their food needs at least to some extent.

An important place is held among these investigations by one carried out at the beginning of 1942 on "Two and a half years of war" on a representative sample basis, to find the answer to the basic question: "What do our educated people think, and what do the other strata of the Jewish people think of the experiences and the experiments of the war period and on the prospects for the future?" This question was put to 50 representative public men, men of letters, scientists, etc., members of tenants' committees and representatives of ordinary Jews: workers, skilled hands, trades-people, etc. We have only part of the answers, which provide faithful witness to the immensely dynamic and positive character of the Warsaw Jews, to their unshaken will to hold out and survive.

The work constantly expanded, the quantities of material collected piled up, yet the whole affair continued to be a secret of the underground. When valuable material had accumulated, the directorate of *Oneg Shabbat* was of the opinion that even if the time had not yet come for an over-all summation, at all events it was now their duty to summarize certain of the most significant processes and phenomena in Jewish life. It was this project that was called, "Two and a half years", since the need was felt to draw up a balance-sheet of Jewish life in Warsaw during the two and a half years of the war. This collective work, which started at the beginning of 1942, was divided into four sections: general; economic; culture, science, literature and art; and social aid. New forces were called in to help with this work, mainly experts in the various spheres. The work was intended to be of the magnitude of over 100 printer's sheets and was to constitute one of the most important documents of the war period.

Material was worked up on the following subjects: the Jewish police; corruption and false measures in the Ghetto; public life; educational institutions; religious life. A questionnaire was drawn up on the way persons active in Jewish cultural life during the war lived and produced their works. The scope of the rest of the subjects was very wide. They covered every field and all the most important phenomena in Jewish life: the legal situation, economic conditions, structural changes, smuggling deals, labour camps, relations between Jews and Poles, the attitude of the authorities to the Jews, questions of nourishment and health, problems of education and culture, religious life, phenomena of corruption and demoralization, the roles of the *Judenrat* and the police in respect to the Jews. Many of the writers had soon made good progress with their compilations; every collaborator had to hand over to the Archives the preparatory material that he had worked up, such as the biographies of young people on the basis of which the author was to write his general essay on the youth as a whole. Thus material of the greatest interest regarding various spheres of Jewish existence in the realities of war-time accumulated in the Archives.

However, at the moment when this work on "two and a half years" was about to become work on "three years", disaster descended on the heads of Warsaw Jews—the *Aktion* of 22 July to 15 September 1942. A beginning was made of collecting material on Treblinka. On the strength of stories told by people who had returned from various camps in outlying districts, an attempt was made to construct a picture of the experiences of Jews from the provincial towns during the great deportation, with the aim of trying to ensure that not a single fact concerning the life of the Jews during the war should remain hidden from the eyes of the world.

So too material reached the Ghetto Archives and was preserved there concerning the doings of the Jewish Combat Organization, the Jewish National Council, the Co-ordination Committee, as well as accounts written by members of the Jewish underground concerning sabotage actions and execution of death sentences on traitors. Finally, *Oneg Shabbat* continued its systematic collection of clandestine publications (manuscripts, newspapers, bulletins) of great value for the history of the passive resistance and mainly insofar as they prepared the ground for armed resistance in January 1943, as well as for the outbreak of the rising on 19 April.

In the final summing up, Ringelblum's Archives (including the Archives of the Jewish National Council) constitute a mine of information for documenting the holocaust and the uprising. The things that were written in the Ghetto are of the greatest value not only because they are live words of witness to the life of those years of abomination, but also for their disclosure of the stand made by those condemned to death, of their sense of history, of their deathless spirit. These works also lay bare whole chapters of the inside story of the Ghettos. In the absence of this material, the very memory would have been lost of many communities of which no official records remain. The clandestine archives are of inestimable importance for research into the story of the Ghetto, amply covering all the details of what happened, the background to events and personal experiences, in order to tear off the veil that covered the deed of extermination.

Thanks to Ringelblum, the heart and soul of the underground archives, with his outstanding professional stature, capacity for work and organizing ability, the stress in the work of *Oneg Shabbat* was not only on affliction and annihilation, but mainly on Jewish life under the conditions of threatened extermination, and first and foremost on efforts at resistance and the manifestations of Jewish will to fight in war and holocaust.

Ringelblum turned his enterprise into an efficient weapon in the hands of the underground. He saw it as one of the arms of the Jewish uprising, and it is noteworthy that during the stage of preparation of the armed uprising in the Ghetto, the Jewish National Council transferred to the authorities of the Polish underground the plan and the map of the hiding-places where the Archives were kept.

To our great misfortune, only a small, a very small part of the works written for *Oneg Shabbat* have been published. These valuable documents, practically all of them, still exist in manuscript only till today, in spite of the desire expressed by Ringelblum, "After the war it will be necessary to speed publication to the utmost". [2]

*

[2] Emmanuel Ringelblum, *Ktovim fun geto*, Vol. II, Warsaw 1963, pp. 76–102; Hirsh Wasser, *Archion hageto—mif'alo shel Dr. E. Ringelblum*, published in *"Yom Yiun lezikhro shel Dr. Emmanuel Ringelblum"*, Jerusalem, Yad Vashem, 1964, pp. 18–25; Joseph Kermish, *Archion "Oneg Shabat"*, op. cit., pp. 26–39.

The great deportation that began on the eve of Tisha B'Av 5702—22 July 1942—opened a new phase in the history of the Jews of Warsaw. The work of *Oneg Shabbat* also changed in character. At a time when people were in imminent danger at every moment of being caught and sent to Treblinka, it was impossible to think about systematic work in collecting material. Only a few writers, Ringelblum among them and Abraham Levin, learned to concentrate even in the midst of danger and horror, in the most appalling conditions, and carried on making their notes day after day. But the giant eviction to Treblinka also swept away and put an end to the writings of the diarists who remained alive, because of the repeated raids and round-ups and the constant sweeps through one street after another. When some kind of quiet returned, work began again energetically in *Oneg Shabbat* with the help of the remnant of writers who remained alive. Ringelblum developed his connections with representatives of the Jewish underground on the Aryan side. After the deportation he himself, sometimes accompanied by other emissaries of the Poalei Zion Party and the Jewish National Council, would join a group of workers going out to the Aryan side, and there he met the members of the underground at the risk of his life.

When Ringelblum was discovered in Trawniki Camp (we do not know the details of how he was caught during the rising and taken to this camp), rescue teams were sent there several times over, until in July 1943 a Polish railway worker, "Theodor" (Pajewski), accompanied by the Jewish contact "Emilka" (Shoshana Kossower), succeeded in getting him out of the camp in railwayman's clothes and bringing him by train to Warsaw. On the trip there were as usual endless controls and examinations of papers, and the slightest hesitation or sign of fear would have been fatal; Ringelblum carried off the journey faultessly, joking and making friends with all the passengers in the carriage. He was taken to the small flat of "Theodor's" sister in Radzymińska Street. Immediately after his arrival, Ringelblum told the Bermans the outline plan of the research work he intended to write about the camp. Two day's later, he joined his wife and son, whom he found in an underground bunker one which a number of public people on the Aryan side had had constructed under the greenhouses of a Polish market-gardener,

Mieczyslaw Wolski, at 81 Grójecka Street. In this bunker there were already 30 Jews. It was agreed that when a suitable flat had been found for Ringelblum on the Aryan side, he would join Jewish underground personalities who were active "on the surface" and would take part in their work. Moreover Ringelblum, a Nordic type with his fair hair, was not in fact obliged to be in hiding at all. But as time passed, Ringelblum and his colleagues came to the conclusion that his work as a historian was more important and that he should therefore stay in the bunker, keeping in touch with people outside by means of women "contacts". Thanks to his efforts, constant communication was set up with the clandestine leadership in Trawniki Camp, which after Ringelblum's escape comprised Dr. Szyfris and Advocates Szulman and Malinowski. Acting on information from Ringelblum about the attempts at resistance and preparations for a rising in the camp, an emissary of the Jewish National Council and the Combat Organization smuggled in a small quantity of arms and explosives, money and maps as well as medicaments to help fight the typhus epidemic that had broken out. The people in the camp planned a break-out to the forest, but on 3 November 1943 the camp was unexpectedly surrounded by a large number of cars with gendarmes and S.S.-men, and in a matter of hours all the prisoners were murdered.

Thanks to extensive correspondence with the camp before its liquidation, Ringelblum had been receiving historical reports according to the system he had established, under appalling conditions, during the three months he was in the camp. After he left, the camp diary was kept up by Advocate Szulman with records and descriptions of events in the Camp, mainly resistance activities, but also songs, anecdotes and "folklore".

It was in the bunker on Grójecka Street that Ringelblum wrote his work on Trawniki (some 200 note-book pages), the first historical and sociological work ever on one of the camps. The work opened with a description of the camp before the arrival of the Jews—it began as the site of mass murder of Russian prisoners; then came a punctilious analysis of the Jews in the camp according to age, occupation, sex, social background, the work systems in the camp (including the means of sabotage devised by the prisoners), daily life, sexual problems, social life, religion and culture. Unfortunately, as has already been related, this work was burnt during the Warsaw rising in August 1944. On the other hand, the work that Ringelblum wrote next, the one on Polish-Jewish relations during World War II, was saved and is in our hands, as well as an entire series of biographies of scholars: Prof. Meir Balaban, Dr. Yitzhak Schiper, Dr. Menahem Stein, Prof. Marceli Handelsman, Shmuel Adelberg, Menahem Linder, Dr. Lipowski, Shmuel Lehmann and others; writers, Yehoshua Perle, Hillel and Elkhanan Zeitlin, Israel Stern, including Polish-Jewish writers, Henryka Lazawert, Gustawa Jarecka, Wladyslaw Szlengel, etc.; pedagogues, Janusz Korczak, Dr. Shimon Lubelski, Yehoshua Brojde, Rosa Symchowicz, Natan Smolar, Aharon Koninski, etc.; public men and leaders of the underground, Shakhna Sagan, Yitzhak Giterman, Mordekhai Anielewicz, etc.; journalists, Aharon Einhorn, Ben-Zion Chilinowicz, and others; advocates, Leon Berenson, Alexander Margolin, etc.; and also actors, painters and so on.

Ringelblum pursued his work energetically all through the autumn and winter of 1943 to 1944. There was constant, indirect contact with Batya Berman through a Christian woman, a sister of the owner of the house on 81 Grójecka St. She would send Ringelblum letters, newspapers, etc., and get back letters and completed notebooks, the fruit of Ringelblum's labours in the bunker.

From time to time, Dr. Berman would visit the market-garden above the hide-out and Ringelblum would be allowed to go out and talk to her for a little while. Discussions took place on the need for Ringelblum to leave and to work "on the surface", since for him to remain in the bunker was extremely dangerous.

The year 1944 began badly for Jewish leaders leading clandestine lives. On 4 January, Dr. Berman fell victim to informers, Gestapo agents. The matter ended in his paying ransom and fleeing from his flat. For months, the Bermans were forced to move from one flat to another, but they continued with their secret work and kept in touch with the underground movement through "contacts". Obviously, contact between the Bermans and Ringelblum became more difficult. Finally, Ringelblum himself came to the conclusion that he should leave the hide-out and take up his post.

In February, the Gestapo uncovered traces of the Jewish Combat Organization, and the matter became urgent. The Commander of the Organization, "Antek" (Yitzhak Zukerman), was forced to go into hiding. "The place of both of them (Dr. Berman and Yitzhak Zukerman) was about to be taken by a man of energy and outstanding merit, Dr. Emmanuel Ringelblum," wrote Colonel Henryk Woliński, the A. K. (Home Army) representative with the Jewish underground to his superiors.

But it was not to be. On 7 March 1944 the blow fell. As a result of base betrayal, the Gestapo uncovered the hide-out.

In the bunker were found Ringelblum, his wife Judith (née Herman, before the war a teacher in the Jewish government school) and their only son, Uri, aged 13, as well as 35 more Jews, most of them people of means, and some of them members of the educated class.

The Gestapo knew who Ringelblum was, and they interrogated him and tortured him for three days in the cellars of the Gestapo Centre on Szucha Avenue to get information from him on the Jewish underground and its leaders. Ringelblum bore himself heroically and said nothing to the end. A few days later he was taken out to the Ghetto ruins and executed, after witnessing the murder of his wife and son. With him died all the other Jews taken together with him.

The last thing Ringelblum wrote is the now famous paper (which first saw the light in *Yivo Bleter,* Vol. 24, 1, Sept.–Oct. 1944, and was first published in Hebrew in the book by Neustadt) on cultural activities in the Warsaw Ghetto, on mutual aid institutions there and on "the marvellous epic of armed resistance". Ringelblum wrote this report while he was in the bunker, in collaboration with Abraham (Adolf) Berman, and he dedicated it to the Jewish Scientific Institute (*Yivo*), the Jewish PEN Club, and four personalities—the writers Shalom Asch, H. Leiwik, Y. Opatoshu, and the historian R. Mahler. This report, whose authors both considered it their testament, was completed on 1 March 1944, and on 20 May 1944 it was transmitted by Dr. Berman alone through the intermediary of the Polish underground to the Government-in-Exile in London. [3]

---

[3] Dr. A. Berman, *Yehudim bezad haari,* published in "Enzyqlopediya shel galuyot Warsha", Vol. I, Jerusalem 1953, pp. 724–730; Dr. A. Berman, *Meyemey hamahteret,* Tel Aviv, 1971, pp. 196–200; Batya Temkin-Berman, .

The problem of mutual relations between Jew and Poles in the period of the German occupation was already a controversial one during the war itself. The question constantly came to the surface as to whether Polish anti-Semitism, with its deep roots, was being attenuated or diminished.

The opinion held by the Jews in the Ghettos was that anti-Semitism had increased during the war, for the majority of Poles were pleased at the disasters that befell the Jews in the cities, towns and villages of Poland. There were Jews who felt that the Poles had received instruction and guidance from the Germans in aggressive anti-Semitism, and that Jew-hatred in its active forms—enclosing the Jews in Ghettos and confiscating their property—was henceforth in their very blood and bones. This belief was strengthened by various manifestations of Polish opinion regarding the Jewish question. In conversation Poles would affirm that after the liberation of their country from the incubus of occupation, there would arise a very serious problem of expropriated Jewish property. On no account were the Poles ready to give up the Jewish property transferred to them by the Germans.

The sharpest accusations against the Poles for their attitude to the Jews came from Mordekhai Tennenbaum, one of those who created the Jewish underground movement in occupied Poland, edited the clandestine papers, "News" and "The Call" *(Der Ruf)*, and commander of the Jewish Combat Organization in the Bialystok Ghetto. He saw on the Polish side "an attitude of hostility, anti-Semitism and extortion" and expressed his astonishment that there were still people "naïve enough to believe in the humanity of this hooligan nation, which rejoices that Hitler has cleared Poland of the Jews for them". Tennenbaum expressed the belief that "if it had not been for the Poles, for their aid—passive and active—in the 'solution' of the Jewish problem in Poland, the Germans would never have dared to do what they did. It was they, the Poles, who called out 'Yid' at every Jew who escaped from the train transporting him

Pan Rydzewski—yemaw ha'aharonim shel Ringelblum, in "Yalkut Moreshet", No. 2/1964, p. 12–16.

to his death, it was they who caught the unfortunate wretches, who rejoiced at every Jewish misfortune—they were vile and contemptible".[4]

It was not only the Jews who were always inclined to see the dark side of things and who expressed such views. Polish authors, and diarists were also of this opinion, adducing sufficiently numeorus facts as supportive evidence. Aurelia Wyleżyńska, a democratic public worker who was active in the underground, aided persecuted Jews and gave shelter in her flat to Jewish officers of the Polish Army, recorded in her daily notes, "A wave of anti-Semitism has engulfed the Polish people", and, "We are surrounded by a nest of wipers, characters from the underworld of crime", and, "For every hundred evil men it is hard to find even one noble soul".[5]

Adam Polewka, one of the righteous among the nations, writing to Michael Borwicz in 1946, declared, "A considerable part of the Polish people displayed an attitude of indifference towards the Jewish holocaust", and he recalled a saying among the Poles under the occupation, "The Germans will throw stones at Hitler dead, because he brought about the downfall of the German people, but the Poles will bring flowers to his grave as a token of gratitude for his freeing Poland from the Jews".[6]

On the other hand, numerous Jews were of the opinion that the war and the terrible blows the Germans inflicted on the country and all its inhabitants—Poles as well as Jews—produced a notable change in the attitude of the Poles towards the Jews and that most Poles were caught up in a philo-Semitic current. They based this view on a considerable number of facts. Many, many accounts from the small towns and villages, written during the war itself, described the warm attitude of the Polish population towards Jewish fugitives. Hundreds of instances were recorded of peasants who for months

4 Mordekhai Tennenbaum-Tamaroff, *Pages from the Fires,* Kibbutz Hameuhad, 1947, pp. 49–50.

5 Aurelia Wyleżyńska, *Z notatek pamiętnikarskich, 1942–1943,* published in "Biuletyn Żydowskiego Instytutu Historycznego" No. 45–46, 1963, pp. 215, 217, 226.

6 Adam Polewka, *To boli,* published in "W trzecią rocznice zagłady getta w Krakowie, Cracow 1946, pp. 159–160.

on end gave food and shelter to Jewish fugitives from small towns
nearby. Ringelblum, writing in his diary on 26 April 1941, speaks
of "bestial anti-Semitism", but in the same breath he points to the
diametrically opposite phenomenon—the rapprochement between
Poles and the Jews, famished and exhausted, to whom they extended
aid.[7]

In Warsaw, evidence accumulated testifying to the fact that at the
beginning of the war Poles were not indifferent to people wearing the
Jewish arm-band and showing that in many instances Poles displayed
warm-hearted sympathy for poor Jews, especially for Jewish child
beggars, to whom Christians gave enough bread and potatoes to
help sustain both them and their families.[8] This was further borne
out by the good relations that prevailed between Polish and Jewish
smugglers; Ringelblum came to the conclusion, "The cooperation
between smugglers on both sides of the wall was one of the finest
chapters occuring between Poles and Jews during the Second World
War".

Many Jewish authors who kept diaries or recorded their memoirs
gave the names of hundreds of Poles, righteous among the nations,
who loved their fellow-men and extended help to the persecuted
at all times with the utmost dedication. They restored the faith in
human nature which had been undermined by the many Poles who
cooperated with the Nazis in the extermination of the Jews.

A member of the underground on the Aryan side, "Wladka"
(Feigel Peltel-Miedzyrzecka), confessed that had it not been for the
help of choice spirits among the Poles, who endangered their own
lives in order to save Jews, the Jewish militants in the underground
would not have been able to maintain themselves and go on acting
either in the period of preparation for the uprising or in general
aid and rescue activities. She described some of the noble Polish
personalities whom it fell to her lot to meet. But at the same time
she pointed out that sad to say such upright, warmhearted Christians
were few in number ... "There is no doubt that more Jews would

---

[7] Emmanuel Ringelblum, *Ktovim fun geto,* Vol. I, Warsaw 1961, p. 251.
[8] H. A. Kaplan, *Megilat yesurim, yoman megeto Warsha,* Jerusalem 1966,
   p. 104.

have been saved if there had been more Poles who were men of heart and conscience".[9]

Ringelblum too sang the praises of dedicated Poles who risked their lives to save Jews. "Idealists", he wrote, "from among both the educated and the working classes, who saved Jews at the risk of their lives and with boundless self-sacrifice—there are thousands such in Warsaw and the whole country. The names of these people, on whom the Poland to come will bestow insignia for their humane acts, will forever remain engraved in our memories, the names of heroes who saved thousands of human beings from destruction in the fight against the greatest enemy of the human race."

It should be pointed out that after the liberation the authors who treated the subject of "Aryan papers" were also divided in their appraisals and their conclusions. There were authors who accused the Poles in the most extreme terms of having no wish to help Jews in hiding. But others, on the contrary, sang the praises of Polish devotion and self-sacrifice in rescuing Jews. It is obvious that both the former and the latter could adduce many unimpeachable proofs to support their conclusions. But for the most part these authors' appraisals and conclusions sprang from their personal prejudices or their political approach.

In the first post-war years, a great deal was written in Poland about the help that had been given by the Poles. Among the testimony witnessing to cases of aid to Jews in hiding there were descriptions and evidence that were not devoid of distortions and falsifications; those who compiled them did not hesitate to ignore some facts and inflate others in order to attribute all the positive phenomena of help for Jews mainly to the Communist Party.

A number of Jewish authors also wrote about the attitude of the Polish public to the problem of saving Jews in Poland under the Hitlerite occupation. Mention should be made here of the works of writers like Philip Friedman,[10] M. Borwicz,[11] T. Berenstein and

9 Wladka-Feigel Peltel-Międzyrzecka, *Meshney evrey haḥoma, ziḥronoteha shel kasharit,* Hakibbutz Hameuhad, Ghetto Fighter's Home, 1963, p. 181, 206, 211.

10 Philip Friedman, *Their Brother's Keepers,* New York, 1957.

11 Michael Borwicz, *Arishe papirn* (3 volumes, Yiddish), Buenos Aires, 1955.

A. Rutkowski,[12] Dr. Datner,[13] and others. The book by Wladyslaw Bartoszewski and Zofia Lewin[14] constitutes the first serious, documented attempt in Polish historical literature to present to the reader the effort made by part of the Polish public to extend aid to the Jewish population and to save it from the sentence of destruction pronounced against it. The editors had recourse, first and foremost, to the testimony, memoirs and accounts of Jews who were helped, in one fashion or another, by Poles. The book treats the various types of aid to Jews very thoroughly, covering the first days of the occupation, the period of the Ghettos and the time of the deportation to the death camps—unorganized, mainly spontaneous aid as well as the aid afforded by the Polish resistance movement through the intermediary of the "Council for Aid to the Jews". The personal experience of Bartoszewski in the Polish resistance movement and in the organized rescue of Jews undoubtedly adds weight to this work of his; most of his research and his writings are devoted to the organized aid activity of the war years, manifestations of solidarity with the Jews and the military assistance rendered them in their revolt.

As against this, no research has been done to throw light on the entire complex of relationships between Poles and Jews, research based on a wide range of testimony, and in the first place on Jewish and Polish evidence from the war period. A scientific treatment of this theme, wide as it is and the object of so much controversy, would require the publication of the most essential documents for a start, and the material regarding this problem that has been uncovered in the archives of the various sectors of the Polish underground— the "Home Army", the "Council for Aid to the Jews", the "Government Delegation", as well as the material to be found in the records of the Polish Government-in-Exile and the Commander-in-Chief, in the archives of the Jewish underground in the Warsaw and

---

[12] Tatiana Berenstein and Adam Rutkowski, *Pomoc Żydom w Polsce 1939–1945*, Warsaw 1963.

[13] Szymon Datner, *Las sprawiedliwych. Karta z dziejów ratownictwa Żydów w okupowanej Polsce*, Warsaw 1968.

[14] Władysław Bartoszewski and Zofia Lewin, *The Samaritans; heroes of the Holocaust*, New York 1970.

Bialystok Ghettos and in what remains of the archives of the political parties.

In 1952, the Jewish Historical Institute in Warsaw published the notes of Emmanuel Ringelblum; the editors falsified the nature of this important source by means of a large number of omissions and alterations. They suppressed many facts and appraisals of Ringelblum that mentioned "bad" Poles who rioted, pillaged and murdered or who were just plain anti-Semites.

Moreover, the trenchant passages from the diary of Mordekhai Tennenbaum-Tamaroff, in which the writer does not conceal his anger at the "hostile attitude . . . the anti-Semitism in every town, big and small, in every single place" (entries of 25 January 1943), have never been published in the Democratic Republic of Poland.

Only after the "thaw" of 1956 in Poland did the Jewish Historical Institute in Warsaw publish a series of documents on the relations between Poles and Jews. The Bulletin of the Institute also published Ringelblum's monograph on this subject in instalments, over the years 1958–1959, in Nos. 28–31, with not a few omissions and mistakes.[15] The Institute later published a Yiddish translations that had appeared in the "Bulletin" of the mangled Polish text in the second volume of Ringelblum's works.[16]

In this work, which covers the whole complex of Polish-Jewish relations in the period of the Hitler occupation, Ringelblum reveals the true countenance of the Polish underground as regards the Jews. He denounces the informers, extortionists and accomplices of the

---

[15] Thus the following important sentence was omitted: "The Council for Aid to the Jews was established on his (Dr. A. Berman's) initiative; while in fact it did not fulfill the hopes set on it, it did cover some 300 families living on the Aryan side whose existence depended uniquely on this Council". The list (drawn up by Ringelblum) of Jewish collaborators who were executed by order of the Jewish Combat Organization was also suppressed from the text without any explanations being given for the omission. Finally, the editors took the liberty of making innumerable changes in style, quite needlessly, and in many instances obscuring the clear language of the author.

[16] Compare too the German edition of Ringelblum's work, where just the same omissions and mistakes are to be found. See: Emmanuel Ringelblum, *Ghetto Warschau—Tagebücher aus dem Chaos,* Stuttgart 1967.

Hitlerite murderers, but of course he did not fail to give their due to those Poles who held out against the prevailing psychosis and who risked their lives to help Jews.

The basis for research on Polish-Jewish relations was laid in the clandestine archives of the Warsaw Ghetto, which were not only purely a centre for documentation but an institute for extensive research, carried on in secret.

Oneg Shabbat concerned itself in the first place with obtaining material on Jewish participation in the September 1939 campaign against the German invaders and on Jewish heroism in battle.

Ringelblum himself displayed a particular interest on the subject of reciprocal relations between Jews and Poles during the fighting and under German occupation. He was a veteran in research in this field, having written works such as, "The Jews seen through the Eyes of the Polish Press (in the 18th Century)" and "Jewish Participation in the Kosciuszko Rebellion" and thus possessing both the experience and the authority needed to deal with this theme. His detailed project comprised the following main chapter-heads, according to the main periods in the development of Polish-Jewish relations during the war: (1) the period of the September 1939 fighting, including the siege of Warsaw; (2) up to the establishment of the Ghetto; (3) the establishment of the Ghetto; (4) the Ghetto, up to the outbreak of war between Germany and Russia; (5) the period of the deportations and mass murder.

Questions were drafted under each chapter-head, typical questions in accordance with the circumstances of the period in question, directed to the crucial issues of the moment; the author, by means of this questionnaire of the project, aimed particularly at elucidating the attitudes of various strata of the Polish population, of parties, institutions and the like—the rise of anti-Semitic currents, their reflection in the Polish press and radio, in conversations about Jews overheard in the streets, in trains, and so on.

It is worth giving some of the chapter heads that exemplify the aim of the entire research project. In treating the stage of the German-Polish war, for example, the project gives the following guidelines for research, *inter alia*: "Reports and appraisals of the role of the Jews on the Polish-German front"; "participation of the Jews

in the works of public institutions and in civil defence"; "manifestations of Polish-Jewish fraternity in city streets". For the period
of the siege of Warsaw, Ringelblum sought to bring out the following, *inter alia*: "The Jewish role in the defence of Warsaw as seen
by the military, as reflected in the press and radio, and in the consciousness of various strata of the public"; "the assistance organized
by the Jewish population for the care of wounded soldiers, victims
of the fires and other fugitives, without religious distinctions (the
various kinds of public assistance, concrete examples)"; "rumours
and stories about Jews during the siege, particularly those dealing
with speculators"; "stories about Jews' being to blame for the fall of
Warsaw, in the view of reactionary elements"; "looting of Jewish
shops in the last days of the siege"; "tremendous increase in anti-
Semitic feeling in the period between the surrender of the city and
the entry of the German forces".

As regards the period under German occupation up till the establishment of the Ghetto, Ringelblum indicates that it is desirable
to examine: "Policies of the German authorities directed towards
undermining relations between Poles and Jews"; "German anti-
Semitic propaganda, its forms and its results"; "Polish-German collaboration in persecuting the Jews". Ringelblum includes the question
of the January 1940 pogrom in this connection: "its course, background, reactions in the street, stand taken by the Polish public and
parties". On the other hand, he was of the opinion that due attention
must be given to something very important at that time, economic
cooperation between Poles and Jews; "Poles as representatives of
and partners in Jewish firms"; "business connections between Poles
and Jews". Besides all these there remained a question which has not
yet been cleared up, "The sad chapter in the record of Polish medicine and public health with regard to the Jews".

For the third stage, the period of the establishment of the Ghetto,
Ringelblum's project included, *inter alia*, clarification of the following questions: "The attitude taken by Polish factors to the establishment of the Ghetto"; "the struggle over boundaries" (that is, the
boundaries of the Ghetto); "exchanges of flats and their exploitation
on the part of Christian tenants"; "the role of Polish reactionary
economic circles in the creation of the Ghetto (the part played by

the Merchants' Association, memoranda of the Polish Artisans)";
"what Polish circles accumulated capital as a result of the creation
of the Ghetto"; "Jewish property entrusted to the keeping of Polish
friends"; and finally, "the problem of Jewish converts to Christianity
and the family tragedies bound up with the creation of the Ghetto".

In the subsequent period as well, "from the establishment of the
Ghetto up to the outbreak of the German-Soviet War", the author
of the project wanted to bring out negative phenomena as well as
and alongside positive manifestations. Among the latter, in his opinion, were, "Polish-Jewish cooperation in smuggling"; "economic cooperation between Poles and Jews—the form, nature and scope of
busines connections"; "signs of feelings of pity shown towards Jews
outside the Ghetto", and finally: "attitude to Jewish beggars outside
the Ghetto walls". Among the negative phenomena he lists: "Theft
of Jewish property, extortion, corruption, collaboration between
Polish Police and the Gestapo"; "the attitude and the behaviour of
the Polish Police towards Jews caught outside the Ghetto", and
"the chapter of hooliganism along the Ghetto walls".

The fifth period, from the outbreak of the German-Russian war
up to April 1942, was characterized by, "Ascendancy of German anti-
Semitic propaganda (its forms and nature)", and thereafter, "The
physical extermination of the Jews—repercussions among the Polish
public; stand taken by workers, artisans, merchants, smugglers, pedlars, and members of the educated classes".

Another objective of the project as planned was to collect material
to show how much the Polish population knew about the German
authorities' planned policy of extermination of the Jews and in what
way the Polish parties in the underground reacted; thereafter—mutual relations between Jews and Poles in the provincial towns and
rural areas; and finaly—the question of the converts in the Ghetto
and still other questions designed to clarify the subject in all its
aspects and from every point of view.

Ringelblum's large monograph, "Relations between Poles and Jews
during the Second World War" (three note-books, in Polish, 217
pages) was written after the final liquidation of the Ghetto, on the
Aryan side, during the second half of 1943, according to the
chapter-heads worked out previously by the author and by the

documentation centre built up by him. This monograph, which was preserved in the Jewish National Council archives (founded by Abraham and Batya Berman) includes not only views and appraisals but also an abundance of factual details, which were known to the author at first hand, the evidence of his own eyes and ears, in the course of his daily contacts with hundreds of public figures, Jews and non-Jews.

Also preserved in the *Oneg Shabbat* archives is a chapter of a work on the theme of mutual relations between Poles and Jews in the period September 1939 to April 1940. In the main, the author treats the trends of thought and feeling among Poles, members of the educated classes, and their attitude towards the Jews; his sources are conversations with representatives of the parties (*Sanacja, liberals, and Endecja*).

Considerable importance is also attached to the over-all survey drawn up by Stanislaw Różycki, "Relations between Poles and Jews" in which the stress is placed on the attitude of various strata of Polish society—police, officials, merchants, the masses of the people— towards the Jews.

The author and journalist, Peretz Opoczyński, too, in the interesting descriptions in his wide-ranging notes, *Goyim in Geto,* discusses economic cooperation between Poles and Jews.

In another work, which was apparently written by the historian Dr. Malowist, and which was also done for *Oneg Shabbat,* on "Assimilated and converted Jews in the Ghetto", interesting remarks are to be found and insights concerning the Polish intellectual elite of Jewish origin that was shut in the Ghetto, and its views on relations between Poles and Jews. Mention should also be made of a series of notes, testimonies and writings on the role of Jews in the September 1939 fighting, on relations between Jewish soldiers and their Polish opposite numbers in German captivity, on the many types of economic cooperation and the like.

Finally, a noteworthy contribution to the subject is comprised in the testimony recorded by Shmuel Breslaw, one of the active members of *Oneg Shabbat,* in the course of interviews with a well-known Polish public figure, a woman. Breslaw, who recorded her testimony, was one of the men who shaped the Jewish underground in Poland.

He was a member of the movement led by Mordekhai Anielevicz, his friend and close collaborator in the underground and war, one of the outstanding publicists of the illegal press; had been in charge and of all publications of original material by the *Hashomer Hatzair* movement, personally editing most of them—writings and bulletins in Polish and Yiddish and a few even in Hebrew, intended for the movement and the general public as well. In this testimony edited by Shmuel Breslav for *Oneg Shabbat* there are recorded the conclusions and evaluations of Poles in every walk of life regarding the whole question of the Jews and the Ghetto.

Ringelblum points to the decisive change that took place in Polish-Jewish relations at the beginning of September 1939, when "anti-Semitism" as an instrument of Hitler's for disrupting Poland vanished off the face of the earth". Unfortunately, this state of affairs did not last for very long, for defeat on the battlefield and the need to find a scapegoat brought anti-Semitism back to life and in Warsaw, for example, led to Jews' being taken out of general army units and to the establishment of special Jewish unarmed battalions, intended only for work on fortifications.

These anti-Semitic trends, whose existence was already felt in the last days of the Polish State, flared up afresh in the prisoner-of-war camps, where Jewish soldiers suffered even worse at the hands of their Polish comrades-in-arms than they did from their German tormentors. In Doessel, on the initiative of the Polish prisoners of war, a Ghetto was set up for the Jewish prisoners. At Woldenburg P.O.W. camp Polish Fascists permitted themselves the pleasure of ridiculing their officers of Jewish origin.

Plenty of facts like these are related in the stories of their experiences told by prisoners of war and preserved in the archives of *Oneg Shabbat*.

*

Finally, it is worth asking where Ringelblum found the material for the many-faceted, extensive descriptions in this essay of his, the most pithy and concentrated of all his articles and essays on the holocaust. The writer affirms at the beginning of his work that he is making an effort to be absolutely objective, that he undertakes the task after much preparation and with reverent fear like that of a scribe of Holy Writ who takes a ritual bath to purify himself before beginning to write a Scroll of the Law. No wonder then that he writes to the point expressing the feelings burning within him in a simple and even restrained style. It is certain that he makes use of every source available at the time, legal and otherwise, for we see that in spite of all the edicts and restrictive regulations, the Warsaw Ghetto was in touch with other Ghettos, with various labour camps and with the Aryan side as well—with well-known personalities and representatives of the democratic parties. The same is true of the underground press which Ringelblum quotes from (often from memory only) as well as the official and German and Polish press. He more than once makes use of letters received by private individuals.

Another source of Ringelblum's information was the news brought by illegal couriers sent by the underground organizations from Ghetto to Ghetto, and in the first place the courageous young women, looking Polish or Ukrainian and carrying Aryan papers, who moved backwards and forwards from town to town in occupied Poland, and brought material back for the *Oneg Shabbat* archives. Another source was information from uprooted Jews, some of them from outside Warsaw, some from small towns nearby and some from places further off—Lodz, Lwow, etc.—who wandered from place to place, mostly by illegal means.

With the help of documents we have been able to illuminate and complete some details that were insufficiently clear in the text because of the brevity imposed on Ringelblum by the stress of events and emergency conditions. The documents have also made it possible for us to give the whole story in matters where Ringelblum could not write fully.

Finally, if we try to analyze and evaluate how far Ringelblum's information was accurate and his conclusions just, we can only wonder at his grasp and range and conclude that he was excellently well informed on the whole subject. Nevertheless, in reading his work we must not forget that what we have before us is not a finished historical work, for the author recorded his facts and his judgements in this concentrated, compressed fashion with the idea that he would be able to work them up and complete them afterwards. There is no doubt that he would not have published this work in its present form, but would have completed it by filling out some of the passages, by polishing and correcting. All the same, this work, unparalleled in its range and its sense of responsibility for the truth in history as it really was, constitutes a testimony to human courage and a memorial for the Jewish historiography of that terrible period.

1

POLISH-JEWISH RELATIONS
DURING THE SECOND WORLD WAR

NOTES AND OBSERVATIONS

When a *sofer*—[Jewish] scribe—sets out to copy the Torah (the Pentateuch), he must, according to religious law, take a ritual bath in order to purify himself of all uncleanness and impurity. This scribe takes up his pen with a trembling heart, because the smallest mistake in transcription means the destruction of the whole work. It is with this feeling of fearfulness that I have begun this work with the above title. I am writing it in a hide-out on the Aryan side. I am indebted to the Poles for having saved my life twice during this war: once, in the winter of 1940, when the blessed arm of the Polish Underground saved me from certain death, and the second time when it got me out of an S.S. labour camp, where I would have met my death either in an epidemic or from a Ukrainian or S.S. bullet.[1] I, in my own person, am concrete evidence of the lack of truth in the assertion made by

---

1 On 19 November 1940 Ringelblum noted down that a letter denouncing him to the Gestapo had come into the hands of two Polish workers in the Post Office, who told him that they had prevented the letter from reaching its destination. After this, Ringelblum went into hiding for a time. (Emmanuel Ringelblum, *Ktovim fun geto, Vol. I (Togbuch fun Warsheyer geto)*, Warsaw 1961, p. 183.)

At the beginning of August 1943, Ringelblum was got out of the Trawniki concentration camp and brought to Warsaw by a regular courier and envoy of the Council for Aid to the Jews, the Polish railway worker Teodor Pajewski, and a brave young Jewish girl, "Emilka" (Shoshana Kosower).

(Rahel Auerbach, *Bemeḥyzato shel Dr. Ringelblum*, in "Enẓiqlopediya shel galuyot Warsha". Part Two, Jerusalem, 1959, p. 351.

Batya Temkin—Berman, *Pan Rydzewski—yemaw ha'aharonim shel Ringelblum*, in "Yalkut Moreshet," No. 2, May 1964, p. 14.

some Jewish circles that the whole Polish population rejoiced over the destruction of Polish Jewry and that there are no people on the Aryan side with hearts that bleed and suffer over the tragic fate of the Jewish people in Poland.[2] On the other hand, Polish circles may be hurt when I say that Poland did not reach the same level as Western Europe in saving Jews. I am a historian. Before the war I published several works on the history of the Jews in Poland. It is my wish to write objectively, *sine ira et studio*, on the problem of Polish-Jewish relations during the present war. In times so tragic for my people, however, it is no easy task to rise above passion and maintain cool objectivity.

I myself am a victim of Nazism: my two sisters and their families, my only brother and his family, four brothers-in-law and their families, not to mention close and distant relatives and no less beloved friends and colleagues, have been taken from me. I am writing this while this murderous war is still going on and the fate of the remaining European Jews is still unknown. The material on

---

[2] Ringelblum more than once, in entries in his diary and in his general surveys as well, records the evaluations and conclusions of numerous Jews in the Ghetto on the subject of relations between Jews and Poles. The opinion was quite widely held in many circles that anti-Semitism increased immensely under the occupation and that the great majority of Poles were pleased at the catastrophes that befell the Jews. (Ringelblum, op. cit. Vol. 1, pp. 189, 251, 3322, 379.)

These circles considered that the Poles took lessons in anti-Semitism from German precept and example, and that Jew-hatred in the practical form of Ghettos and confiscations penetrated to their very bones. (Abraham Lewin, *Mepinqaso shel hamore me "Yehudiya"—Geto Warsha*, Beyt Lohamey Hagetaot, 1969, p. 74.)

On the other hand, we possess excellent documentary evidence on Poles who were ready to face danger and dedicated themselves to saving Jews. In an entry in his diary on 26 April 1941, Ringelblum speaks of bestial anti-Semitism, but in the very same place he notes completely contrasting phenomena—Poles' making sacrifices to save Jews from starvation. More than one of the accounts collected in the "Oneg Shabbat" Archives records the sympathy for Jewish fugitives manifested by the Polish population, and hundreds of cases are on record of Polish peasants' giving food and providing cover for Jewish fugitives from nearby small towns for periods of many months. (Ringelblum, op. cit. Vol. I, p. 251.)

which this work is based is as yet too fresh, too unripe, to permit objective judgement by a historian. Much official information, press material and the like, which will be needed to supplement this work after the war—all this is still lacking.[3] The views given here express the feelings of certain circles among the handful that were rescued from the slaughter of a whole people. As such they will be a contribution to the future historian's history of the Jews in Poland during the World War.

*

Of the nine million European Jews, only two to three millions are left; of the three and a half million Polish Jews only a quarter

---

[3] The historian of today has at his disposal very rich documentary material on this topic. Besides the underground archives of the Warsaw Ghetto founded by Ringelblum (often referred to as the Ringelblum Archives) and the files of the underground press, to which Ringelblum had only partial access, there exist the following basic collections of documents:
1. The records of the Polish Government-in-Exile and its agencies, in the Archives of the General Sikorski Institute and in the Archives of the Polish Underground Movement Study Trust (both in London).
2. The records of the Polish Government Delegate for the Homeland, in the Archives of the Institute for the History of the [Communist] Party (in Warsaw).
3. The records of the Armia Krajowa (Home Army) in the Archives of the Institute for the History of the [Communist] Party (in Warsaw).
4. The records of I. Schwarzbart, member of the National Council of the Polish Republic, in the Yad Vashem Archives (Jerusalem).
5. The records of "Zegota" (the Council for Aid to the Jews) in the Archives of the Institute for the History of the [Communist] Party (in Warsaw).
6. The records of the Council for Matters concerning the Rescue of the Jewish Population in Poland, in the Archives of the Polish Underground Movement Study Trust (in London).
7. The records of the Jewish National Committee.
8. The underground Archives of the Bialystok Ghetto, in the Yad Vashem Archives (Jerusalem), and in the Archives of the Jewish Historical Institute (in Warsaw).
9. Collections of eye-witness reports and memoirs, mainly in the Archives of Yad Vashem, of Kibbutz Lohamey Hagetaot, and of the Jewish Historical Institute in Warsaw.

3

of a million is left,[4] and it is still unknown what their fate will be in the near future. Millions of Jews all over the world, especially Polish Jews abroad, and the whole world with them, are asking how the Polish people behaved during those tragic days when millions of Jews trod a path of torment far worse than Golgotha to Treblinka,[5] Belzec,[6] Sobibor,[7] Auschwitz[8] and Chelmno.[9] What

---

[4] These statistics about Polish Jewry are on the whole accurate. According to fairly reliable data published by the Polish underground movement in the clandestine paper, *Polska*, on 23 September 1943, the number of Jews still alive in mid-1943 in the whole of Poland (frontiers of 1938) amounted to about 300,000, of these 15,000 in Warsaw; 80,000 in the Lodz Ghetto; 5,000 in Lwow; 8,000 in Cracow and Plaszow; 12,000 in the Vilna Ghetto; 20,000 in the Bialystok Ghetto; 1,000 in Czestochowa; 30,000 in Bedzin and Sosnowiec; 5,000 in Tarnow; 24,000 in the forced labour camps in the Lublin region; 20,000 in smaller centres in the Galicia district; 8,000 in the smaller centres in the Cracow district; 12,000 in Auschwitz concentration camp; 50,000 in hiding in the forests and villages.

The author's estimate of the number of Jews in the whole of Europe is less accurate, on the other hand. In May 1943, that is, a year before the annihilation of Hungarian Jewry, there were actually more than four milion Jews still alive in Europe as a whole.

[5] Treblinka (north-east of Warsaw)—mass extermination camp for Jews. Constructed in July 1942, it existed till 2 August 1943, when a revolt of Jewish prisoners took place. About 700,000 Jews were murdered in gas chambers in this camp. In the neighbourhood of this extermination camp, the exact name of which was Treblinka II, there was a penal labour camp, called Treblinka I, built in September 1941, through which about 10,000 prisoners passed, mainly Poles, of whom about 7,000 perished.

[6] Belzec (District Lublin)—mass extermination camp for Jews. Functioned as a forced labour camp for Jews from June to December 1940. In March 1942, an extermination camp was set up here, with gas chambers and crematorium, which functioned till early in 1943. A likely estimate of those murdered in this camp is 600,000 Jews and 2,000 Poles.

[7] Sobibor (District Lublin)—mass extermination camp for Jews. Existed from March 1942 to 14 October, 1943, when a revolt of Jewish prisoners took place. The number of Jews murdered in this camp is estimated at about 250,000.

[8] Auschwitz—in Polish, Oswiecim—the largest Nazi mass extermination camp and a concentration camp at the same time. Set up as a concentration camp, Auschwitz I, in May 1940. The mass extermination

the Polish people is suffering at the hands of the German oppressor is universally known: Auschwitz and Majdanek,[10] Dachau[11] and

camp, Auschwitz II Birkenau (in Polish, Oswiecim-Brzezinka), was constructed from January 1942 on. It is impossible to fix the exact number of Jews murdered there between 1942 and 1944. Historians give different estimates, varying from one to two and a half million Jews. Besides the Jews, anything up to 20,000 Gypsies were also murdered in Birkenau. During the period of greatest activity, 20,000 persons were killed every day. As in other Nazi extermination camps, the victims were taken straight to the gas chambers without being registered, and no records were kept of them. Apart from these unregistered victims of the gas chamber, a total of 405,000 registered prisoners of various nationalities passed through Auschwitz, 340,000 of whom perished there.

(H. G. Adler, H. Langbein, E. Lingens-Reiner, *Auschwitz: Zeugnisse und Berichte,* Frankfurt-am-Main, 1962. L. Adelsberger, *Auschwitz: Ein Tatsachenbericht. Das Vermächtnis der Opfer für uns Juden und für alle Menschen,* Berlin, 1956. J. Sehn, *Konzentrationslager Oswiecim-Brzezinka (Auschwitz-Birkenau) auf Grund von Dokumenten und Beweisquellen,* Warsaw, 1957. O. Kraus, E. Kulka, *The Death Factory: Document on Auschwitz,* Oxford, 1966.)

9 Chelmno on the Ner—in German, Kulmhof, north-west of Lodz, the first mass extermination camp for Jews on Polish territory to be equipped with gas chambers and a crematorium. This camp operated from 8 December 1941 till April 1943 and was set working again for some months early in 1944. About 360,000 Jews, mainly from the western territories of Poland that had been annexed to the Reich, as well as some thousands of Gypsies were murdered in this camp.

(Władysław Bednarz, *Oboz stracen w Chelmnie nad Nerem,* Warsaw, 1946.)

10 Majdanek, a concentration camp and mass extermination camp in a suburb of Lublin. It was also called Lublin Concentration Camp. It was set up in the autumn of 1941, first as a camp for Soviet prisoners-of-war and afterwards as a concentration camp. About 300,000 registered prisoners passed through this camp, mainly Jews and Poles, of whom 160,000 perished, From May 1942 on, the camp also became an extermination camp for Jews; about 200,000 Jews who were not registered at all were murdered there. The greatest slaughter of Jews took place on 3 November 1943, when the Nazis shot about 18,000 persons.

11 Dachau, a concentration camp in Bavaria, was set up in 1933 and existed until the liberation by American forces on 29 April 1945. A

5

Oranienburg,[12] this and other places where all that is best in Poland is being tormented and tortured to death are known far beyond the borders of this country.[13] And yet, in spite of the Polish people's sufferings, the world asks: What did the Poles do while millions of Jews were being led to the stake? What did the Polish Underground[14] do, what did the Home Plenipotentiary of the Polish Gov-

---

total of 160,000 prisoners were registered as having passed through this camp. A very considerable proportion of them perished.

[12] Oranienburg (near Berlin) was one of the earliest Nazi concentration camps in Germany, set up in 1933. It was transferred to nearby Sachsenhausen in 1936, and from then on it was referred to as the Sachsenhausen-Oranienburg Concentration Camp.

[13] Total Polish losses—Jews and non-Jews—are estimated by Polish research workers at 6,028,000 persons, of these about 3,200,000 Jews (90% of the total Jewish population) and about 2,800,000 non-Jews (12% of the total non Jewish population). As regards the non-Jewish Poles, the Nazi terror was directed particularly against the intelligentsia. One of the first terror operations against the Poles was the so-called *Aktion A-B—Ausserordentliche Befriedungsaktion*—in which the Germans murdered about 3,500 representatives of the Polish intelligentsia. In all, in the years of German occupation in Poland 28.5% of the professors, lecturers and teachers in institutions of higher learning were murdered, as well as 27.2% of the Catholic clergy.
(See: *Straty wojenne Polski w latach 1939–1945,* by a joint authorship of: J. Gumkowski, K. Leszczynski, E. Rogozinski, J. Szafranski, D. M. Lewandowska, A. Symonowicz and Sz. Datner, Poznań 1962.)
The Government Delegate's agencies in Poland systematically kept the Government-in-Exile informed about the Nazi terror against the Polish non-Jews in its full dimensions. Through the intermediary of the Polish Government, a steady stream of information reached the governments and peoples of the free world. The peoples of England and the United States received accurate news about this terror in publications of the Polish Ministry of Information in London, and notably in the pamphlet, *The German New Order in Poland,* published in London in 1941, which contained detailed information on German atrocities against the non-Jewish Poles up to the middle of 1941.

[14] By the term, "Polish underground," the author means the clandestine Polish organizations linked with the Polish Government-in-Exile, the seat of which was first—from October 1939 to May 1940—Angers near Paris and after that London. These organizations were directed and their activities co-ordinated on behalf of the Polish Government-in-Exile by the Office of the Government Delegate for the Homeland, a

ernment [-in-Exile] and his agencies in the provinces do, in order to save at least some of their citizens of Jewish nationality? The Polish and Jewish peoples have lived together on the same soil for a thousand years. What did our neighbours do, the moment when the invader, armed from head to foot, attacked the most defenceless people of all, the Jews? When the victims of Nazism fled from the ghettos to the so-called Aryan side, were they afforded asylum despite the prevailing terror, or was the asylum provided only if amply paid for and then withdrawn when the funds were insufficient? In this country where Jews contributed so greatly to the development of commerce and industry, in this country where Jewish labour built houses and factories, workshops and businesses, where whole branches of production were developed over many centuries thanks to the toil of generations of Jews, was all this— the whole world asks—given any thought at the time of greatest danger for Poland's Jews? The Polish people and the Government of the Republic of Poland were incapable of deflecting the Nazi steam-roller from its anti-Jewish course. But the question is permissible whether the attitude of the Polish people befitted the enormity of the calamities that befell the country's Jewish citizens. Was it inevitable that the Jews, looking their last on this world as they rode in the death trains speeding from different parts of the country to Treblinka or other places of slaughter, should have to see indifference or even gladness on the faces of their neighbours? Last

---

clandestine representation of the Polish Government in the occupied country. The qualified advisory body of the Delegate's Office was the *Polityczny Komitet Porozumiewawczy* (Political Co-ordinating Committee), the name of which was changed to *Krajowa Reprezentacja Polityczna* (Homeland Political Representation) in March 1943. It was composed of representatives of the four main Polish political parties: *Stronnictwo Narodowe, Stronnictwo Pracy, Stronnictwo Ludowe* and *Polska Partia Socjalistyczna.* The Government Delegate's Office set up regional and district agencies as its branches in the provinces of the homeland. No representatives of the Jewish population or of Jewish political organizations were included in either the Government Delegate's Office or its provincial branches. This fact decidedly hampered the development of the Jewish resistance movement and limited its possibilities.

summer, when carts packed with captive Jewish men, women and children moved through the streets of the capital, did there really need to be laughter from the wild mobs resounding from the other side of the ghetto walls, did there really have to prevail such blank indifference in the face of the greatest tragedy of all time? A further question is whether some sympathy should not have been expressed during the slaughter of a whole people. Why, we ask, did the Dutch, the Belgians, the French put on arm-bands with the Star of David as soon as this was imposed on the Jews,[15] while in Poland there was no such demonstration as millions of Polish citizens of Jewish descent died at the hands of their tormentors beneath the banner of the "crooked cross"? We ask further, why was it possible to considerably reduce the evil of denunciations, spying and collaboration with the Germans within one's own community, while nothing was done to check the giant wave of blackmail and denunciation of the handful of Polish Jews that had survived the slaughter of a whole people? These and similar questions are being asked every day by the remaining quarter-of-a-million Jews, for whose rescue a miracle is needed.

The Polish and Jewish peoples, co-existing for centuries, had conflicts and quarrels such as occur between neighbours in economic, cultural and political matters. But the question is permissible whether everything that divided us should not have been forgotten, in face of sufferings so extraordinary, sufferings unparalleled in world history? Should not the abyss opened up by the evil agency of the Nazi monster have been bridged over? Will it not be forever a disgrace that in a town like Czestochowa, for example, practically

---

15 In the countries mentioned, cases occurred of non-Jews' wearing the badges, arm-bands, or patches that Jews were forced to wear. This form of protest against racialist regulations provoked strong repressive measures on the part of the Germans. Thus, for example, on 7 June 1942 in northern France, a few score Frenchmen wearing Jewish badges were caught and taken to Drancy concentration camp. In Holland, manifestations of solidarity with the persecuted Jews also took the form of strikes, the most important of them being the famous strike of 25–26 February 1941, which included the main cities of Holland and in the first place Amsterdam.

none of the Jewish inhabitants were saved, only because before the war hostile feelings towards the Jews were current in this town? Why has the Polish anti-Semitic press not stopped its incitement against the Jews even for a moment, and why does the Government press so rarely break its silence on the Jewish question, why does it take so weak a stand in defence of the Jews? Why do the few idealists who defend the Jews and give them refuge so rarely meet with cooperation from the community or the great majority of the community? For those who go day by day to the steam-boiler in Treblinka, to the gas-ovens in Sobibor, to the crematorium in the Lublin concentration camp or to the death-chamber in Belzec, the attitude of the Polish community one way or the other is irrelevant; but to those few who are still alive in some underground cave, in a secret hide-out in some suburb, or living as "Aryans" "on the surface," these questions are not purely theoretical. Whether this small remaining handful of Jews will be able to hold out against the tide of German hatred and the Polish community's passive indifference will depend to a large extent upon the attitude of the Polish community.

Warsaw—"Krysia"—September 1943

2

POLISH-JEWISH RELATIONS BEFORE THE WAR

The Jews are blamed for everything —. "Market stalls" instead
of "Land for the Peasants." — Boycott instead of work for the
unemployed and young people. — Economic anti-Semitism —.
Cultural anti-Semitism —. The attitude of the peasants towards
the Jews—.The working class fights Fascism and anti-Semitism.

In order to understand the structure of Polish-Jewish relations
during the war, we should examine the pre-war period. It will then
become evident that the disastrous mistakes of the *Sanacja*[1] regime
had fatal repercussions for the country and determined the fate of
the Jewish population in Poland. The policy of the ruling *Sanacja*
brought the country to a state of economic and political ruin. This
policy helped unleash such an anti-Semitic hue and cry that Poland
before the war became the leading anti-Semitic country in Europe,
second to Germany alone.

The country's most important problems were neglected, all the
issues being considered "from the point of view of anti-Semitism."
The Jews were blamed for everything, in everything their "interna-

---

1 *Sanacja*—the nickname of the political bloc led by Marshal Josef Pilsudski, which held power in Poland from 1926 to 1939. The name is
connected with the slogan of "moral cleansing" (sanitation) of public
life in the country. After Pilsudski's death in 1935, nationalist and anti-
Semitic trends in the *Sanacja* were strengthened. The *Oboz Zjednoczenia
Narodowego,* created by the *Sanacja,* began cooperating with the extreme
anti-Semitic *Oboz Narodowo-Radykalny.* (The *Sanacja* anti-Jewish policy
is dealt with, among other sources, in the book of Simon Segal: *The
New Poland and the Jews,* New York, 1938.) During the Nazi occupation, military circles formerly connected with the *Sanacja* played a leading role in the strongest Polish clandestine military organization, the
Armia Krajowa (Home Army).

tional power" aiming at control of the whole world was seen. The land question was a most important issue in Poland, a country where two-thirds of the population earned its living from agriculture. Normal development of industry and commerce, urbanization, cultural development, normalization of the country's social problems, etc., depended upon the solution of this problem. Instead of solving the agrarian problem in accordance with the needs of millions of landless peasants and small landholders by division of the *latifundia* of the large land-owning magnates, there was agitation to have the small provincial land-owners take over the Jewish market stalls. Market stalls instead of land,—this was the programme of the united anti-Jewish front, *Endeko-Sanacja*. This agitation, together with frequent pogroms in Przytyk, Brzesc-on-the-Bug, Bialystok, Kielce and other provinces, was aimed at diverting the public's attention from the real, sensitive issues and directing it into false paths of racialism and national hate.[2]

---

[2] When the leadership of the ruling party passed from the Army and its secret police to the associates of Pilsudski, headed by Col. Adam Koc, it was decided to reorganize the government Party for victory over the National-Democrats (N.D.) in the latter's own special field as well—Jew-hatred. It was for good reason that the new Party was called the "Camp of National Unity" (O.Z.N.), a name taken from the National-Democratic political vocabulary. And in fact the "Camp" proved an industrious rival of the N.D. A youth faction "the National-Radical Camp" (O.N.R.), which split off from the National-Democratic Party when their far-reaching programme regarding the Jews proved unacceptable to their elders, enjoyed the support of the "Camp of National Unity" and the Government. Both "Camps" tried to wean the masses from their tolerant opinions and from Communist propaganda by turning them against the Jews. They urged them to take over the Jews' sources of livelihood. This *aggressive anti-Semitism* was meant to serve as a bond between Poland and Nazi Germany, who signed a treaty at the end of January 1934. The National-Democrats then began organizing a campaign by impoverished peasants to take over Jews' market stalls in the small towns. The O.N.R. youngsters would organize disturbances in the small towns on market days and on all other suitable occasions. A wave of disturbances and terror swept over Poland in the years 1935 to 1937. The series of pogroms began in June 1935 with excesses in Grodno, Suwalki and Raciaz. In November 1935, a pogrom took place in Odrzy-

wol and on 9 March 1936 came the notorious pogrom of Przytyk, during which three Jews were killed and 22 wounded. Pogroms took place next in Minsk Mazowiecki (1 to 5 June 1936), in Myslenice (the so-called Doboszynski-march, on 24 June 1936), in Lwow, Piotrkow Trybunalski, Plonsk, Serock (also in June 1936), in Wysokie Mazowieckie (14 September 1936), in Brzesc (13 May 1937), in Czestochowa (19 June 1937), in Mosty, Kamiensk, Zarki, Radomsko, Koniecpol, Kleszczew, Przedborz, Dzialoszyn (also in June 1937), in Przytyk, Odrzywol, Opoczno, Nowe Miasto, Jasinowka near Bialystok (July 1937), in Stok near Wegrow, Dybek near Ostrow, Bransk Podlaski (23 August 1937), in Bydgoszcz (31 August 1937), in Wloclawek, Lublin, Grodno and Lomza (September 1937).

The pogrom of Przytyk, a small town in the Radom district, gained its notoriety because one of the pogromists was killed by a Jew there, a member of a self-defence group. This Jew was arrested and tried before two different courts—and neither court found any justification for the shots fired by a man defending himself from the imminent threat of death. Both courts adjudged this an act deserving of severe punishment. The conclusion implicit in this judgement was that a Jew was forbidden to defend himself. In this matter the law for Jews was not the same as for other citizens of the State, who were permitted to fight for their lives when attacked by would-be murderers. The judgement served as a signal that Jews were free game. At the trial of the participants in the Przytyk disturbances (the sentence was handed down in Radom on 26 June 1936), eleven Jews and twenty-five Christians were found guilty and condemned to various terms of imprisonment. The Government held aloof and for the most part did not intervene unless it was a matter of pogromists' attacking police or of Jews' defending themselves. The judgement against the participants in the Przytyk disturbances came as a profound shock to the whole of Polish Jewry, which took it almost as a declaration of war against itself on the part of the Polish people and Government.

It should be remembered that in order to protest at this pogrom, directed against Jewish pedlars and small traders at the Przytyk fair, a Jewish general strike was organized by the *Bund,* together with the Jewish trade unions. The vast majority of oppressed Jews responded with a truly gigantic demonstration on 17 March 1936, for which the *Bund* also mobilized a large part of the Polish working class and the public opinion of the country's whole proletariat.

(Yiẓḥaq Gruenbaum, *Hagorem haantishemi, in* "Enẓiqlopediya shel galuyot Warsha", Vol. I, Jerusalem, pp. 50–115.

T. Berenstein, *K P P w walce z pogromami antyzydowskimi w latach* 1935–1937, "Biuletyn Żydowskiego Instytutu Historycznego" No. 15–16, 1955, p. 3–74.)

The cities of Poland were in the midst of an economic crisis. Adolescents, graduates of trade and high schools, could not find employment in industry, which was poorly developed and unable to meet competition from abroad because of lack of capital and experience. Foreign capital avoided Poland because of the unregulated social and economic relationships that created a precarious state of affairs extremely unfavourable for normal economic development. Unemployment in the towns and villages, and especially unemployment among adolescents, was one of Poland's major problems.[3] Instead of seeking a solution for this fundamental social problem, the government blamed the Jews. Further, the problem of the underdeveloped third estate, which had existed for ages, was to be solved by means of violence, coercion and force. Economic boycott of the Jews, sanctioned and countenanced by the highest elements in the State (the famous, "All right!" of Prime Minister Skladkowski[4]) was supposed to solve serious national and economic

---

3 Poland was one of the countries with exceptionally large-scale unemployment. Besides a considerable surplus working-age population in the rural areas, estimated in the '30's at several millions, there was mass unemployment in the towns. In 1935, for example, about 20% of the non-agricultural wage-earners were unemployed. Young people in particular suffered from the difficulties of the labour market. In the decade that preceded the second World War, there was a shortage of about 300,000 jobs for young men. Lack of employment caused mass emigration—both seasonal and permanent—which reached a total of over a million in those ten years. Unemployment was particularly severe in the large cities. The economist, Ludwik Landau, estimated the number of unemployed in Warsaw in 1935 at about 100,000. (Ludwik Landau, *Bezrobocie i stopa zyciowa ludnosci dzielnic robotniczych Warszawy*, Warsaw, 1936.)

4 After the Polish Constitution was altered (1935) and the Government's responsibility to parliament abolished, and a new electoral law gave the Government, in effect, power to dictate who should be elected to the Diet or the Senate, all parliamentary opposition on the part of the Jews was crushed. In the new Diet after the elections, anti-Semitic agitation increased, and the method of fighting the Jews by economic means was openly sanctioned by the Premier, Skladkowski, in his famous remark: "Economic war on the Jews—all right." This meant that the Government would protect the Jews against violent outbreaks, restrictions of their rights and oppression, but would willingly see them pushed out and

excluded, their sources of livelihood blocked up and their having to leave the country.

The National Democrats took their stand on the Premier's slogan of "All right" in economic policy directed against the Jews. They claimed that the masses of the Poles suffering from the economic crisis in the small towns were in the power of the Jews, and that it was therefore necessary to break this "foreign" power and take over the sources of Jewish livelihood. They declared that the impoverished masses of the Poles were entitled to use every means to push out the "foreigners" who had taken over so many fields of the economy.

The Government sought to give its anti-Semitic policy an acceptable form, to use legal means to block the sources of livelihood for the masses of Jews and to push them out. It sought to give its measures the appearance of a response to the demands of the developing economy, or to the demands of the Polish masses who were being forced by economic need to pass over to Jewish occupations.

The authorities in the small towns and provincial districts started to change the days fixed for the "fairs" to Saturdays and Jewish holidays, and the locations of the markets to sites outside the towns, so as to make it hard for the Jews and prevent their taking part in the fairs from which they made their living. The authorities began to cancel bus services between towns, services which had been mainly in Jewish hands. The Government began to restrict the rights of Jews in liberal professions, making local examinations harder for Jews who had completed their studies abroad, and making it harder for junior attorneys to become full members of the Bar. It increased the burden of taxes on Jewish merchants and artisans and restricted the grant of credit to Jewish merchants, artisans and small industrialists. This economic policy hit the poorest and weakest strata, and led to bankruptcies and even suicides. Tension increased in the period preceding the second World War, and so did the trend to exclude Jews, under the influence of two social and economic factors: the rise of the Polish bourgeoisie and intelligentsia, and the increased flow of the peasants from the villages to the small towns and the cities. The anti-Semites increased their efforts to push the Jews out of the Polish economy. There was a sharp drop in the Jewish share in agricultural trading and supply of industrial products to the villages, as well as in every branch connected with Government monopolies and export.

What was happening to the Jewish population in this period was accurately reflected in a short but pertinent remark made by the Premier, General Skladkowski, when a delegation of Jewish members of the Diet and representatives of the Merchants' Association protested to him about the Jews' terrible economic situation, and their insecurity—they were being set upon in the streets, beaten up in the universities, their factories and

problems which really required peace and mutual understanding. Economic boycotts allowed the mobs to vent their lowest instincts and riot with impunity, smashing market stalls and small shops, organizing pogroms and committing excesses without hindrance from the authorities. This brought the country to a state of constant turmoil and changed Poland into a Mexico, a country ruled by force and anarchy.[5] The conditions created in the country favoured the growth of Hitlerism and racialism; in other words, modern cannibalism.

Jewish artisans were not allowed to tender for work to be done for government institutions and municipal authorities, even though this meant a rise in prices because of the artificial elimination of Jewish competition. Jewish workers were dismissed from government and municipal establishments, even in those branches of production which they had developed for decades by their toil and labour (such as the Tobacco Monopoly in Grodno and other towns). The characteristic tendency of all economic legislation was to eliminate the Jews from the country's economic life. The Statute of Industries, and especially compulsory membership of guilds, were aimed at eliminating Jews from crafts, some of which had been controlled by Jewish artisans for centuries.

---

shops were being picketed. He answered them in these words, "And what then? These are also means of economic war ... " This was a reference to the famous sentence spoken in the Diet.

For all this, before the outbreak of the war, the Jews in Poland were an organic part of the national economy; they were entrenched in whole sectors of the national economy, and they were widely represented in many economic branches and at every level of the process of production. (Jacob Lestschinsky, *Hayishuv hayehudi behitpaḥuto hakalkalit*, in "Enẓiqlopediya shel galuyot Warsha," Vol. I, op. cit., pp. 125–218. (Gruenbaum, op. cit.)

5 In Polish journalistic phraseology, the expression "Mexico" was occasionally used as a symbol of countries where political instability and disorder prevailed and the situation was exploited by anti-democratic forces. This usage arose out of conditions prevailing in Mexico between 1911 and 1934 (when President Cardenas came to power), a period of constant upheaval and changes of government. The analogy does not hold, of course, for Mexico at a later date.

Alongside so-called economic anti-Semitism in Poland, cultural anti-Semitism began to flourish, a development which seriously damaged Poland's reputation abroad. The O.N.R.[6]—young people infected with the venom of racial hatred—took over the institutions of higher education and began to carry out their "cultural" programme by force. Constant excesses at the universities, touched off by the November anniversary (the anniversary of the death of a student named Waclawski, killed during a student riot in Vilna), the division of lecture halls into left (Jewish) and right (Aryan) sides, boycott and use of physical violence against liberal professors or professors of Jewish descent, strikes in the universities calling for the introduction of *numerus nullus* for Jews, all this changed the institutions of higher education into breeding grounds of predators who enforced their rule by the use of knuckle-dusters, razorblades, knives and clubs. Every year Jewish blood was spilled, Jewish students were wounded or even killed.[7]

---

[6] In 1934, a crisis in the *Stronnictwo Narodowe* (National Party) led to a breakaway by a group of active younger members, who founded a new group called *Oboz Narodowo-Radykalny—ONR* (Radical-Nationalist Camp). This extreme anti-Semitic group, modelling itself on the Nazis initiated the formation of armed bands to carry out pogroms, enforce boycotts of Jewish traders, and demolish Jewish shops and flats; it introduced the so-called Ghetto benches in the universities. A prominent ONR leader at the time was Boleslaw Piasecki (now member of the Polish Council of State). As a result of an internal split in the ONR, two groups took shape—the ONR-Falanga and the ONR-ABC, but they remained identical in their anti-Semitism.

During the Nazi occupation, the ONR-Falanga continued its activities under the name, *Konfederacja Narodu Polskiego,* as did the ONR-ABC group, under the name *Zwiazek Jaszczurczy* or *Szaniec.* Both groups published several papers (*Szaniec, Placowka, Praca i Walka, Zaloga, Walka*), which printed Stürmer-type anti-Semitic articles during the whole period of the Nazi occupation, thus contributing considerably to the growth of anti-Semitic feelings among the Polish people. These two groups also set up a large and well-equipped armed body—*Narodowe Sily Zbrojne*—NSZ, which from the end of 1942 on carried out many attacks on Jewish partisan groups and also murdered Jews in hiding.

[7] The N.D.—National Democrats—launched renewed attacks on the Jews in 1931. They had already entrenched themselves in the institutions of higher education, which became the bastions of nationalist reaction, and

Parallel with this "cultural" activity in the institutions of higher education, *Endeko*-O.N.R. circles put racial teachings into practice, introducing the *numerus clausus* in high schools and colleges. *Numerus clausus*, or rather *numerus nullus* as regards Jews, was in force in government, municipal and public offices. Things reached such a state that the Chief Inspector of Warsaw Public Schools, Wiatr, openly advised the Jewish teachers in the State schools to have a group photograph taken, as they now represented the few

---

they exploited academic autonomy in order to restrict the rights of the Jews and establish percentages for the number of Jewish students in various faculties, especially those which gave access to professions over which the *Sanacja* Government had no control. At the opening of the academic year 1931/1932 skirmishes and clashes broke out between Jewish and Polish students in the institutions of higher education. The Poles were the attackers and the Jews defended themselves.

A Polish student was killed during such a clash in Vilna, and a number of Jewish students were wounded and beaten. The Government condemned this movement and took measures against it. But when the students took to the streets and began attacking Jews and even tried to go into Warsaw's Jewish streets (but were thrown back by Jewish drivers and porters) the Government took no serious steps to repress this movement. The Interior and Education ministers, Pieracki and Andrzejewicz, declared in the Diet that they would preserve order and security, but that it was difficult for them to take control of the situation in the institutions of higher education because of their autonomous rights under the law.

After Pilsudski's death in 1935, the *Sanacja* leaders began to fall into the trap of the slogans and the actions of the National Democrats. The latter continued to incite young Polish students against their Jewish comrades, destined to compete with them as lawyers and doctors. The signal was given, and attacks began on the Jews in Warsaw University. They began to be pushed to the back benches, to be kept out of the anatomy laboratories unless they themselves supplied cadavers, to be harassed all along the line.

As a result of the decree on separate benches for Jews in the universities and institutions of higher education, which opened the way for the Nuremberg Laws in Poland and which was a blow to Jewish university and college students, the "Bund" Party organized an impressive mass protest on 19 October 1938, which demonstrated the readiness of the Jewish masses to fight for their rights.

17

Jewish teachers left in the government educational system. Many *Endeka-Sanacja* social and professional organizations (associations of engineers, doctors, dentists, postal officials, etc.) passed high-sounding resolutions about the Aryan paragraph.[8] The most deserving people were expelled from these associations if their Aryan descent was in doubt. General meetings of these organizations, instead of discussing unity to improve the economic condition of the country, turned into racialist propaganda rallies, much to the pleasure of the country's neighbour to the west. Exponents of racialist "doctrine" and obscurantism from Germany were hospitably entertained in the colleges. The present General-Governor, Dr. Frank, was a frequent guest at the *Alma Mater Varsoviensis,* where he lectured to the assembled men of science about the new theories in German "law" which were being put into practice by modern cannibals in places of slaughter.[9]

---

8 From 1936 on, the Nazi slogan of "Aryanization", that is to say the introduction of the Nuremberg racial decrees into Poland, found a steadily increasing response among members of the liberal professions, tradesmen and artisans. Many of their associations and unions, which were under the influence of the *Stronnictwo Narodowe* (National Party) or the *Oboz Zjednoczenia Narodowego* (Camp of National Unity), passed resolutions in favour of not accepting Jews into their ranks. In the academic year 1937–1938, the autonomous authorities of certain colleges officially recognized the so-called Ghetto benches. After this, Jewish students had their student's pass marked with a special stamp and were obliged to sit on separate benches on the left-hand side of the lecture halls. In January 1939, the members of the Polish Diet representing the *Oboz Zjednoczenia Narodwego*—MM. Stoch and Kieniec—submitted bills to deprive Polish Jews of citizenship.
(Maria Turlejska, *Rok przed kleska,* Warsaw, 1960; see particularly the chapter, *Sprawa zydowska*—The Jewish Question, pp. 147–161.)

9 Poland saw itself torn between two hostile powers, but the fear of Russia was greater than the fear of Germany. Russia had never reconciled itself to the Treaty of Riga and awaited the first opportunity to take over Poland's eastern rural areas (Kresy Wschodnie). The Communist movement was increasing in strength in these rural areas; its programme included secession from Poland and union with the Soviet Ukraine and Byelorussia. Hence Pilsudski's idea of mobilization of the western nations, including Poland, for war against Germany while she was still weak, was dropped. (Incidentally, the West paid no attention to Pilsudski's proposal,

At all events, the anti-Semitic programme of the ruling *Sanacja* was merely part of its general nationalistic policy based on persecuting Ukrainians and Byelorussians, closing down their schools, social and cultural institutions, on the famous "pacifications",[10] on Bereza to make a parade of "representing" the Ukrainian and Byelorussian Kartuska,[11] etc. The *Sanacja* bribed Ukrainians and Byelorussians peoples; these "representatives" recited declarations of loyalty in the name of their peoples in parliament, in the senate and at the

---

for it saw Hitler and his party as a rising force capable of restoring Germany's strength and blocking Russian expansion more effectively than could be expected of Poland.) The treaty between Poland and Nazi Germany was signed at the end of January 1934.

The rapprochement with Germany became closer still after Pilsudski's death, and it was in this atmosphere that Marshall Goering and Minister Hans Frank were received with great ceremony in Poland. Goering paid a short visit to Warsaw on 19 February 1936, and a longer official visit from 15 to 22 February 1937.

Hans Frank, at that time Minister and head of the German Law Academy, visited Warsaw on 12 February 1936. He was received by Beck, Prince Janusz Radziwill and Jan Szembek among others. At the invitation of the Polish Committee for International Intellectual Cooperation, he delivered a lecture on *Zwischenstaatliche Rechtspolitik*—the Rule of Law between States.

[10] The Ukrainians, who constituted the majority of the population in the south-eastern Polish provinces (Wolyn, Podole, Eastern Galicia), had hopes of creating an independent Ukrainian State in this region. These aims were strongly opposed by the Polish authorities, who banned the activities of the extreme anti-Polish Ukrainian Nationalists' Organization. The Ukrainian nationalists responded by terrorist attacks on the lives of Polish officials. In 1931, a prominent member of the *Sanacja* camp, Tadeusz Holówka, was murdered, and in 1934 the Minister of the Interior, Bronisław Pieracki. The Polish authorities, in their turn, applied the principle of collective responsibility, and sometimes burnt down whole villages suspected of sympathizing with the Ukrainian struggle for independence. These measures of repression were called "pacification of the Ukrainian territories."

[11] Concentration camp in Poland set up in 1934. Polish administrative authorities had the power to imprison adversaries of the regime in this camp for up to three months. This period was in fact extended arbitrarily. Many politically active Jews with Leftist views were also held in this camp.

19

farcical *Sanacja* rallies. The *Sanacja* was also "solving" the Jewish question with the help of "its own" Jews from among the Orthodox and from business circles. These Jews obligingly secured seats in parliament for the *Sanacja* and recited declarations in the name of the Jewish people about the benefits they received from the *Sanacja*. To split the Polish community from within, atomize it and weaken its defences in order to exult over the ruins of national unity—this, it was well known both inside and outside the country, was the real aim of all these activities. Racialist and nationalistic hate propaganda was the Trojan horse which Nazism used to invade the Polish community, starting the process of deterioration and inner rot. The *Sanacja* and *Endeko*-O.N.R. leaders, advocating national principles, were unwitting tools in the hands of the foreign agents whose presence these nationalists suspected in everything and everybody but themselves. Inane religious campaigns were used to divert the public's attention from major problems; agitation against ritual slaughter,[12] for example, was propounded by Prystorowa, a member of parliament of the *Sanacja* fraction. This sort of propaganda was an excellent means for duping the larger part of the community and keeping it from dealing with the really important and vital problem of the country's defence system and inner unity.

---

[12] The question of Jewish ritual slaughter was raised in the last Diet; at the beginning of March 1936 there were bitter and stormy debates in the Diet over the law to abolish Jewish ritual slaughter, a law introduced on supposedly humane grounds whose authors and supporters did not bother to hide its real purpose—to push the Jews out of the meat trade and destroy their economic standing. The Government did not see fit to oppose the law against Jewish ritual slaughter but felt itself obliged to sugar the pill, while breaking the Jewish monopoly of trade in slaughter cattle. The Government realized that a Jewish population of three million, most of them observing the ritual food laws of *kashrut*, would not obey a law like this, and it therefore proposed a compromise: Jewish ritual slaughter would not be forbidden, but would be restricted to a certain quota, according to the needs of those observing food ritual laws. It is worth pointing out that in response to a call by the Poalei-Zion Party (Zionist Socialists), and under its direction, a Jewish general strike was held throughout Poland on 17 March 1936 to protest against anti-Semitic violence and aggressiveness (as regards the pogrom of Przytyk, ritual slaughter, etc.). On the same Party's initiative, there was another

The united peasant front (*Piast, Wyzwolenie*[13]) might have understood the danger to the interests of the State and of the working peasants involved in racialism and the market stall ideology, but they were rotted from within by the *Piast* anti-Semitic tradition and lacked the will-power to throw off all disguise and fight the Fascist O.N.R., confederates of the great landlords, on the Jewish question. They were afraid that the peasant movement would be called a Jewish movement and its leaders dubbed the farm-hands and errand-boys of the Jews.

Only the class-conscious workers fought openly and unreservedly against Polish Fascism in all its forms, from the frankly Nazi *Blyskawica*[14] to the O.N.R.-*Falanga*. But Poland being an agricultural

---

Jewish general strike of protest, in which all the Jewish parties participated, on 30 June 1936. In 1937 the *Bund* organized a protest against the ban on Jewish ritual slaughter, which they saw as a deliberate attack on freedom of conscience and on religious consciousness of part of the Jewish population of Poland.

[13] In March 1941, three Polish peasant Parties, which had been separate up till then—the *Polskie Stronnictwo Ludowe "Piast,"* the *Polskie Stronnictwo Ludowe "Wyzwolenie"* and the *Stronnictwo Chlopskie*, came together to form a united party called *Stronnictwo Ludowe*. This new party was decisively influenced by the active members of the former "Piast", who constituted the right wing of the Polish peasants' movement and manifested anti-Semitic tendencies. During the second World War, the *Stronnictwo Ludowe* played an important role inside both the Polish Government-in-Exile and the office of the Government Delegate for the Homeland with all its agencies.

[14] The reference is to a National-Socialist organization which Erazm Samborski and Podgorski had tried to set up in Poland before the outbreak of the second World War. After the German invasion, these two, together with the others—Swietlicki, an active member of the Falanga; Zygmunt Cybichowski, professor of national and international law at Warsaw University and the Academy of International Law in Prague; and Wladyslaw Studnicki—set up a Polish National-Socialist Party in Warsaw, which adopted the official name of *Narodowa Organizacja Radykalna* (NORA for short). This organization's main occupation was propagating anti-Semitism among the Polish population. This Party was liquidated by the German occupation authorities in February 1940 and its headquarters (at 22 Ujazdowskie Avenue) were closed down. (Records of the Government Delegate, Archives of the Institute for the History of the [Communist] Party, Warsaw, file 202/II–22, p. 22.)

country, the labour movement did not have enough strength to cut off the hydra heads of Fascism, especially as the ruling *Sanacja* did everything possible to weaken the movement and split its unity by creating rival *Sanacja* trade unions.[15]

To sum it all up, it must be stressed that when Hitler prepared for war, he chose Poland as the first country that was to be attacked. He therefore made the greatest efforts to conquer it from within before conquering it by military means. These efforts, supported by local elements to a large extent, bore fruit during the war. Fragmented socially, torn by nationalist hatred, demoralized by the campaign against ritual slaughter, the programme for market stalls, boycotts and similar anti-Semitic farces, Poland was easy prey for Hitler. In 1939 the downfall of Poland was brought about not only by an external enemy force but also by an inner enemy that had shattered the unity of the State, its defence system and inner cohesion. This enemy was Polish Fascism allied to anti-Semitism.

---

[15] In order to lessen the influence of the Trade Unions connected with the Polish Socialist Party, the *Sanacja* set up rival trade unions which formed part of the *Sanacja* bloc.

In 1935, when the number of trade union members in Poland totalled 670,000, 243,000 of them were members of trade unions under *Sanacja* influence and 249,000 of unions under the Polish Socialist Party's influence. As regards the other trade unions, their members numbered altogether about 180,000, mostly affiliated to the (right-wing) National Party.

(Data according to Andrzej Micewski, *Z geografii politycznej II Rzeczypospolitej*, Warsaw, 1964, p. 193.)

3

SEPTEMBER 1939

Return to reality. — The Jewish question disappears from the
face of the earth. — Jewish soldiers in the September campaign.
— Polish-Jewish social mutual aid — Jewish Civic Committee.
— Fire fighting by young people. — L.O.P.P.[1] Committees and
Block Committees.

Several months prior to the outbreak of war in 1939, there was
nothing in the Jewish sector to indicate that war was drawing near.
Anti-Semitism throve as if nothing was happening, even in the sphere
where emphasis on national differences should have been avoided,
the military. The attitude towards the Jews in the cadre of young
officers was the same as that of the majority of the Polish educated
class. A Jew could not get a commission however brilliant he was.
A Jew could not rise above the rank of second lieutenant in the
military hierarchy. Jews were not accepted in the professional army
corps. Jews could not tender for army supplies. All this was also
true of para-military training. Young people bred in the spirit of
anti-Semitism in the Universities transferred their attitude to the
army.[2]

---

[1] L.O.P.P. (initials of the name *Liga Obrony Powietrznej i Przeciwgazo-
wej*)—the civilian air defence organization in pre-war Poland.

[2] From the first day of Polish independence, the higher Army echelons
opposed the admission of Jews to the officers' corps and certain élite
units. The Jewish National Council and its representatives in the Diet
fought against this negation of a primary right of the Jews as a citizen.
Before the second World War, the Army in Poland adopted a minorities policy towards the national groups of Jews, Byelorussians and
Ukrainians, instead of classifying the manpower available to the army

Shortly before the war broke out, the Polish community came to its senses. Now it was understood that anti-Semitism in Poland was a weapon in Hitler's hand. Things were somewhat calmer; the anti-Semitic press, apparently on orders, changed its tone and stopped incitement against the Jews. The Jewish question, which had dominated the country's whole life in the shape of market-stalls, ritual slaughter and *numerus clausus* and overshadowed all its really pressing problems, disappeared from the political scene. But all this came too late. Rot and disunity had gone too far for all this to alter the course of the war in any way. Anti-Semitism disappeared as if at the touch of a magic wand. Even the most ardent anti-Semites grasped that at this time Jews and Poles had a common enemy, and that the Jews were excellent allies who would do all they possibly could to bring destruction on the Jews' greatest enemies. The easing of tension could be felt at every step: in the streets, trams and offices a spirit of harmony and cooperation prevailed everywhere. The Jew, who before the war felt himself to be a second- or third-class citizen, a pariah to be beaten, kicked, and insulted at every turn, eliminated from all office or public position, etc., again

---

according to the latter's real needs, and assigning each soldier to his task in his unit according to his physical and mental capacities. The *numerus clausus* was in effect for Jews in the Air Force, the Navy, the armoured corps, signallers' and technicians' corps (construction, bridge-builders and sappers, mine layers, etc.). A very few Jews served in the cavalry and a few in the artillery. In other words, intelligent elements were barred from access to weapons that required intelligence for their use.

According to the Polish Army Code, every secondary school graduate had to go through a reserve officers' training course. A special policy was adopted for Jewish secondary school graduates. Those who registered their nationality as Jewish were in most cases considered as "outside the draft quota" and were not taken by the regular army, because the government wished to keep the number of Jewish officers within limits.

Jews served mainly as medical orderlies, and if they had completed medical training, as doctors. Jewish doctors served as officers in the medical corps in the reserves, but in no instance in regular units.

(M. Canin, *Hayehudim beẓava hapolani*, in "Enẓiqlopediya shet galuyot Warsha", Volume two, op. cit. pp. 509–518.)

Photocopy of a page from
Ringelblum's original manuscript

3 przygotowań. Miljony Żydów we wszystkich
częściach świata, a zwłaszcza Żydzi polscy
zagranicą, a wraz z nimi cały świat pyta się jak
zachował się naród polski w tych tragicznych
chwilach, gdy miljony Żydów szły drogą
uwielokrotnionej "Golgoty" do Treblinek, Bełżca,
Sobiboru, Oświęcimia i Chełmna. Wiadomo
powszechnie jak cierpi naród polski od niemieckiej
ciemiężcy. Oświęcim i Majdanek, Dachau i Oranienburg. – Te i inne miejscowości, w których
katuje się i radością na śmierć wszystko
co najlepsze w Polsce są znane daleko poza
granicami kraju. A jednak pomimo tych
cierpień narodu polskiego zapytuje świat
co uczyniła w chwili, gdy
miljony Żydów polskich prowadzono na stos ofiarny,
co uczyniła Polska Podziemna, Przedstawiciel
na Kraj Rządu Rzeczypospolitej, i jego ekspozytury
na prowincji, by uratować choć część swych obywateli
narodowości żydowskiej. Od tysiąca lat
współżyją ze sobą na jednej ziemi: naród polski
i naród żydowski. Co uczynili nasi sąsiedzi
w momencie, gdy uzbrojony od stóp do głów okupant
rzucił się na najbardziej bezbronny naród,
na Żydów. Czy pomimo istniejącego terroru
udzielono aryjską ofiarom hitleryzmu, uciekającym
z get. na t. w. stronę aryjską. Czy azyl ten
istniał tylko wtedy, kiedy byłon sato
opłacany i kończył się z chwilą, gdy fundusze
się kończyły. Cały świat zapytuje się, czy

became a citizen with equal rights, asked to render help to the common fatherland. One scene provides an illustration. September 1939: A force of twenty soldiers from Poznan province, led by a young second lieutenant, enters the courtyard of the block of flats at 7 Ogrodowa Street. Only Jews live in the block, but within a matter of minutes a feeling of harmony prevails between the men from Poznan province, widely known for their anti-Semitism, and the Jewish tenants. The people in the block entertain the soldiers hospitably, treat them to everything they can possibly find to offer them. For hours on end, the soldiers relate their experiences at the front, the tenants talk about the bombardment of the capital, etc. In short, the vision of Isaiah is realized—the lamb lies down in harmony with the wolf. Similar reports came from Lodz and other provincial towns. The feeling of harmony and cooperation in defence of the country spread throughout all classes and strata of the country.

Intensive participation by the community in all national defence activities characterized September 1939. The social factor, stifled during the reign of the Fascist *Sanacja* regime, came back to life. Cooperation between the army and the community was universal. The basis of community organization was the excellent L.O.P.P., which was developed by selecting the best and most energetic individuals in each block of flats as members. The Warsaw blocks of flats, which had been famous before the war for the fact that their tenants did not know each other and had no community spirit, changed radically. In September, thanks to the L.O.P.P., the Warsaw blocks of flats became the basic unit of communal life. They attended to all the complaints of the tenants, that is, they took care of their personal safety and defence against fires, they saved those wounded in bombardments, distributed food to the hungry, allocated flats to the homeless; they even intervened in the defence of the city, and sought out traitors and spies. In the Jewish quarter, Block Committees came into being as an extension of the L.O.P.P. Committees, and they played a significant part in organizing Jewish communal life during the war. In addition to these tasks, the committees looked after the homeless and the refugees, thousands of whom reach Warsaw from Lodz and other cities affected by the war. In the various "mixed" blocks, Polish-Jewish rapprochement took place. Ideal cooperation came into existence for the sake of benefit to the army and the welfare of war victims, irrespective of religion and nationality.

During the days of the siege of Warsaw, the young people in the various blocks of flats, including considerable numbers of young Jews, performed miracles of heroism. I saw how the young Jews of the block on No. 13 Leszno Street kept on fighting the fires that broke out endlessly in the attic of a five-story building. There was no water. The fire was smothered with sand and put out with water collected from the bathrooms of individual flats. These young people were competing with German pilots, who were dropping incendiary bombs on the block from a height of tens of metres, on the day of the famous bombing of Warsaw, Monday the 25th September.[3] When the pilots saw the tenants trying to put out the fires, they machine-gunned them. From the level of the attic, where I was taking part with the others in fighting the fire, I could clearly see the silhouettes of the pilots. Young Poles and Jews performed prodigies of valour in extinguishing fires, removing incendiary bombs—somtimes scores of them—or isolating the fire and preventing it from spreading to adjacent wings or neighbouring blocks. I remember the tenacity with which the young Poles and Jews from

---

[3] *Cf.* the entry of A. Czerniakow, in his Warsaw Ghetto Diary, for the same day (*inter alia*) : "All night in the air-raid shelter. Another terrible bombardment of Warsaw. On 25 September, very heavy artillery and plane attacks on the besieged city." (See: Adam Czerniakow, *Warsaw Ghetto Diary 6.9.1939–23.7.1942,* Jerusalem, 1968. Hebrew with English introduction.)
An all-night artillery bombardment was followed by air bombing of unprecedented fury, lasting from seven in the morning till dark. About a hundred planes carried out systematic bombing in waves, dropping. explosive and incendiary bombs on the centre of Warsaw. Pilots directed intense fire at the population from aircraft guns. There were some 200 simultaneous fires in the city, some of them covering whole streets. Life in the city was completely paralysed.
(Władysław Bartoszewski, *Warszawa w kampanii wrzesniowej, Kronika wazniejszych wydarzen.* In "Cywilna Obrona Warszawy we wrześniu 1939", Warsaw 1964, pp. XXIV–XXV.)

blocks on Nos. 18, 20 and 22 Leszno Street fought the fire at No. 24 Leszno Street for several days and nights in order to prevent it from spreading to the neighbouring blocks. The common danger, common toil and labour of the Jewish and Polish population amidst the rain of projectiles, the reverberation of the exploding bombs and the bursts of shrapnel, united the tenants of each block in their fight against the common enemy, brought the two peoples closer together and bridged the gulf that had been created by the common enemy.[4]

In the most important sector, the national defence system, the Jews now gave the maximum possible assistance. On the night of the 6th to the 7th September 1939—the night of the evacuation of the Government from Warsaw[5]—the Jewish population took

---

[4] During the siege the civil population displayed great readiness to make sacrifices. Kitchens were set up to supply food to thousands and tens of thousands of refugees, without distinction of creed. In the court-yards of the Jewish quarter, food was given to great numbers of people, including the tenants of whole blocks and Christians among them. At the "points" for refugees and those bombed out of their homes in the Jewish quarter there were many Christians, who were taken into the shelters. "A *rapprochement* began between Jews and Christians in the mixed blocks and thenceforward relations were friendly. The tenants of the block became one large family, and there was even a general idea to organize joint kitchens, but it was not carried out."

In his notes dating from the end of September 1939, in the short phrases with which he used to record things at that time, Ringelblum once more stresses the good relations between Jews and Poles and sees "a fundamental change in psychology. Jews and Christians living together. Jews taking care of Polish soldiers." At the same time, he remembers to note down, "anti-Semitic trends here and there," "the Aryan clause in the shelters, for example in the block of flats on 16 Dluga Street," "scuffles in the queues," which served as targets during the bombardments from the air.

(Ringelblum, op. cit., pp. 27–29.)

[5] At dawn on the morning of 7 September 1939, the Polish Radio announced that the Government of Poland was leaving the capital. The same night, the Army spokesman, Colonel Umiastowski, announced that all men of military age should make their way to eastern Poland, where a new defence line would be established against the enemy attacks. A mass exodus began immediately, mainly on foot. Evacuation of the

part *en masse* in digging trenches in the Wola Quarter. Together with all the rest of the population, the Jews built barricades of overturned trams, cars, crates, broken furniture, etc. Young Jews reported *en masse* to enlist in the regiment for the defence of Warsaw[6] that was formed at the call of the Mayor of the city, Major Starzynski.[7] In the Jewish blocks of flats, ladies' committees organized the so-called halting points, where military detachments returning from the front, tired and hungry, could find hot food, tea, cigarettes, underclothing, etc. After just a few days, the military hospitals were short of everything: there were no bandages, medicines, beds, etc. The Jews took an active part in the collections for the benefit of the hospitals, collections ordered by Mayor Starzynski. Dressing stations came into being to attend to the wounded soldiers for whom there was no longer room in the

---

main government ministries had already begun two to three days earlier.

6 On 12 September 1939, the Mayor of Warsaw, Stefan Starzynski, broadcast an appeal for volunteers to join the Battalion for the Defence of Warsaw which was being set up. In under an hour, thousands of men had presented themselves. Eight hundred of them were attached to the army, and the rest were incorporated in newly organized Work Battalions, which were building defence fortifications. Apart from these Work Battalions, a Volunteer Workers' Brigade for the Defence of Warsaw was created, numbering 6,000 volunteers, mainly workers. The soldiers of this brigade took part in building fortifications and some of them also fought in the first line of defence. In both these formations, Jews probably constituted about thirty to forty per cent.
(See Marian Drozdowski, *Alarm dla Warszawy—Obrona cywilna stolicy we wrzesniu 1939 r.*, Warsaw, 1964.)

7 Acting Mayor of the City of Warsaw since 1934. He stayed at his post after the Government and the main Ministries had left the city. He was the main initiator and heart of soul of the defence of the city. On 8 September, the Commander of the Defence Staff of the City appointed him representative of the civil power in the besieged city with the title Civil Commissioner, attached to the Warsaw Defence Command. The post of Mayor was transferred temporarily to his deputy, Jan Podhorski.
After the surrender, he returned to the post of Mayor. On 27 October 1939, he was arrested by the Gestapo and did not return. He died in Dachau on 17 September 1943.

existing hospitals and army infirmaries. Doctors and nurses did their duty to their country.[8] The Jews of Warsaw were seized with an enthusiasm vividly recalling the year 1861,[9] the period of Polish-Jewish fraternity, when large numbers of young Jews took part in patriotic demonstrations of a religious character, when common patriotic services were arranged in churches and synagogues, and Jewish women, even from Hassidic homes, followed the example of the Polish women and went into mourning for the five victims. We well remember

---

[8] With the first appeal to dig defensive trenches against the German tanks before the siege of Warsaw, Jewish soldiers and civilians presented themselves immediately. The Germans fired their first shells into the Jewish quarters. The story of the rescue of the tenants of the first Jewish block of flats to be hit (on Mylna Street) is a glorious chapter in the story of Jewish fighters. In his first wartime entries in his diary, Ringelblum exalts the courage of the young Jews who put out the fires on the roofs of the buildings. (See above, p. 26.) A similar heroic effort to extinguish incendiary bombs was made at 16 Muranowska Street. (See Ringelblum, op. cit., Vol. I, p. 30.)

[9] In February 1861 recurrent demonstrations began in Warsaw against Russian rule, accompanied by bloody clashes between the population and Russian forces. Five demonstrators were killed on 27 February. On 8 April, soldiers opened fire on the defenceless crowd of demonstrators, massacring about a hundred people. These demonstrations gave birth to a political movement which culminated in the rising that broke out on 22 January 1863 (the so-called January Insurrection). Fighting continued until the middle of 1864 when the Russians drowned the insurrection in blood. Many Jews took part in the demonstrations in 1861 as well as in the January Insurrection. There were numerous instances of fraternization between Poles and Jews. The synagogues of the Jews, like the Catholic churches, became places of political mass meetings, where declarations were heard about the common, fraternal struggle of both religions in the fight for Poland's independence. On the Jewish side, the Warsaw Rabbi, Ber Meisels, played an important part in the movement. Both Poles and Jews were among the demonstrators killed by the Russians. Hundreds of Jews fell in the fighting in 1863 and 1864 and at least a score of Jews were executed by the Russians after the insurrection failed. (A. Eisenbach, D. Fajnhauz, A. Wein, *Zydzi a Powstanie Styczniowe Materialy i dokumenty,* Warsaw, 1963.)

the invitation cards to the common services in the years 1861 to 1863, with pictures on them of a Polish nobleman dressed in a *kontush* kissing a bearded Jew dressed in a caftan. In September 1939, the sight of Jewish detachments marching with shovels on their shoulders, the sight of young Jews rushing *en masse* to the Mostowskich Palace where recruiting was taking place for the volunteer regiment, Defenders of Warsaw, recalled the year 1831, when the Jews of Warsaw formed the Jewish National Guard.[10]

During the siege of the capital, soldiers stationed in the various blocks of flats were given a wonderful reception by the Jewish population. They were invited to the different flats and entertained there. The soldiers reciprocated with whatever they had. They shared their soldiers' bread, a luxury in Warsaw at that time. When the army was getting ready to leave the capital, the military warehouses were opened and provisions were distributed to the population. Jews were treated equally with all the rest of the population. The departing soldiers were given civilian clothes to enable them to avoid capture by the Germans. When the army evacuated the capital in accordance with the terms of capitulation, it was a tragedy for the Jewish population. The departing military detachments were bidden tearful farewells.

The time is not yet ripe for discussing the part played by Jewish soldiers in the September fighting. There is insufficient material on the subject, but it is nevertheless possible to form an opinion on the basis of numerous stories told by those who took part in the September campaign. From these accounts, which in general

---

10 In November 1830, a Polish uprising took place against Russian occupation which went on for about ten months. During the revolt, civilian militia were set up for the defence of Warsaw on the pattern of the French Revolution. There was a National Guard, a Municipal Guard and a Security Guard. Within the framework of these formations, Jewish detachments were organized. Altogether, 1,268 Jews served in the Municipal Guard, 409 in the National Guard and some hundreds in the Security Guard.

(W. Lewandowski, *Materialy do udzialu Zydow w Gwardii Narodowej, Gwardii Miejskiej i Strazy Bezpieczenstwa,* "Biuletyn Zydowskiego Instytutu Historycznego" No. 19–20—1956, pp. 114–138.)

corroborate each other, it follows beyond a doubt that Jewish soldiers on the battlefield displayed fortitude and determination in fighting the Germans. Jewish soldiers distinguished themselves by their bravery and endurance. Aside from the mere fact of his citizenship and devotion to his country, the Jewish soldier's attitude was influenced by his hatred of Hitler. Young Jews who had been through sports and political organizations, who had received paramilitary training[11] and served in the army, wanted to repay the

---

[11] Before the war, the Zionist-Socialist Movement, the Pioneering Youth organizations, the *Bund* and the Jewish Communists all had well-organized, armed defence squads to defend Jewish lives and to maintain morale. Their members were trained and instructed for self-defence against the onslaughts of anti-Semites that developed in Poland in the years 1937 to 1939. They fought the Fascist bands and anti-Semitic hooligans.

It should be pointed out that the Polish workers considered the squads of the *Bund* a desirable reinforcement in their struggle against Fascism, which made no secret of its ambition to destroy the free workers' movement in Poland as well—Jewish and non-Jewish alike.

In the last years before the war, the "Movement for Labour Palestine" in Poland held systematic courses in "physical fitness," which were in fact nothing but intensive self defence courses. In 1937, for example, a course like this was held at which 60 Heḥalutz members received intensive training as instructors. In the report submitted to the World Conference of the Poalei-Zion Union (Iḥud)—the Zionist Socialists—together with the Hitaḥdut group in August 1939, the chapter on the movement in Poland reads: In the winter months 1938–1939, five courses were held in different places in Poland for a total of 170 members of the "Freiheit-Heḥalutz Hatzair" Party (Freedom-Young Pioneers). In the months of June and July 1939, a 6-week course was held at Zielonka near Warsaw with 45 Heḥalutz members taking part. Special instructors from Palestine were in charge of these courses. We know of organized defence in Warsaw that was re-organized afresh and strengthened in 1937 by the Poalei-Zion (Zionist Socialists') Party together with Heḥalutz and the trade unions connected with the Party; and there is no doubt that the same was done by the Left Poalei Zion, Hashomer Hatzair, the other pioneering youth movements and the *Bund*. (Melekh Neustadt (Editor), *Ḥurban vamered shel Yehudey Warsha*, Tel Aviv 1947, p. 38. Nowogrodzki, op. cit.)

In 1937 a military course was held at the Polish Training Centre for members of the National Military Organization (Etzel). This course

31

Nazis properly for all the calamities they had called down on European Jewry. The Jews feared the entry of the German Army into the country and were ready to do everything to prevent it. If we remember all this, the exceptionally outstanding role of the Jewish soldier in the September campaign will not surprise us.

A correct attitude towards the Jews was the rule in the army, but there was a reversion to certain anti-Semitic tendencies regarding Jewish soldiers. Some of the events of this period need airing, episodes which should receive attention from the courts when the country is liberated. Sabotage and anti-Semitism—blood-brothers—contributed to producing condemnable incidents even in the sector of the defence system. Anti-Semitic saboteurs made difficulties in the recruitment of Jews for active service. Only a certain number of Jewish doctors were mobilized, so that they had to report by themselves. For incomprehensible reasons only a small number of non-commissioned officers, limited to specialists, were called up in Warsaw (this information comes from an official of the Regional Recruiting Office in Warsaw). In mid-September something in the nature of a new Jablonna[12] was created. Jewish soldiers were removed from some battalions and concentrated in a purely Jewish work battalion.

---

gave "Etzel" its first commanders with professional military training. The "Betar" youth movement adopted a military spirit in theory and in practice, and with the help of the Polish Army authorities courses were given in practically every cell of the movement in the handling of fire-arms, mainly pistols. For the first time in the history of Polish Jewry, parades were held in the open of young Jews carrying arms on their shoulders. The Betar World Executive organized and maintained schools for defence training in different parts of Poland under the direction of Yerimiyahu Halperin.

(A. Remba, *Hatenua harevizyonistit,* in "Enẓiqlopediya shel galuyot Warsha," Volume two, op. cit., pp. 185–212.)

[12] From the very first days after the proclamation of the Polish State in 1918, the top Army leadership opposed admitting Jews to the officers' corps and even to the ranks. It is not surprising therefore that when the Russo-Polish war was at its peak in 1920, thousands of Jews were imprisoned in the Jablonna camp, including many who had volunteered for the Army. The prisoners in the camp were not sent back to the Army and were only released after the end of the fighting.

In September 1939 the Metropolitan Committee of Mutual Social Aid (S.K.S.S.[13]) came into existence to bring help to the victims of the war. The government allocated large funds for mutual social aid. The S.K.S.S. helped by distributing provisions among the refugees that came from various regions of the country, and also by allocating flats to the homeless victims of the capital bombing and to the refugees. In the first days of the war, Jewish social welfare organizations ("Centos"—the Society for Jewish Child Welfare, the Central Rescue Committee, and others) with the American "Joint" (American Joint Distribution Committee) at their head, had already created a branch of the S.K.S.S. with functions analogous to those of the general Committee. It was called the Co-ordination Committee. That the Jewish aid societies were affiliated to the S.K.S.S. is typical of the new era of Polish-Jewish rapprochement. While before the war, Government circles strove to eliminate Jews from joint organizations by means of the so-called "Aryan paragraph," official factors now gave their consent to incorporating Jewish aid organizations within the framework of the general Committee. The Co-ordination Committee (K.K.), which attended to the districts with a Jewish majority, concerned itself with the fate of all refugees irrespective of nationality. In the beginning, relief stations for refugees were mixed, Poles and Jews together, but the K.K. was soon forced to separate them according to nationality, as refugees from the Poznan district, known for their anti-Semitism, could not remain under the same roof with Jews. The K.K.'s aid activities went on throughout the month of September until the entry of the Germans. One of the first orders given by the Germans was to prohibit the Jewish K.K.'s from giving aid to Aryans. The K.K. officials wore blue crosses

---

13 At the beginning of September 1939, the Polish Government set up the "Metropolitan Committee for Mutual Social Aid"—S.K.S.S. The Committee had nine members, and was presided over by the Polish historian, Artur Sliwinski. The Jews, who were not represented on this Committee, set up the "Co-ordinating Committee"—"K.K." This was done at a meeting of all the Jewish organizations in the city—a meeting called by the "Joint" office in Warsaw immediately on the outbreak of war.

like most of the officials of this institution [the S.K.S.S.]. It should be emphasized that the head office of the S.K.S.S. adopted a very loyal attitude towards the Jewish section. A sum of about 50,000 zloty was paid over in order to meet the needs of the Jewish charity organizations. Provisions were granted equally to the Jewish and Christian refugees and homeless. The K.K. officials at that time did their duty with great self-sacrifice, standing in line at the Post Office Savings Bank building, which was being incessantly bombed by the Germans. There were several casualties among those standing in line at this time. The K.K. began energetic action to obtain housing. This was a very difficult task, practically a labour of Sisyphus. The refugees and the homeless had to be transferred from one point to another every day, because of incessant bombing. Although the falling bombs and the shrapnel did not differentiate between Jews and Christians and thousands of Jews and Poles slept their last sleep together in common improvized cemeteries—green spaces, public squares, gardens, courtyards and the like—the venom of anti-Semitism started spreading again, even into relief work.

The Jewish educated class of Warsaw and especially the teachers of the capital reported for work with the S.K.S.S. in response to the appeal of the authorities. Many of them were then referred to various welfare sections, which accepted Jewish candidates very reluctantly. Those who were accepted were harassed to such an extent that they were forced to resign.

The Jewish Civic Committee [14] was created the moment the war

---

[14] On the first day of the war, 1 September 1939, representatives of all the Jewish parties and social and economic organizations met in the Jewish Community building and decided to set up a "Jewish Public Committee of the Warsaw Jewish Community for affairs concerning the defence of the State." A declaration to this effect was issued to the press on 3 September, signed by the "Provisional Executive: Adv. Apolinary Hartglas, Consul Maximilian Friede, Engineer Moshe Kerner, Dr. Salomea Lewite, Leon Lewite, Chairman Maurycy Mayzel, Member of the Diet Adv. Shimon Seidman, Prof. Moshe Schorr, Senator Rafael Szereszewski, Dr. Henryk Szoskies, Member of the Diet Yaakov Trokenhajm, Editor S. Wolkowicz, Dr. Abraham Weiss, Senator Zdzislaw

broke out. One of its members was the engineer Adam Czerniakow, later Chairman of the Warsaw [Jewish] Community. The Civic Committee was made up of representatives of tradesmen and artisans only, without any representatives of the workers, the working intelligentsia, etc. The activities of this committee were confined to delivering various declarations of a political nature to Mayor Starzynski. The Civic Committee did not maintain contact with the community and was not very popular. It kept its distance from the quite extensive relief work that was done, and disbanded on the entry of the Germans. Its "demise" went unnoticed by the general public.

Even before Warsaw fell, the hydra of anti-Semitism began raising its head again. It was a common occurrence for Jews not to be allowed into the air-raid shelters in purely Polish blocks of flats, even during bombing. I was able to observe this in September 1939 in a certain block on Dluga Street, where I was serving in the Civilian Air Defence. The commanding officer of our shelter refused, on principle, to allow Jewish passers-by into the shelter. At 13 Leszno Street, across from the block at No. 18 Leszno Street, where I lived during the bombing, there was a shelter of the timber firm, "Paged". When a wing of our block was hit by a bomb, the tenants sought refuge in the shelter at 13 Leszno Street. We were refused because of anti-Semitism, although there was no shelter at all in our block. People were also turned away from shelters in many blocks of flats which had a majority of Polish tenants.

Then conflicts arose between Jews and Poles standing in the

Zmigryder-Konopka. (See *"Cywilna Obrona Warszawy we wrześniu 1939,"* Warsaw 1964, p. 16.)
Since many of the members of this Committee left Warsaw at the time of the mass exodus, public figures met again during the siege to set up a fresh Jewish representation *vis-à-vis* the Polish authorities. It was set up this time under the name, "Jewish Citizens' Committee of the Capital, Warsaw", and its members were Abraham Gefner, Hartglas, Adam Czerniakow, M. Lichtenbaum, Kerner, Weiss. The Committee was legally authorized by Mayor Starzynski on 15 September. (*Cf.* Czerniakow Diary, entries for 11–15 September.)

endless queues at the bakeries or the few grocery stores that were still open and where only a limited number of food products were being sold. Anti-Semitism was also demonstrated in the long queues at the Vistula, where water was distributed to the city's inhabitants. At the demand of anti-Semitic hooligans, separate queues were created for Jews and Aryans. For every fifty Aryans, only five Jews were given access to water. Jews coming back with water would be knocked down, beaten and bruised, and their water would be spilt. The result was that after a long day of waiting in the queue, the Jew would return home wounded and without water. There was hunger in the city. Most of the bakeries were closed down. At the few bakeries that were open, the queues were so long that one had to stand for hours and hours. Nobody was scared off by the fact that German bombers strafed the town with impunity, as it was bare of anti-aircraft defences, and aimed at the long queues in front of the bakeries. After every bomb that fell, there were pools of blood left on the pavement, but after a little while the queue formed anew. Death from a bomb was preferable to slow death from hunger.[15]

---

[15] In the three weeks' siege of Warsaw in September 1939, the population of the capital suffered enormous losses through German air and artillery attack, some 10,000 killed and over 50,000 wounded. (This figure does not include the losses of the Polish armed forces defending the capital.) (According to W. Bartoszewski, entry in *Wielka Encyklopedia Powszechna,* Vol. XII, Warsaw 1969, p. 122.)

4

AFTER THE GERMAN INVASION

National-Socialist Social Welfare. — Round-ups for forced labour. — Street trading. — The anti-Semitic scum of society controls the streets. — Pillaging of houses and shops. — The Germans film and photograph. — Raids on the railways. — The pogrom of February 1940. — Condition of the Jewish prisoners in German camps, and the attitude of the Poles.

After the German invasion, there was a revival of anti-Semitism in the full sense of the term. It was manifested in the relief work carried out by the N.S.V. (*National-Sozialistische Volkswohlfahrt* —National-Socialist Social Welfare[1]). In the public squares, enormous N.S.V. trucks distributed free bread and soup (made from commandeered Polish produce) to the starving population of Warsaw. For the first few days, the Jews were not excluded from this

---

[1] With the surrender of the city after its heroic stand, the Nazis signed an "agreement" with Warsaw representatives. Under this agreement, the Nazis promised to distribute 160,000 soup rations a day to the hungry population, and so Germans trucks went through the city streets distributing not 160,000 rations according to their undertaking, but only some 40 to 50,000. The Germans did not lose on this deal. On the morrow, the Nazis came to the Municipality and demanded that the City Council pay them an "advance" of a million in gold for the charity-soup, and the Council was obliged to pay.

The agreement promised that this soup would be distributed to all the inhabitants, without distinction of origin, but contrary to this promise, the Nazis pushed Jews out of the queues right from the beginning. On 15 October 1939, a notice was published signed by the Mayor Starzyński and by Janowski, the Nazi in charge of NSV activities, officially excluding the Jews from receiving any relief.

relief. But this was primarily for the sake of the films that were being made in the newly conquered capital. On Muranowski Square I witnessed how the Jews who had been given free bread and soup for the sake of the filming were immediately afterwards beaten up by the German soldiers and how the queue, which the Germans themselves had caused to be formed, was made to disperse. The anti-Semitic mob would pick out the hungry Jew standing in line before the N.S.V. trucks and would point out who was a *Jude*—the one German word the hooligans learned at once.

Very soon round-ups began for the various military formations that needed skilled workers for jobs of various kinds. As the Jews were not yet wearing special badges, it was difficult for the German blood-hounds to distinguish between Jews and non-Jews. The anti-Semitic scum came to their aid and obligingly pointed out the Jews to the Germans. Thus was the first bond sealed between the Polish anti-Semites and the Nazis. The platform that united them was, as usual, the Jews. These first performances of the Polish anti-Semites came as a severe shock to the Jews. They had imagined that when the enemy, this incarnation of the baseness and perfidy of the Teutonic Knights, the ruthlessness and treachery of the Prussians, the savagery of the Vandals, the morality of Hottentots, the cruelty of Mongols, the barbarism of the Tartars and the brutality of the Huns, entered the capital which they had conquered after such a heroic defence, they would be met with the universal and silent contempt of the whole nation. Of course no one accuses the Polish nation of not having adopted a befitting attitude towards the enemy. The nations must pay homage to the Poles for the indisputable fact that despite the dreadful terror, not one single prominent personality was to be found willing to play the part of a Polish Hacha.[2] This makes it even more distressing that this attitude

---

2 Emil Hacha (1872–1945), Czech politician known for his pro-German attitude. He became president of Czechoslovakia after the conference of Munich in September 1938. On 15 March 1939, without authorization Berlin handing over power in Czechia to Hitler and wiping out the independence of Czechoslovakia. With the entry of the German Army into Czechia, Hacha became the puppet-president of the so-called Pro- from the Czech Government or Parliament, he signed a declaration in

was not adopted by the whole nation. As early as October there were a considerable number of anti-Semitic elements who collaborated with the Germans in waging war on the Jews. This collaboration was manifested in many ways and it encompassed larger or smaller domains, depending on external circumstances. The anti-Semitic feelings were intensified after the return of thousands of Poles from the territories that were first occupied by the Soviets and later by the Germans, with their stories of atrocities committed by the N.K.V.D. (itself described as Jewish, of course); atrocities like Katyn,[3] in spite of the many Jewish names on the

---

tectorate of Bohemia and Moravia. Arrested after the defeat of Nazi Germany, he died in prison.

In Poland, the well-known Germanophile Gisbert Wladyslaw Studnicki, member of the Polish Council of State during the first World War, tried to play a similar role. In November 1939, Studnicki presented Goering with a memorandum asking for the establishment—under German leadership—of a rump Polish vassal State and a Polish Army to be used as auxiliary to the German Army in the event of Germany's waging war on the Soviet Union. Studnicki's proposal was rejected by the Third Reich. His book entitled, *Rzady Rosji Sowieckiej we Wschodniej Polsce, 1939–1941* (Soviet Russian Rule over Eastern Poland, 1939–1941), extremely anti-Semitic in tone, appeared in Warsaw in 1943.

(Czeslaw Madajczyk, *Generalna Gubernia w planach hitlerowskich*, Warsaw, 1961.)

3 Katyn: a place near Smolensk in the Soviet Union. In the middle of April 1943, the Germans officially announced that they had discovered mass graves in the forest nearby, in which were buried some thousands of officers of the Polish Army who had been captured by the Russians in September 1939. The Soviet authorities never admitted responsibility for this mass murder. The Nazis launched a large-scale anti-Semitic propaganda campaign among the Polish population, playing up alleged Jewish participation in the Katyn crime. They were not in the least disturbed by the fact that among the over 4,000 names of victims who were identified, many scores of names were those of Jews who had also been murdered. The Polish writer, Jozef Mackiewicz, a member of the enquiry commission sent to the site of the crime by the Germans, wrote as follows:

"I made one further discovery at Katyn which, though indirectly, throws further light on the identity of the true culprit. It was the scores of Jewish names which appeared in these lists of victims published by the Germans. While I was looking through these lists, I could not resist the

lists of the victims. The enormous anti-Jewish propaganda connected with this and the breaking off of diplomatic relations between the Polish Government-in-Exile and the Soviets, etc., also exerted their influence in helping to increase anti-Semitism. The first smile to be seen on the face of a Polish anti-Semite nodding to a German was in response to a blow dealt to a Jewish passer-by, who had been caught for forced labour by a German with the help of a Polish anti-Semite.

Mass pillaging of Jewish shops and homes began.[4] Bands of

---

temptation of saying to the German officer standing beside me: 'H'm . . . Quite a number of Jewish names here?'—'Yes. Quite so . . . Well, what? Is it worth while stressing it?' Nor did I stress it, I only stated a fact. Whoever is acquainted with that blind, raving anti-Jewish propaganda may imagine how reluctantly they must have made the concession of publishing scores of Jewish names on the list of Katyn victims."

(Joseph Mackiewicz, *The Katyn Wood Murders*, London, 1951.)

[4] In the first days after the entry of the Germans, groups of S.S.-men appeared in the streets and began picking up Jews as labourers, especially elderly men with beards, wearing caftans. Bands of street urchins and riff-raff surrounded the Germans and with cries of *Yid, Yid,* pointed out Jewish passers-by in the street. As for the mob—its attitude remains as before. Many of them go with the Germans through the streets pointing out where Jews live and helping them rob them. Sometimes they also help them beat up the Jews in the streets.

In the first days after the fall of the city, soldiers and officers accompanied by young Polish women would go into Jewish shops and take goods without paying for them. After two days of pillage, an order was issued by the Army Commander that soldiers were forbidden to enter shops without a special permit. This calmed the Jews somewhat, but the order remained a dead letter and in fact the robbery went on as before. Private houses were robbed as well, both by day and by night. There was no question of complaining; if anyone lodged a complaint, he either received a very rough answer or else disappeared completely. When soldiers came to rob the jeweller Stefan Luksemburg, he began to shout, thieves, thieves. The soldiers left, but later others came, searched the place, found bullets from a German gun—which of course they themselves put there—and he was executed.

If anyone reported a theft, the Germans investigated the accuser and proved that he had insulted the authorities. So the Jews preferred not to report robbery. The businesses on Franciszkanska Street (the centre of the leather trade in Warsaw) were pillaged in the course of a few weeks.

German soldiers went from one flat to another and emptied them of everything. A local element acquainted with the terrain was needed here, which could play the part of an intermediary. This commendable role was played by the anti-Semitic mob, which served as informer giving information as to which homes and shops belonged to wealthy Jews. The Germans took the porters of the blocks of flats and the doormen of shops to help them as informers. Among these informers were also some of the dregs of Jewish society. Assisting in the plundering Jewish homes, shops and warehouses was just one step short of regular collaboration with the Gestapo, the German police, etc. Later on, these individuals became the personnel of the various kinds of *Lagerschutz*,[5] whose task it was to keep watch over the Jewish labour

---

Lorries would drive up day after day and load up with merchandise from morning till night. To bring out the goods and load them, the Germans utilised the Jewish shop-owners and workers provided by the *Judenrat*. From day to day, maltreatment of passers-by in the streets grew increasingly frequent and serious, as did breaking into flats at night. Official confiscation of furniture and other movables also increased. Unofficial robberies went unpunished.

On 12 December 1939, representatives of the unit in charge of foreign currency (*Devisenschutzkommando*) told the chairman of the *Judenrat*, Czerniakow, that the community was to hand over addresses of rich Jews, so that their furniture, lamps, bed-linen, etc. could be confiscated.

In sum, from the first moment Jewish property was considered the booty of the conqueror. According to the order of 18 December 1939, the Jews had to register all their property; they were forbidden to utilise it or to sell their real estate. All their bank accounts were frozen. In general, Jews were forbidden to hold more than 2,000 zloty in cash. All the rest of their money had to be put in frozen bank accounts.

(A. Hartglas, *Meḥodashim harishonim bekibush hanazi*, in "Enzyqlopediya shel Galuyot," Volume two, op. cit., pp. 493, 505. *Sefer hazewaot; teudot, aduyot*, Jerusalem, 1945, p. 23–26, 30, 34, 42–43, 45.)

5 By an Order of the Warsaw District Governor of 27 February 1941, volunteers were recruited from among Poles, Ukrainians and Byelorussians for a Nazi auxiliary police formation, to be called the *Lagerschutz* (Camp Guard). The purpose of this force was to guard the forced labour camps for Jews. Its members often behaved towards the Jewish camp prisoners with the greatest cruelty. A number of leaflets put out by the Polish underground press called on the Poles not to volunteer for this formation. (Cf. Em. Ringelblum: Notes: Vol. I, p. 233.)

camps. They tormented and tortured the Jewish prisoners with impunity, pitilessly wounding and killing anyone without sufficient money to buy off the torturers.

From the moment the Polish anti-Semites helped the Germans drive the hungry Jews away from the soup vats, the "street" became a link between the Polish anti-Semites and the Nazis. The "street" supplied them with steady prey. These professional informers made up the future teams of *schmalzowniks*[6] and blackmailers who were to terrorize the Jews on the Aryan side and who, next to the police agents and the Polish police,[7] were to

---

6   *Schmalzowniks*: The greatest danger threatening Jews in hiding and those who gave them shelter was the plague of blackmailers and informers. Whole gangs of blackmailers went around in Warsaw and its environs trying to trap Jews. These gangs included Polish police, Polish agents of the Gestapo and the Kripo, smugglers, speculators, criminal underworld types and members of the Polish anti-Semitic and Fascist movements as well, such as "Szaniec", "Miecz i Plug" and others, who did this work for its own sake and not for reward. These blackmailers and informers (popularly called *Schmalzowniks*) brought disaster to thousands of Jews who had succeeded in escaping from the clutches of Hitler's murderers. More than once, the blackmailers' victims returned to the Ghetto to meet their end there. In their report, "The Destruction of the Warsaw Ghetto", written in October 1942, a few weeks after their escape to the Aryan side, the Berman couple describe how they were blackmailed three times over on the very day they left the Ghetto. (A. Berman, *Hayehudim beẓad haari,* in "Enẓiqlopediya shel galuyot Warsha", Vol. I, op. cit., p. 686.)

7   The Germans set about creating the Polish Police Force (known to Polish patriots as the "blue police" because of the colour of their uniforms) immediately after the conquest of Warsaw. Its members became notorious to Jews as agents and accomplices of the Gestapo in all its crimes and deeds of horror and to the Poles as German spies and accessories in the struggle against the Polish underground. The force was not so bad at the beginning, and many former policemen joined it and had their previous rights restored to them. But in the course of time, many honest people were excluded from the force and were replaced by *Volksdeutsche,* criminals, and weak characters poisoned by anti-Semitic indoctrination. (A. Hartglas, op. cit., p. 500.) The Polish police played a shameful role in the war waged by the German authorities on the hundreds of indigent women and children who infiltrated

be the Germans' most faithful ally in their hunting down of Jews. Their jeering laughter, their coarse jokes and sneers and even songs composed for the purpose—*"Hitler kochany, Hitler zloty nauczyl Zydow roboty"* ["Dear Hitler, golden Hitler—taught the Jews to work"] were to accompany the Jews employed in work-posts[8] on

into the Aryan side in order to beg for alms or a crust of bread. "They (the Polish police) stop carts in the street and extort money. They visit the bakeries where there is more flour than allowed under the quota. They go into shops and extort large sums. The Air Defence regulations also provide them with a good opportunity to extort money from Jews. The Polish clandestine press even gives the numbers of policemen who mercilessly beat up women and children for leaving the Ghetto or for begging. Their treatment of Jews is generally rude and often far worse than that of the Germans." Things reached the point that in June 1942 Polish police stations in the Ghetto were arresting Jews without the slightest pretext and demanding money ransom from them. (Ringelblum, op. cit., Vol. I, pp. 279–280, 373.)

Finally, note must be taken of the humiliating role of the Polish police, both uniformed and plain clothes, in serving the occupying forces by constantly blackmailing Jews who escaped to the Aryan side and then handing them over to the Germans.

In his diary, the Polish teacher, Żemiński, points with heartfelt bitterness to the part played by the Polish police in the murder of Jews who were trying to hide away from deportation to the extermination camps, calling them "animals".

(S.Żemiński, *Kartki z dziennika nauczyciela w Łukowie z okresu okupacji hitlerowskiej*, "Biuletyn Żydowskiego Instytutu Historycznego", No. 27, 1958, pp. 105–112.)

Dr. Klukowski writes in the same way about the liquidation of Jews in Szczebrzeszyn in his diary on 21 October, 1942: "Many people took an active part in hunting down the Jews. They pointed out the places where the Jews were hiding; boys even ferreted out little Jewish children, whom the Polish police then killed on the spot in front of everyone."

(Zygmunt Klukowski, *Dziennik z lat okupacji Zamojszczyzny*, Lublin, 1959, p. 290.)

[8] "Outpost" workers were employed at "work posts" outside the Ghetto. They went out to work and returned from it to the Ghetto *en masse,* under guard. This outside work was generally hard and dangerous, but afforded possibilities of smuggling food and establishing contact with the outside world. The number of these work sites outside the Ghetto reached 48 in May 1942, 54 in mid-June, 75 in mid-July (employing

their way to work. The street, from then on, became the realm of the anti-Semitic rabble, ruling there with the approval of the Germans.

In the autumn of 1939 there is very lively street trading in Warsaw.[9] Thousands of people who have lost their possessions in the Warsaw bombing come out onto the streets to sell whatever they have left. Most of the shop-owners have closed down at this stage for fear of being robbed by the Germans, who took their best wares for a song under the pretence of buying them. At this time one could buy anything and everything on the streets for next to nothing. Anti-Semitic hooligans made it their business to point out the Jewish street vendors to the Germans. Together with these pillagers, the Germans took everything away for nothing or for a few pence. I often witnessed how Jewish women—the pedlars were all women because the men were afraid to go out on the streets—wailed aloud when these German-Polish companies of robbers took everything away from them, depriving them of all

---

about 6,000 Jewish workers), and included S.S. and Wehrmacht installations and railway workshops.

[9] Jews in Warsaw were permitted to trade in the streets without restriction only in the Praga quarter, and in the other quarters, only in certain streets. The Jews' share in street trading was relatively small, because Jewish pedlars were more exposed to the risk of robbery and it was more dangerous for them to move about the city in general than for the others. Street trading was a permanent feature in the Jewish quarter. Emaciated children and young girls sold food (mainly bread) and products such as matches and cigarettes. Besides these things, there was also an illegal trade in various industrial products which came under requisitioning orders. Vendors of articles like these had only samples and patterns with them in the street, hidden under their clothes; for example, a vendor would have with him one shoe, one pair of stockings, a piece of leather, samples of thread, cloth, linen. Only after the transaction was completed, would the vendor bring the buyer the goods.

The Ghetto population also dealt in various home-made products and substitutes, such as soap, candles, paper, writing materials, drugs and medicaments, and food products.

(T. Brustin-Berenstein, *Hitlerowskie dyskryminacje gospodarcze wobec Zydow w Warszawie przed utworzeniem getta,* in "Biuletyn Żydowskiego Instytutu Historycznego", No. 2(4), 1952, pp. 178–179.)

possibility of further livelihood. These constant street robberies drove the Jews off the streets of the city. Street peddling passed almost completely into the hands of the Poles.

These ruffians did not confine themselves to attacking street vendors but pointed out shops and warehouses to the Germans. Cooperation between German soldiers, the Gestapo and the *Volksdeutsche* on the one hand and Polish anti-Semites on the other yielded a bountiful harvest in the shape of deserted Jewish shops and warehouses, which were pillaged and stripped bare in the course of a few months. By then the Germans had taken away fortunes which had been accumulated by the toil and labour of many generations. Some Jewish shop and warehouse owners in a fit of despair distributed their wares free to passers-by. There was plundering of shops regularly: it was enough for a German with his girl friend from the red-light district to go into a shop for the rabble to follow him and strip the shop completely of its contents. In many cases, a German gendarme would become the protector against the attacking native anti-Semites!

The Germans realized what excellent propaganda material was provided by their role as protectors against Polish aggression. This was a remarkably effective psychological propaganda trick. The Jews, the Germans claimed, are a harmful, destructive, unproductive element. They are hated by the Polish population, as is proved by the frequent attacks on the Jews. The Germans are instrumental in restoring law and order. They defend the Jews and put them to productive work. Photographs depicting Germans in their role of protectors against attacks by Poles, pictures sometimes authentic and sometimes faked and staged for this purpose, were proof of the fact that the Germans were *Kulturträger* in the "Wild East", where they were introducing elements of civilization and culture. The photographs of Germans saving Jews from the aggression of the Poles would from then on be repeated with every possible variation. A very important propaganda success was thus achieved. News was reaching the outside world of German atrocities in the occupied Polish cities, of mass murders of the civilian population and especially of Jews, of the burning down of towns, etc. By reproducing pictures of the Germans as defenders of the

Jews, evidence would be given of the Germans' humanitarianism. Illustrations depicting the positive German role in the East were apparently in great demand in the *Heimatland,* since the photographing of such scenes has gone on all the time without a break. It must be conceded that the level of the *Heimatland* itself was evidently not so high, as they even photographed Germans . . . being beaten by Jews . . .

This photographing and filming took place not only in the capital but also in the provinces.[10] In the first months of the war, a film was shot at Lubartowska Street in Lublin. One sequence of this film depicts a scene with Jews beating Germans. A German lies on the ground and a Jew is tormenting him. About this film the following anecdote was told: One day the Germans assembled the whole Jewish population in a public square and ordered them to wait there. Standing there the whole day, bare-headed, the assembled people were in a very gloomy state of mind, fearing something disagreeable, some repression. After prolonged waiting, the crowd was grouped in a variety of poses and the people were then ordered to sing. The song that the film operators liked best was a very simple folk-song with an easy, familiar melody, beginning with the words, *Lomir zich iberbeit'n* (Let's make up our quarrel), The crowd sang it with a growing enthusiasm that reached

---

10 German propaganda made use of films to help justify the policy of repressing and isolating the Jewish population. In Lodz, for example, the Germans filmed the transfer of the Jews to the Ghetto and described the operation as a peaceful and humane one.
(Ringelblum, op. cit., Vol. I, p. 129.)
On the other hand, in the Warsaw Ghetto they wanted to make a propaganda film consisting mainly of scenes staged in different places in the Ghetto—in the streets, restaurants, and places of amusement (a party with dancing), and even including descriptions of a Brith Milah (circumcision) ceremony, a Mikveh (ritual bath), a wedding, a funeral, etc., with the aim of displaying Jewish degeneracy. In May 1942, films were taken to show how the Jews were living in luxury: rich Jews guzzling and ignoring the fate of their starving brethren. Czerniakow raised the question of the films with the German authorities, and asked, "Why don't they film the school, and so on". (Entries for 12, 13 and 19 May 1942.)

ecstasy. Eye-witnesses relate that this extraordinary mood which came over the Lublin Jews can be explained by the fact that instead of singing, *Lomir zich iberbeit'n,* the Jews were singing, *"Mir weln zay iberleb'n"* ("We shall survive them"), which of course did not come true as far as the Jews of Lublin were concerned! The winter of 1939/40 arrived. The shameless street ruffians ran riot in the city streets. They attacked Jewish passers-by with impunity, especially those with beards and side-curls. For the Germans, bearded Jews in caftans constituted an extraordinary attraction.[11] There were specialists who stopped orthodox Jews and cut

---

[11] During the first period of the Nazi conquest, pious Jews, wearing traditional garb, with beard and side-curls, suffered more than other Jews. The Nazis cut off their beards and side-curls in the cruellest manner. During this time, they attacked the home of the elderly Rabbi Shlomo David Kahana, one of the most respected Rabbis of Warsaw, took the Rabbi, cut off his beard and side-curls and ordered him to sing and dance. The Rabbi fell ill from sorrow and shame. The same thing happened in the home of Rabbi Yehoshua Gutschechter, also an eminent old man, and the home of the Gaon Rabbi Menahem Zamba. (*Sefer hazevaot,* op. cit., p. 23.) In his survey, "The first months of the Nazi conquest", Hartglas writes, *inter alia,* "In Marszałkowska Street I saw with my own eyes three high-ranking officers, not Gestapo personnel but regular Army, one of them a Major, stopping an old Jew. One of them took from his pocket a small pair of scissors, which he apparently had ready for the occasion, and cut off half the white beard of the Jew. An officer with the rank of Captain stood to one side and photographed the spectacle. Apparently they wanted to have a picture from the front line to send home to their families, to raise their morale." ("Enziqlopediya shel Galuyot Warsha", Vol. II, op. cit., pp. 493–494.) At times soldiers, officers, and police held up bearded Jews and took them to barbers, who shaved off the beards of these pious Jews, and afterwards forced them to pay the barber for his work. But for the most part, the soldiers themselves acted as barbers. "It very often happened", writes Rabbi Shimon Huberband, "that when they caught bearded Jews, they also arrested well-dressed Jewish girls or women, and made them cut off the Jews' beards in the street. They often forced the Jews to swallow their beards after they were cut off. Very often, this cutting off of beards was accompanied by shameful maltreatment. Thus for example, the writer of these lines (Rabbi Huberband) was picked up for forced labour on the eve of Tisha b'Av 5400 (1940) as

off their beards with scissors and more often with a knife, together with pieces of flesh. The local ruffians followed the German example; shrieking with laughter, they helped their knife-wielding kin in their "cultural activity" of civilizing the Jews. Sometimes there was division of labour: the Pole would point out a bearded Jew, the German would stop him and the Pole would then hold

---

he was walking in the street accompanied by the journalist, A. Steier. Two other Jews were picked up at the same time, one with a long black beard and one with a long blond beard. A well-dressed young woman was also caught and forced to cut off our beards. While doing so she wept at the public desecration of the honour of Israel by evil men. They put the two of us together with the others on a lorry. Some Poles who were there dealt us some good blows while this was going on. The lorry drove to Nowolipki Street near Smocza Street, where it stopped. Some of the Poles and Germans went into Jewish houses in order to confiscate furniture, and we stayed in the lorry with Germans and Poles guarding us. They redoubled their blows on the other two Jews. They gave the black-bearded Jew a pair of scissors to cut off half the beard and half the moustaches of the blond man. The way he performed this task did not find favour in the eyes of his supervisors, and he was beaten up unmercifully. Then they gave the scissors to his blond companion, and the same spectacle was repeated. All this went on in an open lorry, in full view in the middle of the street, before the Ghetto was set up. Poles of the neighbourhood split their sides laughing at the sight of the Jews' being baited and tormented. And that wasn't enough for them. Not far from the spot where the lorry stopped was a barbershop. They called the owner and ordered him to use an electric clipper to shave off bunches of hair from the remaining half beards. The barber did as he was told, and when he finished his work, they made each Jew pay him two gold coins as a fee for his trouble. Steier and I were also obliged to pay the barber a similar sum, because he had not done any work on us ... When the faces of the Jews appeared in their ridiculous condition, the leading bully told them, "Well, now you're handsome skirt-chasers, now you can go and kiss beautiful Jewesses. At once one of them jumped out of the lorry, stopped some Jewish girls and made them kiss the Jews with the cut off beards in the street in front of hundreds of Poles who gathered at the spot. The assembled Poles laughed uproariously with pleasure at the sight."
(Shimon Huberband, *Kidush hashem, Ktavim meyemey hashoa*, Tel-Aviv, 1969.)

him while the German cut off his beard. Following the German example, the Poles would stop Jewish passers-by and beat them up mercilessly. For fear of the "decent" Germans who sometimes protected Jews, the hooligans were obliged to limit their activity during the daytime. The night, however, was their exclusive realm. That was when they could hold their revels freely. There were streets where a Jew could not show his face if he did not want to return home beaten bloody, robbed of his money and even his clothes. The Saski Gardens, famous for anti-Semitic excesses before the war, was now the sole domain of the anti-Semitic bandits. Here, even during the day, a Jew could not show himself and get away unscathed. One of those gangs that beat and robbed everyone ruthlessly awaited him there.

From the city streets, the hooligans' activities were transferred to the trams. In the beginning there were separate cars "For Jews Only" (*Nur für Juden*); afterwards the Jews were not allowed to travel on the trams at all. On orders from the anti-Semitic hooligans, the conductors stopped the trams, and the hooligans dragged out the Jewish passengers, throwing themselves by scores on their outnumbered and helpless Jewish victims. It was very rare for the conductors to summon up enough courage to resist. We know of a case where a German ordered a tram-driver in the Praga Quarter to run over a Jew who was forced to lie down spread out over the rails, but the driver refused, despite the fact that the German pointed a gun at his head.

The same thing that was happening on the streets of Warsaw was also happening on the trains, where Germans would enter the carriages and shout, *"Alle Juden raus."* There were always obliging Aryans to denounce the Jewish passengers and give them away to the Germans, who usually killed them on the spot. People who returned from the eastern territories conquered from the Russians by the Germans did their part in increasing the hostile attitude towards the Jews. According to an eye-witness report, they told unbelievable stories in the trains about the terrible things the Jews did to the Poles while the Bolsheviks were there. They rejoiced that now Hitler had come to take the Jews in hand and repay them for everything. Hundreds of Jews were rounded up on the

49

trains by the Germans and were victimized as a result of this propaganda.[12]

Meanwhile, the numbers in the anti-Semitic gangs increased daily. Derelicts made their living this way. Single attacks were no longer enough. The organization supporting those bandit elements, undoubtedly one of the O.N.R. branches, decided to put on a show for Warsaw such as the anti-Semites had been wanting for a long time. They had received *panem* from the N.S.V. and now they wanted *circenses*. There were several outbreaks during the winter.[13] The best known was the pogrom of February 1940.

---

[12] Dr. Zygmunt Klukowski entered the following note in his diary on 11 January 1940 (*Dziennik z lat okupacji,* op. cit., p. 94) : "Today I was called to a sick Jew with frozen feet. He had been travelling by train from Warsaw with goods he had bought. He told me, in tears, how Polish travellers robbed him of part of his goods and threw him out of the carriage while the train was still in the station in Warsaw. The railway guard then put him in a luggage van, where he travelled to Rejowiec, and from there on for a further twelve hours, this time in a carriage, but also not heated. German methods have found fertile ground among certain strata of the Polish population."

[13] Disturbances took place in the Jewish streets on 16 and 17 December 1939, and on 15, and 27–30 January 1940 and the beginning of February, at the end of March, on 15 and 16 May (in the suburb of Praga) and on 31 May, and again on 19 August and 26 October. The armbands with the Shield of David, which at first served the Germans as a means of recognizing Jews so that they could pick them up for the labour camps, gradually turned into a sign for the Polish rabble authorizing them to beat up the wearers of the armband and maltreat them mercilessly. In these pogroms, Polish bullies, among them school pupils, armed with sticks and all sorts of heavy implements, would fall upon passers-by, regardless of age or sex, and deal them murderous blows. They would break the few remaining display windows and loot whatever they found in the houses and shops, and so on. The Polish police observed the rioters with equanimity. Sometimes the attackers were held off by Jewish workers. In the disturbances of March 1940, the Germans photographed the spectacle of the pogrom and put up a show of defending the Jews; the photographs were published in the press of the Reich, with the stress on the Polish people's anger at the Jews.

It is true that members of the Polish intelligentsia as well as representatives of workers' organizations condemned the outbursts. At that time the attitude of the Polish intelligentsia towards the Jews, according to

Anti-Semitic gangs, made up mostly of minors, were directed by a German who protected their rear and oversaw the "action". The armament of these bands consisted of sticks, clubs, crow-bars, etc. The assailants' battle-cries were: "Kill the Jews", "Down with the Jews", "Long live independent Poland without Jews", etc. On their way they broke the plate-glass windows of shops marked with the Star of David, burst open the iron shutters, broke into the shops and pillaged them. They punched and knocked down Jews who crossed their path and beat them unconscious. The last act of the pogrom and its real aim was pillaging the shops. The pogrom lasted several days. No one intervened. The Polish Police, responsible for the safety of the population, kept silent. So did the Polish independence organizations. The pogrom, directed by a hidden hand, came to an abrupt end, as if by order. Everything returned to normal.

An eye-witness of the excesses at Franciszkanska Street in February 1940 relates: A crowd of 200 to 300 people, armed with sticks, clubs and crow-bars, moved along under the command of young airmen with guns in their hands. Older Aryans brought up the rear of the procession; they directed the disturbance, were in constant communication with the Germans and gave instructions to the band of rowdies. The mob broke plate glass windows on the way. Inside the entrances to blocks of flats stood groups of Jews armed with sticks and clubs, ready for defence. At the corner of Franciszkanska and Walowa Streets, the herd of hooligans came up

---

a reliable Jewish source, was one of "open support, and of opposition to the pogroms". But on the other hand, there was no public Polish expression of disassociation from the pogromists, nothing to weaken the impression that the whole Polish population supported the anti-Semitic excesses committed by the Poles who collaborated with the Germans. All along, apart from the pogroms, Polish hooligans threw stones over the Ghetto walls and did not shrink from smashing tombstones with hammers in the Jewish cemeteries of Okopowa and Praga. Thus, for example, the tombstone of Zvitkover was badly damaged.
(Ringelblum, op. cit., Vol. I, pp. 78, 79, 81, 83, 103, 104, 105, 107–109, 133; see also Czerniakow's entries for the dates mentioned above, and also the entries from 30 June to 9 July 1940; *Sefer hazevaot*, pp. 34, 45–47, 49, 53, 55.)

against a group of a few score Jewish workers, armed with the picks they use to break up ice. Fighting broke out in which one hooligan was killed and two Jews. At the same time another pogrom with German airmen participating was taking place on Grzybowska Street. The Germans kept shooting their guns into the air to celebrate. A band of German soldiers followed the hooligans' procession, pleased with their performance. The hooligans profaned the name of Poland by shouting. "Long live free Poland without Jews". Many Jews fell victim in this pogrom. Here too, the Jews stood ready to defend themselves inside the entrances to the blocks of flats. The courageous attitude of the Jewish population deserves to be emphasized. They did not succumb to terror of the anti-Semitic bandits and took suitable measures to defend themselves.

The pogrom of February 1940 was a profound shock to the Jewish population of Poland. From then on the Jews feared a coalition between Polish anti-Semites and the Germans, who would want to take advantage of the Poles' deep-rooted anti-Semitism to make them do their dirty work for them. Warsaw Jews feared that the Germans would make the pogroms a pretext for evicting the Jews from the city. They feared that the Germans would take seriously the slogan that echoed in the streets—"We want a Warsaw without Jews"—and would drive the Jews out. The Warsaw Jews were deeply pained that no reaction against these things came from the Polish community. It did sometimes happen that an elderly Christian would stop a Jew in the street and warn him that they were beating up Jews on such and such street. But it never happened that passersby dared to actively oppose the excesses of the hooligans. I witnessed pogroms on many streets. I would take off my badge and follow the raging mob. Only once did I see someone stop the rowdies, an elderly woman on Bankowy Square, who reproached them for profaning the good name of Poland and for aiding and abetting the Germans. Sneering laughter was the ruffians' only answer to this Polish woman's noble words.

To sum up: The period from October 1939 to November 1940 —that is, up to the creation of the Ghetto—was a period of constant anti-Jewish agitation, which steadily increased. It started with attacks on individual Jews and ended with uncontrolled pillage of Jewish wealth and recurrent pogroms in different parts of Warsaw. No one will accuse the Polish nation of committing these constant pogroms and excesses against the Jewish population. The significant majority of the nation, its enlightened working-class and the working intelligentsia, undoubtedly condemned these excesses, seeing in them a Germain instrument for weakening the unity of the Polish community and a lever to bring about collaboration with the Germans. We do, however, reproach the Polish community with not having tried to dissociate itself, either in words—sermons in the churches, etc.,—or in writing, from the anti-Semitic beasts that cooperated with the Germans, and for not having actively opposed the constant excesses, for not having done anything whatsoever to weaken the impression that the whole Polish population of all classes approved of the performances of the Polish anti-Semites. The Polish Underground's passivity in face of the filthy tide of anti-Semitism was the great mistake in the period preceding the creation of the Ghetto, a mistake which was to take its revenge in the later stages of the war.

*

The condition of Jewish prisoners-of-war captured in the September 1939 campaign was characteristic of Polish-Jewish relations. I heard reports from a series of prisoners who had been in different *Stalags* [P.O.W. camps], and their accounts agreed completely. On the whole, these accounts are very saddening, for they show that Polish anti-Semites in military uniform carried out their anti-Semitic programme to the letter, even in the face of the common enemy. They forgot that military regulations, to which they were still subject, prescribed fair treatment for all soldiers, irrespective of descent or nationality. Anti-Semites in uniform decided to make up for the break of one month—the month of September—in anti-Jewish activities, and with redoubled energy began harassing their companions in distress. On the basis of very detailed written statements, giving names of places, dates, precise circumstances, etc., we can form an idea of the hell which Jewish prisoners went through at the hands of their Polish companions in the prisoner-of-war camps. There were several instances of Polish prisoners' taking the Jews' clothes, shoes, etc. away from them, which was then tantamount to death in the winter cold. More than once a German guard would become the Jews' protector, delivering them from the clutches of raging Polish anti-Semites. That Polish Fascists should behave this way will not surprise us when we recall the basic principle of the O.N.R.—"Beat the Jews, always and everywhere". So they beat them and tormented them, even in captivity, to the joy of the enemy.[14] Relations were

---

[14] We possess information on numerous manifestations of anti-Semitism in prisoner-of-war camps, culled from various reports collected by Ringelblum (Ringelblum Archives, Part 1, Eye-witness Reports, Nos. 423, 710, 763, 1,701) as well as from many reports written after the war. Ludwik Landau, the chronicler of the Polish Underground, writes about anti-Semitism in P.O.W. camps as follows (entry of 27 February 1940): "An afflicting sign of life is the permanence of a phenomenon which —it would seem—ought to have disappeared from the present political scene: anti-Semitism. By chance I heard some observations on this subject today, remarks made in different places—in railway carriages on the main line and the narrow-gauge suburb one, in the queue in front of a shop; the Jews are a constant subject of conversation, of complaint; fears are expressed that maybe Jews will get something forbidden them by the invaders, the same invaders indeed, who are persecuting the Polish Christian population too! The Jewish prisoners of war returning from German camps (there have been frequent instances recently of Jews' being freed, and not only Jews) also talk of the anti-Semitism displayed by their companions in distress; there are said to have been cases of Christian prisoners' asking the Germans to separate them from the Jews in the camp. It is symptomatic that anti-Semitism is said to be much more strongly felt in the officers' camps than in those for other ranks." (Ludwik Landau, *Kronika lat wojny i okupacji*, Vol. I, Warsaw 1962, p. 303.)
In some P.O.W. camps, in Doessel for example, a Ghetto was set up for Jews in the camp on the initiative of anti-Semitic P.O.W.s. The one and only pre-war Polish General of Jewish origin, Bernard Stanisław Mond, describes the conditions prevailing in this camp: "...I went through the inferno of a life-time, caused both by the Germans and my own fellow-prisoners". (Excerpt from a letter from General Mond to Ignacy Schwarzbart. Yad Vashem Archives, file M-2, D-17.)
The Polish military historian, Col. Jan Rzepecki, former member of the Home Army General Staff, writes of the situation in another P.O.W. camp: "From the political point of view, the dominant organization was the O.N.R., being the most alert and the noisiest, with its great influence among the young officers, both reservists and professionals. In the camps, the Germans put their racialism into practice only to the

better in camps for civilian prisoners, most of whom came from the educated class. Here mutual assistance prevailed and equal treatment for all, irrespective of descent.

The situation of Jewish prisoners-of-war only improved considerably when they were assigned to work in factories, on estates, with peasants, etc. The Germans, who were unacquainted with Jews, had imagined them, along *Stürmer* lines, to be usurers, parasites, bloodsuckers and similar harmful elements. And now it appeared that the Jewish prisoners provided first-class experts in all fields of handicraft and industry. The Jews were also outstanding in farming the land, as if this had been their occupation from the day they were born. Under the influence of contact in everyday life, obscurantist superstitions disappeared, and the German population's attitude towards the Jewish prisoners changed radically. The Director of the American Joint Distribution Committee, Mr. Giterman,[15] who had been

---

extent of collecting officers of Jewish origin into half of one encampment; but our native Fascists permitted themselves to jeer at the Jews and attack them verbally, and even to institute a social boycott."
(Jan Rzepecki, *Wspomnienia i przyczynki historyczne,* Warsaw, 1956, pp. 300–301.)

[15] Yitzhak Giterman, born in Hornostopol, in the Ukraine, active in public life and one of the first members of the "Joint" in Warsaw, continued his public activity in the Ghetto, and served on the executive of "Oneg Shabat" and the enterprises of YCOR ("Yiddische Cultur-Organizazie", which was established in the Ghetto on the initiative of the economist, Menahem Linder, with the aim of encouraging Yiddish language and culture in the public life of the Ghetto; it organized lectures, celebrations of centenaries of Jewish authors, artists' meetings, etc.).
He succeeded to organizing large-scale assistance and in mobilising large sums of money for the tens of thousands of war fugitives and victims. He organized aid and welfare for the Jews of Vilna after the first "actions" and also for the Jews of Lublin after the first "expulsion" to Belzec.
The chairman of the *Judenrat* in the Warsaw Ghetto, Czerniakow, accepted Giterman's suggestion that very substantial means should be mobilised for assistance. In this activity under Giterman's leadership there took part, among others, public workers L. Bloch, M. M. Kohn, and Dr. Ringelblum; coercion was brought to bear to put fugitives in the flats of rich people and get them work. For these things over a million zloty were raised. However, the main purpose was not achieved,

a civilian prisoner in German hands for some months, told me the following very characteristic expression of this change of attitude in the words of a German: *"Ihr seid hierher gekommen als verfluchte Juden, ihr kehrt zurück nach Hause als gelobte Kinder des Volkes Israel."* (You came here regarded as accursed Jews, you're going home as esteemed children of Israel.)

The Jewish prisoners—private soldiers—left Germany shortly afterwards and returned to their native towns, except for the Jews from the eastern borderland, who remained in the province of Lublin, where a considerable part of them were exterminated.[16]

---

because "the milieu of the chairman (Czerniakow) did everything possible to block the idea of levying compulsory taxes from the new-rich war profiteers".

Giterman was one of the few public figures of long standing who in the spring of 1942 responded to the call of "Hehalutz" for self-defence; he supported the setting up of a Jewish combatant force in Vilna, and together with Dr. Ringelblum, Lipa Bloch, Menahem Kohn and David Guzik, he was a member of the finance committee of the Jewish Co-ordination Committee which saw to mobilising financial means for the Jewish Combat Organization. He was murdered by the Germans in the "action" of 18 January 1943.

(Emmanuel Ringelblum, *Ktovim fun Geto*, Vol. II, *Notizn un ophand-lungen*, Warsaw 1963, p. 122–141. Yizhak Zukerman, Moshe Basok (Editors), *Sefer milhamot begetaot, beyn hahomot, bemahanot, beyaarot*, Tel Aviv, 1954, p. 716.)

16 At the beginning of 1940, Jewish prisoners of war, both privates and N.C.O.'s, whose homes were in Nazi-occupied territory, were freed from the P.O.W. camps. Those whose homes were in Soviet-occupied territory were brought together to a P.O.W. camp in Lublin (7, Lipowa Street), called the Lipowa Camp. All Jewish officers, no matter where they came from, were kept in P.O.W. camps until the end of the war. The first group to be brought to the Lipowa Camp, in December 1939, numbered about a thousand. At the end of December they were transported in the direction of the new German-Soviet border, and nearly all of them were murdered *en route* by the S.S. escort. At about the same time, the turn of the year 1940–1941, more Jewish P.O.W.'s—about 2,500—were brought to this Camp, where they remained until October 1943. Here in Lipowa, there was a great deal of clandestine activity, aimed mainly at organizing prisoner escapes with the help of the Polish underground, the prisoners' intention being to join the partisans. In

all about 400 prisoners managed to escape, about 250 of whom were caught by the Germans and killed soon after escaping, while another 50 or so were treacherously murdered by members of the Polish underground who had promised to help them join the partisans. Only about a hundred got to the partisans, mainly Jewish partisan units commanded by Samuel Jegier and Samuel Gruber, acting in the framework of the Polish *Gwardia Ludowa*, and the majority of them perished in the fighting. The prisoners still left in the Lipowa Camp were brought to Majdanek concentration camp on 3 November 1943 and shot there. (Reports of former P.O.W.'s in the Lipowa Camp: Samuel (Mieczysław) Gruber, Roman Fiszer, Josef Reznik, Josef Sterdyner and others. Yad Vashem Archives.)

57

5

POLISH-JEWISH ECONOMIC QUESTIONS

The Ghetto is formed. — Intentions and reality. — The Ghetto, a concentration camp. — The Ghetto works for the Aryan side. — Old clothes influence the Ghetto balance of payments. — Safe-keeping of belongings and goods on the Aryan side. — Police agents. — Money exchange. — Tribute to the Unknown Smuggler. — Sale of Jewish real estate. — Résumé.

The Ghetto is formed[1] and a new era begins in Polish-Jewish relations. In organizing the Ghetto, the Germans aimed at isolating the Jewish population completely and segregating it entirely from the Aryan population. The Ghetto was to be isolated and reduced to such a state that the Jews would have no air to breathe and would die of starvation.

The process of eliminating the Jews from the economic life of the country began as soon as the Germans invaded. Jews were removed from all posts in government, municipal and public institutions and business concerns. Aryan firms were forbidden to employ Jewish workers and officials. Jews were forbidden to use public and

---

[1] The Nazis began setting up Ghettos on Polish soil in the very first months of the occupation. An order for the establishment of a Ghetto in Piotrkow Trybunalski was posted on 28 October 1939. By the end of 1939 orders had also been issued for Ghettos in Puławy and Radomsko. The order to set up a Ghetto in Lodz, the second biggest Jewish community in Poland after Warsaw, appeared on 8 February 1940. Numerous Ghettos in the regions of Kielce and Lodz were set up in the spring of 1940. It was in October 1940 that the Nazis proceeded to make preparations for a Ghetto in Warsaw, and many Ghettos came into being in the Lublin district at this time. The Ghettos in the Cracow district were set up relatively late—in the spring of 1941. The Ghetto in Cracow itself was set up under the Nazi order of 3 March 1941.

private libraries, to go to theatres, cinemas, etc. They were not allowed to use state or municipal means of transport (railways, suburban trains, buses, trams). Young Jews were not given access to public schools nor, of course, to private Aryan schools. All economic and cultural contact between Jews and the Aryans was to be broken off completely. In practice, social relations with Jews were forbidden, although regulations were never issued to this effect. Forming the Ghetto was to be the Germans' crowning achievement, the completion of the process of segregation, From now on the Jews would be able to communicate with the Aryan world only with the approval of the authorities, who would control and supervise all economic contacts. The Ghetto was to be hermetically sealed off.

The Aryan world—the *Umwelt* in official terminology—is a foreign country, separated from the Ghetto by a frontier customs post. Economic exchange between these countries is based on the principles of clearance agreements. The clearing institution is the *Transferstelle*,[2] an *ad hoc* creation. The Ghetto was to receive food provisions according to the amount of labour provided. At the time the Ghetto was formed, there were other co-existant ideas, which, if realized, would very soon have led to disaster. The Ghetto was

---

[2] On 20 November 1940, the *Judenrat* was ordered to supply furniture for the twenty rooms of the *Tranferstelle* Office by 1 December 1940, and to pay 10,000 zloty a month "for administering the affairs" of the new office. It was also necessary to prepare a place close to the railway station for the loading and storage of goods in wholesale quantities and for food provisions.

Though the order regarding the *Transferstelle* was issued only on 14 April 1941, it was already in force within the Department for Population Transfers (*Abteilung Umsiedlung*) when the Ghetto was closed off (16 November 1940). Under this order of the general-governor, "The *Transferstelle*, as a corporate entity under public law, makes arrangements, in accordance with the regulations laid down by the head of the province (governor), for the economic relations of the Jewish residential quarter (the Ghetto) with the world outside it". Actually, the main activity of the *Transferstelle* for many months was preventing food imports into the Ghetto.

(See Czerniakow, Diary, entries for 19 December 1940 and 3 May 1941 and *passim*.)

59

to pay for provisions with currency, valuables and gold. Fortunately, neither of these ideas was ever realized. The Commissioner of the Jewish District, Auerswald,[3] somehow couldn't tackle this problem, and he let things take their course. In practice, the Ghetto was something in the nature of an autonomous territory with a local municipal authority, its own Order Service, Post Office, prison, even its own Bureau of Weights and Measures. The Jews defined it as a concentration camp, bounded by a wall and barbed wire, the only difference being that in the Ghetto the inhabitants had to pay for their keep out of their own pockets.[4]

---

[3] Advocate Heinz Auerswald (born in Berlin on 26 July 1908), who joined the ranks of the S.S. as early as 7 June 1933, joined the "Protective Police" (*Schutzpolizei*) in October 1938 and took part in the September 1939 campaign. He remained in the police till February 1940, reaching the rank of *Polizei-Oberwachtmeister*. In spite of the recommendations of Warsaw District Governor Fischer, Auerswald was transferred to service in the civil authority. (See J. Wulf, *Das Dritte Reich und seine Vollstrecker*, Berlin 1961, p. 314.) He was at first Head of the Welfare Department of the Warsaw District Governor. On 1 May 1941 he was appointed by the District Head (*Distrikts-Chef*) in Warsaw as "Commissioner for the Jewish Quarter". In order to carry out his appointed tasks, the Commissioner, who was subordinate to the District Head, made use of the *Transferstelle* in Warsaw and of the Chairman of the *Judenrat*. In the Commissioner's Office a department was established for General Administrative Affairs and a Department for Economic Questions.
Auerswald was one of the most oustanding enemies of the Jews. On 17 November 1941 eight Jews, six of them women, were executed in the yard of the Jewish prison; they had left the Ghetto to hunt for scraps of bread for their hungry children. Auerswald also signed a declaration of 30 June 1942 on the killing of 110 persons, 10 of them Jewish policemen, as "reprisals" for the increased Jewish opposition to orders of the German police, an opposition that on occasion took the form of forceful resistance. The Jewish policemen were included for having attempted to give bribes, helping smugglers and for breaches of discipline.

[4] In setting up the Ghetto, the Germans had two clear aims: to isolate the Jews and to starve them out. To the outside world, the Ghetto was simply the Jewish quarter, just as there was a Polish quarter and a German quarter. But the real truth of the matter was that the Jewish Ghetto in Warsaw was nothing but a concentration camp for half a million people, without any link to the outside world, for it was closed off like a prison by high walls, with twenty-four openings guarded

The formation of the Ghetto produced great consternation in the Jewish community. It was estimated that in a year, at most, the Ghetto would have no means of payment left, for everything would have been transferred to the other side as payment for provisions. Official food supplies were sufficient for a few days in the month at most; the other days had to be covered by smuggling. It soon became apparent that dry theory is one thing and that the "tree of life" is another and very different. The Germans wanted to tie down the Ghetto in a Procrustean bed of production for the benefit of their Army. But in spite of the special *Sonderdienst* watching the Ghetto from the outside, in spite of the Gendarmerie, the Blue Police, the S.S., the S.D., the *Transferstelle* and the Jewish Order Service,[5] it became evident that the resilience of Jewish economic

---

by police to check entry and exit. It was forbidden to bring in food provisions or goods of any description.

The Warsaw Ghetto, like other Ghettos, was treated by leading Nazi officials as a temporary concentration camp. At a conference of the general government administration on 15 October 1941, the head of the Department for the Economy, Dr. Emmerich, said of the Warsaw Ghetto: "It is to be a temporary concentration camp up to the moment it is possible to move the Jews out" (*"Es soll ein zeitweiliges Konzentrationslager sein bis zu dem Zeitpunkt, an dem die Juden abgeschoben werden können"*).

5 When the Ghetto in Warsaw was finally closed off, the head of the *Judenrat* was in fact vested with the authority of Mayor of that part of the city and he was moreover obliged to assume responsibility in spheres that in more orderly times belonged to the State, such as the administration of justice, posts, etc. In order to rule so large a mass of population, the *Judenrat* had to establish a suitable militia, which was called in German *Jüdischer Ordnungs-Dienst* (Jewish Service for the Maintenance of Order, generally referred to as the Jewish Order Service). On the one hand, this Service was subject to the orders of the head of the *Judenrat* and on the other to the Polish Police which in its turn was subordinate to the German Police. The Order Service was created at the time of the creation of the Ghetto in Warsaw, November 1940. Up to that time there was only a police detachment numbering about a hundred men, which served as escort for the Jewish workers' groups on their way to their work-places for the Germans, and for the maintenance of order on the premises of the *Judenrat*. This detachment was attached to the Labour Department, and was not considered a separate

61

authority. After the Ghetto was closed off, the Polish Police were withdrawn from the police stations bit by bit, and the whole Ghetto gradually passed to the authority of the *Judenrat* and its Order Service.

The Ghetto was divided into six districts, each under a "District Command" with four platoons of police, plus one platoon attached to the community premises. There were in addition reserve units. The Order Service men received special technical training, they wore special caps and carried rubber truncheons. They received ranks according to their tasks and wore badges of rank accordingly. The Commanding Officer of the Jewish Police was the convert, Józef Szeryński, a former Colonel in the Polish Police. His appointment to the command was intended to point to a desire to maintain contact with former Polish government circles and with the Polish population. But with the passage of time it became clear that the appointment was a mistake from every point of view.

At first, only members of the intelligentsia, men who had matriculated from Polish secondary schools, served in the Warsaw Jewish Order Service. In the officers' cadre of the force there were many well-known barristers, some of them former officers in the Polish Army. Most of them had come forward to serve in the force in the belief that by doing so they would be able to serve the tormented Jewish public. In his notes in the first days of the setting up of the Ghetto with its Jewish regime, Ringelblum stressed the good qualities of the Jewish policemen—instead of ordering and demanding, they requested, persuaded, talked with the people.

As time passed, the *Judenrat* and the Jewish Police cut themselves off more and more from their own people, whom they had previously said they were serving. In the last resort, little by little, they became the willing instruments of those who had vested authority in them and they carried out the will of the rulers. They began by standing on street corners and controlling the movement of passers-by. Then they went on to bring in Jews who had not presented themselves for work, and finally it came to breaking into shelters and hide-outs to fetch out women and children and hand them over to the hangmen during the "action". If a policeman did not produce five "head" of victims for the Germans, they would take his wife, his children, and him too, and it was for this —to sacrifice the lives of innumerable people in order to save his own— that he was trained by those who gave him authority. Some individuals who realized in time what was happening drew back and resigned, while later on it became impossible to retreat. As time passed, the only people who stayed in the force were pliable characters who became the actual executors of all the German operations and the direct instrument of extermination. Every new anti-Jewish decree of the authorities the Jewish police turned into a source of income for itself. The vilest of all were the

life, Jewish energy and initiative, professional competence and ancient tradition, and the will and desire to live of four hundred thousand Jews had brought about a miracle: the Ghetto proved capable of independent economic life. A year after the Ghetto was formed, when an attempt was made to strike an annual balance, even the most ferocious pessimists who had forecast the darkest prophecies—financial exhaustion of the Ghetto and general starvation of the Jewish population—had to admit that their expectations had not been well founded.[6] The main fault in their reasoning was their assumption that the exchange of products between the Ghetto and the Aryan world would be carried out solely on official lines,

---

blackmailers among the police, including many brutes among them who decided the next victims for the torture camps. "Who said that the Jewish police did not carry arms?" wrote one of the Ghetto diarists. "Their fists, well developed by means of corruption and extortion, are enough to easily overpower little groups of starving children, who fall to the ground like match sticks at the first blow, especially when it's a blow from a rubber truncheon."

As a matter of course, the Order Service men fought against the Ghetto underground, and only a few of them made use of their positions to help the Jewish underground combatants.

The Jewish Order Service plumbed the depths of vileness during the deportation of summer 1942, when it carried out German orders; there was not a single word of protest from its members against the abominable role they played in bringing their fellow-Jews to be killed. It is not surprising, therefore, that after this "action", the surviving remnant in the reduced Ghetto demonstrated their burning hatred of the Jewish police (there remained only 300 police to keep guard over the Ghetto).

It was with satisfaction that the public learnt of the death penalty inflicted on the Police Commander Yaakov Lejkin by the Jewish Combat Organization on 20 October 1942.

(E. Ringelblum, Vol. II, op. cit., pp. 31–37. Naḥman Blumental, *Geto Warsha wehurbana*, in "Enziqlopediya shel galuyot Warsha", Vol. I, op. cit., pp. 605–607. Joseph Kermish, *Nigudim maamadiyim begeto Warsha*, in "Enziqlopediya shel Galuyot Warsha", Vol. II, op. cit. p. 573.)

6 What the author has to say in this passage applies only to the Warsaw Ghetto. It should be recalled that in other Ghettos such as Lodz (160,000 inhabitants) the Nazis succeeded in isolating the Jews completely from the outside world and in cutting off all unofficial economic contacts between the Ghetto and the Aryan side.

that is, through the specially created *Transferstelle*. In practice it became evident that the ratio of official exports to unofficial was in proportion to the ratio of official food supplies to the real ones. It turned out that the Ghetto continued to carry out lively economic transactions with the Aryan side as before, and that economic ties created long before the war were not cut off, even when the walls that separated the Ghetto from the Aryan world were raised higher and still higher. Apart from what was produced officially for the needs of the German Army and the German market in general, the Ghetto continued to produce for the Polish market, utilizing the stock of raw materials in the Ghetto and raw materials smuggled into the Ghetto. These raw materials were acquired, illegally of course, from firms in custody in Tomaszow Mazowiecki, Czestochowa, Lodz, etc,, out of these firms' quotas of raw materials. Jewish industrialists and artisans displayed unprecedented ingenuity in contriving substitutes to replace scarce materials. Everything that had been manufactured for the Aryan market before the war was being produced now as well. The weaving plants produced excellent woollen fabrics with wool stolen from factories in Czestochowa, the "Wola" factory in Warsaw and from other towns. Prayer shawls were dyed and made into scarves, sweaters, etc. Production was started of women's kerchiefs, jerseys, peasant's overcoats, etc. These were made out of old clothes that could be bought wholesale on the enormous square on Gesia Street (the so-called Gesiowka), where there were mass sales of things that had belonged to the Jewish population, which was being reduced to poverty. Day after day, special agents of various firms would buy up thousands of kilograms of old sheets and all sorts of old clothes in general. In this market Polish merchants sold a large transport of old clothes (20,000 kilograms) bought from the Lublin *Werterfassung*[7] after the liquida-

---

[7] *Werterfassung*: The German office that collected Jewish property for the benefit of the German economy after the owners had been killed or expelled to concentration and extermination camps. An elaborate machinery was set up for this purpose, and a labour force which included the Jews themselves. It was a typical German invention to have Jewish labour clear out the Jewish houses that had been left abandoned.

The head of the *Werterfassung* was Franz Konrad, who more than once

tion of the Ghettos in the District of Lublin. All these old clothes were dyed and printed with various patterns in the dye house set up specially for this purpose on Niska Street or in private flats. A flourishing textile industry was organized by former Lodz entrepreneurs. Woollen stockings and mixed cotton and wool gloves were produced. The production of fancy articles made from wool, cotton and leather also flourished. Cardboard from various kinds of castoff packaging and the covers of old account books was pressed and made into fibre suitcases. The brush industry was greatly developed. Apart from real bristle, the brushes were made from old carpet beaters, goose feathers and similar refuse, which was assiduously collected in the Ghetto. This industry employed several thousand workers. Mattresses made from all sorts of materials were produced for the army and for the Aryan side. Illegal tanneries processed the leather that was being smuggled into the Ghetto. Children from the age of ten, even six, made mass-produced toys in private flats, lofts, cellars, etc. An aluminium industry—bowls, spoons, etc. —was developed, utilizing fragments of planes imported into the Ghetto. In addition, the Ghetto produced stoves, hinges and other metal articles. House-slippers with wooden soles and cardboard tops were produced in mass quantities. Beautiful pipes, cigarette holders

---

made use of his pistol. Though he also did private deals, he was able to see to it that the Third Reich should not lose either through the extermination of Warsaw Jewry. Transports of furniture and cars and various raw materials were sent off at regular intervals. The warehouses were never empty. Konrad set up dozens of warehouses—for furniture, for feathers, for horsehair mattresses, for household utensils, for crystal, china, etc., etc., even a warehouse for books and even one for musical instruments. These warehouses he set up by choice in places of worship, such as the church on Nowolipki Street and the great synagogue on Tłomakie Street, where he held regular sales for the Polish population of the lowest grade of belongings or broken and battered furniture.

It should be pointed out that the Jewish *Werterfassung* workers did their work as badly as possible, deceiving the Germans in as many ways as possible, if only in order to prolong their "work" as much as they could. Apart from this, they committed acts of sabotage whenever possible.

(Rahel Auerbach, op. cit., pp. 240–242.)

and fancy articles in general were made from wood. The chemical and pharmaceutical industry, processing of fats, soap factories, etc., were all flourishing. The wood industry—sawmills and furniture manufacturing, the rubber industry, etc., were expanded. Even after the "action" of July 1942,[8] when three hundred and fifty thousand Jews were deported and all this industry collapsed, the Ghetto kept on producing on a smaller scale for the needs of the Polish market. This production took place under cover of the newly-organized workshops, where the remaining Warsaw Jews were employed. In these workshops, thousands of pairs of trousers were produced for the rural population out of military trousers, which were first dyed of course. Wind jackets were also made out of trousers. This went on in almost all the workshops. Supply of the materials as well as delivery of the finished articles was done by smuggling; the *Transferstelle,* created for the official exchange of goods with the Aryan side, was of great help in this. These factories, or rather workshops, were concealed in cellars, camouflaged rooms, and specially built hide-outs.[9] During the day it was impossible

---

8   What is referred to here is the great deportation from the Warsaw Ghetto to the mass extermination camp of Treblinka, which began on 22 July and ended on 13 September 1942. By this deportation the Nazis murdered nearly a quarter of a million inhabitants of the Ghetto.

9   It should be pointed out that an illegal industry functioned in the Ghetto for export. In spite of tremendous difficulties and obstacles, Jewish persistence and ingenuity succeeded in obtaining the raw materials for production. The Jewish industrialist and craftsman also succeeded in finding raw materials within the Ghetto itself or in importing them illegally from the Aryan side. These materials were worked up and the goods were then smuggled out again to the Aryan wholesalers on the Polish side, and the money earned was also smuggled back into the Ghetto. Jewish rag-collectors who were allowed to trade in rags and old clothes took advantage of their permits to move around freely outside the Ghetto. In the main they did not hand over all the stuff they gathered but hid considerable quantities for the needs of the Ghetto industries. Officially they were collecting for the Germans: rags and junk metal, broken glass, down and feathers; at the same time they collected things that the producers in the Ghetto were interested in: used paper, bones, mattresses, seaweed, horse-hair, baskets, bamboo reeds, watches, cog-wheels, etc. The carpentry branch in the Ghetto developed so well that the monthly

to see that a factory was at work there at night. The owners of these workshops had to bribe a variety of bloodsuckers who preyed on the Jewish economic organism. The Gestapo branch in the Jewish District, called the Office for the Struggle against Usury and Profiteering (the so-called "Thirteen"),[10] as well as the *Preisüberwachungs-*

---

revenues in the first half of 1941 reached five to seven million zloty, and so did brush-making—approximately three million zloty. Alongside carpentry, the turning branch produced tent and flag poles, boards, brush handles, etc.

Brush production was even more extensive. From mid-1941 on, about two thousand families made their living from this work, which also gave rise to increased employment in the string industry, turning, and so on. This production reached its peak in the months of September and October 1941, when the Ghetto was supplying about 25,000 brushes daily.

Apart from carpentry and brush making, the Ghetto also exported very large quantities of upholstered goods and metal products. The Jews also supplied wholesalers on the Aryan side with metal and leather, knick-knacks, toys and paper goods.

In the winter of 1941, producers in the Ghetto manufactured gloves made of rabbit skins, which were brought from the Cracow area. The skins were worked in the Ghetto and a secret tannery was set up for this purpose.

When the demand for hospital beds rose in the second half of 1941, Jewish locksmiths undertook this work and were obliged by the lack of raw materials to use all sorts of piping, old gas pipes and the like.

All this merchandise passed to the Aryan side illegally.

Besides illegal industries working for export, there also existed industries working on a far smaller scale for the needs of the internal market. Illegal mills ground flour and grits from wheat and barley, and artificial honey, jam, sweets and the like were also produced.

(N. Blumenthal, op. cit., pp. 621–624.)

10 The nickname for the Gestapo branch in the Warsaw Ghetto established by Avraham Gancwajch in December 1940 at No. 13 Leszno Street—hence the name. This office had an independent special police force of 300 men attached to it, wearing green-striped caps. Gancwajch provided the Germans with fortnightly reports on life in the Ghetto. He and his henchmen extorted sums of money from Jewish merchants who imported goods into the Ghetto as well as from Jews whose relatives had been arrested by promising them that those arrested would be freed. Ringelblum called the "Thirteeners"—"Jewish Gestapoists".

(Ringelblum, Notes, Vol. I, p. 269; Abraham Rosenberg, *Dos Drei-zehntel,* in "Bletter far Geschichte", Vol. V, Leaflets 1–2, 3.)

stelle[11] and also police agents active in the Polish Police Station in the Ghetto belonged to these bloodsuckers. There were more agents now than there had been before the war. In the Police Station No. 4, where there had been only four police agents before the war, there were twelve during the war. All trade and industrial establishments functioning in this district, the legal ones as well as the illegal, had to bribe them. In these lawless times even legitimate shops and factories were exposed to searches by these agents, who simply concocted false accusations of crimes. Under the pretext of searching for arms, they searched everywhere and took everything. Every factory within the bounds of the Fourth Police District paid at least 1,000 zloty a month, while some establishments paid up to 20,000 and even 50,000 zloty a month. The mill at 33 Nalewki Street, although an absolutely legitimate enterprise, producing for the *Judenrat,* paid 20,000 zloty a month. The agents went from one flat to another searching for hidden wares. Even if the wares were legal, the agents claimed they were stolen, etc. When the decree about furs came out, they searched everywhere for furs.[12] The fur

---

11 Official German name of the so-called "Thirteen" (see note 10).

12 On 24 December 1941, the Head of the Security Police and the Security Service (*S.S.* and *S.D.*) in the general government, Karl Schoengarth, issued an order for the confiscation of all furs and articles made of fur in the possession of the Jewish population.

These furs were intended to be sent to the German Army units on the Russian front.

On the same day, 24 December, the Head of the *Judenrat,* Czerniakow, received an order that all furs, both men's and women's, were to be handed over by 28 December, and he was to be "personally responsible" for the order's being carried out. According to Ghetto Commissioner Auerswald, the confiscation order applied not only to Jews of the General-Government, but also to Jews who were foreign nationals. The only exceptions were Jewish citizens of neutral countries, such as Sweden and Switzerland. On 25 December, the chairman of House Committees received a warning notice from the Jewish Police that all furs and fur articles in Jewish possession, including pieces and collars, were to be handed over to the Germans, in the Community building, from 26 to 28 December. Any Jew in whose home furs of any description were found after that date would be shot on the spot.

On 31 December 1941 Auerswald extended the deadline for handing

exchange at Walowa Street had to pay them 1,000 zloty a day. The police agents were like a plague of locusts, stripping the Ghetto bare. Bribery was nevertheless worthwhile. Manpower in the Ghetto was very cheap, the illegal factories did not pay taxes, and so production was profitable.

At the suggestion of a few industrialists, a special association came into being in the Ghetto called *Jüdische Produktion,*[13] to set up

over the furs to 3 January 1942, and by the latter date 713 men's furs, 2,828 women's furs, 4,441 fur linings for men, 4,020 fur linings for women, 236 silver fox furs, 265 blue fox furs, 1,016 red fox furs, 5,123 cuffs, 44,528 collars, 7,690 skins and 2,481 sheepskins were handed over. The total number of receipts issued by the *Judenrat* was 28,403.

On 5 January 1942, the furs that had been collected were sent to the *Umschlagplatz* (loading station) packed in paper bags, for sorting. The transfer was supervised by the Ghetto Commissioner and by the Gestapo man Jesuiter. An armed guard on a motor-bicycle followed each car.

The anti-Jewish decree on furs, which left thousands of people without overcoats, caused ruinous loss to the Ghetto, valued by economists at between 30 and 50 million zloty. At the same time, it should be pointed out that a large number of furs were hidden in the Ghetto, many Jews destroyed furs rather than hand them over to the enemy, and a large number of furs were smuggled over to the Aryan side to be hidden there or were sold to Poles for a song. "The Ghetto was surrounded by thousands of Poles who bought furs for a few pence and smuggled them to the 'Aryan side'. Mink, Persian lamb, silver fox, furs that even before the war cost many, many thousands of gold coins, were sold now for hundreds or even tens ... Poles celebrated Christmas drunk with joy because of the Jewish furs they had got for next to nothing." Shimon Huberband, op. cit., pp. 118–119.)

(See also Czerniakow, entries for the days from 24 December 1941 to 5 January 1942; Ringelblum, op. cit., Vol. I, pp. 330–331.)

[13] The administration of the General-Government made use of the most sophisticated forms of economic exploitation of the Warsaw Ghetto, the largest segregated Jewish centre under Nazi occupation. As a deliberate policy, the German authorities decided to interest Jewish *entrepreneurs* in the possibility of establishing private, profitable factory production in the Ghetto. These factories were to bring in huge profits to the Germans who would place orders for production in the Ghetto. Only a small number of Jewish enterprises were given the right by the Nazi authorities to import raw materials into the Ghetto and export the finished goods. As a result, these enterprises had a great number of smaller factories and workshops dependent on them, and this contributed to a con-

centration of production in the Ghetto. It was a concomitant of this exploitation of productive forces in the Ghetto that for a certain limited time the invader prolonged the Jewish entrepreneurs' right to use and make a profit from their property, which in any case was soon to fall into Nazi hands with the "liquidation" of all the Jews.

On 16 August 1941 a limited liability company called "Jewish Production" was formed by Jewish businessmen; it completely took over from the *Judenrat* the job of organizing production. The shareholders of the new company were three directors of the *Judenrat's* "Production" Department: Mieczyslaw Orlean, Beniamin Gliksman and Dr. Salomon Eiger, and they constituted the board of directors of the company. These three shareholders provided 44,000 zloty, i.e. over half of the total capital of 80,000 zloty (40 shares of 2,000 zloty each). As appears from the articles of the Company, the aim of the enterprise was to organize and support Jewish production in the Ghetto. It would accept production orders from public authorities and institutions and private persons and allocate them to Jewish factories and workshops. It would also buy and sell on commission all kinds of raw materials, semi-manufactured goods and machinery and tools, as well as supporting concerns dealing with the purchase, sale and storage of merchandise, raw materials and machinery.

The newly founded Jewish Production Company was legalized by the *Judenrat's* Production Department in September 1941. From 1 October 1941, the Company began to take over from this Department its workshops and warehouses, its central office and the division for non-workshop production. The Production Department retained only its supply division and its central card index files. The Department was closed down completely in December 1941.

A special session of the *Judenrat* devoted to the problem of production took place on 13 October 1941. A resolution was passed in favour of reviving the board of directors of Jewish Production by bringing in new members.

In order to ensure a high standard of production in the workshops and to protect itself against sabotage, Jewish Production set up a Receiving Control Commission to supervise the completed products.

Jewish Production directed workshops which in general filled orders for armament concerns. The workshops that had been set up by the *Judenrat's* Production Department were taken over by the company, gratis. The Ghetto diarist, Peretz Opoczynski, compares the Ghetto workshops with the prison workshops described by Dostoievsky in "The House of the Dead". Opoczynski also wrote a description for the Ghetto clandestine archives of the tragic conditions in the linen workshop at 65 Niska Street. A hundred workers worked there, almost 80% of them women. The wages for a 12 hour working day amounted to five to

workshops for the needs of the German Army. Industry in the Ghetto constantly expanded, providing employment for more and more workers and artisans.[14] Shortly before the "resettlement ac-

---

seven zloty, from which 2.80 zloty were deducted for the scanty food ration of bread and soup. Thus after an exhausting day of piece-work, the worker was left with three zloty in his pocket, not enough even to buy 250 grams of bread.

Ghetto production took place under conditions of brutal exploitation made possible by the cruel terror of the invader. Ghetto businessmen could exploit the Jewish workers without hindrance, because the number of unemployed was very high and because they had no need to fear a workers' srike for better wages and conditions since they were protected from the workers' demands by the Nazis.

(A. Czerniakow, op. cit., entries of August 1941 and 13 October 1941; T. Brustin-Berenstein, *O hitlerowskich metodach eksploatacji gospodarczej getta warszawskiego*, in "Biuletyn Żydowskiego Instytutu Historycznego", No. 4 (8), 1953, p. 44.)

[14] According to the figures given by Czerniakow, "the number of persons employed in various occupations at the end of April (1942) was 79,000. (This number does not include people whose occupations are barred from inquiry.) At this time (the beginning of July 1942) there were 95,000 workers (apart from the second group), 4,500 among them in points outside the quarter; 50,000 in industry, crafts and household production". (Czerniakow Diary, *ib.* pp. 321–2.)

According to the Ringelblum Archives, of the 404,300 Jews in the Ghetto in September 1941, there were only 33,762 who were economically active, that is to say: for every one person working there were 13 who were not working. The social structure of the economically active appears to have been, according to this description, as follows:

	Independent	Wage-earners	Total
In industry	3,558	3,600	7,158
In trade	6,157	1,625	7,782
In public institutions	—	9,100	9,100
Other occupations	9,264	201	9,465
Domestic servants	—	257	257
Total	18,979 (55%)	14,783 (45%)	33,762

This number of persons earning a livelihood (33,762) had to support the large army of persons without a source of livelihood, thirteen times their number [it was estimated that in 1939, out of the 351,445 Jews in

71

tion" a very significant article appeared in the *Warschauer Zeitung* on the economic role of the Warsaw Ghetto. It pointed out that 80,000 Jews were active in their trades, producing for the German Army and for the Polish market. The various branches of production that had been developed in the Ghetto were described in highly appreciative terms. In accordance with the general line of German propaganda, all this was, of course, the doing of the Germans. Until their arrival, the Jews had busied themselves with trading and had cheated the Christians. Only the Germans had taught the Jews how to work and, thanks to them, a productive Ghetto had come into being. This reminds us of the naive propaganda articles in the German press, from which it followed that the Polish population is indebted to the Germans for everything modern in the General-Government, even electric light in the cities, gas lighting, water supply, etc. The article in the *Warschauer Zeitung,* published after the Jews had been deported from Lublin,[15] the

---

Warsaw there were 150,874 earning a living (42.9%) and in September 1941 in the Ghetto, not more than 8.3%].

These figures should not be considered fixed or stable, they were valid only for the period when the research was done; changes took place constantly, just as the whole life of the Ghetto changed completely from one day to the next. Throughout the period that the Ghetto existed, the situation was never static for any length of time.

It should be pointed out that the above figures were gathered for internal purposes only: the German authorities were given different figures, in accordance with their dictate that all Jews had to work.

In a report that the *Judenrat* prepared for the Commissioner of the Jewish quarter for the year beginning 15 May 1941 (the day the Commissioner took up his appointment) to 15 May 1942, the following figures are given: end of April 1942, 40,000 Jews worked in the workshops; this number does not include workers in "factories for army production" working for the *Wehrmacht* directly (the number is not given). Besides these, 40,000 Jews are working in other economic spheres: for the *Judenrat,* in social aid, etc.

In spite of the fact that the number of Jews working in the workshops had increased because of the fear of deportation from the Ghetto and because of the expansion of the workshops themselves, these figures must be judged exaggerated. (N. Blumental, op. cit., p. 619.)

[15] The first mass deportation from Lublin began on 16 March 1942. In

first town in the General-Government affected by this "action", made a great impression at the time. This article was regarded as a sign that the Germans intended to leave the capital in peace, precisely because of the productive nature of the Ghetto. The hopes connected with this article proved vain. Warsaw was not spared the fate of Lublin. The *Warschauer Zeitung* article was merely publicity for the *Transferstelle*, which was showing off its diversified activity in the sphere of exports.

What was happening in production was happening in trade as well.[16] The Jews kept up active trade relations with the Aryan

---

this deportation, about 30,000 Jews were transported to Belzec extermination camp or else murdered on the spot.

16 Imprisonment of the Jews behind the Ghetto walls was really brought about in order to put an end to exchanges and trading between Jews and non-Jews. The producer was cut off from the consumer and connections became difficult, if not impossible. But the Jewish industrialists, merchants, artisans and craftsmen did everything to overcome the obstacles and the restrictions of the Nazi regime and secure the necessary raw materials in order to create profitable industries, whose sole customers were Christian merchants.

Apart from bakeries (official and secret), mills, and factories for jams and sweets, and brushes (25,000 brushes produced a day!), the Ghetto soon began to produce trinkets, knick-knacks and haberdashery, leather bags and gloves; it organized workshops for knitted goods, household linen, textiles, furniture, etc. Contact with the outside world became so sensitive that the various raw materials which appeared occasionally on the Aryan side would reach the Ghetto at once. There were periods when production in the Ghetto attained tremendous proportions. The Jews were not so naive as to hand over their products to the official *Transferstelle*, at official prices, but based their calculations on prices on the free market. Practically the only things that went through the *Transferstelle* were the products of the workshops (tailoring, shoemaking, furs, etc.) run by German firms alone.

The official exports of the industrial establishments in the Ghetto, which constituted only a fraction of the commercial exchanges effected, and which were carried out through the *Transferstelle*, reached the sum of 1,200,000 zloty in November 1941. Monthly unofficial exports can be estimated at over ten million zloty (30 to 40 per cent of which were profits for the Ghetto).

According to Czerniakow's data on the balance of payments, at the end of 1941, food provisions entered the Ghetto legally through the

Transferstelle to the amount of 1,800,000 zloty monthly, while the total through smuggling reached as much as 70 to 80 million zloty (reckoned according to black market prices).

A considerable part of the Jewish population survived for a long time by selling property. Although with the closing of the Ghetto the Jews were deprived of the Wolowka market for second-hand goods, the trade in old clothes and other belongings flourished at the beginning of the winter of 1941, and it expanded till it spread from the square in the Ghetto that was its centre to additional streets. A barter trade was carried on in furniture, clothes, shoes and even jewellery in exchange for bread. People who were deprived of their livelihood with the creation of the Ghetto sold everything they had. For every three Jews who sold their belongings in order to eat there was a fourth who lived by trading in these goods. A new type of middleman came into being on the Polish side as well as on the Jewish side: an intermediary between the Jewish seller and the Polish buyer. Most of the middlemen were Poles who were allowed to enter the Ghetto (people who had permits to cross the "border", tram-drivers, gas and electricity account collectors, tax-collectors, etc.). Apart from this, Christians would get into the Ghetto with sacks, and buy second-hand goods in order to sell them in the Wolowka, in Karcelak Square on the Aryan side (the "flea-market" close to the border of the Ghetto). According to the survey of the secret Archives of the Ghetto ("Oneg Shabbat") carried out in the autumn of 1941 in the Warsaw Ghetto the average amount of clothes and furniture sold monthly amounted to 20 million zloty.

The Jews would first sell clothes and furniture, then household and bed-linen, and finally kitchen utensils. On 18 May 1942 Avraham Levin remarked on this phenomenon in his diary: "My attention has recently been attracted to certain types of smugglers, Christian women, both young and old, who come towards evening laden with sacks full of cooking utensils—pots and pans, frying-pans, basins, and wash-tubs and so on—which they have bought in the Ghetto; they smuggle out their merchandise through gaps or over the wall to the Aryan side. Apparently these Christian women specialise in this field. They are buying up Jewish kitchens. This spectacle has not seen before. It began with the Jews' selling their last clothes, furniture and afterwards linen, beds and pillows, and now the time has come for pots and wash-tubs. The poor Jew and Jewess will stay without a pot to cook their thin soup in, without a wash-tub to wash their last shirt in."

Illegal exports from the Ghetto and the mass trading in personal belongings to a certain extent covered the tremendous gap in the balance of payments for food (according to the "Oneg Shabbat" research, "The energy value, in calories, of food supplied on ration-cards in 1941 amounted to only 220 calories per head per day, about 15% of the

side, both large and small scale. Wares that had escaped German pillage and requisitioning were sold. The process also began at the time when individual households sold linen, clothing, household articles, etc., which had been accumulated for generations. The sale of household articles had a favourable influence on the Ghetto balance of payments. It was an undeniable fact that from this time on, the sale of personal belongings was to be one of the most important items in Ghetto economy. Until the last moment of the Ghetto's existence, this sort of sale was to maintain tens of thousands of Jewish families. Unfortunately there would be more and more of these belongings. The more Jewish families that disappeared as a result of the various "actions", "selections", etc., the more belongings would pass to the remaining members of the family, despite the intense activity of the *Werterfassung*, which was the official heir to properties left by the Jews murdered in Treblinka.

From July 1942 on, old clothes would be the most important export article of the Ghetto. Old clothes would also be the most important, possibly even the only trade article of Jews employed in the workposts, who took their own things or things they had bought out of the Ghetto in rucksacks and bags every day. Hundreds of Polish smugglers would come into the Ghetto through openings in the walls or through the guardposts (by paying bribes valued in scores of zloty). Old clothes would be the livelihood for hundreds of families of Polish workers employed in various workshops on Ghetto grounds (Brauer, 28–38 Nalewki Street; Kurt Roehrich, 105 Zelazna Street; K. G. Schultz, 76 Leszno Street, etc.). These Polish workers would come to the Ghetto in the morning and would leave in the evening after buying old clothes. Individuals not wearing arm bands were leniently treated at the guardposts. During the morning hours before work began, crowds of Poles and Jews could be seen trading in old clothes on Leszno and Zelazna Streets and

---

quantity needed to keep someone alive and capable of working").
Without this the Ghetto population would have died of hunger in a
very short time.
(J. Kermish, *Nigudim maamadiyim begeto Warsha*, op. cit., pp. 561–
563; Czerniakow Diary, entries of 6 and 8 December 1941; Avraham
Levin, op. cit., p. 36.)

in the courtyards of Nalewki Street, where the Brauer workshop was situated (nos. 28–38). The Polish old clothes peddlars would often spread rumours with the aim of lowering prices; for example, the date of the liquidation of the Ghetto or the workshops, and so on. The point was to create an atmosphere to make the Jews fear a new "action" and put more things on the market, which would naturally lower prices. They often said to the Jews employed in the workposts, "They'll turn you into leather anyway—sell your jacket and buy yourself something to eat." The Germans fought this trade energetically. Patrols of gendarmerie would round up the Christian old clothes traders in the Ghetto, and some paid with their lives.

Apart from the old clothes trade, there was trade in currency, valuables, gold, silver, etc. A black market money exchange functioned in the Ghetto, fixing a daily rate of exchange for "hard"—gold dollars, "soft"—paper dollars, "pigs"—golden roubles, etc. Rumours circulated that on Pawia Street, where currency trading was concentrated before the "resettlement action", there was a secret mint where gold dollars were produced. I was unable to establish how much truth there was in this. The Ghetto Exchange played the important role of a National Exchange, where the dollar rate of exchange was established for the whole country.[17] Currency trading in the country took place through the intermediary of the so-called *bukses,* couriers who carried the currency about the country on their persons, and often "in their persons" (in the rectum), etc. From Warsaw the currency was distributed not only throughout the country but also abroad. Fearing depreciation of the German mark, the Germans would not infrequently buy dollars or jewellery.

---

[17] Ringelblum exaggerates somewhat here. The flow of foreign currency from the Warsaw Ghetto was not on a large enough scale to influence the Polish rate of exchange. The decisive influence on that rate of exchange was exercized by the Home Army Command, which threw the largest amounts of foreign currency onto the black market. It is a well known fact that during the war, the Home Army received more than 30 million dollars from abroad. This sum was exchanged on the black market in order to pay the salaries of those employed in the Polish underground, to buy weapons illegally and for other expenditures by the Polish underground.

Between the exchange in the Ghetto and the exchange on the Aryan side, there was usually a difference on the minus side for the Ghetto —that is, the dollar rate of exchange was always higher on the Aryan side. The trade in gold was usually carried on by the Blue Police, the gas and electricity account collectors, tax collectors and officials from the different institutions and establishments who got passes for the Ghetto in general.

One of the most important economic matters in the field of Polish-Jewish relations was the problem of Jewish possessions and goods left with Poles for safekeeping. This practice dated from before the formation of the Ghetto, and was prompted by the constant searches made by the Germans in Jewish flats. Then the only resort was to hand over these belongings or goods to Aryans for safekeeping. At this time it was done on a mass scale. Belongings were given for safekeeping to former clients, partners and to Christian acquaintances in general. Goods had to be given to Aryans for safekeeping because of several anti-Jewish decrees—registration of all textiles, leather goods, etc. Jewish merchants recorded only a minimum quantity of goods in these registers, leaving the rest with Aryans. When the decree about handing over of furs by the Jews was issued, the Jews turned over the furs to Aryan friends for safekeeping. In many cases the Jews entered into partnership with the Christians, handing over their warehouses and stocks on condition that the Jew should be a partner in the business. It usually turned out very badly for the Jew. The war had demoralized people who had been honest and decent all their lives; now they appropriated the Jews' possessions unscrupulously, in most cases not wanting to share even part of them. The Jews were treated as "the deceased on leave" about to die sooner or later. Thus there was no need to take them into account. I know of cases where Aryans withheld payment of debts during the "resettlement actions", hoping that their Jewish creditors would sooner or later fall into the German net. In an overwhelming majority of cases, perhaps 95 per cent, neither goods nor personal belongings were returned. Stock explanations were usually given that the things had been taken away by the Germans, stolen, etc. These Jewish belongings more than once supplied a motive for blackmail and denunciation. In order to eliminate an unwanted claimant, someone would turn him over to the "competent authorities". But we also know of many cases where belongings, furniture, goods, valuables, etc. were kept safe without recompense, even when it meant trouble for the Aryans in the form of denunciations, searches, etc. These noble Poles have saved and to this day are still saving the lives of Jews on the Aryan side for whom these belongings are often their only source of maintenance. However, as happens in war, baseness predominates. The number of noble individuals who have resisted the temptation to appropriate other people's possessions is small, as is the number of idealists who keep Jews alive in hiding.

During this war, conditions have been created which hamper Jews with restrictions at every turn. The force of every order of the German authorities has been directed against the Jews. When stamping of paper banknotes by the Issue Bank was decreed in the winter of 1940,[18] thousands of Jews found themselves in very

---

[18] On 17 January 1940, an Order of the General-Governor was posted up in Warsaw streets announcing the withdrawal from circulation of notes of 500 and 100 zloty and on the need to deposit them in the "Reich Credit Fund" (*Reichskreditkasse*) by 31 January. Only offices of the Finance Ministry were authorized to accept payment in these notes. At the first moment, it was not known whether the intention was to exchange these notes for new ones or to confiscate them without compensation. In the end these notes were exchanged for signed notes of 100 zloty and for notes of smaller denominations that remained in circulation. Over a period all these notes were exchanged for new ones issued by the General-Government's Issue Bank.

This Order created tremendous difficulties for the Jews. On 20 January 1940, Czerniakow noted in his diary, "On account of the order to deposit 500 and 100 zloty notes in the banks, business life is reaching a state of paralysis. In the [Jewish] community I can't buy coal for the hospitals, food provisions, etc."

It was not until 26 January that the Chairman of the *Judenrat* received a letter from the "Reich Credit Fund" regarding the exchange of 500 and 100 notes for smaller denominations. In actual fact, on 31 January the Credit Fund exchanged only 70,000 zloty belonging to the community for smaller denominations; the rest—some 115,000 zloty—was retained on deposit. It was not until the beginning of May that the pre-war zloty were exchanged for new notes, which were also called "zloty". The

difficult circumstances, since a former decree had ordered the Jews to deposit all sums above 2,000 zloty in *Sperrkonto* in the banks. Thus the Jews were now not allowed to exchange more than 2,000 zloty, and even this was difficult, since Jews were taken out of the queues in front of the Issue Bank. The only thing left to do was to seek help from Aryans. This yielded large profits for some Aryans, who took a percentage of the sums they exchanged, at the beginning ten per cent and later twenty or more. In the end, the individual who made the exchange, jointly with a suitable bank clerk, took three quarters of the sum for the two of them. At this time thousands of Jews lost their fortunes through lack of Aryan middlemen to exchange their money.

Smuggling of food into the Ghetto, as well as the smuggling of goods out of the Ghetto, was a very important part of Polish-Jewish cooperation.[19] The smuggling began the moment the Jewish residential area was fixed, and rations were fixed at 180 grams of bread a

---

new notes were nicknamed "Młynarki" after the head of the Issue Bank, Feliks Młynarki, formerly head of the "Bank Polski".

Evidence of the difficulty of carrying out the exchange was afforded by the queues outside the "Bank Polski" stretching for several blocks. (*Cf.* Notes of Czerniakow for the days 20–31 January and also on 6 May 1940.)

[19] The most important diarists, Ringelblum, Czerniakow, Kaplan, Levin and others, devote long passages to the well-organized smuggling that was done on such a large scale, and especially to the courage of the smuggler children who supplied the Ghetto with food.

German hopes that the Jews would starve in short order were disappointed. The Jews used every means that came to hand to defeat the various decrees and restrictions. The Ghetto developed and constantly improved techniques of smuggling over the walls and roofs, through the cellars of houses that were on the border, in the tramway carriages, through every spot hidden from the occupiers. Professional smugglers frequently acted with the help of the police—German, Polish and Jewish— who were well rewarded for their silence. On 2 December 1940 Kaplan made an entry in his diary recording the transfer of a large quantity of provisions "over the walls, over the roofs, through the Jewish cemetery on Gesia Street, through cellars under houses situated on the border... With smuggling like this going on, we have for the time being an abundance of all sorts of provisions". It goes without saying that these smuggled goods were very dear and only the well-off could afford them. Masses of poor people were also occupied in smuggling by slipping though the entry points; crossing the Ghetto borders was the mainstay of thousands of persons, Jews and non-Jews. Children were active in smuggling because they could slip through every hole and gap in the Ghetto wall. The cemetery served as a transfer point for small-scale smuggling. The poor came here, miserable youngsters and even children in rags whose needs were few and whose job it was to smuggle in a kilo or two of potatoes or onions. It was just these miserable "small fry" among the smugglers who brought in small quantities of provisions across the walls, who were killed off by the score. The large-scale smugglers from whom the German gendarmerie received enormous sums of money ran no risk. The smuggled goods were brought in trucks through the entry-points guarded by these same gendarmes.

Czerniakow noted in his diary on 19 January 1942 that 443 persons were being held in prison for crossing the Ghetto border illegally as well as 213 children and youngsters who had tried to get across the wall to bring food to their parents. In his entry of 26 February he writes: "At 12:30 I was waiting for Auerswald in the Housing Bureau in Nowolipie Street. Just as he arrived—some parcel or other that had been thrown from the other side of the wall flew over his head". The entry of 9 April records that a smuggler's truck had been detained near the "Wacha"; it had been entering the Ghetto over a long period with false number plates of the gas company. On 3 July 1942, Czerniakow again records, "Someone threw a sack of smuggled goods over the wall".

In spite of the large number of victims among the smugglers in May and June 1942, smuggling went full steam ahead as though nothing was happening. "This pioves", wrote Abraham Levin in his diary on 11 June 1942, "that in present circumstances smuggling is a *sine qua non* for existence, that the demands of life are stronger than death". A joke circulated in the Ghetto that four things were invincible: the German Army, the British Navy, the American postal service, and Jewish smuggling.

It should be noted that many Polish common people displayed human magnanimity as regards smuggling and were ready to make sacrifices for the sake of the Jews. Poles too were shot for smuggling things into the Ghetto (as early as 19 November 1940 a Pole was shot for smuggling in a sackful of bread); "Jewish and Polish blood spilt together cries out to heaven for vengeance", wrote Levin.

An over-all survey of smuggling in the Ghetto, written in 1943, reached the conclusion, "The part played by the smugglers in the struggle against the criminal plans of the occupying authorities to starve out the Jewish population is so important that they deserve to be ranked in the foreday, 220 grams of sugar a month, one kilogram of marmalade, half a kilogram of honey, etc. It was estimated that the official food supplies did not satisfy even ten per cent of the regular demand. If the whole Ghetto population had really been forced to restrict themselves to these official supplies, they would all have been bound to die of starvation in a very short time. And in fact these minute supplies of food, in addition to a typhus epidemic, were the cause of an alarming increase in the death rate, which reached 5,000 to 7,000 a month, while before the war, with a slightly smaller population, about 1,000 Jews died annually in Warsaw.[20] The real aim

front of the struggle against the oppressor." (M. Passenstein, *Szmugiel w getcie warszawskim*, "Biuletyn Żydowskiego Instytutu Historycznego", No. 26/1958.)

The writer Rahel Auerbach also included the Jewish and Polish smugglers in the "list of saints and heroes of our dark age" in her diary, "those who supply food, even if only in part, to the masses condemned to perish by starvation. The smugglers do what they do in order to eat themselves, it is true; but in spite of this—and perhaps just because of this—they are among the most important and determined combatants in the unequal fight waged by our city, bound hand and foot, against a cruel and criminal power".

The poem written in Polish, "The Little Smuggler", by the young poetess, Henryka Lazowert, was often read in public at educational and sports events in the Ghetto, voicing as it did admiration for the thousands of four- to five-year old smuggler children who risked their lives several times a day in order to maintain themselves and the Jewish community. The whole matter of smuggling was a very positive and well developed phase of Jewish passive resistance to the German policy of isolation, starvation and physical and moral collapse. It was an outstanding phenomenon of Jewish dynamism, initiative, intelligence and courage. (Czerniakow, op. cit.; Ringelblum, op. cit., Vol. I, pp. 184, 188, 189, 191, 193, 200, 210, 212, and *passim;* Vol. II, p. 187. Hayim Aharon Kaplan, *Megilat Yesurim — Yoman Geto Warsha*, Jerusalem 1966, pp. 405, 408, 411, 448-9, 485, 486; Rahel Auerbach, *Baḥuzot Warsha 1939-1943*, Tel-Aviv, 1954, pp. 36-39; Levin, op. cit., pp. 75, 81, 174, 190-191.)

20 According to official *Judenrat* statistics, mortality in the Ghetto was over 5,000 (5,550-5,560) in the two months of July and August 1941. In 1941, 43,137 deaths were registered, that is, about 10% of the population, of these 13,781 in the last quarter of the year alone, representing a rate of 14% a year as against the average rate of 1.2% mortality for the years 1931 to 1935.

in creating the Ghetto was to starve the Jewish population. If this slow death of the Ghetto did not succeed, it was certainly not the fault of the Commissioner of the Jewish District, Auerswald, who did everything he could to carry the diabolical German plan to completion. The credit for its failure goes to the smuggling organized by Jews and Poles. No matter what our opinion may be of the moral worth of those people who provided the Ghetto with food by smuggling and who after the liquidation of the Ghetto changed over to blackmailing the Jews on the Aryan side, we approve of the attitude of the distinguished counsel for the defence of the fighters for independence during the partition of Poland, the attorney Leon Berensohn,[21] who died during the war. He proposed to erect a monument to the memory of the Unknown Smuggler. The same positive attitude towards smuggling has been adopted by the Polish Underground. The Underground press urges the Poles to support smuggling, as it thwarts the invader's policy regarding food provision, a policy aimed at despatching all food resources out of the borders of the General-Government. Without smuggling, stresses the Underground press, the cities of Poland would be bound to die, and smuggling should be supported.

The German authorities did their best to seal off the Ghetto

In the course of a year and a half—from January 1941 to June 1942—a total of 69,357 persons in the Warsaw Ghetto died from hunger and epidemic diseases, i.e. about 17% of the total population (about 410,000 persons in January 1941). In comparison in the last six months before the war 2,348 Jews died in Warsaw. Thus, mortality was nearly ten times as high as before the war.

(See. J. Kermish, *Nigudim maamadiyim begeto Warsha*, op. cit., p. 569; T. Berenstein, A. Rutkowski, *Liczba ludnosci zydowskiej i obszar przez nia zamieszkiwany w Warszawie w latach okupacji hitlerowskiej*, in "Biuletyn Żydowskiego Instytutu Historycznego", No. 26/1958.)

[21] Leon Berensohn (1885–1941), a leading advocate, connected with the Polish Socialist Party, famous as counsel for the defence in big political trials in Poland. In the Warsaw Ghetto, he took part in the activities of the Jewish Mutual Aid and collaborated with Ringelblum's underground Archives. He wrote a diary during the period he lived in the Ghetto, but only a few cards from this diary remain.

(*Cf.* Ringelblum's biographical note in: Ringelblum, E., *Ktovim fun geto*, Vol. II, pp. 230–232.)

hermetically so as not to allow one gram of food to enter. The Ghetto was encircled by a wall on all sides, and no open space was left. Several stretches where the borderline went along the roofs of houses were taken out of the Ghetto, and the line was drawn in the middle of the road. Barbed wire and broken glass were put on the walls. When this did not help, the *Judenrat* was ordered to make the walls higher, and this, naturally, at the expense of the Jews, who were constantly forced to pay hundreds of thousands of zloty to cover expenses connected with the building and upkeep of the walls. Several kinds of sentries were put to guard the walls and the exit points; their number and kinds were constantly being changed and increased. The walls were guarded by the Gendarmerie jointly with the Blue Police, and the Ghetto gates were guarded by a triple cordon of Gendarmerie, Polish Police and Jewish Order Service. The *Sonderdienst,* called *junaki* by the Ghetto population, used to patrol the Ghetto looking for cars with smuggled goods. The *Transferstelle* clerks also controlled the circulation of goods at the exist gates. To all this we must add the Gestapo, who often appeared at the Ghetto gates together with the S.S. and who guarded the Ghetto jointly with Ukrainians, Latvians and Lithuanians during the "resettlement actions". To sum up, the Ghetto walls were guarded by six kinds of formations from three, and sometimes six, nations—Germans, Poles, Jews, and in the case of the "resettlement actions" Ukrainians, Lithuanians and Latvians.

The mildest punishment for smuggling is death, carried out on the spot.[22] A gendarme catching anyone on or near the walls will kill him on the spot. Scores of hundreds of passers-by have fallen

---

[22] On 10 November 1941, a public notice signed by Warsaw District Governor L. Fischer was posted, announcing the introduction of the death penalty for leaving the Ghetto illegally. The same penalty would apply to non-Jews who gave shelter to Jews who had left the Ghetto. The first death sentences carried out under these regulations were announced a week later, on 17 November, when eight Jews, six of them women, were executed for leaving the Ghetto illegally. Jewish children who engaged in smuggling became the main victims of this legalized murder. A description of the actual trapping and shooting down of these children is to be found, among other sources, in the famous book by Curzio Malaparte, *Kaputt.*

victim to this German ruthlessness. There were gendarmes like the notorious one whom people called "Frankenstein" (because he acted like the well-known film character).[23] They daily "removed" several victims from among the smugglers or more often still, from among passers-by. A Silesian, Boruta, was this kind of monster in human form; he maltreated the Jews employed in the workposts and would often kill someone for the slightest offence, such as not stating the correct sum of money, etc. The victims among the smugglers were mostly Jews, but Aryans were not lacking. Mr. Auerswald also made use of the severest repressive measures in order to put an end to smuggling. Repeatedly, smugglers were shot at the Central Gaol on Gesia Street; once there was literally a hecatomb— a hundred persons were shot in the vicinity of Warsaw.[24] Among

---

[23] The name "Frankenstein" was given by the Jewish police to one of the German gendarmes, and the Jewish and Polish smugglers adopted it from them, as did even his German comrades. At his post on the corner of Zelazna and Leszno Streets, he was trigger-happy, always ready to open fire on smugglers or Jews. On different days he would fire according to different "criteria".

In the first half of June 1942, the number of Frankenstein's victims was pretty high. Czerniakow entered in his diary on 10 June 1942, *inter alia*: "I have raised the question of 'Frankenstein' with the Gestapo—he fires at people day after day at one of the exit points (from the Ghetto)." (*Cf.* also Rahel Auerbach, op. cit., pp. 60–62.)

[24] On July 1942, 300 copies of a proclamation signed by the Ghetto Commissar, Auerswald, were posted in the Ghetto giving notification of the killing of 110 persons, ten of them policemen, as reprisals (*Vergeltung*) for the increasing number of manifestations of resistance by Jews to orders of the German police, a resistance offered sometimes even by force. The Jewish policemen were included among the 110 for not having maintained the required level of discipline, "they try to give bribes, they help smugglers and they commit breaches of discipline". The administration of the Jewish prison was ordered to prepare 100 persons (including ten women) from among the prisoners. The intervention of the Chairman of the *Judenrat*, Czerniakow, had no effect on Auerswald and Brandt of the Gestapo; he had asked for the release of the ten Jewish policemen (three of them had been arrested in the street to serve as hostages in place of three others who had been ordered to appear and had disappeared; and apart from them, there were others on the list who had no connection at all with smuggling). Between 4 and 6 o'clock

the Jewish smuggler victims were scores of Jewish children aged five or six, whom the German bandits shot down *en masse* at the exits and near the walls. Apparently the Düsseldorf murderer[25] had millions of followers in Germany! And yet, in spite of these victims, smuggling did not stop for a moment. While the pavement was still slippery with fresh blood, other comrades would set out on the job again as soon as those keeping "cave" gave the sign that the coast was clear. Only during the "resettlement action", when the walls were closely guarded and picketed by new watchmen who had not yet been "cultivated" by the smugglers, was there a break in smuggling across the walls, but not a total break.

Smuggling was done: 1) across the walls; 2) at the exit points; 3) through underground tunnels; 4) through the sewers; and 5) through the houses on the borderline. Smuggling through the exit gates was the most important, as it was carried on almost officially, in full view of everyone. A "fiddler" (Jewish policeman who bribed gendarmes) would make contact with the Gendarmerie and the Polish Police, and they would then fix a lump sum for the period a particular gendarme was on duty or, more frequently, a sum according to the number of carloads smuggled in. As the car was driven through the gate, it gave the gendarme a password that had been fixed in advance. It occasionally happened, however, that the gendarme was surprised by an unexpected Gestapo or S.S. inspection, and then the car would be confiscated or, to use the smugglers' terminology, would be "burnt". The greater part of the smuggled goods went through the exit points in enormous trucks, which would drive quickly into some block entrance where the wares would swiftly be reloaded into other cars. Lots of goods were also smuggled into the Ghetto across the walls, usually at night or at dawn. However, there were daredevils who did smuggling over the walls in the daytime as well. In the initial period of the Ghetto's

---

on the morning of 2 July 110 people were taken out of the prison and shot in three batches.

(See Diary Czerniakow, entries for 30 June, 1 and 2 July 1942.)

[25] The reference is to a pervert who became notorious at the end of the 1920's because of the numerous murders of children he committed in Düsseldorf, Germany.

existence, food provisions and goods were smuggled in through holes in houses bordering on the Aryan side. These holes were bricked up every day but the smugglers were constantly breaking them open. The smugglers were organized in Polish-Jewish bands, which operated on the basis of a common "pool". Their profits were large, but the risk was also great, for their lives were in danger. The price difference between the Aryan and Jewish sides was fairly large, reaching as much as a hundred per cent, but this could not be helped, as smuggling was the only means of subsistence of the Jewish population in the Ghetto. After the "resettlement action", smuggling largely abated, and some of the smugglers turned into *schmalzowniks*. To sum up: Polish-Jewish cooperation in the field of smuggling has been one of the finest pages in the history of mutual relations between the two peoples during the present war. This cooperation has taken place not only in the capital but also in almost all the other Ghettos of the General Government; these Ghettos would most certainly have swiftly perished without the help of Polish smugglers.[26]

A propos of Polish-Jewish economics, it is not inappropriate to

---

[26] There was of course no question of deliberately organized assistance in the proper sense. The Polish and Jewish resistance movements realized the value of the smuggling that went on, but no one connected with clandestine political or social activity undertook or organized anything of the kind. The smugglers were not motivated by humanitarianism for the starving Ghetto population—they were simply out to make profits. Smuggling between the Ghetto and the Aryan side brought profits to various groups of Jews and Poles—Jewish workers employed outside the Ghetto, Poles employed on Ghetto territory, Jewish children, police officials, Gestapo agents. Smuggling also brought profit to certain German officials in the Nazi administration. Some of the people connected with smuggling even became very rich indeed.

An exhaustive study of the various forms of smuggling into the Warsaw Ghetto was written by M. Passenstein, while in hiding. (He was later killed by the Nazis.) This study, which the author passed on to the clandestine Archives of the Jewish National Committee, is now to be found in the Archives of the Jewish Historical Institute in Warsaw. It was published in a somewhat shortened form in the "Bulletin" of the Institute. See: Biuletyn Żydowskiego Instytutu Historycznego", No. 26, 1958.

mention the hundreds of sales of Jewish property in Warsaw to Aryans. Before the war, real estate was a very important source of livelihood for thousands of Jewish families. This ended the moment the Germans invaded. On the instructions of the authorities, administration of real estate was taken away from the Jews. Jewish real estate owners, suddenly deprived of their former means of subsistence, were forced to sell their properties in whole or in part. This was done through agreements which were drawn up by attorneys or even by public notaries and entered in the books with a date prior to 1 September 1939, and which were founded on mutual trust. The basis of these agreements was a loan, with the house as security, repayable one year after the war, either in gold or according to the price of grain or some other commodity. In the event of the Jew's not repaying the debt on the date fixed, the building or part of it would pass into the hands of the Aryan.

Polish-Jewish economic relations were very much alive in spite of the constant obstacles and hindrances created by the invaders. Neither the restrictions on the liberty of movement of the Jews on the Aryan side nor the walls, rising higher and higher, were of any avail. Normal, healthy economic relations were maintained. The Aryan side forgot about the economic boycott which had been so fervently propagated before the war and raised to the level of the highest civic virtues. The most fervent antagonists of the Jews recognized the weakness of the barrier that had been artificially built. The original German plan to subjugate the whole economic life of the Ghetto and to use slave labour to support its Army was thwarted. Healthy economic principles overcame. The Jews were able to break out of all the cages in which economic life was to have been confined and were able to continue producing for the needs of the Aryan market as they had before the war. The evil designs of Polish anti-Semites who proclaimed an economic boycott of the Jews and the evil designs of the invaders who aimed at a slow death of the Jews in the Ghetto were defeated. Economic life knows no national and racial distinctions. After the establishment of the Ghetto, and later, when the normal exchange of commodities came to an end between the Ghetto and the Aryan side, a substitute offered itself in the form of smuggling as an excellent means of exchange. Across walls and barbed-wire entanglements Poles and Jews traded raw materials and manufactured goods in order to defeat the invaders' plan to starve four hundred thousand people walled up alive in the narrow confines of the Ghetto. Extraordinary ingenuity and energy on both sides, combined with the greedy corruption of the "invincible" German Army and its auxiliary formations, resulted in defeating the infamous plan of Auerswald, Commissioner for the Jewish District.[27]

---

[27] Not even the most energetic smuggling of foodstuffs and illegal trading of all kinds could still the hunger of the Warsaw Ghetto to any marked degree. The catastrophic dimensions of the starvation that prevailed are seen in the statistics given in footnote.[20] In Ringelblum's notes we find the following description of the results of the famine in the Warsaw Ghetto:

"People use horse-carts, hand-carts, bicycles-carts, litters, etc. The horse-carts are loaded with corpses, both inside and on top. Two or three boxes full of the dead are piled up. In some blocks of poor Jews (e.g. in Wolynska Street) whole families die. There are instances when the last member of the family dies and lies there in the house for days until the neighbours smell the stench of the corpses. There was a case of a mother's hiding her child's corpse, so as to make use of the ration cards for as long as possible. In some blocks of flats on Wolynska Street, there were cases of rats' eating the corpses left lying in the flats for several days. In the block on No. 7 Wolynska Street, ten flats remained empty because all the tenants had died. In general, it is a frequent thing for whole families to die within a few days of each other. The number of orphans increases with tremendous speed because of the fact that the adults die first, particularly the men. On the whole, children under the age of two all die because there is no milk at all for babies or their mothers. If things go on like this, the Jewish question in Warsaw will soon be solved."

(Ringelblum, op cit., Vol. I, p. 288.)

6

AFTER THE CLOSING-OFF
OF THE GHETTO

The telephone the only link with the Aryan side. — The electricity "racket" in the Ghetto. — Individual and collective passes, — Who goes across to the Aryan side?—The work posts fix the Jews up on the Aryan side. — Getting past the guard-posts, across the walls, through sewers and tunnels, by Gestapo cars and by cars of German firms escorted by *Begleiters*.

After the 15th of November 1940, the date when the Jews in the Ghetto were no longer permitted access to the Aryan side, Christians were still admitted to the Ghetto for a few days' longer. At that time the streets were filled with masses of Poles who had come to say farewell to their Jewish friends for the last time, bringing food with them. The astounded gendarmes saw Aryans and armband-wearers kissing each other at the exit points. From then on a Christian could only enter the Ghetto if he had a pass and the only link between the two worlds was the telephone. The Germans knew very well that the Jews were communicating with the Aryan side by telephone, and they knew that economic, social and other contacts were also being maintained over the telephone.[1] Smugglers,

---

1 Connections between the Ghetto and the Aryan side were kept up mainly by telephone as long as there was any telephone link at all. Representatives of the Jewish underground on the Aryan side were in constant contact with the Ghetto by telephone, using a code language. (See A. Berman, op. cit., pp. 685, 690.)

Aurelia Wyleżyńska made the following entry in her diary on 29 January 1942:

"Now the Ghetto has to hand over its furs—not only entire furs but even the smallest articles made of fur—on pain of death. So telephone calls, more diplomatic than ever before, flash from one side to the other,

merchants, industrialists, etc. communicated this way. With the crossing over of Jews to the Aryan side the telephone became an important factor in maintaining family connections across the Ghetto boundary. Because of this, the Germans tried to steadily reduce the number of telephones in the Ghetto. Finally the point came where all private phones in the Ghetto had disappeared and the only ones remaining were those in some offices of the Jewish community and social institutions. There were whole blocks and whole streets without telephones; there were none even in the pharmacies. The Jewish population coped with this situation as far as possible. So-called fake telephones came into being, constructed by engineer specialists. These telephones were not registered with the telephone exchange, but they nevertheless operated without a hitch. Telephone calls would be made to the Aryan side from official telephones in the Jewish community offices and social institutions after office hours. The charge for a phone call was from 5 to 10 zloty, while on the Aryan side a phone call cost only 40 to 50 grosze.[2] For fear of wire-tapping, telephone conversations with the Aryan side required some camouflage. Polish names and surnames would be used in these conversations, causing more than one *quid pro quo*. It was impossible to know whom was meant when Stanislaw was asked for instead of Szyja, or Wisniewski instead of Kirszenbaum.[3] Jews and Aryans carrying on a conversation with someone in the Ghetto had to be masters of the art of apparently banal conversation in order to arrange such important matters as fixing up a child on the Aryan side, the date of crossover, the dispatch of belongings, etc., and to do so without letting anyone waiting in the

---

'Come to work tomorrow in your coat', someone is told who works in the Ghetto or has a pass for the Ghetto. Generally, we have learned to speak in agreed-on word-symbols."
(Aurelia Wyleżyńska, Z *notatek pamiętnikarskich,* "Biuletyn Żydowskiego Instytutu Historycznego" No. 45–56, 1963, pp. 215, 217, 226.)

[2]   100 grosze = one Zloty.

[3]   ...Wisniewski instead of Kirszenbaum: a play on words in the two languages, Polish and German. "Wisnia" in Polish and "Kirsch" in German both mean "cherry".

queue for the phone suspect that what was actually meant was of vital importance to the Ghetto and the Jews.

Besides the telephone, municipal officials and officials of public institutions also served as connecting links between the Ghetto and the Aryan side. They were not very good at it and they caused the Ghetto population a lot of trouble. The collectors for the electricity works enjoyed *ex lege* status in the Ghetto and went around collecting electricity payments for past years. Municipal gas works collectors did the same, threatening to cut off the gas in case of non compliance with their demands. In the winter of 1941/42, the municipal power-station workers invented a new source of income for themselves by connecting and disconnecting electric lines: if you wanted to have a constant flow of electric current, you had to bribe the electricians, who charged a few hundreds or sometimes thousands of zloty a week for their trouble. This however did not ensure the block of flats against an interruption in the flow of current, because when one electrician had connected the wires in return for the bribe he had received, another one would disconnect them until he received a given sum. It was like the situation described by the 18th Century jesters, who said that if a member of the Diet spoke in favour of the Jews, he was doing so because he had received a bribe from the Jews, and if a member spoke against the Jews, it was because by so doing he was endeavouring to receive a bribe. In the end, the bands of electricians operating on the Ghetto terrain came to terms with each other: they divided the Ghetto into districts, assigning a defined district to each group for exploitation. Commercial or industrial establishments which depended on electricity in order to function had to pay larger bribes. The Jews were forced to pay tribute for electricity until the "resettlement action". There was no electricity "racket" in the workshops built after that, because the gas and electricity bills were paid by German contractors, and the electricity works employees did not dare start a quarrel with them.

The tax-collectors were a real nightmare in the Ghetto.[4] They

---

4 The lawless behaviour of tax officials towards the Jews in the Ghetto took the form of outright thefts. Abraham Levin in his diary on 26 May

plundered the Jewish population mercilessly, demanding payment of taxes on commercial or industrial establishments that had been pillaged, burnt or bombed. They demanded taxes for past years, well knowing that most receipts had disappeared during the bombing of the capital. If someone would not or could not pay the taxes on the spot, the tax-collectors would take things away from his flat and at the same time search his person. Tax collection had all the attributes of ordinary robbery. Searches were carried out in the following manner: All the tenants of a given flat would be brought together in one room, and the tax-collectors would take whatever objects they liked, on their own in the absence of the landlord or any other witnesses. They would appear in the courtyards of the Jewish blocks of flats armed with guns, for fear that the wronged Jews would take their revenge. They behaved like the Germans, lashing about them indiscriminately with whips. In case of resistance, they arrived in German cars and took away everything they could find in a flat or warehouse. Cashiers of the different tax offices collaborated with these robbers: they "fixed" the Jewish clients in such a way that they were unable to pay the taxes they owed within the time limit set by tax office. The next day, of

---

1942 noted the following event: "This morning they closed the exit of the court-house on Leszno Street, where the Ghetto *Steueramt* is (the German Tax Office, where Polish officials worked), and a search was made in the things carried by all the Jews in the waiting-room. All the cash found was confiscated and they were given receipts. This is open theft under the fig-leaf of receipts. Pillage like this, with the Jews as free game, could only happen under the Hitler regime." (Levin, op. cit., p. 54.)

In his notes of October 1941, Ringelblum censures the mockery of official action by Polish tax officials, who instigate personal searches in flats, and make no distinctions between the main tenant and the sub-tenant, imposing collective responsibility on all the tenants without exception. "There are houses where they instigate outright pogroms." In shops that owed taxes, the tax officials would confiscate all the money to be found not only on the owners but also on the customers themselves. On the other hand, Ringelblum singles out for special praise those noble tax officials who were devoted patriots, showing Jews how to avoid paying, so as not to increase Germayn's revenues.

(Ringelblum, op. cit., Vol. I, pp. 308–309, 373.)

course, the tax-collectors appeared and confiscated everything they could find in the flat. There were cases of tax-collectors who had no authority whatsoever to work in the Ghetto and who acquired illegal passes for thousands of zloty in order to be able to plunder the Ghetto without hindrance. The collectors of the 15th, 16th and 17th Tax Offices distinguished themselves by their special zeal for this sort of robbery.

I shall give an example to illustrate the corrupt practices of the tax-collectors. A number of functionaries of the 14th Tax Office came to a Mr. Schoenberg, living at 14 Muranowska Street, and demanded payment of taxes on a piece of real estate belonging to his father-in-law, Scherman. When Schoenberg's wife declined to comply with the officials' wishes, they threw her on the floor and beat her until she was bleeding. Since they had no choice, the family paid the robbers 7,000 zloty plus some valuables. This did not satisfy them, however, and they demanded payment in kind . . . from the daughter of Mr. Schoenberg; she was supposed to report to them. When the daughter did not present herself, they came back and threatened the family with the consequences.

There were, however, some rare decent and trustworthy people among the officials of public institutions, who assured liaison with the Aryan side; they not only took care of correspondence with the Aryan side but even accepted such dangerous missions as the distribution of illegal newspapers.[5]

Jews went across to the Aryan side either singly or in groups. Individual passes to the Aryan side were usually available to officials of the *Judenrat,* to industrialists who had economic "connections" with the other side and last but not least to the Jewish Gestapo-men. In the beginning, a great many individual passes were available, as many as a thousand or even more. As time went on the German authorities, in their attempts to weaken the ties

---

5 Ringelblum wrote in his diary (in October 1941) about the distribution in the Ghetto of underground literature smuggled in by some of the Polish police and the street sweepers. He noted incidentally that supporters of the P.O.W. (Polish Military Organization) were active in a very limited sector of the Jewish population.
(Ringelblum, op cit., Vol. I, p. 308.)

connecting the Ghetto with the Aryan side, kept cutting down the number of passes until they had reduced them to a minimum. The obstacles became so great in the course of time that merchants and industrialists interested in staying on the Aryan side had to buy passes from Jewish Gestapomen for 10,000 to 15,000 zloty a month. Collective passes were issued to Jewish work posts to enable their workers to go across to the Aryan side.

Before the Ghetto was set up, only a few Jews appeared in the registration books as Aryans and so they did not wear the Jewish armbands. Some did this because they foresaw rigorous anti-Jewish regulations. Even then there were already conscienceless individuals who went hunting Jews without armbands and Jews appearing as Aryans in the registration books. A sentence of up to nine-months' imprisonment was the penalty for not wearing the armband, but it often happened that the offender went with a transport to Auschwitz. A telegram would arrive in a few weeks' time notifying the family of his death as the result of a heart attack or pneumonia or the like. This deterred many Jews from passing as Aryans.

After the Ghetto was set up, only a small number of Jews and converts went across to the Aryan side. As to the converts, they were governed by the same regulations as the Jews, provided that both the parents were Jews. Converts and assimilated Jews of the educated class, total strangers to Jewish life, returned to the Aryan side. Individuals tied to the Aryan side by marriage also returned. In Poland there were relatively few mixed Polish-Jewish marriages before the war. We shall not now analyse the causes of this phenomenon in Poland, in contrast to the state of things in the West —in Vienna, for example, half the marriages contracted by Jews were mixed marriages. Mixed marriages contracted in Poland by Jews of the educated class were characterized by their outstanding permanence, in contrast to Germany, where the majority of such mixed marriages broke up. Aryan mothers did not shrink from saving their children from the laws governing "halfbreeds" at the price of their honour by declaring that they were illegitimate children by an Aryan father, with whom they were deceiving their Jewish husbands. German decrees against the Jews could not break up Polish-Jewish marriages. Aryan families tried to safeguard their Jewish members; they got proper Aryan papers for them, or simply hid them, or moved to a different district or town in order to cover up all trace of them. It can be taken as axiomatic that if a Jew had Polish relatives, he could count on their help, even if the family was anti-Semitic. Polish anti-Semites did not apply racialism where relatives or friends were concerned. On that score the old maxim prevailed: every Pole, even the greatest anti-Semite, had his own Jew of whom he was fond.

Hundreds of Jewish children, mostly orphans or so-called street children, sought their livelihood on the "other" side by smuggling provisions or by begging.

The date when the "resettlement action" began, 22 July 1942, marks the beginning of mass Jewish crossing to the Aryan side.[6]

---

6 At the time the Ghetto was created, the number of Jews on the Aryan side was negligible. Completely assimilated Jews and even converted Jews resided in the Ghetto for fear of the penalties. On the Aryan side remained only a tiny handful of people of Jewish origin, all of whose ties were with family connections in the Polish milieu, and who were utterly unable to summon up the strength to wear the Jewish armband. The Hitlerites would not infrequently catch these "criminals" and send them to prison or to Auschwitz.

Only with the beginning of the "action" to liquidate the Ghetto on 22 July 1942 did a considerable number of the Jews in the Ghetto begin to pass over to the Aryan side. Among the first to go across were part of the Jewish educated class who had friends and close acquaintances among the Poles. Likewise, a number of well-off people went across. This wave increased after the second "action" to liquidate the Ghetto in January 1943, when the hope of being saved in the Ghetto became feebler and feebler. At this time the wave included different social strata, and even part of the socially active leadership. Passage to the Aryan side became a mass phenomenon. Mainly people went over, ostensibly to work in the work posts, many of which were outside the Ghetto walls. They would bribe the Polish and Jewish police and would leave through the Ghetto gates, or climb over the walls, or pass through the sewers and so on. At the time of the third and last "action" in April 1943, during the Ghetto revolt and after it was repressed, a certain number of Jews saved themselves by escaping to the Aryan side. There was also a number of Jews there, mainly young people, who had jumped from the railway trains on the way to Treblinka. (Berman, op. cit., p. 685.)

Two groups crossed over: a large group of the wealthy who were plentifully supplied with enough foreign currency and valuables for them of live out the war, and a smaller group of working intellectuals, connected with the Aryan side by long-standing ties of friendship and social relations. Typical of some of the types who would cross over to the Aryan side: the owner of a block of flats to his porter, with whom he had lived side by side for decades; a director of some establishment to his caretaker or other employee towards whom he had been humane and helpful all his life; a factory owner or a master to the worker whom he had cared for all his life; private or government clerks to the colleagues with whom they had worked side by side—in short, people who had been bound by ties of friendship for many years now showed their real feelings. The majority of the Polish friends drew back; they were terrified of the consequences of having their Jewish friends stay in their flats or in an Aryan hide-out, and they refused to harbour them on one pretext or another. The pretexts were varied: a bad neighbour; a *Volksdeutscher* or a Gestapo man as a neighbour; the wife or the relatives object; too many visitors come to the flat, and so on. The only real reason was fear, fear of the Germans, fear of punishment for hiding Jews. Only a few rare exceptions—mainly people who were not well-off—showed courage and saved their Jewish friends without fear for the consequences.

The work posts played a decisive role in setting up Jews on the Aryan side. In view of the lack of manpower on the Aryan side, various military institutions (the airport at Okecie), railways (*Ostbahn*), other formations (the S.S., Gestapo, *Transferstelle*) and concerns working for the German Army (Steyer-Daimler), etc. willingly availed themselves of the services of Jewish workers who came every day from the Ghetto to their place of work, generally accompanied by German guards (the railway work posts were under the escort of "the blacks", as the railway guards were called). Besides permanent work posts, there were also temporary ones, which were dissolved at the conclusion of a specific job. The wage of those employed at the work posts was a quarter of a loaf of bread and some soup, and the only remuneration of the Jews employed in the work posts came from smuggling provisions into the Ghetto and from the profit made by selling the old clothes they brought across to the Aryan side. Workers at these work posts went across to the Aryan side even while the "resettlement action" was in progress. At a charge of 50 to 100 zloty, the group leader in control of a work post would let outsiders join the group. Aryan acquaintances and friends, notified by telephone or letter, would come to the site of a particular work post so as to meet this one-day employee and settle conditions with him for the Jewish family's stay on the Aryan side. The crossing over to the Aryan side generally took place through the work posts. It was managed somehow, in spite of the fact that the guards at the exits counted heads as people entered and left the Ghetto. The crossing itself was done like this: our one-day employee would "break loose" from the work post, or on the way to it, provided there were no *schmalzowniks* hanging about. It was usual for Aryan acquaintances or friends to come along in order to take a given person away with them. In order not to arouse the suspicions of the *schmalzowniks* that infested the work post, the worker's clothing would be changed and he would be given a hat instead of the cap worn by Jews in the Ghetto. Sometimes he would stay at the work post for the whole night and go to the new flat only at dawn. A Polish policeman would often be bribed to accompany runaways to the address fixed for them. It was estimated that over a period of several months, hundreds of people left the Ghetto daily by means of the work posts. People on the Aryan side whose flats were "burnt" would return to the Ghetto, again through the work posts.

Some Jews got across to the Aryan side with the help of the Polish work posts in the Ghetto. At that time there were German factories in the Ghetto (Kurt Roehrich, K. G. Schultz, Brauer and others) which employed Polish workers as well the Jewish ones, with the understanding that the Poles were supposed to replace the Jews in the future. Jews provided with Aryan papers would join the groups of Polish workers. There were, however, many cases in which the Poles betrayed their Jewish fellow workers to the guards, so this method of crossing to the Aryan side was rarely used.

The second way of going across to the Aryan side was over the walls that surrounded the Ghetto. In this case one only needed to bribe the wall guards, who were Polish Police after the July "action". The crossing would take place either at daybreak or in the evening. At a sign from the guard, you went over the wall by a ladder set against it, or through a hole in the wall. On the other side of the wall an Aryan smuggler would be waiting for the crossing and would take you to some hide-out, whence you went to the new address.

The third way of crossing—not a very common one—was through an underground tunnel constructed under the paving to connect two cellars, one on each side of the wall. Ramified smuggling of goods took place this way as well. The fourth way of crossing was through the underground sewers, although this technique entailed considerable difficulty. Under the direction of a guide, one had to walk underground, stooping (the height of the sewers was 85 centimetres) and ankle deep in water and mud, for an hour or two or sometimes longer. Water trickled down the walls so that one's clothing got drenched and soiled with mud. Getting lost on the way meant death in appalling torment. Getting out of the sewers in muddy and drenched clothing through a man-hole in the middle of the street was far from safe. I once saw such an underground procession. The ghastly sight of people with their coats and hats turned inside out in order not to have their outer clothing soiled, carrying candles in their hands, their faces pale and fearful, brought to mind illustrations depicting the underground meeting of some Freemasonry Lodge. During the "resettlement action", all the other ways of crossing over were impossible and only the sewers remained. But during the April "action", the invaders saw to this as well by poisoning the sewers with gas or surrounding all their exits.[7] Many people who tried to escape through the sewers in April

---

[7] In spite of the fact that the Germans had blocked the outlets of the sewers, two separate groups of the Jewish Combat Organization managed to escape from the Ghetto through the sewers during the uprising. The first group of some 40 persons, commanded by David Nowodworski, got out on 28 April 1943, guided through the sewers by Jewish Combat Organization liaison agents, Regina Fuden and Salomon Barczynski. Another liaison agent of the Organization, Symcha Ratajzer, led another

met their death by asphyxiation from the gas which the Germans had let into the sewers or by drowning.

The king of the sewer guides was Szemrany Maniek, who carried over quite a number of people from the Ghetto on his back. He had members of the uniformed police force at his disposal at Krasinskich Square, where a sewer exit was situated. The sewer guides were the sewerage workers employed by the City Sanitation Authority and their job was to check the normal functioning of a given section of the sewers.

In the period after September 1942, an excellent way of crossing over to the Aryan side was provided by the so-called *Begleiters*—Germans escorting Jews on the Aryan side. The authorities gave orders to the effect that even Jews equipped with passes were not allowed to move freely on the Aryan side without an Aryan *Begleiter* to accompany them. This constituted an extraordinary blessing to the Jewish population, which could now, thanks to these *Begleiters,* go across to the Aryan side in mass numbers and move about freely.

---

group of 34 Jewish combatants out through the sewers on 10 May 1943. Thanks to the help of Lieutenant Gaik of the Polish "People's Guard", both of these Jewish groups managed to reach Lomianki Wood near Warsaw, and from there they later passed to partisan fighting in the Wyszkow forests. The experience of the Jewish Combat Organization's liaison personnel was used again, during the Polish revolt in Warsaw in August and September 1944. Jewish liaison men and women led out several units of rebel fighters on different occasions from one quarter of the city to another through the underground sewers. For example, Henryk Poznanski led out the Home Army General Staff together with the Commander-in-Chief, General Bor-Komorowski; Shoshana Kosower led out units commanded by Colonel Seweryn, and at the end of the revolt, Zofia Friedental led out relatively large combat units from the centre of the city to the Czerniakow quarter.

EMMANUEL RINGELBLUM

7

ON THE ARYAN SIDE

Jews "under the surface" — Aryan papers.[1] — What does a
"good" appearance mean? — Admonitions and instructions for
a Jew "on the surface". — Hide-outs on the Aryan side. — It is
not good to be ill, still worse to die. — Recklessness and daring.
— *Schmalzowniks* and blackmailers — Wasps and vultures. —
Denunciations. — Honourable *schmalzowniks*. — "Little Feliks"
of Parysow. — Blackmail on a large scale and with impunity.
— Anti-Semites left without prey. — Hiding Jews in the countryside. — The crimes of the Blue Police.

When a Jew found himself on the Aryan side, he had two possibilities: to remain "above the surface" or to go underground. In the
first case, the Jew turns into an Aryan: he provides himself with
Aryan papers and lives legally, registered in an appropriate registry
office. In the second case, a Jew with a Semitic appearance hides
either in a hide-out or in a camouflaged room, where he stays illegally, not registered. Jews on the Aryan side would generally make
use of Roman Catholic papers. In rare instances, a Jew would pose
as a *Volksdeutscher*—if he had the blond appearance of course and
possessed an excellent knowledge of the German language. In the
East, Jews posed as Ukrainians. It was very rare for Jews to pass
themselves off as Germans—then only if they were German Jews
familiar with and assimilated to the German environment.

Life "on the surface" is not at all easy. A Jew on the surface
lives in constant fear, under constant tension. Danger lurks at every
step. In the blocks of flats—the landlord, smelling a Jew in every

---

[1] The life led by Jews holding forged documents in order to pass as non-
Jews is described in a large three-volume work by Michael Borwicz,
entitled *Arische papirn* (Aryan Papers), Buenos Aires, 1955.

100

new subtenant, even if he produces a guarantee of Aryanism from a trustworthy source; the gas and electricity account collectors; next, the manager and the porter of the block, a neighbour, etc.— all these constitute a danger for the Jew "on the surface", because each of them can recognize him for a Jew. Yet there are far fewer dangers than the Jew imagines. It is these imaginary perils, this supposed observation by the neighbour, porter, manager or passer-by in the street that constitute the main danger; because the Jew, unaccustomed to life "on the surface", gives himself away by looking round in every direction to see if anyone is watching him, by the nervous expression on his face, by the frightened look of a hunted animal, smelling danger of some kind everywhere.

Another prerequisite for survival on the Aryan side is an occupation. A Jew "on the surface" must be employed somewhere, otherwise he will give himself away sooner or later. Thus the majority of the Jews on the Aryan side are employed in various callings. Jewish women, often with a university education, work as servants, housemaids,[2] in factories, hospitals, shops, even in educa-

---

2 Remarks of some interest on the fate of these Jewesses are to be found in the diary of Mieczyslaw Pokorny, who writes:

"Many Jewesses, women and girls, wanted to escape death but were not wealthy enough to set themselves up independently on the Aryan side, so they looked for work as housemaids. To get an Aryan to accept a Jewess for a servant, she had to have Aryan papers, and to pay a certain sum of money right away for her keep and as compensation for the danger involved. Furthermore, this Jewess would have to work very hard, cleaning the flat, washing the linen of the master and mistress, cooking meals and washing up, like a real servant. In return, she had to suffer constant humiliations of all kinds, silently and with resignation, because otherwise she would be thrown out into the street, which would mean death. As time went on, many Aryans—fearing the consequences of hiding Jews—took every precaution to avoid having a Jewess slip into their home when they engaged a new housemaid. Thus a typical advertisement in the papers under the "Housemaids wanted" heading would include the following: "Aryan documents will be checked." This was intended to frighten off Jewesses who might apply for work. It was not a rare thing for people who had had large beautifully furnished flats before the war, with many servants, to become servants themselves in order to save their lives. Maybe in this way a certain

tion. As it became known that Jewish women look for work as housemaids, candidates for the calling of housemaids have recently been required to produce a guarantee of their Aryanism from suitable persons. Jewish women also work as secretaries in German firms. Jews are in trade, they work as artisans or in industry, even in public institutions. Some Jews, in order to be in contact with the Ghetto, worked as Aryans near the Ghetto walls or in German firms that employ Aryans in the Ghetto. Some who were being hounded sought refuge outside the borders of the General-Government. Many Jewish women volunteered for work in Germany. There have been many such cases, certainly hundreds of them and maybe even more. It became known in the *Arbeitsamt* that Jewish women were looking for a way to get to Germany as workers, so a special agent, a Jew, was brought in to pick out the Jewish men and women. Men apply for work in Germany less often than women because of the medical examination required for qualification. But this can also be got around. One buys the papers of an Aryan who has already been classified, or one sends an Aryan for the medical examination. In view of the difficulties connected with leaving for Germany, the Jews have to look for other ways. They go to various work posts in the east, where the workers get special treatment. Some go to the region that was formerly Galicia. Recently, medical examinations have begun to be held there frequently to pick out the Jews.

A Jew "on the surface" has to possess Aryan papers, for it is only on the basis of these that he can get work. Baptismal certificates, fabricated in Warsaw, usually give as the birthplace parishes that have been burnt down, mostly in the eastern borderland. On the basis of such a certificate and the counterfoil of the register, one receives a genuine *Kennkarte* (identity card) from an appropriate registry office, or else one buys a faked *Kennkarte*. Other documents, such as work papers, diplomas of institutes of high edu-

---

number of women will survive this war and manage to save themselves, but no chronicler will ever tell how many will have perished, denounced by neighbours."

(Mieczyslaw Pokorny, *Dziennik*, p. 154, Yad Vashem Archives, File 0-25/105.)

cation, etc., can be acquired from competent printing firms. If a Jew does not work, he must at least keep up every appearance of working. He must leave his flat in the morning in order not to give rise to suspicions. Many inspections take place in parks and public places, so Jews spend long hours riding in tramways in order to pass the time somehow till lunch time or till the evening.

Individuals who are getting ready to cross to the Aryan side try to adapt themselves to their future environment while they are still in the Ghetto by growing a moustache; so the joke went round the Ghetto that a Jew on the Aryan side could be spotted by a moustache, knee boots and a *Kennkarte*.

Only individuals with a so-called "good"—that is, Aryan—appearance can survive "on the surface". Scientific research has ascertained that only a certain percentage among the Jewish population have Semitic features. According to data assembled by Professor Czekanowski,[3] at least twenty per cent of Polish Jews belong to the Nordic group, a large percentage are of the Mediterranean type, and only part belongs to the Semitic group. In the Ghetto, "studies" were carried out in order to establish what features a Jew or Jewess can be recognized by. The results of these "studies", these incessant discussions in the Ghetto, were as follows: a Jew can be recognized by his nose, hair and eyes. As for the Jewish nose, usually long and curved, some people had surgical operations performed. However, conditions in the Ghetto were not suitable for this, and besides it was very expensive. It was difficult to change a Jewish nose —it stayed on, and in the Ghetto as a result of insufficient nourishment it became even longer and even more Jewish than before. People had their characteristically Jewish dark hair bleached, but this did not help much either, because the agents checked the roots. In practice it turned out that platinum blondes gave rise to more suspicion than brunettes. Jewish eyes, the experts claim, can be recognized by their melancholy and pensiveness. The whole suffering

---

3 Professor Jan Czekanowski (1882–1965), prominent Polish anthropologist. His main works published before the second World War were: *Zarys antropologii Polski* (1930) and *Czlowiek w czasie i przestrzeni* (1939). In the latter work, Prof. Czekanowski sharply criticized Nazi racial theories.

of the Ghetto, the many years of torment, the loss of the family—all this was concentrated in them. It was told that a certain Aryan in a train spotted a Jew who had a first class Aryan appearance by his sad eyes. My acquaintance solved this problem too. Whenever he was planning to leave the Ghetto for the Aryan side, he assumed a grim facial expression and, so he says, his eyes darted angry glances. Women disguise themselves by wearing mourning, bleaching their hair, combing it out smooth, etc. There are some people who have a first class Aryan appearance but know little Polish or pronounce Polish badly, people who cannot even pronounce their Aryan surname properly. This can also be got around —one pretends to be a deaf-mute and wears an armband saying *taubstumm*.

Jews on the Aryan side have to act like real conspirators. No one knows their addresses. One brother does not know the address of the other, children do not know the addresses of their parents—they use the addresses of go-betweens. Visits are undesirable as they can lead to exposure. Jews usually meet at tramway stops, in cafés, etc. It is forbidden to write down the addresses—they must be learnt by heart or put down in some code form.

Jews on the Aryan side are least unwilling to go out after dark, since then it would be difficult for a *schmalzownik* to distinguish between Jew and non-Jew. Crossing to the Aryan side takes place after nightfall or at dawn. Blessed darkness! It has saved the life of many a Jew on the Aryan side. But the *schmalzowniks* get around this too; they walk about the streets in the evening and light up the faces of passers-by. However, the Jews have found a way of countering this as well—they turn their faces away from the light.

There are Jews "on the surface" who not only move around in town but travel round the country in trains. Some show bravado by going to restaurants and cafés, travelling in tramway cars reserved *nur für Deutsche* ... However, they get caught in the end.

To illustrate I shall give the characteristics of a few persons on the Aryan side. One, 190 cm. tall, not very Aryan looking, has a moustache and wears a green jacket. He carries Aryan papers belonging to a Pole killed during the bombing. He stayed for some time in Kolomyja, where he was hidden by a Ukrainian woman to whom he had rendered many services during the period when the Bolsheviks were there. He was engaged in trafficking in dollars, gold and valuables, which he brought from Kolomyja to Warsaw. Later he found a way to get into the *Rohstofferfassung*, and he received a work-card on the strength of which he could travel through the whole country. After he was "nabbed" in Kolomyja, he took refuge in the vicinity of Czestochowa, where he is still living.

A lawyer from Warsaw used to arrange Aryan papers for people with the help of house-managers who were acquaintances of his. He acted as intermediary in the sale of building lots, he traded in currency and building materials, engaged in the sale of real estate, etc. He received his clients in a café—he had swarms of clients. No wonder that with such numerous contacts he was "nabbed" and denounced by one of his acquaintances.

Miss U. has a "good" appearance. She is a genuine blonde, and she is brave and daring. Before the war she studied abroad. She came home for Easter in 1939. This looked suspicious to the sages of the *Defensive*,[4] who interrogated her several times and finally did not let her leave again. When the war broke out, she decided to go into business. She did not remain in the Ghetto, but registered on the Aryan side. Over a long period she travelled to and from Deblin, taking various kinds of goods there and bringing back food provisions. She occasionally slipped across the Ghetto wall at night to see her parents, who lived near the wall to be able to keep in contact with her. The parents smuggled goods across the wall; the daughter sold them on the Aryan side. Miss U. made arrangements on the Aryan side not only for her family but also for women acquaintances and friends. She helped them financially as much as she could. When contacts with the Ghetto were broken off after the liquidation "action" of April 1943, Miss U. established trading relations with a certain group of foreigners, through whom she imports goods which she sells to the shops.

Mrs. I.[5] is a very interesting type of Jewish woman "on the sur-

---

4 "Defensive" was a nickname of Polish Counter-Espionage in the period between the two world wars.

5 Batya Temkin-Berman; born in Warsaw in 1907. Her whole life was

devoted to public work. For a short while she was a member of "Ha-shomer Hatzair", and after that she joined the Left Poalei-Zion. During her years at high school she was active in the Jewish Students' Socialist Federation, "Jugend". She played a large part in the creation of the students' united front against Fascism.

How great was her devotion to books and the calling of librarian (before the war she was in charge of one of the branches of the Warsaw Municipal Library) can be judged from the notes of Dr. E. Ringelblum, in which he reports that during the days of the siege of Warsaw and the terrible bombardments, only one branch of the Warsaw Public Library remained open: the branch in the Jewish residential quarter run by Batya. About 30 children and young people came to the library day after day in spite of the great danger involved. Under Ghetto conditions as well she set up a library for the most wretched of all, the child fugitives without a home, and she ran it for them all the time she stayed in the Ghetto. Children's institutions, orphanages, clandestine courses, etc. received aid from this library.

Apart from the field of books and the library, she played a great part in political life—for example, in Jewish underground activity and in the anti-Fascist block.

Alert, courageous and forceful—with these qualities she contributed much to the Jewish underground. After she left the Ghetto at the beginning of September 1942, she knew how to evade mortal perils when carrying out missions for the underground on the Aryan side.

Though her features were not Aryan, Batya ("Barbara") would move about with absolute freedom, doing things and getting things done, hastening to every place where Jews were in hiding and awaiting help. She became one of the central figures in welfare aid to the Jews persecuted by the Nazi foes and their accomplices. She organized some hundred welfare cells among Jews and Poles, who helped over 2,000 Jews who came over to the Aryan side stripped and destitute; it was necessary to provide them with papers of various kinds, find them flats and pay the rent, find new flats when these were "burnt", and provide help in money and clothes. She created a whole movement of helpers, men and women, Jews and Poles. Special friendships were created between her and some of the Polish women underground activists, such as the directress of the institution for special pedagogy, Maria Grze-gorzewska, the psychologist, Janina Bukolska, the well-known actress, Irena Polska, Professor Ossowski and his wife, the political leader Irena Sawicka, Dr. Zofia Podkowinska, and others, who endangered their lives to help Jews. These friends of Batya's helped to save many Jews from death. Beside her daily, constant welfare activities, she lent a hand in collecting material for the archives of the underground on the Aryan side. She got many people to record what they remembered about those

face". A librarian by profession, she went to endless trouble to open a public library for children in the Ghetto. Despite mounting difficulties at every step, she succeeded. She was active in a child

---

times; she also helped others to rescue experiences from oblivion and write them down and she looked after what had been written with the most jealous care, transferring the records from place to place under the nose of the Gestapo and their agents. During her few free hours she took the trouble to record things herself in order to preserve their memory. "We shall certainly be lost"—she would write—"but it is our duty to leave behind us documents, testimony, records, which will tell the truth about our disaster and the cruelty of the Hitlerite criminals." That was how the underground archives of the "Jewish National Committee" were created, the documents of which were collected and hidden with the utmost devotion and sacrifice and part of which were saved from destruction. Batya used to transfer a great part of the archive material from place to place personally and hide it (in hermetically sealed boxes) in the cellars of houses where she was living or in the gardens of her Polish friends.

In recognition of her many great deeds in the days of the Nazi occupation, the Polish Government awarded her a high decoration after the war—"Polonia Restituta". With the liberation, Batya at once returned to public activity. She was appointed director of the Central Jewish Library in Poland. She enthusiastically devoted herself to the work she loved: Jewish books and literature in general. She dedicated a great amount of time and effort to rescuing Jewish books from beneath the piles of rubble of the Ghettos of Warsaw and other cities. In a short time she had collected about 100,000 books, including extremely valuable works, which later came under the authority of the Jewish Historical Institute (many copies of religious works and duplicates were even sent to the National Library in Jerusalem). In 1948 she took part in an all-European congress in Paris of people active in the field of Jewish culture, and there a proposal was made to establish a centre in Europe to deal with questions connected with Jewish books. In 1950, she emigrated to Israel and began to record her memories. She was elected to the ruling body of the Mapam Party, and in the last period of her life she took part in founding the "Left Socialist Party" and the Israel-Poland Friendship League in spite of her failing health. She died on 30 April 1953, a few days after the mass memorial assembly in honour of the heros of the Warsaw Ghetto in the Beit-Ha'am in Tel Aviv.

(Batya Temkin-Berman, *Yoman hamaḥteret*, Tel-Aviv, 1956,)

care association under the aegis of the "Centos".[6] When the "resettlement action" started, she several times found herself at the *Umschlagplatz*,[7] and by a miracle escaped the journey to "the East", as Treblinka was called in German terminology. A day before the Niska Street "kettle"[8]—as they called the quadrilateral of Gesia-

---

[6] "Centos" is the acronym of the Polish title: Centralne Towarzystwo Opieki nad Sierotami: a society for the care of orphans, headed by Dr. Abraham (Adolf) Berman.

At the end of 1940 there were 50 towns under the jurisdiction of the General-Government with special facilities for the care of 32,000 children, 25 orphanages with 2,300 children, and, in addition, 100 open care centres for 90,000 children (children's kitchens, children's corners, feeding centres): 50 in Warsaw and about the same number in other towns. Only 32,000 babies (out of 200,000 in need) received additional food.

Simultaneously with the depletion of the Jewish population was an increase in the number of children's institutions, and according to the list drawn up on 12 July 1942, there were 61 orphanages (23 of them in Warsaw) for 5,267 children (3,352 of them in Warsaw), 24 children's corners (where children received two to three meals a day) for 4,949 children (1,527 of them in Warsaw), 236 children's clubs (one meal a day) for 47,907 children (17,151 of them in Warsaw) under the jurisdiction of the General-Government.

(Michael Weichert, *Yiddische Alleinhilf 1939–1945*, Tel Aviv, 1962, pp. 301–311, 319–323. *Cf.* Kaplan, op. cit., p. 305.)

[7] *Umschlagplatz*: A square in the approaches to the Warsaw Ghetto adjacent to the goods station. It was through this square that the goods produced in the Ghetto for the Germans were transferred and others were brought in, in exchange for food supplies for the Ghetto. At the time of the liquidation, the square and an adjacent school building were used as the concentration point for loading Warsaw's Jews onto the trains as they were expelled and deported to Treblinka and the other death camps.

[8] On the night of 5 to 6 September 1942, the Deportation Command published a notice announcing that Jews living in the big Ghetto must all present themselves, without exception, in the reduced Ghetto comprising Smocza, Gesia, Zamenhoff, Szczęśliwa Streets and Parysowski Square for registration. "Anyone remaining in the Ghetto (outside the area designated for registration) after 10 a.m. on 6 September will be executed." That night, before dawn on 6 September, Jews were permitted to move through the streets. The Jewish police cordoned off the new, reduced area of the Ghetto with ropes. The Jews nicknamed it, "the Kettle". The workshop workers also came here, marching together from their former

Niska-Smocza-Zamenhoff Streets where the whole population was concentrated—Mrs. I., as if seized by a prophetic spirit, crossed to the Aryan side with her husband. The *schmalzowniks* who preyed on the misfortunes of the Jewish population were guarding the Ghetto no less conscientiously than the Ukrainians and the Latvians. These were the people Mrs. I. had to bribe twice. The second time, she even sat in a café and had coffee with the gentlemanly *schmalzowniks*. Having acquired her spurs of Aryanism in this way, Mrs. I. did not lose heart, as usually happened in such cases, and hide "under the surface", nor did she return to the Ghetto. Mrs. I. is endowed with character, she is firm and consistent in pursuing her goal. She told herself: there is no return to the Ghetto, which has been condemned to death. Mrs. I. does not have an especially "good" appearance, but she knows that it is not one's face but one's behaviour that determines whether one can survive "on the surface". She always keeps calm and cheerful, is not afraid of anyone and always smiles. She wears mourning in order to appear more dignified. If anyone glances at her in the tramway, she looks boldly back, and if anybody observes her intently, she walks up to him and asks what time it is. Mrs. I. works all the time; in the beginning she worked as a housemaid for an anti-Semitic employer, who tried to indoctrinate her with hatred for the Jews. Her main occupation is saving her numerous Jewish friends in the Ghetto.

---

living quarters. Some tens of thousands of people were pressed and crowded into these few streets in the new Ghetto. The "registration" carried out by S.S. men took a whole week, till Saturday 12 September. During this week, 50,000 Jews were seized and sent to Treblinka. The workshop teams that had been screened were sent back to their factories and their living quarters. During the "registration", the Jewish hospital in Stawki Street was liquidated, patients and staff, about 1,000 people all told. The streets were full of Jews who had been executed: 2,648 Jews were shot during the "registration" period, while 60 committed suicide. On 15 September the Jewish underground in Warsaw reported what had happened to the Polish Government in London.
(*Cf*. Levin, op. cit., pp. 121–122.)

Mrs. I. is not one of those people who, after escaping to the "other" side, lock themselves in hermetically and discontinue all contact with the Ghetto in order not to expose themselves, God forbid, to personal danger. Our Aryan in mourning has been an active member of a workers' party for many years. There she imbibed the principles of altruism and duty to society, there she was taught to endanger herself for the sake of others and to work for the good of the whole community. True to this doctrine, good Mrs. I., helpful, cheerful and brisk, energetic and resourceful, is constantly active saving comrades with whom she worked for a score of years. Mrs. I.'s work is exceptionally hard. Her clients are people who all their lives were used to doing public work for the good of society, people who always depended on their own resources, never depended on others for help and do not want to do so now. People who are bound up with social work by thousands of ties cannot and do not want to give up this work in order to hide on the "other" side. And yet these people have no choice—only the Aryan side can save them. Since 5 September 1942, Mrs. I. has not passed through the Ghetto gates. She does all her campaigning over the telephone. One can only admire the masterly skill with which she conducts a conversation in such a way that her Jewish interlocutor can understand her while the Aryans listening to the loquacious Mrs. I.'s endless chatter suspect nothing. The first stage in her campaign is propaganda, and the next is assistance for those who have already come across. Intellectuals—and these constitute the majority of Mrs. I.'s clients—have no money to pay inflated rents: cheap living quarters have to be obtained from educated Poles. Then comes the matter of help for those who are already living on the Aryan side—finding new flats for those whose lodgings are "burnt", and thousands of other everyday problems in the difficult lives of Jews "on" and "under the surface". An important part of Mrs. I.'s work is seeing to the care of children whose parents have been killed in the various "actions". All day long Mrs. I. is busy. Scores of people owe their rescue to her. It was from Mrs. I. that the author received lessons on how to behave "on the surface", and it is thanks to her cooperation that he was rescued from a labour camp.

Mr. Michael[9] is one of the most interesting people "on the surface". A modest teacher in Warsaw secondary schools, he was at the same time working for the Committee for Jewish Handicrafts

---

[9] The man in question was Dr. Adolf-Abraham Berman, the leader of the Left-wing Poalei Zion in prewar Poland, one of the directors of "Centos" in the Ghetto, one of the organizers of the Jewish underground on the Aryan side and one of its first activists. He also served as secretary of the "Council for Aid to Jews".

As representative of the underground Jewish National Committee, Berman kept contact with the Polish underground movement through a young woman active in the underground, head of the Child Care Department of the central Polish Social Council, Dr. Ewa Rybicka, who also helped rescue children from the Ghetto.

Representing the Jewish National Committee on the Aryan side, he maintained contact with the Ghetto by liaison personnel, by telephone and by personal contact with emissaries of the Ghetto combatants. For a long stretch of time, the underground activity on the Aryan side was a continuation and reflection of the Ghetto underground, of its problems and its struggle, right until it ceased to exist. Only when the Ghetto had been destroyed was there a change in its methods. Dr. Berman took the under-cover name, "Adam Borowski", and it was under this name that he signed most of the documents sent abroad. To preserve secrecy in operation, he was in fact obliged to use two more aliases: "Joseph" in Catholic circles, particularly when Jewish children were handed over to institutions, and "Ludwig" in contacts with the Polish Workers' Party.

In the first three months of 1944, the Jewish underground on the Aryan side was hit very hard as a result of discoveries by the Gestapo. The Headquarters of the Jewish Combat Organization was paralyzed, and the Commander of the Organization, Antek (Yitzhak Zukerman), was sought by the Gestapo. Dr. Berman was also unable to move. Only in April 1944 did Dr. Berman come out of hiding and renew his "activity on the surface". He went about in disguise and changed his appearance completely; day and night he trod a narrow path between life and death, but never lost his faith in the coming liberation. Berman and his comrades fought against any manifestations of anti-Semitism on the part of Government representatives. They rejected a proposal of the Government representation that the Jewish organizations should join the "Council of National Unity", which was a sort of substitute for a secret parliament alongside the Government representation. Tense relations reached their pitch when a unit of the Jewish Combat Organization near Koniecpol in the Czestochowa region was

set up by the American "Joint". Mr. Michael had belonged to a
Jewish workers' organization; he did very intense organizational work
on its behalf; and he delivered lectures on social psychology and
economic aspects of Jewish life in Poland. Mr. Michael is one of
those assiduous, persevering people who pursue their aims with
great persistance. He obtained his doctorate and went on to do
research in his beloved psychology, endeavouring to treat it from
the social point of view. He remained in touch with his university
professor, under whose guidance he went on with his research.
The war brought this unassuming psychologist into a prominent

massacred by a gang of the "National Armed Forces" (N.S.Z.). Berman
demanded an end to the murderous abominations of the N.S.Z. and
proposed that the Government Delegate publish an open condemna-
tion of the murders and censure all manifestations of anti-Semitism
and blackmail. But the Government Delegate was of the opinion that
this was not "the right time" for it.

In view of the new situation, the Jewish underground organizations
decided to begin independent action. In May 1944, they published the
leaflet, "A year in Treblinka", by Jakov Wiernik and sent it abroad
secretly. A small collection of poems, "From the Abyss", was also
published, dedicated to the martyrdom of the Jews and their fight. On
22 July 1944, a year after the destruction of the Warsaw Ghetto, the
Jewish National Council distributed a programmatic manifesto, "A
call from the Depths", which included passages about the attitude of
the Polish underground to the Jews.

Among those whom Dr. Abraham Berman and his wife Batya made
efforts to save from the Ghetto or from the extermination camps
were: Dr. Emanuel Ringelblum, his wife Yehudit and his son Uri;
Pola Elster, her sister Wanda Elster, Hirsch Berlinski and Eliahu
Erlich (all of them combatants of the Jewish Combat Organization);
Antoni Natan Buksboim (Secretary General of Left Poale-Zion in
Poland), his wife Batya and his son; Yosef Gitler-Barski (director
of Centos), his wife and his son; Koppel Piżyc (a Zionist worker), his
wife and two daughters; Yonas Turkow, his wife Diana Blumenfeld
(both of them actors) and daughter; Hirsch Wasser (Dr. Ringelblum's
secretary) and his wife; Yosef Sack (member of Poale-Zion—Zionist
Socialists), his wife and daughter; Genia Silkes; Aviva Finkelstein.

In January 1945, Dr. Berman succeeded in reaching Lublin, and became
one of the heads of the Central Jewish Council of Polish Jewry. By late
1946, he was a member of the Diet, and from early 1947 head of the
Central Jewish Council. He emigrated to Israel in 1950.

position in the public life of Warsaw Jewry. Before the war he had directed the Vocational Guidance Department in the *Centos*—the Society for the Protection of Jewish Children, and he took a deep interest in the life of Jewish children, their needs and difficulties. When war broke out in 1939 and the *Centos* administration left Warsaw for the east, Mr. Michael remained at his post. When thousands of children lost their parents in the bombing, he organized "flying" boarding schools, where he collected homeless orphans wandering about in the ruins of wrecked houses, in staircase wells, cellars, etc.. These boarding schools were called "flying" since they had to change premises every few days because of the bombing. In the days of the heaviest bombing of the capital, he stayed at his post in accordance with the dictates of his socialist conscience, which would not let him leave a public post. After the bombing of the capital, the problem of the Jewish orphans and children was one of the weightiest in the life of the Jews. Hundreds of thousands of homeless refugees appeared in Warsaw and other towns,[10] and the *Centos* had to take their children under its protection. The extermination policy of the Germans caused a terrifying increase in the death rate, and the number of orphans increased to calamitous proportions. More and more new problems kept emerging for the *Centos;* the refugees' children, the street children, the war orphans, etc. As director of the *Centos,* Mr. M. set up more and more new boarding schools and part-time boarding schools; he grew in stature together with the expansion of the child protection organization. When the "resettlement action" started, the structure erected

---

[10] Homeless refugees and people who had been "resettled" (i.e. deported) constituted a considerable percentage of the inhabitants of many Ghettos under the General-Government. In the Warsaw Ghetto, for example, their number reached a total of about 130,000 in April 1941.

(See Ruta Pups-Sakowska, *Opieka nad uchodzcami i przesiedlencami zydowskimi w Warszawie w latach okupacji hitlerowskiej,* "Biuletyn Zydowskiego Instytutu Historicznego" No. 65–66—1968, pp. 73–104.) This part of the Ghetto population was in the worst position of all and their mortality rate from hunger and disease was the highest. Some monographs on the life of these people in the Warsaw Ghetto were written by the poetess Henryka Lazowert, who helped create the clandestine Ringelblum Archives.

by the *Centos* collapsed. The refugees' children went on the first day. Even the boarding school for refugees' children, where older children had been doing productive work, was not spared disaster. In the first days of the "action", the *Centos* management had secured a promise from the command of the Order Service to the effect that the children's boarding schools, which had been cared for with such love and devotion by the teachers and technical staff, would not be thrown on the "scrap heap"—that is, Treblinka. But the Moloch demanded new victims every day. The boarding schools did not escape disaster; the children went to the *Umschlagplatz* together with the staff. Together with the hundreds of thousands of Warsaw Jews taken to Treblinka, the whole structure erected during the three years of war crumbled. Mr. M. remained at his post till the last minute. He several times found himself at the *Umschlagplatz* and only by a miracle avoided the trip to "the east". To make things worse, the Jewish Council displayed an adverse attitude towards the officials of the Jewish Social Care. During the so-called "selections", the workers in the child protection institutions had been decimated and their number reduced to a minimum; the rest went to the *Umschlagplatz*.

Mr. M. left the Ghetto a day before the famous "kettle" at Niska Street. He was able to hold out thanks to the help of friends in scientific circles. True to his duty to society, he did not shut himself up in his flat but started the work of enlightening Polish intellectuals. He informed them about the tragedy of Warsaw Jewry, gave talks on the slaughter of Jewish children and young people, called on them to give help to the intellectuals in their agony. A Council for Aid to the Jews[11] was set up on his initiative; admittedly it has not fulfilled the hopes placed on it, but nonetheless it encompassed three hundred families, who have been able to stay on the Aryan side on the basis of help from this Council. Mr. M. became the mouthpiece for the Warsaw Ghetto's needs and pleas. Thanks to his exceptional ability, personal tact and cultivated intellect, he succeeded in winning the esteem of key circles. But this was not much help towards securing a helpful attitude in the circles of the

---

[11] On the Council for Aid to the Jews, see Introduction.

Government [-in-Exile] regarding the problems of arming the Ghetto, giving practical help to a people in its death throes, etc. Mr. M. is the personification of assiduous, unbounded activity. During the period when the work posts were the only connection between the Ghetto and the Aryan side, Mr. M. went to the different work posts several times a week, regardless of the great danger involved, infested as they were with *schmalzowniks*. There he met the representatives of the Ghetto social organizations, and listened to their reports on what the situation required, in order to pass the information on to government agencies. The protection of three hundred families of the Jewish educated class on the Aryan side with the help of twenty intermediary links requires him to move about the city constantly. It is thanks to him that the Polish Underground got to know the details of the Warsaw Ghetto's fight to defend the honour of a dying people. Recently, the scope of Mr. M.'s work has expanded considerably to include labour camps in Lublin province and other regions, where the last quarter of a million Polish Jews now live,[12] saved as yet from the slaughter of the whole people. Mr. M. sends emissaries to these camps, he secures the release of valuable individuals from there, organizes camp defence, gives news of Jewish life in the country, keeps people's spirits up and saves them from moral collapse. Mr. M. is the soul of the Jewish National Committee, representing the last remnant of Polish Jewry. Together with Mr. Mi.,[13] he represents Jewish public opinion in the eyes of influential Polish circles; in the name

---

[12] This figure refers to the number of Jews still alive in the whole of Poland at the beginning of 1944, including the Lodz Ghetto, then still in existence, with its 80,000 inhabitants, and the Jews still alive in forced labour camps. In the labour camps in the Lublin District— Trawniki, Poniatowa, Biala Podlaska, Zamosc, Budzyn, Krasnik, Pulawy, Deblin and others—there were at most 24,000 Jews still alive in October 1943, that is, shortly before the liquidation of the majority of these camps. There was a much smaller number of Jews in the forced labour camps in the Radom district (Skarzysko-Kamienna, Ostrowiec Swieto-krzyski, Radom, Piotrkow, Czestochowa) and in the Plaszow concentration camp. Emissaries of the Jewish National Committee managed to make contact with all these Jewish forced labour camps.

[13] Dr. Leon Feiner ("Mikolaj", "Berezowski"), native of Cracow, a left-

of the Jewish National Committee, he [Mr. M.] formulates Jewish requirements and demands that the Jewish population be given its rights. Mr. M. is a magnificent example of the social worker "on the surface", who remains at his post despite imminent and omnipresent danger.

The majority of Jews on the Aryan side remain "under the surface". They live either in a hide-out, or simply in a back room. I have heard from someone who has lived for six months in a back room in a flat how much skill is needed to prevent neighbours and acquaintances from knowing that a Jew is staying there. If someone is paying a visit, one has to resort to stratagems and move from the room to the kitchen or to other rooms in such a way as to enable the visitor to see the whole flat and not allow him to realize that a Jewish family is hidden there. I heard about a Jewish family that lived for five months in a two room flat without there ever being a single collision, despite frequent visits from friends and relatives of the owners. But these Jews had to leave that flat, as the owners' mother could no longer stand the nervous tension connected with the Jews' stay there, and moreover this street was frequently

---

wing leader of the *Bund*, one of the advocates who defended leftists in political trials.

At the time of the German occupation, he was Chairman of the *Bund* Central Committee in the underground and its moving spirit. He was one of the central personalities in Jewish underground activity in Warsaw. It was he who wrote most of the reports of the *Bund* underground in Poland which reached the West from 1942 on, reports with descriptions of horror and cries of despair that gave the world some idea of the fate of the Jews of Poland.

He lived on the Aryan side of Warsaw under the name Berezowski. He was Vice-Chairman of the Council for Aid to the Jews that was set up by the Polish Government Delegation in Warsaw.

He survived all the hardships and dangers of the period of the German occupation but, with the liberation of Warsaw and his rescue in Lublin in January 1945, his strength gave out and he was taken straight to the clinic of the University Hospital. He was suffering from a fatal illness, but he retained full consciousness to his last moment. Even in hospital he maintained contact with his comrades and took part in discussions on the political line of the *Bund* in the new Poland. He died on 22 February 1945 at the age of 59.

cordoned off by gendarmes searching for arms and there was no place to hide in the flat.

There were no such hide-outs on the Aryan side as there were in the Ghetto. In the Ghetto, there were experts who specialized in building hide-outs, and they achieved extraordinary results in this field. Some hide-outs in the Ghetto constituted whole underground flats, with toilets, washrooms, gas, bathrooms, radio, electric light, etc.[14] It was impossible to build such hide-outs on the Aryan side because of the need for secrecy. For this reason, hide-outs were built mostly in flats in the districts where Jews had lived previously, mainly in the so-called "Little Ghetto".[15] These flats,

---

[14] After the deportations ended in September 1942, the Warsaw Jews began *en masse* to build different kinds of underground hide-outs and shelters, for they were convinced that sooner or later the Germans would start new deportations. (Ringelblum gives a detailed account of these bunkers in his *Ktovim fun geto*. See entry for 24 December, 1942. Vol. II, pp. 48–53.) Early in 1943, besides bunkers, underground tunnels were dug to permit contact between the different parts of the Ghetto and between the Ghetto and the Aryan side. In a report written in imprisonment in Warsaw after the war, Nazi General Stroop wrote as follows about the bunkers and the means of communication in the Warsaw Ghetto:
"A whole underground communications network had been established, which permitted contacts between all parts of the Ghetto. The sewerage system, particularly the main sewer going through the centre of the Ghetto, was skillfully utilized for this purpose. Jewish combat groups and the Ghetto inhabitants could therefore change their positions unobserved, something of prime military and purely organizational importance in conditions of house-to-house and street fighting. As far as I remember, underground communication routes had not been adequately developed and built up because there had not been enough time for this, but nevertheless the Ghetto had made preparations for a months-long defence." (Quoted from Josef Wulf, *Das dritte Reich und sein Vollstrecker. Die Liquidation von 500,000 Juden im Ghetto Warschau.* Berlin, 1961, p. 184.) During the uprising, Stroop reported to his superior, General Krueger, that the Nazi forces had uncovered and destroyed a total of 631 bunkers and underground hide-outs, all built in secret. (See: *Report of Jurgen Stroop concerning the Warsaw Ghetto Uprising and the Liquidation of the Jewish Residential Area,* Jewish Historical Institute, Warsaw, 1958, p. 28.)
[15] The "Little Ghetto" was the southern part of the Ghetto which included,

allocated by the Living Quarters Bureau, were in poor condition, and this was used to build hide-outs in these flats. Among the most popular kinds of hide-outs were parts of rooms that had been cut off, disguised rooms, recesses, cut-off parts of attics, cellars, etc. In ground floor flats, the cellars were converted into hide-outs, which were connected with the flats by trap doors. In other parts of the city, building hide-outs presented great difficulties. Bricks had to be carried in briefcases to avoid suspicion by the neighbours. One bricklayer, an expert in building hide-outs, carried the bricks on a push-cart, on which there was an iron stove that served to simulate the need for using the bricks. Building a hide-out required a lot of money, tens of thousands of zloty and sometimes even more. The expenses were both one-time and permanent. The one-time expenses were first of all the bribes for the officials of the Living Quarters Bureau for the allocation of the flat; next, the expense of repairing the flats; a one-time fee to the Aryan family which provided "cover" for the given flat, etc. In principle, one stayed in the flat all the time, and only if strangers arrived (friends rang the bell in a specific way settled beforehand) did the Jewish tenants go to the hide-out.

There are hide-outs in suburban villas; Jews would often buy these villas for their Christian "dummies". A "dummy" is usually a Christian but sometimes a Jew of "good" appearance. In addition to a monthly payment of usually one to two thousand zloty per person, the Jewish subtenants support their Aryan landlords.

Sometimes prison serves as a hide-out. This is no fantasy but actual fact. A Jew is in a Warsaw prison as an Aryan on a criminal charge. Legal proceedings have been under way for a long

---

inter alia, Grzybowska Street, where the Community premises were. The Little Ghetto (23% of the over-all area) stretched from south Chlodna Street (on the odd numbers side) to Zlota Street. But the borders were not fixed, since Zlota Street was cut off from the Ghetto and later the odd numbers of Sienna Street. The main Ghetto (77% of the over-all area) stretched from north of Chlodna Street (on the even numbers side) as far as Dzika Street, Niska and part of Pokorna Street. The two parts of the Ghetto were connected by half of Zelazna Street (cut in half down its length; the second half—the western side—was outside the Ghetto).

time and are constantly being adjourned until ... the end of the war.

Jews "under the surface" often live in the flats of Party members. In a flat like this, one lives among ethical people who do not fear German threats and will not betray a Jew despite the threat of death. When such a flat is "blown" because of the illegal activities conducted in it, the Jewish subtenants go to their death together with their Aryan landlords. Regardless of this danger, the Jews willingly seek flats recommended by the Party, because there is a hundredfold more danger of blackmail and denunciation than of a "mishap" from political causes.

Since March this year, many blocks of flats have been searched for arms or unregistered tenants. The Gendarmerie cordons off blocks and conducts searches in the flats. These blockades take place frequently and in more and more blocks of flats, and large numbers of unregistered Jews are being discovered as a result. It is becoming more and more imminently dangerous to live illegally without a hide-out.

The position of a Jew on the Aryan side becomes particularly difficult if he is taken ill. There have been cases of betrayal by Aryan doctors to whom Jews were forced to turn for help. In one particular case, a Jew hiding on the Aryan side, a former high official of the Ministry of Agriculture, had a serious heart attack. An Aryan doctor was called and he stayed up the whole night with the patient. In the morning, the doctor discussed the patient's further treatment with his wife. He advised her to have the patient hospitalized, to which the wife—half unconscious after her sleepless night—replied that it was impossible to put him in hospital for certain reasons. Half an hour later, the Gestapo arrived and sent the couple to the *Umschlagplatz* as part of the "resettlement action" then in progress. The husband went to Treblinka, and his wife managed to escape.

It is still worse if a Jew dies on the Aryan side. In a certain hide-out a little girl died, and she was buried in the adjacent garden. When the Ghetto was still in existence, Christian undertaking establishments would smuggle the bodies of deceased Jews to the Jewish cemetery. After the liquidation of the Ghetto, the situation became more difficult. However, for a few thousand zloty the deceased "on the surface" will find eternal rest "under the surface".

Even in the tragedy of Jews on the Aryan side, there were comic moments. I heard of a certain Jewish engineer, who had been working on the railways for a building firm. He travelled round the country for this firm, equipped with the necessary papers. In Chelm he ran into a German railway inspector who boasted about being able to spot any Jew. Social considerations obliged our engineer to go to the bath house with his colleagues. The engineer employed all available means in order to hide his "shame"—he soaped the "infamous" place, wriggled around discreetly, moved away when necessary, in order not to be "nabbed". "Social" obligations were met, and the Jewishness of the engineer was not exposed. But he was spotted later on; he barely saved his life and had to give up his important and safe position and take shelter in a hide-out.

The stay of a Jew on the Aryan side means the torment of constant fear, day and night. Every murmur at the entrance of the block of flats after curfew, the sound of an automobile hooter, a ring at the door, every sound and every noise in general cause the heart to beat faster for fear of an informer, blackmailer or gendarme. For Jews on the Aryan side to be "nabbed" or denounced is an everyday affair. The Polish agents of the criminal police, Gestapo-agents and Polish Police are all under orders from the German authorities to pursue Jews. When the police—both agents and uniformed policemen—were deprived of their ample takings in the Jewish District, where the scope for their activity was constantly dwindling, they passed over to the "Jewish region" on the Aryan side. It was not so much a matter of giving the Jews away to the Germans as of making profits, and ample ones at that, for themselves. Jews of limited means, who were not able to buy themselves out of the hands of their tormentors, were given away to the Gestapo.

Jews on the Aryan side are "nabbed" for a variety of reasons. The most important one is denunciation. Denunciations come from different quarters, mostly from neighbours hostile to the Jews, Volksdeutsche, informers, Gestapo-men, etc. A very frequent way of being "nabbed" is registration. There are Polish Police officials who systematically inspect particular blocks of flats and look through the registry books, which serve them as basis for various inquiries. Jewish belongings are a frequent cause of blackmail or of being "nabbed". The person with whom belongings have been deposited looks for a way to get rid of their owner and the simplest way is to report the hiding place of the Jew to the suitable quarters. Belongings are a source of disaster for another reason as well. Blackmailers follow the belongings from the Ghetto, and the belongings lead them to the flats of the Jews on the Aryan side. The most frequent way of being "nabbed" is by accident. There was one case when neighbours heard some suspicious noises from a locked flat, and suspecting there were thieves there they broke the door open and uncovered the Jews. In one case Jews were discovered in house-to-house searches after an attempt on the life of a German. In another case, the "give-away" was caused by a quarrel among the Jews in hiding which was overheard by the neighbours. Sometimes the "nabbing" is caused by romantic reasons: a Polish-Jewish marital triangle, disappointed love, jealousy, etc. Jews often unmask themselves by their unsuitable mode of life: wealthy Jewesses often show off their rare and valuable furs, put diamond rings on their fingers, squander their money, drive around in rickshaws[16] and carriages. The results of such a way of life are surveillance, searches and finally arrests. Jews are often "nabbed" as a result of their own recklessness and imprudence, for example by meeting in large numbers in given restaurants or cafés. Some move about the streets of the capital too frequently, until an Aryan acquaintance gives someone away to the authorities. A wedding held by Jews in the St. Alexander Church on Trzech Krzyzy Square belongs to this category of reckless performances. The Gestapo received information about this wedding, surrounded the Church and arrested everyone

---

16 Rickshaws appeared in the streets of Warsaw as early as the first year of the occupation, after cars had been confiscated and many of them completely wrecked during the September 1939 fighting. The rickshaws were commoner in the Ghetto than on the Aryan side, especially after the trams stopped running; they became a source of livelihood for people of different social strata who had been ruined. For a certain period, the rickshaws were the only vehicles in the Ghetto for both passengers and goods.

assembled there. In this case the bride and groom, who had already been married according to Jewish law for a long time, wanted to acquire the first authentic document which would establish their legal existence in the eyes of other tenants and the neighbours. Also in this category is a collective dinner party of eleven Jews at Swider, near Warsaw. The German authorities were notified and those present were arrested and subsequently shot.

Police agents and police in uniform have made great progress in spotting Jews. As far as men are concerned, it is not a difficult matter: the trousers are pulled down and there is the evidence, and the trousers are pulled down at every turn without ceremony. Aryans suspected of being of Jewish origin are often checked this way. A remedy was sought for this too. Some people are of the opinion that it is possible to make a Jew's male sex organ look like an uncircumcised one by means of an operation. The attempt has been abandoned for the most part, because of sexual disorders connected with this very costly operation. In some cases the authorities required medical examination of suspected Jews. If the doctor happens to be a decent man, he will certify that so-called *phimosis* was performed, that is, the removal of the foreskin, as the result of veneral disease. A medical certificate like this has saved the life of many a Jew. More than one Jewish Aryan walks around with this certificate of *phimosis.*

The agents have much more trouble in spotting Jewish women, though rumour has it that they recognize Jewish women by a protruding bone in the neck or by the ears, a notion with a striking resemblance to the eighteenth-century folk belief that Jewesses give birth after their death. But the agents find ways here too. A Jewish woman of even the "best" appearance can rarely give references about her family. The agents also know of another weak point of Jewish women, namely their purely superficial knowledge of Catholic religions rites. To the question, "What does the priest do after confession?" very rarely will a Jewish woman answer that he taps the confessional. Sometimes a Jewess is trapped and ruined by so simple a question as, "When is your nameday?" The newly christened Maria or Stefa has not yet had the time to look at a calendar in order to check when her nameday is.

Next to the police agents, the blackmailers and the *schmalzowniks*
are an endless nightmare to the Jews on the Aryan side. There is
literally not a Jew "on the surface" or "under the surface" who has
not had something to do with them at least once or more than once,
who has not had to buy himself off for a sum of money.[17] There is
even a joke about it: one Jew meets another Jew on the Aryan side
with a suitcase in his hand. He asks his acquaintance, "Where are
you going? What's happened?" The answer is, "Oh, it's nothing,
just a spot of blackmail". Extortion by *schmalzowniks* begins the
moment the Jew crosses through the gates of the Ghetto, or rather
while he is still inside the Ghetto gates, which are watched by
swarms of *schmalzowniks*. Every Jews who leaves the Ghetto is a
prey for a *schmalzownik*. In *schwalzownik* terminology a Jew is a
"cat" slinking through the city streets. These voluntary police agents,

---

17 Ringelblum's observations are confirmed by the reports of practically
all the Jews who left the Ghetto and managed to survive on the Aryan
side, living through harrowing dramas, subjected to blackmail over and
over again. There are hundreds of such reports in the Archives of Yad
Vashem, and many official Polish documents also bear witness to the
plague of blackmail. One of them is the striking appeal made to the
Government Delegate for the Homeland by the Council for Aid to the
Jews in April 1943. It reads as follows: "To the Government Delegate
for the Homeland: We once again bring up an urgent problem of
burning importance to us—the fight against blackmail. This phenomenon
is on the increase at an appalling rate—both as regards its size and the
forms it takes. Not a day passes without many cases of blackmail, of
victims' being robbed of their last money and belongings. There is
hardly a single family or individual who has not been subjected to this
vile proceeding. And often—very often—there are cases of the very same
family or person's becoming the victims of blackmail two, three or many
more times. It is not infrequent for these cases to end with death—by
suicide or through the liquidation of the victims by the authorities into
whose hands they are delivered by the blackmailers.
This increasingly wide-spread type of crime haunting our streets day by
day cancels out the Council's attempts at assistance, in fact renders them
impossible, and is also evidence of the proliferating gangrene of demoralization."
(Archives of the Institute for the History of the [Communist] Party in
Warsaw, Files of the Government Delegate's Office, 202/XV–2, p. 300.)

the *schmalzowniks*, keep their eyes glued on the Jew so that at the right moment, when he takes off his armband and goes into the entrance of a block of flats, they will be able to catch him red-handed and demand a suitable ransom. A more cunning *schmalzownik* will make a note of the number of the flat and will join forces with a policeman to raid the Jew and the Christians who are his hosts. The *schmalzowniks* operate in every place where Jews have some contact with the Aryan side—at all the posts near the walls, at the exit gates, along the routes to the work posts, at the work posts, etc., in short, wherever Jews try to "break loose", to detach themselves from the work post and go to a flat on the Aryan side.

The *schmalzowniks* walk around in the streets stopping anyone who looks Semitic in appearance. They frequent public squares, especially the square near the Central [Railway] Station, cafés and restaurants, and the hotels where Jews who were foreign citizens used to be interned. The *schmalzowniks* operate in organized bands. Bribing one of them does not mean that a second will not appear in a little while, then a third and so on, a whole chain of *schmalzowniks* who pass the victim on until he has lost his last penny. The *schmalzowniks* collaborate with police agents, the uniformed police and in general with anyone who is looking for Jews. They are a real plague of locusts, descending in their hundreds and maybe even thousands on the Jews on the Aryan side and stripping them of their money and valuables and often clothing as well. A *schmalzownik*, like a real street thief, will sometimes take not only his victim's money away from him but his belongings as well. But fortunately a *schmalzownik* is usually satisfied with moderate booty or, to be more precise, whatever [money] the victim has. The *schmalzowniks* are usually juvenile delinquents under twenty years of age, who hunt Jews for lack of anything else to do. It must be added that among the *schmalzowniks* there are also so-called honourable individuals. Such a *schmalzownik*, having received his "tip" from his Jewish client, will even accompany his victim home and guard him from the aggressiveness of his colleagues. Even a gentleman is sometimes to be found among the *schmalzowniks*. A gentleman of this kind turned out to be the ring-leader of the *schmalzowniks* on Parysow Square: "Little Feliks of Parysow". A certain young Jewess, who was active in the Combat Organization, was accosted by "Little Feliks"; she did not haggle with him and gave him the 1,000 zloty demanded without a word. "Little Feliks" was so struck by this extraordinary behaviour on the part of this Jewess, who was on the Aryan side arranging a number of dangerous matters (transporting arms to the Ghetto, etc.), that he promised her safe-conduct in his district. If she was accosted by anyone, she was to mention his name,

The *schmalzowniks* feel great respect for the Party[18] and are in deadly fear of it. I know of a case where a Jewish woman was accosted by *schmalzowniks*, and had no alternative but to threaten them with revenge from the Party, which she said had sent someone to follow her. To prove it, she winked to a man passing by, and in this way she escaped the *schmalzowniks*. It happens that persons threatened with denunciation by a porter or neighbours actually approach the Party, which then steps in and uses its influence to safeguard the Jewish family on whose behalf the appeal has been made. Obviously, these are very rare cases.

The Jewish "pastime" is a very convenient thing for the *schmalzowniks* and for blackmailers. Quite often blackmailers use it with regard to Aryans, whom they accuse of Jewish origin. The subjects of their blackmail are usually single women, who are unable to protect themselves against the pressure and the impudence of these wartime robbers. A case like this was brought to court in the summer of 1943, according to the *Nowy Kurier Warszawski*. Blackmailers called on two single ladies and threatened to accuse them of Jewish origin, swindling them out of 5,000 zloty. A few days later they demanded another 20,000 zloty and the women brought the case to court. The blackmailers were sentenced to a year in prison.

The Jewish factor is taken advantage of by Germans, police agents and uniformed police, etc., when running down people who are politically involved. It is enough to shout, "Catch that Jew!" for obliging passers-by to give the fleeing "Jewish criminal" to the representatives of hostile authority who are pursuing him. The pass-

---

18 In popular Warsaw slang of the period of Nazi occupation, the word "Party" often referred simply to the underground.

ers-by find out too late that they have been taken in and that they have betrayed a combatant of the Polish Underground to the enemy. This trick has recently been practised on such a large scale that the illegal press has found it advisable to bring it to the notice of the whole community. The large-scale nature of the practice is the best evidence of how active the anti-Semitic mob is and how attractive anti-Semitic slogans are among the Polish population.

An even more dangerous plague for Jews on the Aryan side is constituted by bands of blackmailers. The difference between the *schmalzowniks* and the blackmailers is that the former's area of activity is the street and the latter's is the flat. Through surveillance in the streets, in the cafés, by collaborating with the *schmalzowniks,* the blackmailers find their victims; they call on them in their flats together with agents and uniformed police. If the *schmalzowniks* are wasps that sting their victims, the blackmailers are vultures that devour them. The demands of the informers-police-blackmailers partnerships are set very high and come to at least thousands of zloty and oftener to tens of thousands. An instance is known where sixteen Jews caught in a suburban villa paid half a million zloty. Only the very rich can afford to buy themselves out of the blackmailers' hands. Usually, there is only one thing left to do—to escape, leaving all one's belongings to the landlord, who is usually collaborating with the blackmailers.

While the Ghetto still existed, one could observe the return of great numbers of blackmail victims to the Jewish district, broken in spirit, stripped of belongings and money, cursing the Aryan side which had deprived them of their last haven. The returning Jews kissed the earth of the Ghetto, blessed every day spent there and claimed that there they could rest without continually watching out for the police and the "Black Maria" with the Gendarmerie. Some people returned to the Ghetto even without having been blackmailed, just for fear of this nightmare which prevented Jews on the Aryan side from sleeping at nights and imbued them with deadly fear. Some people returned to the Ghetto for a holiday: their shattered nerves could no longer stand the constant tension. After a short period of rest for their nerves, their mental stability returned, the situation was analysed and the paradoxical conclusion was reached:

—for a Jew there is no escape, there is merely a choice of the kind and place of death. There are four kinds: (1) death in a Ghetto bunker; (2) death on the Aryan side; (3) death in the S.S. labour camps in Trawniki or Poniatow, and (4) death in an internment camp in Vittel (Alsace).[19] Some Jews, in their disappointment with the Aryan side, having neither the health nor the wealth needed to return there, proceeded voluntarily to the S.S. camps set up by Toebbens and Schultz. A small handful of privileged people with considerable funds at their disposal sought their way to Vittel as foreign citizens. Some recovered from their fright and realized that it is after all a fact that Jews have better prospects of surviving the war on the Aryan side than in the Ghetto, sentenced to extermination. Such wanderings backwards and forwards continued without stopping from now on. Thousands went to the "other" side but thousands also returned to the Ghetto for fear of blackmailers.

---

[19] Vittel: A spa in eastern France in the neighbourhood of Nancy. During the war, whole families of British and American citizens—about 2,000 souls—were interned there. Vittel remained a concentration centre for foreigners from the occupied zone of France until January 1943, under the supervision of the International Red Cross.

In the summer of 1943, some 200 Warsaw Jews reached Vittel on the strength of dubious "rescue passports" of South American countries, which had been sent to Warsaw from Switzerland. When these "papers" arrived, practically all the Jews they were intended for were no longer alive. The Gestapo decided to sell them (or part of them) to other Jews, still in hiding after the liquidation of the Ghetto. A Jewish committee was set up to decide who was to receive these "papers". Most of those who received them paid large sums for them, but a minority got them for little or nothing. Part of the moneys collected in this way was needed to bribe the Gestapo men, and the rest was handed to the Jewish Aid Committee.

On the first day of the "deportation" of 18 April 1944, about 170 Jews with "rescue passports" were sent from Vittel to Drancy. Among them was Yitzhak Katznelson, the poet who wrote the great lamentation of the holocaust. From Drancy they were sent to Auschwitz extermination camp. A second transport left Vittel on its way to Auschwitz on 16 May 1944.

(Natan Eck, *Hatoyim bedarkey hamawet,* Jerusalem, Yad Vashem, 1954, pp. 146, 156, 161, 188, 190, 193, 217, 218.)

The blackmailers have sophisticated methods of operating, characteristic ways of trapping Jews. One of them is to publish advertisements in the press offering vacant rooms. A gang like this was operating in Senatorska Street, advertising vacant rooms in the papers. If a Jewish family turned up as a result of the advertisement, other members of the gang presented themselves and forced the Jews to escape by threatening them with denunciation—naturally, the Jews had to pay a large sum of money and leave all their belongings behind. After they disappeared, a new advertisement was published, and so it went on and on.

Blackmailers, *schmalzowniks,* agents, uniformed police and all sorts of other scoundrels held and still hold their revels with impunity in the streets of the capital. The murder of thousands of Jews, sentenced to death by the Gestapo after being caught, is their handwork. Yet no harm befalls them. They know that where Jews are concerned, there is no law and no punishment, nobody will stand up for them. Jewish political and social organizations constantly demand that extortion and blackmail be fought. The Polish Underground, however, has as yet done nothing to save the handful of Polish Jews on the Aryan side. The Home Plenipotentiary of the Polish Government [-in-Exile] has indeed issued a very belated warning that blackmailing Jews is a crime, which the Government will punish now and after the war. Words have not been followed by deeds. Though energetic action was taken to liquidate denunciators and informers, very little has been done in the sphere of fighting blackmailing of Jews. This complete impunity for the blackmailers and the *schmalzowniks* has wounded and still wounds the handful of Jews, who see in this a clear sign that nobody is anxious to save Polish Jews.

The united anti-Jewish front of agents, uniformed police, blackmailers and *schmalzowniks* gets considerable help from the anti-Semitic propaganda which has built up the ideological basis for the disgraceful deeds of these unified scoundrels. Anti-Semitic propaganda,[20] which is discussed elsewhere, provides this gang with

---

[20] In pursuing their policy of persecution and extermination of Polish Jewry, the Nazis made use without scruple of anti-Semitic propaganda on a large

material which, in the eyes of the Polish population, mitigates the criminal nature of handing over Jews to the Germans. With regard to this propaganda material, these are hard times for the anti-Semites. They are now short of prey for their pro-Nazi, anti-Jewish propaganda. There are almost no Jews left in Poland and those who do remain are locked up in S.S. camps or are in hiding on the Aryan side. It has now become difficult to reproach the Jews with buying up all the food, with being responsible for the high cost of living, for taking bread away from the Poles, for taking over all the jobs, etc. And still, the Polish anti-Semites would like to help

---

scale, calculated to appeal to the basest instincts of certain strata of the Polish population. The venomous Polish-language Nazi press (e.g. the newspaper, *Nowy Kurier Warszawski*)—which was boycotted by Polish patriots—continuously incited the Poles against the Jews. Posters were put on the walls of buildings, in railway stations, in trams and other public places in the towns, with illustrations depicting the Jews as loathsome.

With the invasion of Russia, the German occupation authorities began a frenzied campaign of anti-Jewish incitement throughout the whole country. The German press was full of stories of "Jewish criminal deeds against the Church", "Jewish murders of the Polish intelligentsia" and similar fabrications. Anonymous leaflets in Polish were distributed among the Polish rabble, full of poisonous agitation directed against "the Jewish Bolsheviks." German agents carried this propaganda even into the villages, and spared no efforts to work up hatred against the Jews. The main task of the Polish-language German press was to spread anti-Semitism among the Polish population. The anti-Semitic infection was spread in every conceivable medium, such as the radio, public loud-speaker system, special anti-Semitic exhibitions, illustrated brochures, leaflets and posters, all permeated with anti-Semitic poison.

The question remains whether the hostile attitude of the general Polish population to the Jews was due to German propaganda. A reply comes from a sufficiently authoritative Polish source, which affirms that "there was a general reaction against German propaganda, including anti-Semitic propaganda, as a matter of course. But it is another matter that it had its effect on the sub-conscious all the same, and perhaps even to a considerable extent. Thus the poster, 'Jews — lice — typhus', did its work, and there was no little poison in the existing atmosphere".

(Ringelblum, op. cit., Vol. I, p. 228. See also, "An unknown Note of Shmuel Breslaw", *Yalkut Moreshet,* No. 11, 1969, p. 105; Wylezynska, op. cit., p. 212.)

the Gestapo by exposing Jews, would like to carry out Hitler's programme a hundred per cent. That is why they still look for arguments against the Jews. Thus a variety of stories are invented and inflated about Jewish partisans who rob the Polish peasants and strip them of their belongings. Despite the small number of Jews in the guerilla movement,[21] all the sins of the Polish partisans[22] are

---

[21] The statement that there were relatively few Jews in the partisan movement refers only to the situation as it was from late 1943 onwards, when thousands of Poles joined the partisans. No more young Jews were entering the partisan formations at this time because of the mass extermination of the Jewish population, and because the overwhelming majority of Jewish partisans who had been in the forests since 1942 had already perished in the constant fighting. This is why the number of Jews in the partisan movement from late 1943 on amounted to only a small percentage.

In the preceding year, from mid-1942 to late in 1943, the situation had been quite different. The Jewish partisan movement came into being in the summer of 1942 as a result of spontaneous escapes into the forests by masses of Jews during the first deportations to the extermination camps. At this time, there was practically no Polish partisan movement in existence yet, and the Jewish fugitives in the forests were the pioneers of the partisan movement in Poland, side by side with Russian soldiers who had escaped from P.O.W. camps. The Polish historian of the resistance movement, Bogdan Hillebrandt, writes: "In 1942, the number of people hiding in villages and forests increased greatly as a result of escapes from the Ghettos. These followed on the ill-famed *Aktion Reinhardt* which began in the summer of this year [in fact, it had already begun in March 1942—Ed.] and the aim of which was to deport hundreds of thousands of the Jewish population, closed in inside the Ghettos, to the extermination camps to be murdered there. Many Jews, particularly young people, foresaw the fate the Nazis had in store for them and escaped from the Ghettos, hoping to find asylum with the Polish population. These dauntless men constituted an excellent element for the partisan movement."

(Bogdan Hillebrandt, *Partyzantka na Kielecczyznie*, Warsaw, 1967, pp. 65–66.)

From the end of 1942 on, better-organized escapes took place from the Ghettos, forced labour camps and even from the concentration and death camps. Groups of combatants from the Warsaw, Vilna, Bialystok, Cracow and Czestochowa Ghettos also carried out partisan activities. A certain number of those who took part in the risings in Sobibor and Treblinka death camps also reached the ranks of the partisans.

The Polish underground began creating partisan units in the forests only at the end of 1942. By mid-1943 partisan units under the command of the Home Army numbered only 2,000 soldiers in all (Rawski and others, *Wojna Wyzwolencza Narodu Polskiego w latach,* 1939–1945, p. 401), and the units under the *Gwardia Ludowa* ("People's Guard") 1,500 people (*Dwadziescia lat Ludowego Wojska Polskiego, II sesja poswiecona Wojnie Wyzwolenczej Narodu Polskiego,* Warsaw, 1967, p. 140). Up to mid-1943, Jews played a very large part in the whole partisan movement on Polish territory. In the four districts alone of the "General-Government"—Warsaw, Lublin, Radom and Cracow—more than 30 Jewish partisan units were active in 1942 and 1943, some of them on their own and some under the Polish *Gwardia Ludowa* (and this number does not include the smaller armed groups of just a few men each). Moreover, the Jews constituted a considerable percentage of those units of the *Gwardia Ludowa* that were of mixed nationality—Polish-Jewish, Polish-Russian-Jewish and Russian-Jewish. Some hundreds of Jewish partisans were even members of Polish units of the *Gwardia Ludowa,* the *Armia Ludowa,* the Home Army, the *Socjalistyczna Organizacja Bojowa,* the *Bataliony Chlopskie* and other lesser-known Polish and military organizations. Jews also took a considerable part in the raids by commando units that shifted their operations from liberated territories to behind the German lines. And, finally, scores of Jews were to be found among the commanders of the Polish partisan movement. (These data are taken from the work by S. Krakowski on the Jewish resistance movement under Nazi occupation, part of a research project being carried out by the Institute of Contemporary Jewry at the Hebrew University in Jerusalem.) Exact data are not available on the Jewish partisan movement in the rest of Poland.

22 There are no quotation marks in the original, but without any doubt the expression, "the sins of the Polish partisans", is used here figuratively, not literally. The author is referring to the difficult, complex problem of German repression in reprisal for partisan activities. The Polish organizations connected with the Government Delegate's Office and the Home Army—and these constituted the greater part of the Polish underground—regarded partisan warfare in 1942 and 1943 as premature and harmful, since such activities would needlessly expose the Polish population to the danger of repressive measures on the part of the occupiers. The propaganda service of these organizations called on the Polish population to adopt a waiting attitude and avoid clashes liable to provoke repression. These organizations also accused the Russian and Jewish partisans, and later on the Polish *Gwardia Ludowa* (People's Guard) as well, of provoking unnecessary fighting, which would finally turn out against the interests of the Polish population. Thus, for example, when a Nazi punitive expedition came to the village of Laszczew in the Lublin region

attributed to them. Legends are spread to the effect that Jews who are caught by the Germans ruin their Aryan landlords by affirming that the latter knew that their sub-tenants were of Jewish origin. These rumours and others like them are spread on purpose, constantly and secretly. As a result, the position of Jews "on the surface" and "under the surface" gets worse every day. The number of Jewish victims shot down pitilessly becomes larger and larger. Woe

---

on 25 December 1942, and shot 87 of the inhabitants, it was regarded as a reprisal for the killing two days earlier of two Nazi gendarmes at the Laszczew railway station by Russian partisans. (See Report of Government Delegate's Office for 11 November 1942 to 23 January 1943, Yad Vashem Archives, microfilm JM/2843.)

Reports sent to the Polish Government in London, as well as articles and proclamations in the underground press, used an accusing tone blaming the partisans for causing the Polish population unnecessary suffering. The following passage from a proclamation of 26 July 1943, put out by the "A" Agency (one connected with the Government Delegate) is an example in point: "Basing ourselves on partisan activities in the region of Lublin, Kielce and even Warsaw, we see how such doings end up for the Polish population of the towns and villages. The Germans usually avoid clashes with armed units, but with full Teutonic fury they attack, burn and murder the peaceful Polish inhabitants. Who can be interested in bleeding our people like this in a premature and needless struggle? Only our enemies and no one else. Therefore, notwithstanding all the show of "pro-independence" and "national" attitudes on the part of the Communists from the *P.P.R.* and the *Gwardia Ludowa,* these people constitute a hostile force which we shall have to fight against just as we fight against what is the greatest hostile force at this moment —Germany."

(Quoted from files of the Government Delegate's Office, in the Archives of the Institute for the History of the [Communist] Party, Warsaw, 202/II-24, p. 22.)

There is however no direct evidence of repressive measures' being taken against the Polish population in reprisal for Jewish partisan activity. And the Jewish partisans, on their side, created their movement as a result of the deportations—it was not a matter of choice, of deciding on the right moment. The Jews could not postpone flight to the forests. The Government Delegate's Office, however, did nothing at all to help or guide the numerous Jewish fugitives who escaped into the forests, where they sought to evade deportation to the death camps and to take up arms against the Germans.

to the Jew whose flat is getting "hot". Even for money it is difficult to find an Aryan willing to hide a Jew in his flat. A Jew who has lost his flat will not find shelter anywhere, even for a day or two. He has to hide in the ruins of bombed buildings or in open fields, with his life in danger until he finds a flat, which costs more every day. While in January of this year it was possible to find a flat with board for a hundred zloty per person per day, now they are asking two hundred and over. The noose is constantly tightening round the neck of Warsaw's remaining Jews, and there is no prospect of help from anywhere.

In August of this year, organizations fighting for Polish independence issued a proclamation which stressed that Germany is trying to make the Polish population bear joint responsibility for the murdering of the Jewish population in Poland. The proclamation refers to the appeal made formerly by the Home Plenipotentiary of the Polish Government [-in-Exile] and calls on the Poles to give the Jews active support. These appeals do not, however, reach wider circles and they do not evoke the right response, for reasons which will be discussed in a separate chapter.

The Polish Police, commonly called the Blue or uniformed police in order to avoid using the term "Polish", has played a most lamentable role in the extermination of the Jews of Poland.[23] The

---

[23] The Polish Police functioned only on the territories in central Poland forming the so-called General-Government—the regions of Warsaw, Lublin, Kielce, Cracow and Eastern Galicia. This Police was subordinate to the German *Schutzpolizei* and constituted the second-biggest armed force (after the German *Ordnungspolizei*) used for anti-Jewish measures. At the end of 1942, it numbered 14,300 men in all, about 3,000 of whom were stationed in Warsaw. The part played by the Polish Police in the liquidation of the Jews is confirmed from many sources. The Government Delegate's Office reported as follows on 31 December 1943: "The Polish Police (the so-called Blue Police) is thoroughly corrupt. The taking of bribes and blackmail of persons of Jewish origin—and even sometimes of unquestioned Aryans—are an everyday affair... The occupiers do not use the Polish Police for political activities, but nevertheless the part played by this Police in anti-Jewish measures, for example in the liquidation of the Warsaw Ghetto in April and May 1943, or in the tracking down of non-Aryans has been considerable." (Archives of the Institute for the History of the [Communist] Party,

uniformed police has been an enthusiastic executor of all the German directives regarding the Jews. The powers of the uniformed police in the sphere of collaborating with the Germans concerning the Jews were as follows: (1) guarding the exit gates of the Ghetto as well as the walls and fences enclosing the Ghettos or the Jewish districts; (2) participating in "resettlement actions" in the capacity of catchers, escorts, etc.; (3) participating in tracking down Jews who were in hiding after the "resettlement actions"; (4) shooting Jews sentenced to death by the Germans.

In Warsaw and in several other cities, the Blue Police were on

---

Warsaw, 202/II-8, p. 18.) Another report of the Government Delegate's Office, of 1 May 1943, states: "...The 'Blue Police' have again received an order to track down Jews; they have been promised a reward for every Jew caught, namely, one third of his property." (Archives of the Institute for the History of the [Communist] Party, Warsaw, 202/II-21, p. 13.) Numerous sources testify to the zeal displayed by the Blue Police in anti-Jewish activities. Thus for instance the underground paper, *Agencja Prasowa,* No. 51 (142) of 30 December 1942, reported: "In Lukow county, the Blue Police have shown exceptional zeal in catching Jews in hiding." Similar observations were made by Dr. Zygmunt Klukowski, a Polish chronicler connected with the Home Army. In his note of 22 October 1942 describing the liquidation of Jews in the town of Szczebrzeszyn, he states: "The gendarmes from outside and the S.S.-men left yesterday. Today, 'our' gendarmes and the Blue Police are at work; they have been ordered to kill every Jew they catch on the spot. They are executing this order with great zeal. Since morning, they have been bringing the corpses of the Jews killed from different parts of the town, mostly from the Jewish quarter, 'Zatyly', on horse-drawn carts to the Jewish cemetery, where they dig large pits and bury them. Throughout the day, Jews have been routed out from the most varied hide-outs. They have been shot on the spot or brought to the Jewish cemetery and killed there." (Zygmunt Klukowski, *Dziennik z lat okupacji Zamojszczyzny, 1939–1944,* Lublin, 1959, pp. 289–295.) Plentiful information about the catching and shooting of Jews in hiding in forests and villages by the Blue Police is to be found in the answers to questionnaires regarding execution sites throughout Polish territory issued after the war by the Central Commission for Research on Nazi Crimes in Poland. The data collected from these questionnaires have been recorded by Kazimierz Leszczynski in Bulletins Nos. VIII–IX published by the above-named Commission (*Biuletyn Glownej Komisji Badania Zbrodni Hitlerowskich w Polsce*),

guard at the exit points from the moment the Ghettos were established. In Warsaw, in the period after the first "resettlement actions", the Blue Police were posted at intervals around the Ghetto walls, while at the same time German police patrols supervised their activities, checking to see that the [Polish] Police were not neglecting their duties and allowing smugglers into the Jewish district. The Blue Police treated Jews passing through the exit gates with definite hostility and brutality in order to ingratiate themselves with their German supervisors. However, for the price of an ample bribe, the uniformed police permitted themselves to be induced to take an active part in smuggling, both through the exit gates and over the walls and fences. The greater part of the bribes that made smuggling possible was swallowed up by the uniformed police, who took sixty per cent of the whole "pool" for themselves.

The uniformed police has had a deplorable role in the "resettlement actions". The blood of hundreds of thousands of Polish Jews, caught and driven to the "death vans" will be on their heads. The Germans' tactics were usually as follows: in the first "resettlement action" they utilised the Jewish Order Service, which behaved no better from the ethical point of view than their Polish opposite numbers. In the subsequent "actions", when the Jewish Order Service was liquidated as well, the Polish Police force was utilized. It was like that in Biala Podlaska, for example, where the Polish Police conducted the extermination "action" against the Jews in October 1942. I heard from an eyewitness of this "action" that the local fire-brigade, jointly with the uniformed police, discovered sixty Jews in the house where my woman informant was staying, herself among them. The uniformed police [usually] maltreated captured Jews terribly. They would hand over captured Jews to the Germans, who would shoot them on the spot. This time, thanks to the large amount of the bribe offered, the captured Jews were not shot but were sent to Miedzyrzec Podlaski, where the remnant of the Jews from Biala Podlaska were being concentrated. This remnant was shortly afterwards sent to Treblinka.

In Czestochowa the Polish Police, together with Ukrainians, guarded all the exits during the "resettlement action", and took the deported Jews to the railway station; after the "action", they tracked down the Jews and discovered them and, unless given bribes, handed them over to the Germans.

The Blue Police took an active part in the "resettlement action" in Lublin. The police spied on Jews who had been hiding on the Aryan side and caught them. They went about their persecution of the Jews energetically; they would stop passers-by in the streets whom they suspected of being of Jewish origin and take them to Polish police stations.

In Lukow, Blue Police searched the flats of Jews during the "resettlement action", and took away the Jews they found hiding there. The same thing happened in other places. The Blue Police took an active part in the "resettlement actions" everywhere. It was the rule for them to look for Jews in the various towns after the "liquidation". Without aid from local elements, it was difficult for the Germans to look for Jews who were hiding. They had to be sought in attics, cellars, sheds, barns, etc., and for this, it was best to utilise police who were familiar with the terrain, with the lay-out of the flats, etc. This follow-up "action" would go on for several weeks and even sometimes for as long as several months, and as a result greater and greater numbers of Jews would be discovered. As I have mentioned elsewhere, punishment for hiding Jews and rewards for giving them away also helped. It is difficult to estimate the number of Jews in this country who fell victim thanks to the Blue Police; it must certainly amount to tens of thousands of those who had managed to escape the German slaughterers. As regards the Blue Police's carrying out death sentences on Jews, we know of a particular case in the winter of 1941 to '42. Over twenty people, mostly women, and a ten-year-old child, accused of illegally crossing the border of the Warsaw Ghetto, were shot by the Polish Police in the backyard of the Central Police Station on Gesia Street. We do not know whether this was an isolated occurrence in Warsaw, nor whether similar cases occurred in the rest of the country as well. The prominent part taken by the Blue Police in blackmailing Jews was discussed above.

Besides the Blue Police, the fire brigade also played an active part in "resettlement actions" in the country by cordoning off Jewish blocks of flats, hunting down the Jews hiding in attics, cellars, etc.[24] We have specific knowledge of fire-brigades' participation in "liquidation actions" in Kaluszyn and Biala Podlaska. It must be said in favour of the fire brigades that they did save some few Jews during the so-called "kettle" at Niska Street in Warsaw. They hid them in the firemen's cars and drove them away from the danger spot.

As regards Jews' hiding in the countryside, this proves to be a difficult matter, as in small towns and particularly in villages everybody knows everybody else and a stranger arouses general curiosity. The Germans knew very well that after every "resettlement action", some Jews would be hiding at their Christian neighbours' or in the near vicinity in the country side. To clear the surrounding area of Jews, the Germans would employ two methods: the method of rewards and the method of threats. Financial rewards and rewards in kind were put on the head of every Jew captured, in addition to which the clothes and belongings of those captured were also assigned to the captors. In Western "Little Poland", in Borek Falecki, Wieliczka, Bochnia and Swoszowice, for example, 500 zloty and a kilogram of sugar were given for every Jew captured. These tactics resulted in success for the Germans. The local population in great numbers turned Jews over to the Germans, who shot these "criminals". In Volynia, three litres of vodka were given for every Jew denounced. Vodka as a reward for denouncing Jews was repeated in the countryside in other provinces as well. Besides rewards, the Germans also utilized a system of punishments for hiding Jews. Posters threatening capital punishment for this "crime" appeared with the start of every "liquidation action" against the Jews in any given locality. These threats and rewards, however, did not always achieve the desired effect. In small towns where Jews had lived with the Christian population in harmony for centuries, Jews found refuge with Polish neighbours, friends and acquaintances whom they

---

24 This report is confirmed, among other sources, by the underground paper, *Agencja Prasowa* (No. 51/142 of 30 December 1942), which wrote:
"In the Krasnik district, the volunteer fire brigade was called on to look for Jews in hiding. All the firemen readily undertook these degrading and horrible tasks."

had known and been friendly with for long years and even for generations. A peasant or a burgher would give a Jewish fugitive shelter. However, the length of time that it was possible to go on hiding a Jew depended on two things—the German terror and the surrounding atmosphere. Where the environment had been infected with anti-Semitism before the war, hiding Jews presented great difficulties, and denunciations by anti-Semitic neighbours were more to be feared there than the German terror. But this terror was intensified day by day. Whole districts were being thoroughly cleared of the Jews in hiding, mass searches were carried out, and landlords hiding Jews were punished—that is to say, shot. In Kielce Province, known for its exuberant anti-Semitism, the local population in great numbers denounced the Jews hiding there. In Czestochowa and the vicinity, some Jews were in hiding after the "resettlement action". They were paying 50 zloty or more for one night's accommodation in barns, toilets, etc. In accordance with its tradition of anti-Semitism, the Polish population hunted down the Jews hiding there. Czestochowa, where 40,000 Jews were living during the war, is today, according to information from an expert in this field, a town free of Jews. In Lukow, the Jews hid in the surrounding woods for some time after the "resettlement action". It was a frequent occurrence for Polish children playing there to discover groups of these Jews in hiding; they had been taught to hate Jews, so they told the municipal authorities, who in turn handed the Jews over to the Germans to be killed.[25] In Hrubieszow prov-

---

[25] Confirmation of the flight of numerous Lukow Jews to the surrounding forests, as well as the part played by the local population in tracking down the Jews and denouncing them, is to be found in the diary of a local Polish teacher from Lukow, S. Zeminski, who wrote in his entry of 8 November 1942:

"On 5 November, I passed through the village of Siedliska. I went into the cooperative store. The peasants were buying scythes. The woman shopkeeper said, 'They'll be useful for you in the round-up today.' I asked, 'What round-up?' 'Of the Jews.' I asked, 'How much are they paying for every Jew caught?' An embarrassed silence fell. So I went on, 'They paid thirty pieces of silver for Christ, so you should also ask for the same amount.' Nobody answered. What the answer was I heard a little later. Going through the forest, I heard volleys of machine-gun

ince, a score of Jewish families which had fled during different "resettlement actions" took refuge in a quarry. They bought their food from the peasants, who tolerated these Jewish groups in hiding. The village guards also knew of their presence. A peasant betrayed one of these Jew, and rumour had it that this Jew, when he was being interrogated, said that this peasant possessed a radio! For this, the peasant was arrested. In revenge for this betrayal, the village guards called in the uniformed police, who arrested all the Jews after robbing them of their belongings and valuables. Some Jews hid in large provincial towns as well. There are many Jews hidden in Cracow, despite the large number of police contacts and informers there who hunt the Jews down mercilessly. In the territory of "Little Poland", Polish-Jewish relations had been friendly for a long time, and this naturally had an effect on the rescue of Cracow Jews. It should be added that many Jews from larger provincial towns (Lwow, Cracow, Grodno and others) have been hiding for a year or perhaps more on the Aryan side in Warsaw.

---

fire. It was the round-up of the Jews hiding there. Perhaps it is blasphemous to say that I clearly ought to be glad that I got out of the forest alive.

In Burzec, one go-ahead watchman proposed: 'If the village gives me a thousand zloty, I'll hand over these Jews.' Three days later I heard that six Jews in the Burzec forest had dug themselves an underground hideout. They were denounced by a forester of the estate."

S. Żeminski, *Kartki z dziennika nauczyciela w Lukowie z okresu okupacji hitlerowskiej*, "Biuletyn Zydowskiego Instytutu Historycznego" No. 27— 1958, pp. 105–112.)

8

JEWISH CHILDREN ON THE ARYAN SIDE

The children keep their origin secret. — Betrayal through the
horse-drawn tram. — The epic of the smuggler-children on the
Aryan side. — Those with power to decide do not give much
thought to Jewish children. — A discussion on convents.

Jewish families rarely crossed to the Aryan side together. First the
children went, while the parents stayed on in the Ghetto in order
to mobilize the necessary funds for staying on the Aryan side. Very
often the parents gave up the idea of going across to the Aryan
side, as they did not have the money to fix up the whole family.
The cost of keeping a child on the Aryan side in the summer of
1942, when the number of children being sent over was at its peak,
was very high, about 100 zloty a day. A sum was demanded for
six months or a year in advance, for fear that the parents might be
deported in the interim. Thus, a sum of several tens of thousands
of zloty was required to fix up a child on the Aryan side and only
very wealthy people could afford to do so. Parents of limited means
and especially working intellectuals were forced to see their children
taken as the first victims in the various "selections" and "actions".
Not all Jewish parents wanted to send their children to the Aryan
side. There were those who weighed the question of survival for the
children, especially the youngest ones, when no one knew what would
happen to the parents at the next "selection". Some parents argued
that a child deprived of its parents' care will wither like a flower
without the sun. There were children who strongly opposed being
sent to the Aryan side. They did not want to go to the other side
alone, but preferred to die together with their parents. It took me a
long time to convince my son that it is in the interest of our people
that as many children as possible should survive the war. I know

140

ten-year-old twins, who put up stiff opposition for several months and refused to go over to the Aryan side, despite the fact that there was a worker's family which was to keep the children at the cost of a workers' organization. The children declared emphatically that they would not go over to the Aryan side without their mother, as they did not want to survive the war on their own, alone. After a long period of conflict, the mother won, and the children went across to the Aryan side, where they are to this day. The mother died in a sewer trying to get through to her children during the "action" of April 1943.

The majority of children, however, agreed to go across to the Aryan side, as living conditions in the Ghetto were terrible. They were not allowed to leave their flats, they stayed for whole weeks in stuffy, uncomfortable hide-outs, they did not see daylight for long months. No wonder then that they let themselves be tempted by the promise of going out into the street, of walking in a garden, etc., and agreed to go to the Aryan side by themselves.

I knew a twelve-year-old boy who jumped with joy at the Ghetto wall, which he was about to cross to get to the Aryan side, and shouted, "I'll survive the war". This boy has suffered greatly on the Aryan side. Far away from his parents, whom he did not see for months, he did not go out into the street at all. He stayed in a one-room flat belonging to very noble people; if somebody came, he had to hide in a cupboard, behind a sofa, in the toilet, etc., and stay there for hours without moving until the guests departed. Though the boy was very much liked, he had to leave this flat, since the landlord's anti-Semitic relatives did not acquiesce in hiding a Jew, and considered it a sin against the Polish people. The boy had been there throughout the "hottest" time for the Jews, the April "action". When the Ghetto where his father lived was burning and the explosions reverberated as walls were dynamited, the boy had to listen to anti-Semitic conversations, with the talkers frankly expressing their great satisfaction at the Nazi solution of the Jewish problem.[1] This boy is clever and understands political problems,

---

[1] After the big deportation in the Warsaw Ghetto, on 29 September 1942, Aurelia Wylezynska noted in her diary: "Some Poles are glad that the

and he had to listen to this anti-Semitic drivel without being able to react. The boy is now together with his parents and they are staying in a hide-out on the Aryan side. He has again been confined there for many months, among nervous people exhausted by their experiences. He is losing ground physically, but for all that he is lucky to have his parents with him.

I know an eight-year-old boy who stayed for eight months on the Aryan side without his parents. The boy was hiding with friends of his father's, who treated him like their own child. The child spoke in whispers and moved as silently as a cat, so that the neighbours should not become aware of the presence of a Jewish child. He often had to listen to the anti-Semitic talk of young Poles who came to visit the landlord's daughters. Then he would pretend not to listen to the conversation and become engrossed in reading one of the books which he devoured in quantities. On one occasion he was present when the young visitors boasted that Hitler had taught the Poles how to deal with the Jews and that the remnant that survived the Nazi slaughter would be dealt with likewise. The boy was choking with tears; so that no one would notice he was upset, he

---

Germans have done their dirty work for them. They felt no need even to spare their nerves by putting cottonwool in their ears to muffle other people's groans." (A. Wylezynska, op. cit.)

S. Zemiński, the Polish author of another diary, written in Lukow (Lublin region) during the occupation, gives a similar report. On 16 November 1942 he writes: "There are many who condemn the German crimes with revulsion. There are some who just sink into despair at the spectacle of the German excesses. But there are also some who regard all this as very cruel and disagreeable, but also, to tell the truth, as a service rendered us by the Germans—they are solving the Jewish problem. Our *Endecja* with all it comprises can be proud of its offspring." (S. Żemiński, op. cit.).

Adam Polewka also writes: "A considerable part of the Polish population was indifferent to these monstrous things [i.e. the extermination of the Jews—Ed.] and some even faced them with a certain satisfaction, expressed thus: 'Although we don't approve of such methods, we have to admit that Hitler has done the job for us, because we should not have been able to carry it out so completely.' These people regarded the mass murder of the Jewish population committed by the German Fascists as a national gain."

hid in the kitchen and there burst out crying. He is now staying in a narrow, stuffy hide-out, but he is happy because he is with his parents.

The situation is much worse for the children who have lost their parents, who were taken away to Treblinka. Some of their Aryan protectors have meanwhile taken a liking to the children and keep them and look after them. But these are only a small percentage of the protectors, generally people of limited means in whom Mammon has not yet killed all human feeling. People like these have to suffer on account of the Jewish children but they do not throw them out into the street. The more energetic among them know how to fix themselves up and receive money subsidies from suitable social organizations. We know of cases where the governesses of wealthy children took care of them after their parents had been taken away to Treblinka. They keep these children out of their beggarly wages and don't want to leave them to their fate. Some of these Jewish orphans were fixed up in institutions, registered as having come from places affected by the displacement of the Polish population (Zamosc, Hrubieszow, Poznan, Lublin, etc.). A considerable percentage of the orphans returned to the Ghetto, where the Jewish Council fixed them up in boarding schools; they were taken away in the "resettlement actions". There were frequent instances, when the "protectors", having received a large sum of money, simply turned the child out into the street. There were even worse cases where the "protectors" turned Jewish children over to the uniformed police or the Germans, who sent them back to the Ghetto while it was still in existence.

There were also cases of Jewish children, especially very small children, who were adopted by childless couples, or by noble individuals who wanted to manifest their attitude to the tragedy of the Jews. A few Jewish children were rescued by being placed in foundling homes, where they arrive as Christian children; they are brought by Polish Police, who, for remuneration of course, report them as having been found in staircase-wells, inside the entrances to blocks of flats, etc.

There were no problems with Jewish children as far as the need for keeping their Jewish origin secret. In the Ghetto Jewish children went through stern schooling for life. They experienced a Gehenna without equal in world history. They knew and felt that the sharp edge of Nazi hatred was aimed at them. The Jewish children went through the hard school of round-ups and "selections". They learned to control themselves, even outdoing adults in this respect. They learned to keep silent for hours at a time and even to hold their breath when the enemy was approaching. They learned to sit motionless for hours at a time since the slightest movement might be heard by a Ukrainian or an S.S.-man during a search and this could bring disaster to the whole hide-out. They learned to stay in the hide-out for months at a time and not see daylight, for fear of the S.S. torturers. They ceased to be children and grew up fast, surpassing their elders in many things. So when they were sent to the Aryan side, their parents could assure their Aryan friends and acquaintances that their little daughter or son would never breathe a word about his Jewish origin and would keep the secret to the grave. I know of a young girl who was dying in an Aryan hospital, far from her parents. She kept the secret of her origin till her death. Even in those moments of the death agony, when earthly ties are loosed and people no longer master themselves, she did not betray herself by a word or the least movement. When the nurse who was present at her death-bed called her by her Jewish name, Dorka, she would not reply, for she remembered that she was only allowed to respond to the sound of the Aryan name, Ewa.

Even the youngest children were able to carry out their parents' instructions and conceal their Jewish origin expertly. I remember a four-year-old tot who replied to my asking him treacherously what he was called before—a question often put to children by police agents—by giving his Aryan name and surname and declaring emphatically that he never had any other name.

In spite of this, "give-aways" by children do occur, for several reasons. I know of a case of a five-year-old Jewish child, who had been living on the Aryan side for a long time and had been playing the part of a Christian very well indeed. One day there was a conversation at table about horse-drawn trams. The grandfather related that in his youth there were trams like these in the streets of the capital. The Jewish child present at the table said suddenly that he too had seen a horse-drawn tram, in ... Zamenhoff Street.² After this "give-away", the parents had to take the child away and fix him up somewhere else.

A "give-away" of a seven-year-old girl with a "good" appearance, who had been living in a village for a long time, happened because of nonsensical rumours spread by unknown persons to the effect that every Jew possesses enormous fortunes in gold, valuables, dollars, etc. All of a sudden a rumour spread through the village by word of mouth that the little girl from Warsaw was Jewish and that kilograms of gold had been handed over for keeping her. For fear of denunciation, the girl had to be sent quickly to her parents in Warsaw.

A "give-away" can sometimes occur with a Jewish child because of so innocent a question as, "Are you going to school?" A Jewish child, deprived of systematic schooling since the beginning of the war, has large gaps in his education and has difficulty in extricating himself when asked questions like this by a visitor or acquaintance.

I have heard of a case of a four-year-old Jewish child who secured his return to his parents..., though blackmail *sui generis.* The child was longing for his parents, from whom he had been separated for a long time, and one day he declared that if he were not allowed to return to his parents, he would go to a German and tell him he was from the Ghetto. The blackmail succeeded and the parents had to take the child back.

Unfortunately Jewish children were not spared real blackmail either. There have been cases where they were kidnapped by black-mailers and held until the parents bought them out of the hands of the worst type of criminal.

The circumcision of Jewish children is an important obstacle to fixing them up on the Aryan side. The number of uncircumcised is very small. Pressure from religious parents and relations, together with the judicial difficulties presented by the Jewish Community and municipal authorities, were so great that very few parents,

---

2 A horse-drawn tram was introduced in the Warsaw Ghetto by the Germans and was the only means of public transport there.

even the most progressive ones, could manage not to have their children circumcised. One simply was not given a birth certificate, and the child was exposed to humiliations and difficulties in school.

I know an uncircumcised Jewish boy who has suffered a great deal on the Aryan side. He has been living there for ten months and has already moved to his fifteenth place. Something always goes wrong. He complains that anti-Semites harass him. He has had to listen to more than one Jew-devouring lecture from his "protectors", who were not informed of his Jewish origin.

Children of parents who are not well off are also to be found on the Aryan side. This dates from the first moment the Ghetto was formed. Many poor parents managed to live on the smuggling done by their four- to five-year-old children, who went across *en masse* to the Aryan side. Every day one could see hundreds of Jewish children hanging around the exit gates in masses in order to get through to the Aryan side. The children would wait for a "good" guard so as to get through to the "other" side. Some went through holes in the walls or fences. To hide the things they were smuggling, the children would wear jackets or dresses with a double lining; after these had been stuffed with potatoes or other produce, they looked like crinolines. These children went through several times a day, laden with goods that often weighed more than they did. Smuggling was the only source of subsistence for these children and their parents, who would otherwise have died of starvation. Nothing could discourage the children from smuggling, not even blows by the Jewish Order-men. The children were not frightened off by shots from gendarmes vexed by their importunity, by their wanting to get to the Aryan side at any cost. Even when the gendarme on guard was shooting into the crowd and the pavements were wet with the blood, the children would only hide inside the entrances of the neighbouring blocks of flats for a short while in order to attack the Ghetto exit a moment later. Only a Frankenstein-type criminal, a mate of the Düsseldorf murderer, could pass indifferently by the bodies of innocent children. Pitiless gendarmes would often stop the little smugglers and bring them to the sentry-posts, where they would take everything away from them and beat them mercilessly. The screams and pitiful cries of these innocent children could be heard all around, but this had no effect on the German gendarmes, who were utterly brutalized and devoid of all human feeling.

The children who were smuggling had the most extraordinary and fantastic courage, which I often admired at the Ghetto exits. Once, at the corner of Zelazna and Chlodna Streets, I saw how a gendarme took smuggled wares away from a six-year-old boy. The boy was choking with tears and, despite the blows falling on his small shoulders, kept going back to the sentry-box where his treasure lay, treasure probably bought with his last pennies. The Aryan mob that gathered on the other side of the exit was watching the fight between the gendarme and the Jewish boy with satisfaction. The laughter of the street ruffians heartened the gendarme and encouraged him to drive the boy off more and more energetically. With everyone turned against him—the gendarme, the uniformed police, the Aryan mob and even the Jewish Order Service, the boy did not give up the fight, and kept renewing his efforts to retrieve the confiscated wares. I watched the uneven struggle for quite a long time and saw in it the energy and endurance of the Jewish masses, who persist in the obstinate defence of their rights even when they know that excessive importunity may mean a bullet put through their heads.

The hard life of the smuggler children is reflected in this poem by a young Polish-Jewish poetess, Henryka Lazowert,[3] who was taken to Treblinka during the "resettlement action" of July 1942:

---

3 Henryka Lazowert (1910–1942), Jewish Polish-language poetess. She had earned fame before the war with her collections of poems, *Zamknięty pokój* (1930) and *Imiona świata* (1934). During the war, she helped create the clandestine Ringelblum Archives. A victim of the great deportation from the Warsaw Ghetto, she perished in Treblinka in August 1942.

(*Cf.* the biographical article by Ringelblum in *Ktovim fun geto,* Vol. II, pp. 186–187.)

THE LITTLE SMUGGLER

Past walls, past guards
Through holes, ruins, wires, fences
Impudent, hungry, obstinate
I slip by, I run like a cat
At noon, at night, at dawn
In foul weather, a blizzard, the heat of the sun
A hundred times I risk my life
I risk my childish neck.

Under my arm a sack-cloth bag
On my back a torn rag
My young feet are nimble
In my heart constant fear
But all must be endured
All must be borne
So that you, ladies and gentlemen,
May have your fill of bread tomorrow.

Through walls, through holes, through brick
At night, at dawn, by day
Daring hungry, cunning
I move silently like a shadow
And if suddenly the hand of fate
Reaches me at this game
'Twill be the usual trap life sets.

You, mother
Don't wait for me any longer
I won't come back to you
My voice won't reach that far
Dust of the street will cover
The lost child's fate.
Only one grim question
The still face asks—
Mummy, who will bring you bread
Tomorrow?

I heard a report from a woman working in the *Centos* about the life of a group of young smugglers. There were more than ten in this group, living at 28 Mila Street. They were full of energy and *joie de vivre*, and talked jokingly and with satisfaction about their life and its many thrills. In the beginning they made 200 to 400 zloty a day each. They engaged in "looting" in the "Little Ghetto" (the locality of Wielka, Ciepla, Twarda and Sienna Streets). In winter they lived by trading in wood, which they tore from the floors, attics, etc. of deserted houses. At that time they made 40 to 50 zloty a day each. The children shared between them the task of keeping house. Two of them would stay at home to prepare the meals and clean the room. When the *Centos* worker proposed that they move into a boarding school, the children refused, declaring that they were managing very well by themselves. They said that the *Centos* should put starving children in the boarding schools.

Many homeless children, orphans whose parents had died at the so-called refugee "points" or in the "death houses" where the very poorest lived, used to go begging on the "other" side. They were well received there and were not refused alms or food. Even the Germans used to give them alms. Some children returned to the Ghetto for the night, others would spend the night in attics, back yards, etc. The Germans, with the help of the Blue Police and native anti-Semites, fought the swarms of Jewish children on the Aryan side. Every day they would drive them *en masse* to the Jewish gaol at Gesia Street. The prison director of "Gesiowka", Rudnianski, whom the Germans later shot, tried to ensure humane conditions for the children; he taught them gardening and trained them for productive work. When the "resettlement action" came in July 1942, "Gesiowka" was the first victim that fell to the S.S. bandits, who sent the children to Treblinka. When the daily round-ups for children did not help much, and the number of smuggler children increased from day to day, rigorous repressive measures were employed. Children were drowned in the Czerniakow lake—at least, so rumour had it.

"Looting", that is, stripping deserted houses of all their contents, done by the smuggler children, was a very dangerous occupation.

The Germans considered the possessions of Jews taken to Treblinka their property, and looting was therefore punishable by death. S.S.-men or gendarmes who caught people looting put them to death on the spot. Thus, looting was usually done at night or at daybreak. The children would afterwards sell the looted goods on the Aryan side for a few pence. Sometimes a homeless child like this would become adjusted to the Aryan side, which afforded him shelter. I knew a five-year-old orphan who had lost his parents in the "action". He lived on the Aryan side permanently and paid 5 zloty for a night's lodging. The boy sold newspapers, which he smuggled into the Ghetto from the Aryan side, making a profit of a few zloty on each copy. Some children earned their living by singing in the streets or courtyards. They assimilated to their environment to such an extent that they even sang the anti-Semitic songs that came into being during the war. Some children were able to live on the Aryan side thanks to the Jewish work-posts, which used them as errand-boys, sent them to do shopping in the streets, etc.

Attempts were made to settle a certain number of children as wards in institutions, but this activity had to be suspended after a short time because of fear of denunciation from their staffs. A few girls were placed in these institutions. The clergy took some children in their institutions, generally the very young ones. These few cases did not help the general condition very much. Polish Fascists and anti-Semites were to blame for the prevailing atmosphere which was not favourable for rescuing the children or adults. Fear of the anti-Semitic hue-and-cry was even greater than fear of the Germans and this discouraged attempts to rescue the children. We accuse the Polish anti-Semites and Fascists of spilling the blood of the innocents who could have been saved from the Huns of our time.

For the sake of history, we mention a project to settle a few hundred Jewish children in convents, in accordance with the following principles: the children would be aged ten and upwards; the annual charge of 8,000 zloty would be paid in advance; a card-register would be kept of the children, recording their distribution throughout the country, so that they could be taken back after the war. This project was discussed in Jewish social spheres, where it met with opposition from Orthodox Jews and certain national groups. The objection was raised that the children would be converted and would be lost to the Jewish people for good. It was argued that future generations would blame us for not rising to the necessary heights and not teaching our children *Kiddush Ha-Shem* (martyrdom for the faith), for which our ancestors died at the stake during the Spanish Inquisition. The discussion on the matter among social workers reached no agreed conclusions, no resolutions were accepted, and Jewish parents were left to decide for themselves. The project was not carried out because of a variety of difficulties, but mainly because the Polish clergy was not very much interested in the question of saving Jewish children.

9

PENALTIES FOR HIDING JEWS

As soon as the Ghetto was formed, a decree was issued forbidding free movement of Jews on the Aryan side on pain of death. Further, the Jews were forbidden to buy in Aryan stores; both buyers and sellers would be punished.

This decree was repeated during the "resettlement actions" in July 1942, and January and April 1943. Decrees were issued several times on the Aryan side threatening the Poles with heavy prison sentences or capital punishment for hiding Jews voluntarily, facilitating their escape or affording them aid of any kind.[1] Jews who were registered did not constitute a danger for their Polish landlords, who could claim if interrogated that they did not know that their tenants, who possessed Aryan documents, were of Jewish origin. I was unable to ascertain whether there were any cases in Warsaw of Poles' being executed for hiding Jews. I know of a case of a Polish family which was sent to the Majdanek concentration camp because the family of a Jewish doctor was found in their home.[2]

It should be stressed that before each "resettlement action" in the Ghetto, rumours would be spread by unknown persons about the collective responsibility of the whole block of flats if a Jew should be found there. During the April "action", rumours were

---

[1] In mid-1942, the Nazi authorities posted notices in several places in Poland announcing the introduction of the death penalty for aid to Jews. A notice of this kind, signed by the Warsaw District Chief of the S.S. and police, was posted in Warsaw on 5 September 1942.

[2] Stanislaw Wronski and Maria Zwolakowa, authors of the work, *Polacy-Zydzi, 1939–1945* (Warsaw, 1971), drew up a list of about 270 cases of Poles who were murdered for giving help to Jews; 17 of these cases were in Warsaw. The authors do not give the sources of their information.

152

spread in Warsaw to the effect that this collective responsibility would be incurred by the two neighbouring blocks as well, which would be burnt down. Definite instances were cited of Aryan houses' being razed as punishment for the discovery of Jews there. The basis of these rumours was undoubtedly the burning of the Aryan, odd-number side of Swietojerska Street (the stretch between Nalewki and Nowowiniarska Streets). This may have been done because of the close proximity of the Aryan blocks of flats to the Jewish blocks on the even-number side of Swictojerska Street. It is not difficult to guess that the Gestapo had a hand in spreading these rumours in order to make it more difficult or impossible for the Jews to find asylum on the Aryan side. Under the influence of rumours like these, anti-Semitic tenants would conduct a search at their neighbour's on their own account to try and find Jews hiding there. The more zealous tenants, like those of 39 Panska Street, for example, revealed the Jews' presence to the Germans. It is very typical that in this case the Jews who were "given away" had already come to an understanding with the Gendarmerie that they would leave them alone in return for an ample bribe. In spite of this, the zealous friends of the Nazis dragged the three Jews they had caught to the nearest police station. On the way they met two Germans in uniform and a Polish policeman, who however did not want to deal with the captured Jews. Even this did not abate the Jew-devouring zeal of the inhabitants of 39 Panska Street, who got the Jews to the Gestapo in the end, through a station of the Polish Police.

Penalties inflicted upon Jews for crossing over to the Aryan side without passes were much severer that those inflicted upon Poles. In Warsaw the following punishments were meted out: 1) arrest; 2) death by shooting; 3) "resettlement" in Treblinka, i.e. death *modo germanico;* 4) despatch to the so-called *Werterfassung* in the Ghetto; 5) deportation to the labour camps in Trawniki and Poniatow, i.e. death by slow agony.

The conduct of the German authorities as regards Jews caught on the Aryan side was not consistent. The degree of punishment depended on the circumstances at the time or simply on the whim of the authorities at the given moment. Death by shooting was carried out in the courtyard of the Central Gaol at Gesia Street as early as a few months after the formation of the Ghetto. In March 1941, the Commissioner for the Jewish District, Auerswald, had the Blue Police execute the death sentence on some tens of persons, mainly women, plus a ten-year-old child, who were caught smuggling on the Aryan side and put in prison at the Central Gaol at Gesia Street. This sentence made a staggering impression. At that time, death for seeking bread on the "other" side was too much, even in terms of Nazi justice. At the time of intensified terror that preceded the July "action", the Gestapo often brought in Jews at night who had been discovered on the Aryan side, and they were then shot at the entrances to blocks of flats, mainly in the vicinity of Pawiak [Prison].[3]

At this time the Ghetto was in general the site for executions— every night death sentences for Aryans were carried out there. The bodies of the Aryans who were shot were buried anonymously in mass graves in the Jewish cemetery.

In the first months after the formation of the Ghetto, those caught on the Aryan side were gaoled at the Central Gaol at Gesia Street. In the first days of the July 1942 "action" the Gesia Street Gaol was cleared of prisoners and they were sent to Treblinka. From then on it became the rule that a Jew caught on the Aryan side during a "resettlement action" should go to the *Umschlagplatz* and from there to Treblinka. During the period between the "actions" of July 1942 and January 1943, Jews from the Aryan side were

---

[3] "Pawiak" was the nickname of the Warsaw prison at 24/26 Dzielna Street. When the Ghetto was closed off, this prison was included in it. From October 1939 to August 1944, the "Pawiak" was used by the Nazi Security Police (*Sicherheitspolizei*) for "investigation". In all, nearly 100,000 prisoners passed through the "Pawiak" during this period; 37,000 of them were executed and about 60,000 deported to concentration camps. A considerable proportion of the victims were Jews.

Any Jew arrested on non-political grounds or any Jew who had tried to pass as Aryan and had been discovered was held in the death-cell for a few days at most and taken out to be shot.

With the advance of the Soviet front, the last of the prisoners were murdered; in July 1944, the Germans blew up the Pawiak buildings.

(Wladyslaw Bartoszewski, *Warszawski pierscien smierci 1939–1944*, Warszawa, 1967, p. 17; *Wspomnienia wiezniow Pawiaka*, Warzawa, 1964.)

handed over to the *Judenrat*, which either let them go free or sent them direct to the *Werterfassung*, which was engaged in stripping the flats left by the deported Jews. This sending Jews back to the Ghetto after their cover on the Aryan side has been "blown" led to the grim conclusion that it was a sign that the Ghetto was doomed to liquidation. When there were not enough people for the transports to the labour camps at Trawniki and Poniatow, persons serving sentences for being on the Aryan side without a pass were taken and sent there.

Since April 1943, the date of the liquidation of the Warsaw Ghetto, every Jew caught on the Aryan side is shot on the spot. In July 1943, a strict check was carried out at the "Polish Hotel" in Dluga Street, where Jews interned as foreign nationals were living. Of the 400 persons living there, 340 were shot, as they could not produce foreign documents. These were mainly Jews living on the Aryan side whose flats had become "burnt".

Up till July 1942, the authority which Jews caught on the Aryan side were handed over to was the Commissioner for the Jewish District. From the moment the "resettlement action" began, the office of Commissioner ceased to exist; from then on the only authority over the Jews was exercised by the S.S. and the Gestapo jointly in the so-called *Befehlsstelle* at 103 Zelazna Street. From then on the life of every Jew caught on the Aryan side was disposed of by the *Befehlsstelle*, with its famous big boss, Brand, at its head. The *Befehlsstelle* death sentences were usually carried out in the courtyard of the block on 101 Zelazna Street. The sentences were carried out *modo teutonico*: the condemned, who were first stripped of all their possessions, were made to lie down on the ground and they were killed by a revolver shot in the back of the head. It often happened that gendarmes who caught a few Jews on the outskirts of the town would deal with them on the spot. From time to time Poles were also the victims of executions like these.

Information laid against someone to the effect that he has been hiding Jews is enough to call down strict repressive measures. A short time ago, the family of a Warsaw Polish doctor (Dr. Mroczko) were murdered near Warsaw by mistake as the result of a false accusation that they were Jewish.

10

THE "RESETTLEMENT ACTION" IN WARSAW AND THE ATTITUDE OF THE POLISH POPULATION

The Polish population's indifference over the July "action". — Why did the Ghetto not defend itself? — Awakening to reality after the July slaughter. — The Combat Organization prepares its cadres. — What the Jewish arsenal looked like. — General Stroop—master-executioner of Warsaw Jewry. — "Little Stalingrad" defends itself. — Rumours about the Ghetto struggle. — Cooperation with the Aryan side. — Fighting on the Aryan side. — Conversations among Poles about the April "action". — The anti-Semitic keynote: "The bugs are burning."

At the beginning of the July "action", when the Polish public did not know what was happening to the deported Jews and when it was still thought that the transports were really headed for the East, for colonization, the Polish population was not very much interested in the "resettlement". The situation changed when they learned that the Jews were being "resettled" in Treblinka. Then on the Aryan side they spoke very ill of Warsaw's Jews, disparaged them, accused them of cowardice and lack of national pride.[1] "Why

---

[1] Supporters of the Jews on the Aryan side criticized them for not defending themselves. Instead of committing suicide, they said Jews should have attacked the murderers if only with their bare hands. An article that appeared in November 1942 in the underground paper, *Wiadomosci Polskie,* the organ of the Home Army General Staff, blamed the Jews for obeying and giving in, for agreeing to wear the Jewish armband, for accepting "autonomy"—the *Judenrat* and the Jewish Police, and for not preventing social collapse—class differences grew into an abyss between those who ate and those who starved, those who lived and those who died.

(*Cf.* A. Wyleżyńska *op. cit.,* p. 220.)

In the heated debates that took place on the Aryan side, the Jewish

didn't you defend yourselves?" "Why did you go like sheep to
the slaughter?" "Why didn't you attack the Germans once you knew
death was inescapable?" "We wouldn't let ourselves be led to
the slaughter, with us they'd have a difficult job to carry out and
they wouldn't dare"—this is what the Jews were told. These and
similar opinions were to be heard at every step, mainly at the work-
posts where Jews came into contact with Poles, where they informed
each other about what was going on on their respective sides of the
walls. This theme demands a comprehensive elucidation, which would
make it evident that though the accusations against the Jews were
justified to a certain extent, it should not be forgotten that part of
the blame lies with the Aryan side. For several months the Jewish
community had been demanding arms for the Ghetto from the Government. After long, very long efforts, arms were received, but in
such a small quantity and of such bad quality that there was no
possibility of undertaking any defensive action. The "resettlement

---

underground leaders, who were well aware of the situation in the Ghetto,
were more than once obliged to stress that in the conditions of murderous
terror prevailing in the Ghetto no population could display mass
resistance, not even one trained for revolt. This terror, combined with
the cunning tactics of the Hitlerite deportation machine would have succeeded for a time in breaking the will of any population, especially
one which had been kept under prison conditions in a giant concentration camp for years. In debates and discussions like these, the Jewish
leaders passed on information about the Jewish underground movement
and currents of resistance, which would burst into the open at a given
moment, when the Jewish masses' will to fight had matured.
(Berman, *op. cit.*, p. 697.)

In a letter of 31 August 1942, the head of the underground Central
Committee of the *Bund*, L. Berezowski (Dr. L. Fajner), told a member
of the Polish National Council in London, Shmuel Zygielbojm, that
cases of active resistance had occurred here and there during the deportation, and that some blocks of flats had been barricaded by the
tenants. But these were isolated instances. Such attempts at resistance
were met with immediate liquidation. Dr. Fajner gave the following
reasons for lack of active mass resistance: the illusions fostered by
the Nazis, the collective responsibility of the Jews, the absence of any
help from outside the Ghetto walls.
(Bernard Mark, *Walka i zaglada warszawskiego getta,* Warsaw, 1959,
pp. 188–189.)

action" lasted forty-four days, and there was no reaction from the Aryan side. On the Aryan side complete silence reigned while the drama was enacted before the eyes of hundreds of thousands of Poles. There was no appeal from the Government calling for defence, there was no word of comfort, there was not even a promise of at least moral support. Only the P.P.R. issued a proclamation to the Jewish population, which was distributed in the area of the "Little Ghetto", and which began with the words, "Don't give in."[2] The proclamation informed the Jews of the real aim of the "resettlement", it told them that seventy-thousand Jews had already been

---

[2] The P.P.R. (*Polska Partia Robotnicza*) also called on the Jews in the Warsaw Ghetto to resist the Nazis. In an article entitled, *Pogrom Zydow w Warszawie,* published in the Party's clandestine paper, *Trybuna Wolnosci,* on 1 September 1942, one passage reads as follows:
"The invaders are merciless and relentless. The Jewish population should be equally unrelenting in defending its existence. The Jews must summon up heroism, courage and contempt for death. Only uncompromising resistance in every situation, only action—and not passive waiting for the slaughter—can save possibly thousands and tens of thousands, though it may claim victims. Let the heroic resistance of Nowogrodek and other towns serve as an example. Individual heroism meant saving thousands who were being led to their deaths. Force must be used to get out of the bounds of the Ghetto and of Warsaw—to get to the forests in order to fight the foe. The Police must be met with resistance. Every block of flats must become a fortress. The guards must be overcome and people must escape and make for the partisans. These things are not easy to do, but they are possible. It is the only way to be rescued."
It should be pointed out that given the conditions prevailing at the time of the deportation, this paper did not reach the population, and so the call of the P.P.R. had no effect in the Ghetto. But what is more important is that in mid-1942 the Warsaw Jews did not in fact have even the slightest possibility of offering significant resistance. The Ghetto was without weapons. In the immediate environs of Warsaw there were no forested regions that could provide shelter for fugitives from the Ghetto. The partisan movement hardly existed as yet in Poland. In these circumstances, this appeal with its argument that individual heroism could save thousands of Jews was utterly unreal. The example given of resistance of Nowogrodek actually had not happened at all—it was nothing more than a legend spread for propaganda purposes. Finally, this call for resistance was not accompanied by any concrete help from beyond the Ghetto walls.

gassed in Treblinka, and it summoned the whole Jewish population to resist. Regarding the arming of the Ghetto, the military took a negative stand, which has continued to this day. The rumoured explanation is that officials have no confidence in the loyalty of the Jews and fear that these weapons would be used against Poland. I do not know how much truth there is in this rumour, but how else can one explain a consistently maintained attitude like this regarding arms for the Ghetto? Beautifully phrased resolutions proclaimed that it was the duty of the military to help arm the Ghettos for a struggle against the invaders. In reality, these resolutions have remained on paper.

This is not the right place to discuss the inner reasons for the passivity on the part of the Jews during the July "action". The best evidence proving that this passivity was a temporary phenomenon and the consequence of outside factors is furnished by the actions of January and April 1943, when Jewish resistance evoked general esteem. The most important reason for the Jews' passivity in July 1942 was the excellent German strategy, which deceived the Jewish population as to the real aim of "resettlement". The fairy tale about the "resettlement in the East", supported by the *Judenrat* and by the band of Gestapo agents brought in from Lublin,[3] was so widely accepted by the Jews that thousands of people who were starving as a result of the constant cordons and the complete stoppage of smuggling presented themselves at the *Umschlagplatz* voluntarily,

---

[3] One of these was Shamai Greier, a Lublin man, a barber by trade. At the time of the Ghetto, he kept a restaurant where Gestapo men and their Jewish collaborators met. In the spring of 1942, Greier—"trusty" of the Germans, blackmailer and informer—was sent to Warsaw to work for the Gestapo.
On 25 May 1942, the following warning appeared in the underground paper of the *Dror* movement, *Yediot* (News) : "A Gestapo man, Shamai Greier, has arrived in Warsaw." A second warning was printed in the issue of 2 June 1942, in the following terms: "The head of the Jewish Gestapo men in Lublin has arrived in Warsaw, the notorious Shamai Greier. We warn the Jewish population against this individual."
Greier helped murder the Jews of Lublin. He was killed by the Germans in November 1942.

in order to be sent to work in the East. I personally saw how a few weaklings of the Jewish Order Service, without assistance from Ukrainians or S.S.-men, led a group of porters to the *Umschlagplatz*, men as tall as oaks, with broad shoulders and muscles of steel. If these men had dreamt that they were being led to their death, it would have been enough for one of them to raise a finger and the whole set of the Order Service would have vanished into thin air. It is to be regretted that the government, which was certainly informed of the fate of the Jews of Lublin, deported to an unknown destination a few months earlier, before Warsaw, and which was certainly aware of the real intentions of the S.S. regarding the Jews of the capital, did not warn the Jewish community. It is possible that private individuals and Jewish organizations did not know what the fate was of the Warsaw Jews taken to the East. But the Home Plenipotentiary of the Polish government [-in-Exile] had agencies—did he not?—dispersed all over the country, from which he could get information on what Treblinka was. Why was the Jewish population not warned that the so-called "resettlement" was in reality large-scale murder, a monster-murder? This was a cardinal mistake, which determined the fate of four hundred thousand Jews, the largest Jewish community in Europe. Only when a few individuals escaped from Treblinka, to which were despatched all the transports from the capital, were the eyes of the Jews opened, only then was the real destination of these journeys revealed to them.

The Combat Organization, which came into being at the moment when the Warsaw Jews reached the lowest depths of prostration, issued several proclamations in August 1942, giving information about Treblinka and calling for resistance. German terror, exhaustion from the constant round-ups, resignation, and the crazy paralysis of the Jewish masses were so great that this unconfirmed news coming from Treblinka was not believed. It was difficult for normal, thinking people to accept the idea that on this globe it was possible for a government calling itself European to murder millions of innocent people just because they were Jewish. A normal, sane mind could not comprehend the morbid, apocalyptical ravings of degenerates, sadists and congenital Düsseldorf-murderers. No wonder then that the appeals of the Combat Organization calling for resistance[4] were considered a piece of German provocation, the aim of which was to produce a resistance which would serve as pretext for the complete destruction of Warsaw Jewry. With heartache and in despair, the Combat Organization, not equipped with arms and at that point unable to evoke a response from the population, had to watch passively while hundreds of thousands of physical and intellectual workers, the socially, culturally and politically active members of society, the best young people, innocent women, children, etc., were led to the slaughter. We are not trying here to excuse the socially and politically active members of Warsaw Jewry for not coming up the mark, for letting themselves be terrorized by the S.S. and for allowing the mass murder of Warsaw Jewry to happen without shedding a drop of blood of the Germans and Ukrainians. We claim emphatically that if authoritative Polish elements had given moral support and had supplied the Ghetto with arms, the Germans would have had to pay for the sea of Jewish blood shed in July, August, and September 1942.[5] I wish to stress that I have

---

4 The first proclamation of the Jewish Combat Organization (Z.O.B.) to the Jewish population was issued in order to make it known that "resettlement" meant Treblinka, and that Treblinka meant death; and that the Jews must hide their women and children and resist the German orders.

(See: Neustadt, *op. cit.,* pp. 78–91.)

A. Levin noted briefly in his diary on 21 August 1942: "Today fly-sheets (leaflets, proclamations) were distributed against the Jewish police, who helped to take out 200,000 Jews to be killed. Sentence of death has been passed on the entire police."

(Levin *op. cit.,* p. 109.)

This proclamation was published by the Jewish Combat Organization, and it said: "The Commanding Officer and the officers as well as the men of the police force have been declared accused, and accordingly an attempt has been made on the life of Józef Szerynski. Further repressive acts of the same kind will be carried out with the utmost severity."

5 When the author uses the expression, "the authoritative Polish circles," "elements" or "government", he is referring to the Polish Government-in-Exile and its subordinate agencies in the Homeland, especially the Government Delegation in the Homeland and the Home Army Command. During the whole period of deportations from the Warsaw Ghetto (July–September 1942), no initiative was taken in these quarters to organize any help for Jews who managed to escape from the

Ghetto, or to make it possible to organize resistance in the Ghetto itself. The quarters referred to confined themselves to a mere protest in the form of an Appeal issued by the Directorate for Civilian Struggle on 17 September 1942—that is, five days after the end of the deportation of Jews from the Polish capital, which had lasted nearly two months.

This Appeal reads in part as follows:

"Side by side with the tragedy experienced by the Polish community, which is being decimated by the enemy, a deliberate, monstrous slaughter of Jews has been going on, on our soil for nearly a year. This mass murder is without parallel in the history of the world; all the cruelties committed in recorded history pale beside it. Babies, children, young people, adults and the old, the infirm, the sick and the healthy, men and women, Catholic Jews and Jews of the Mosaic persuasion, for no other reason than their belonging to the Jewish people, are being ruthlessly murdered, poisoned by gas, buried alive, thrown down from high buildings. Before their death they must go through the additional pain of slow agony, a hell of misery and homelessness, sufferings caused by cynical maltreatment at the hands of their tormentors. The number of victims killed in this way is already more than a million and is growing every day.

"*Being unable to actively oppose this,* [our italics—the Editors] the Directorate for Civilian Struggle voices its protest in the name of the entire Polish community at the crime that is being committed against the Jews. All Polish political parties and social organizations join together in this protest. Just as in the case of the Polish victims, the physical responsibility for these crimes will fall on the hangmen and those who collaborate with them."

(This Appeal was published in the clandestine periodical, *Biuletyn Informacyjny,* No. 37 [141], 17 September 1942.)

For the purpose of covering up the fact that no initiative was taken to defend citizens of Jewish nationality in mid-1942, a fictitious version of what happened was produced later on. The author of this version was the Second-in-Command of the Home Army and afterwards (from mid-1943) its Commander-in-Chief, General Tadeusz Bor-Komorowski. He wrote:

"As early as July 29 [1942] we got news from the railwaymen that the transports of Jews were going to Treblinka concentration camp, where they disappeared without a trace. There was no longer any doubt that these deportations were only the first stage in a planned liquidation. "Rowecki [at that time Commander of the Home Army] made his decision quickly, as usual, recognising that we could not look on passively at what was happening and that we must offer the Jews help to the fullest extent possible. With this aim, he convoked the inner

162

Staff committee for briefing. Some of those present had doubts, however. They argued: If America and Great Britain, with huge armies and air forces at their disposal, equipped with every means of modern warfare, are not able to prevent this crime and must look on helplessly while the Germans commit all kinds of monstrosities in the occupied countries—how are we to stop them?

"To this Rowecki replied that the lack of any resistance would encourage the Germans to carry out further mass liquidations. This opinion prevailed.

"In our organization we had a Department charged with protecting Jews, helping those who had managed to escape from the Ghetto, and distributing among them the monies sent us for this purpose from London. This Department was headed by a certain 'Waclaw'. Rowecki instructed him to make his way into the Ghetto and get into contact with the Jewish leaders. He was to inform them that the Home Army was willing to assist the Jews, to give them arms and ammunition, and to co-ordinate its own activities, under outside leadership, with the resistance of the Jews inside the Ghetto. But the Jewish leaders rejected our offer. If we keep quiet—they explained—the Germans will deport or murder 20,000 or 30,000 of us, perhaps even 60,000, but they will not wipe out 400,000—that's impossible. If we start to resist, however, they really will annihilate all of us.

"When Rowecki got this answer through 'Waclaw', he decided to step up sabotage of German lines of communication, so as in this way to delay the deportation of Jews."

(Tadeusz Bor-Komorowski, *Armia Podziemna*, London, 1950, pp. 99–100.) The following comments are called for:

1) In mid-1942 there was no department in the Home Army charged with protecting Jews; no help was afforded Jewish fugitives from the Ghettos by the Home Army; no money for aid to Jews was distributed. There was only a Jewish Section in the Information and Propaganda Department at the H.Q. of the Commander-in-Chief of the Home Army. The head of this Section was Colonel Henryk Wolinski, *alias* "Waclaw". The activity of this Section in this period was confined to collecting documentary material from the Warsaw Ghetto and from provincial centres and all kinds of other documents that might possibly be of use concerning the situation of the Jews in occupied Poland.

(*Cf.* Bartoszewski Wladyslaw, *On Both Sides of the Wall,* published in "Righteous Among Nations—How Poles Helped the Jews. 1939–1945." London, 1969, p. xxxvi.) It was only at the end of 1942 that this Section began to concern itself with providing some help for the Jews, mainly as a result of the efforts of Colonel Wolinski.

2) Colonel Wolinski has never confirmed the above version of General Bor-Komorowski.

not dealt here with the problem of resistance as a whole. I have limited myself to elucidating this particular question only in its relation to the attitude of those Poles who had influence.

As soon as the round-ups stopped in September 1942 and numerous reports started arriving from eye witnesses of the mass slaughter in Treblinka,[6] the terrible awakening took place.[7] The

---

3) This version is contradicted by numerous documents of the period under discussion, among them the Appeal of the Directorate for Civilian Struggle quoted above.

4) The Home Army never carried out any sabotage operations calculated to delay the deportation of Jews.

6   In his essay *Oneg Shabbat*, Ringelblum points out that immediately after the big "action" in the Ghetto, the *Oneg Shabbat* people started to recapitulate what had happened during the deportation and to collect material on the extermination camp of Treblinka. The authoress Rahel Auerbach, one of the permanent collaborators and active members of *Oneg Shabbat*, was charged with taking evidence from Abraham Krzepicki, who was in this death camp for 18 days during the months of August and September 1942 and succeeded in escaping from it. The talks went on between R. Auerbach and Krzepicki week after week, and resulted in a long article in Yiddish called, "A man escaped from Treblinka." This manuscript was found in December 1950 in the second section of the Ringelblum Archives; it was reproduced in its notebook form on microfilm, and was given to Yad Vashem. (*Cf.* A Krzepicki, *"Treblinka," "Bletter far Geschichte,* Vol. IX, Nos. 1–2, 1956, pp. 71–141.)

7   Material found in the second part of the Ringelblum Archives affords important documentary illustration of the profound shock suffered by the remaining Jews in the Warsaw Ghetto after the deportations to death in mid-1942, and of the resultant deep alteration in attitudes. Documents have been preserved bearing witness to the general reaction on the morrow of the "action" of pain and sorrow over the fact that "deportees" offered no resistance, not even to the Jewish Police. "We should have gone into the streets and burnt everything down"—in these words Dr. Ringelblum sums up the mood of the people—"we should have broken through the wall and crossed to the other side; the Germans would have taken revenge and it would have cost us tens of thousands of lives—but not three hundred thousand." "What's it mean to say 'They'll come and take us away'? said one man, just a man in the street, not even one of ours," wrote Mordechai Anielewicz himself, when he was trying to find out what ordinary people were thinking. " 'No, they won't manage so easily. We'll shut ourselves in the

Jewish public understood what a terrible error had been made by their not offering resistance to the S.S. It was argued that if on the day the Warsaw "resettlement action" was announced, everyone had rebelled, if the Germans had been attacked with knives, sticks, spades and axes, if hydrochloric acid, melted tar, boiling water, etc., had been poured over the Germans, Ukrainians, Latvians and Jewish Order Service, in short if men, women and children, young and old, had begun a mass rising, there would not have been three hundred and fifty thousand murdered in Treblinka, but only fifty thousand shot in the streets of the capital. Husbands tore their hair because they had let the Germans, unharmed, take away those dearest to them, their wives and children; children loudly reproached themselves for allowing their parents to be taken away. Oaths were sworn aloud: Never again shall the Germans move us from here with impunity; we shall die, but the cruel invaders will pay with their blood for ours. Our fate is sealed, people were saying. Every Jew carries a death sentence in his pocket, handed him by the greatest murderer of all time. Thus we must think not so much of saving our lives, which seems to be a very problematic affair, but rather of dying an honourable death, dying with weapons in our hands.[8] The oath that was sworn in the name of the beloved victims

---

houses. We'll fortify the entrances to the blocks of flats, and arm ourselves with picks and axes. Oh no, let them try and overwhelm us, let them shower us with grenades and bombs, let them lay mines and explosives, just let them come and take us. We won't go out and walk in file. And if one of them tries to get in, he won't get away from us alive. If they find where I'm hiding, I'll fight on. It'll be him or me, if I've got to die I'll die like a man, not like a sheep in the flock.' "

(See: Nachman Blumental, Joseph Kermish, *Resistance and Revolt in the Warsaw Ghetto. A Documentary History,* Jerusalem, 1965 (Hebrew, with English Introduction), p. 51.)

8 Between 22 July and 13 September 1942, the Nazis deported 237,954 persons from the Warsaw Ghetto, 225,991 of whom were sent to Treblinka and killed there, 11,580 to forced labour camps, and 383, considered unfit to work, were shot in the Jewish cemetery during the first days of the deportation. (These figures are taken from semi-official statistics contained in two documents, a statistical entry and a report dated 15 November 1942, in the Ringelblum Archives, Part 2, No. 195;

was kept. The Ghetto began to arm itself and to prepare for the new blows that were expected at any moment. Underground bunkers were dug to serve as shelter in time of danger. The Ghetto was purged of local traitors, the Jewish Gestapo-men, who had spread false tales during the "resettlement action" in order to forestall any thought of resistance, stories that the "action" would end, that

these two documents have been utilised by T. Berenstein and A. Rutkowski for their article, *Liczba ludnosci zydowskiej i obszar przez nia zamieszkaly w Warszawie w latach okupacji hitlerowskiej,* "Biuletyn Zydowskiego Instytutu Historycznego" No. 26, 1958.)

Another 9,274 Jews were shot (1,620 of them between 22 and 31 June, 4,517 during August, and 3,137 between 3 and 13 September 1942) as a means of imposing Nazi terror and breaking the passive resistance of the general Jewish population. (Report on the situation in occupied Poland, No. 1/443, Polish Ministry of the Interior; copy in Yad Vashem Archives. I. Schwarzbart Records, M-2/H-14.) These mass executions, as well as the cutting off of the Ghetto from all sources of food supply, were what caused the majority of the Warsaw Ghetto population to present themselves at the *Umschlagplatz* (deportation loading point) in the belief that deportation might not necessarily mean death, whereas remaining in the Ghetto appeared to mean certain annihilation. Any armed resistance, even a token one, was of course out of the question —the Nazis were armed with automatic weapons while the Ghetto had no suitable arms at all.

When the deportation was completed, and the surviving Jews learnt of the enormity of the tragedy, they fell victim to a pathological sense of guilt over their failure to resist the Nazis. This psychosis born of despair brought many Jews to the brink of absurdity. Thus Ringelblum suggests that the Germans (armed with machine guns) could have been attacked with knives and axes or by pouring melted tar and boiling water on them. Hence too the notion, "an honourable death with weapons in one's hands", while such a death was not possible in the Ghetto in 1942 because there were no weapons to be had. Even during the rising in April and May 1943, in spite of months of energetic preparations, it was only possible to arm a fraction of the Ghetto's inhabitants. The overwhelming majority perished without any possibility of resisting deportation, arms in hand. The psychosis of guilt, of self-accusation, which developed out of the tragic trauma caused by mass annihilation, is still being exploited by some historians and writers who favour anti-Semitic interpretations so as to be able to blame the Jews themselves for their misfortunes by pointing to their alleged passivity in the face of Nazism.

people were being moved to the East where children were being given fresh milk. They were now shot like dogs for spreading tales about camps in different places for Warsaw Jews, camps for Warsaw children, etc., in order to lull the suspicions of the Jewish population. The Combat Organization dealt, in the first place, with the people who had conducted the "resettlement action". The head of the Jewish Order Service, Colonel Szerynski, a converted Jew and a former Polish Police officer, had given the Germans loyal service. For his energetic conduct of the "resettlement action", he was seriously wounded by a combatant. His deputy, the advocate Lejkin, whose head had been turned by power and who had exceeded all bounds in his loyalty to the Germans, was "finished off" by the Combat Organization, to the great satisfaction of the whole Jewish population.[9] The Combat Organization set about preparing

---

[9] The first shot fired by the Jewish Combat Organization was at the height of the deportation to Treblinka on 20 August 1942. Israel Kanal, one of the heads of the "Akiva" movement, seriously wounded the Commander of the Jewish Police, Józef Szerynski. An attempt on the life of another Jewish Police Officer, Schmerling, one of the most industrious executors of the deportation, was unsuccessful.

Even before the "Coordinating Committee" was set up on 30 October 1942, the Jewish Combat Organization decided to purge the Ghetto of the enemies within the gates by wiping out the most corrupt of those who had sold themselves to the Germans, and so to cow the *Judenrat* and the Ghetto Police.

The Second-in-Command of the Jewish Police, Yaakov Lejkin, was executed on 29 October 1942 by Eliahu Różański-Alek (with the help of Mardek Grubas and Margalit Landau). This served as a warning to his comrades in the Police. The same is true of the death sentence on Israel Fuerst, a go-between between the *Judenrat* and the Gestapo, carried out on 29 November 1942 by David Shulman (with the help of Berl Broido and Sarah Granatstein).

The public announcement of the Combat Organization on the day after the execution stated: "Further reprisal measures will be taken with the full rigour of the law", and it informed the population that the following categories of people would be placed in the dock: 1) The Warsaw *Judenrat* and its presidency for collaboration with the Germans and help afforded them in carrying out the deportation; 2) workshop foremen and their staffs for exploiting and maltreating the workers; 3) the group leaders and officials of the *Werkschutz* (the body that

cadres for the coming struggle with the invaders. Government elements were again approached for help with arming.

At this time two Combat Organizations were active in the Ghetto and in the workshops: the Combat Organization of the Coordinating Committee, which, with the exception of the Revisionist-Zionists, united all the Jewish groups (*Hashomer Hatzair*—the Jewish scouts'

---

guarded the German concerns; it included some Jews) for their cruel attitude towards the workers and the "illegal" Jewish population.

In January 1943 (before the deportations began again) the Combat Organization acted to terrorize persons guilty of sins against the Jewish community, punishing them by pouring acid on them.

A network of secret agents of the Gestapo spread throughout the workshops, but the Jewish Combat Organization only had exact information on the misdeeds of some of them. Most of them succeeded in covering up their actions so well that their role was revealed only by chance.

The Combat Organization declared a war to the death against the treacherous German collaborators; when it passed a death sentence on them, it was only by fleeing to the Aryan side that they could evade the judgement of the Organization. The biggest sweep to clean out Jewish enemy agents, with fifteen men taking part, was carried out on 21 February at 16:45 hours at No. 38 Świętojerska Street at the end of the brush-making district; all but one of the condemned —Leon (Lolek) Skosowski—was shot to death; Skosowski was seriously wounded. The others were Pawel Wlodarski, Adek Weintraub, Mangel, Lidia Radziejewska (Ania). The combatants took possession of a pistol of the type M.N. 7657 and seven bullets, the property of Skosowski.

The head of a group of Gestapo agents, called "Urich", supposedly the editor of a clandestine radio bulletin, was also executed in the brush-industry area by two members of *Hehalutz*. A Gestapo card was found on him as well as a large sum of money.

The clean-up of traitors and spies also took in those *Werkschutz* members who maltreated the workers in the workshops. One of the much-hated German *Werkschutz* who was shot was a man called "Fat". In each case, a special public notice was posted announcing the death sentence. As a result of these actions, the Combatants were also called the "People's Avengers". The Z.Z.W. (the military arm of the Jewish Revisionists) also did not shrink from carrying out several death sentences on traitors who collaborated with the Gestapo. Among others they executed the policeman Skokowski.

(Joseph Kermish, *The Ghetto Fight on Two Fronts*, "Yad Vashem News" No. 30, 1963.)

organization, *Hechalutz*, the left wing of *Poale Zion*, the right wing of *Poale Zion*, the *Bund*, the *Gordonia*-Organization of Zionist youth, *Hitachdut*, the left wing of the trade unions); and the Jewish Military Union (Z.Z.W.), which was under Revisionist influence and tended towards Italian-style Fascism. It is clear that the O.B.K.K.[10] commanded much more allegiance in the community than the Z.Z.W. When the "action" began, coordination took place of the efforts of both organizations. I visited one of the combat stations of the O.B. a few days before the "action". It was a two-room flat with a kitchen at 32 Swietojerska Street; the *Wache* of the German *Werkschutz* was situated three floors below. Ten persons stayed on these premises, day and night, prepared for anything. That was where the arms were. The combatants were not allowed to leave the premises, they received their food on the spot. Entrance to the premises was through the attics of the neighbouring blocks of flats, and there was an agreed way of knocking on the door. Three women combatants in the flat prepared the meals and also carried out various dangerous missions and orders of the O.B. Discipline and order were exemplary. The group under the influence of the left wing of *Poale Zion* had several successful expropriations (so-called "exes")[11] to its credit for the sake of arming the Ghetto, etc.

At the same time I also saw the Z.Z.W. arsenal. It was situated in an uninhabited, so-called "wild" block of flats at 7 Muranowska Street, in a six-room flat on the first floor. There was a first-class

---

10 O.B.K.K. The initials stand for *Organizacja Bojowa Komisji Koordynacyjnej*—the Coordinating Committee's Combat Organization already referred to.
O.B. stands for *Organizacja Bojowa*—Combat Organization—the full title of which was, *Zydowska Organizacja Bojowa*—Jewish Combat Organization, generally called by the initials, Z.O.B. All these names refer to one and the same organization.

11 "Exes"—short for "expropriations": freezing or confiscation, forcible transfer of property of foreigners; descending on people or places in order to rob. Combatants in the Ghetto and in Warsaw also used the word for the imposition of fines or levying of monies from collaborators, Ghetto profiteers, the *Judenrat*, etc.
(*Cf. Sefer milḥamot bagetaot*, p. 760.)

radio in the command room, which received news from all over the world, and next to it stood a typewriter. I talked to the people in command for several hours. They were armed with revolvers stuck in their belts. Different kinds of weapons were hung in the large rooms: light machine guns, rifles, revolvers of different kinds, hand grenades, bags of ammunition, German uniforms, etc., all of which were utilized to the full in the April "action". There was great activity in the command room, as in any army headquarters; fighters received their orders for the "barrack-points" where future combatants were being brought together and instructed. Reports arrived of expropriations of wealthy people carried out by individual groups for the sake of arming the Z.Z.W. While I was there, a purchase of arms was made from a former Polish Army officer, amounting to a quarter of a million zloty; a sum of 50,000 zloty was paid on account. Two machine guns were bought at 40,000 zloty each, and a large amount of hand grenades and bombs.[12] In answer to my question as to why the premises were not camouflaged I was told that there was no fear of betrayal from their own followers, and in the case of an undesirable visitor, a gendarme, for example—he wouldn't leave there alive.

Various other groups and individuals besides the O.B. were also arming themselves.[13] Arms were flowing into the Ghetto in large

---

[12] As regards arms purchases, it must be pointed out that the Jewish resistance movement had to pay prices three times those paid by the Polish underground organizations on the black market, because of the higher risks involved in smuggling the arms into the Ghetto and in the very fact of contact with Jews under the conditions of the Nazi occupation. As a result, the Jews paid 10,000 to 20,000 zloty for a single pistol, 40,000 zloty for a machine gun, while the top prices paid by the Home Army were 4,000 and 12,000 zloty respectively. This constituted a very real limitation on the possibilities open to the Ghetto resistance movement, which received no financial help from government circles.

(See: *Polskie siły zbrojne w drugiej wojnie światowej,* Vol. III—*Armia Krajowa,* London, 1950.)

[13] The two armed organizations in the Warsaw Ghetto—the Jewish Combat Organization and the Jewish Military Union—had only limited possibilities and could not take in everyone who wanted to fight.

quantities. Groups of workers in separate workshops were arming themselves together with their foremen; porters, carters, smugglers, work-post labourers, etc., were arming themselves. In addition to a radio, many hide-outs possessed weapons bought with common hide-out funds. The O.B. was preparing not only arms but a large quantity of bottles filled with explosive liquids, which were to be used to cause panic among the Germans, to set fire to buildings, to the storage rooms belonging to the workshops, etc. Bottles of explosive liquids were used successfully in some shops before the April "action"; thus, for example, the O.B. burnt down and destroyed a large storage room full of furniture meant for the German Army in the Hallman workshop at 55–83 Nowolipki Street. Separate hide-outs also prepared bottles like these and substitute weapons as well, such as axes, clubs, etc. The O.B. did not attach much importance to these spontaneous arming activities, assuming that German tactics would paralyse all attempts at defence on the part of individual hide-outs. The O.B. reckoned on the Germans' using surprise tactics, and that is why the Combat Groups remained on the alert for several months, prepared to step forward at any moment. It was not thought, of course, that the Ghetto would be able to defend itself for long. It was understood that it would be the struggle between the gnat and the elephant, but national pride commanded that Jews offer resistance and not let themselves be led helpless to the slaughter.

We shall not here describe the history of the "resettlement action" of January 1943. For the 10,000 persons deported, approximately 1,000 were shot on the spot because of the energetic resistance put up by the population of entire blocks of flats. To the glory of the O.B. it should be stressed that the S.S. had to go into the Ghetto as if to a battlefield, armed with small tanks, small field guns, hand grenades, light machine guns, machine guns, etc.

Hundreds of Jews therefore organized themselves on their own in loose groups (sometimes called "wild groups") and tried by themselves to secure the arms needed in order to fight. During the Warsaw Ghetto rising, these groups, for the most part equipped with small arms only, offered considerable resistance in defence of particular bunkers and hide-outs.

Army Headquarters were set up in Muranowski Square, with maps of the Ghetto spread out on tables; despatch riders on bicycles and motorcycles darted to and fro with instructions to the various detachments located in the blocks and squares of the Ghetto. The gendarmes and the S.S.-men operating in the Ghetto were so afraid of the combatants that they would not go into the Jewish flats and instead sent ahead scouting parties consisting of functionaries of the Jewish Order Service. Only after the Jewish Order Service had made sure that there were no armed Jews in a given flat would the Gendarmerie enter in order to conduct a thorough search. Jews who were caught were ordered to put up their hands, like prisoners-of-war at the front. We do not know the exact number of German and Ukrainian victims, but I am sure that there were scores.

Polish public opinion was intensely interested in the defence put up by the Ghetto. The Underground Press spoke of the heroic attitude of the Ghetto with great esteem. January 1943 was compared with July 1942, the passivity of the Warsaw Jews at that time was compared with the active stand they now took after their previous experience. All this, however, brought no change in the attitude of the Government elements towards the defence problems of the Jews. In spite of constant appeals on the part of the Jews, arms were supplied only in very small quantities.[14]

---

[14] According to data published by the General Sikorski Historical Institute in London ("*Polskie siły zbrojne w drugiej wojnie światowej*", Vol. III — "*Armia Krajowa*", p. 326), the Home Army supplied the Jewish Combat Organization with the following arms: 90 pistols with two magazines and ammunition; 500 defensive hand grenades; 15 kilograms of explosives with detonating fuses and detonators; 1 light machine gun; 1 automatic pistol; *materiel* for incendiary bottles; sabotage *materiel* such as time bombs and safety fuses. These figures are a little higher than those given by Col. Henryk Wolinski (in his report on the activities of his Department for Jewish Affairs at Home Army Headquarters), by Zivia Lubetkin, *Aharonim al hahoma*, Eyn Harod, 1946, p. 31 and by Marek Edelman, *Getto Walczy*, Łódź 1945, pp. 47– 48. The leaders of the Jewish resistance movement demanded greater quantities of *materiel*, affirming that the supplies received were utterly disproportionate to the needs of the Jewish Combat Organization and

April 1943 was approaching, a memorable date in the history of Warsaw Jewry, the date of the liquidation of the Jews in Warsaw. The illegal government of the Ghetto, the O.B., prepared energetically for its defence. Considerable funds were obtained by terror from war profiteers who would not have given a penny voluntarily. The unwilling ones or their families were kidnapped in broad daylight and taken to secret flats until they paid the levy,

---

to the supplies available to the Home Army. The Home Army High Command admitted that the arms allotted went nowhere near meeting the needs of the Ghetto but argued that they did not dispose of any considerable quantities of arms. However, data published by Polish historians after the war bear witness that the demands of the Jewish Combat Organization were certainly not excessive. At the end of 1941, the Home Army possessed secret arsenals of arms from Polish Army stocks hidden before the capitulation of September 1939, containing: —566 heavy machine guns; 1,097 light machine guns; 31,391 rifles; 6,492 pistols; 40,513 grenades; 28 anti-tank guns; 25 anti-tank rifles; over 5 million units of ammunition. Of the arms enumerated in the above list, the following were stocked in arsenals in the Warsaw region: —135 heavy machine guns; 190 light machine guns; 6,045 rifles; 1,070 pistols; 7,561 grenades; 7 anti-tank guns; about 1,200,000 units of ammunition. (Organizational Report No. 79 of the C.-in-C., Home Army, 1.3.1941–1.9.1941. *Loc. cit.,* pp. 324–325.) Some Polish historians maintain that these large amounts of arms listed as being in the possession of the Home Army were no longer usable in 1943, having deteriorated completely under unsuitable storage conditions in the secret arsenals. According to these historians, this explains the minute quantity of arms allotted to the Jewish Combat Organization, a quantity bearing no relation whatsoever to the quantities of arms available in the Home Army arsenals. (See for example, article by Adam Ciolkosz, *Bron dla getta Warszawy* in "Zeszyty Historyczne", No. 15/1969.) That this argumentation is false appears, among other sources, from a memorandum on the Home Army's possibilities of action, presented to the Supreme Command of the Allied Forces in plenary session by the Polish Military Attaché in Washington, Col. Mitkiewicz, on behalf of the Prime Minister of the Polish Government-in-Exile, General Sikorski, on 2 July 1943. According to this memorandum, the Home Army possessed the following arms in the spring of 1943 (i.e. at the time of the Warsaw Ghetto rising): 600 heavy machine guns; 1,000 light machine guns; 25,000 rifles; 6,000 pistols, 30,000 hand grenades.
(Leon Mitkiewicz, *Powstanie warszawskie — z mojego notatnika w Waszyngtonie,* "Zeszyty Historyczne", No. 1/1962, p. 113.)

amounting to tens of thousands and sometimes even hundreds of thousands of zloty. War was declared on informers, Gestapo-agents who helped the Germans in production, foremen who exploited Jewish workers for the benefit of German production, *Werkschutz* who oppressed the people living in the workshops, the directors of the shops, and those who made propaganda for voluntary departure to the S.S. labour camps in Trawniki or Poniatow. Death sentences were carried out in front of everyone; announcements and explanations of the sentences were posted on workshop walls and Ghetto walls. These death sentences made a deep impression on everyone. The authority of the O.B. grew, securing the obedience of the population by propaganda and by bullets. This had to be taken into consideration by the "kings" of German industry, Toebbens and Schultz, who polemized with the O.B. on the walls of the workshops, calling on their workers to go to Poniatow and Trawniki. I remember a conversation I had with the commander of the O.B., member of the Council of the *Hashomer Hatzair* (Jewish scouts organization), Mordekhai Anielewicz (pseudonym "Marian"— Mordekhai), who was killed in the April "action". He gave an accurate appraisal of the chances of the uneven struggle, he foresaw the destruction of the Ghetto and the workshops, and he was sure that neither he nor his combatants would survive the liquidation of the Ghetto. He was sure that they would die like stray dogs and no one would even know their last resting-place. After repeated heroic deeds in January and April 1943, he was killed, a few weeks after the April "action" began, in a hide-out with five entrances, suffocated by gas which the Germans threw in before they broke into the hide-out from all five sides.[15]

The April "action" broke out. O.B. patrols circulated in the Ghetto streets on the night between Sunday the 17th and Monday the 18th of April, calling on the population to take to their hideouts. The hopeless struggle began. A German army of six thousand soldiers appeared in the streets of the Ghetto, armed with modern

---

15 Anielewicz perished on 8 May 1943, in the command bunker of the Jewish Combat Organization at 18 Mila Street. Several scores of his comrades-in-arms perished with him.

motorised equipment.[16] This modern army was opposed by a handful of desperate young men, armed with poor-quality revolvers, who knew that extermination awaited them.[17] We shall not describe

---

[16] For the Ghetto fighting of April 1943 the Nazis formed a special battle group composed of the following units:

Waffen-S.S.: 3rd Battalion of Armoured-Car Grenadiers. 1st Battalion of Cavalry.

Ordnungspolizei: 1st Battalion of the 22nd *S.S. Ordnungspolizei* Regiment. 3rd Battalion of the 22nd *S.S. Ordnungspolizei* Regiment.

Wehrmacht: One battery of the Light Anti-Aircraft Artillery. One detachment of the Armoured-Train Sappers' Battalion. One detachment of the 14th Sapper Reserve Battalion.

One Battalion of the Polish Police. One Company of the Polish Fire-Fighting Police. Supplementary technical assistance.

Other units: A Battalion made up of Ukrainian, Latvian and Lithuanian auxiliaries.

Moreover, in the closing stages of the fighting, the 3rd Battalion of the 23rd *S.S. Ordnungspolizei* Regiment was also put in.

No exact data are available on the manpower of this group, because its Commander, General Juergen Stroop, gives only the *Durchschnitts-Tageseinsatz* (mean daily effective forces), and not, as is the general rule in operational reports, the total effectives employed. According to Stroop, these "mean daily effective forces" (not counting the 3rd Battalion of the 23rd S.S. and Police Regiment) amounted to 2,090 men, of whom 36 officers, 2,054 NCO's and other ranks.

(See: *Es gibt keinen jüdischen Wohnbezirk in Warschau mehr*—Exhibit U.S.A. 215 [1061-PS], Neuwied 1960.)

According to data from Home Army Intelligence (Report No. 149 of 20 April 1943, Internal Affairs Department, Office of the Government Delegate), the battle group operating against the Ghetto totalled about 5,000 men. The manpower and armament of the *Waffen-S.S.* Battalions were practically the same as those of *Wehrmacht* units at the front. The other units were armed with infantry weapons and machine guns. Furthermore, the German battle-group had at least 15 armoured cars, as well as a certain number of anti-aircraft guns (fired directly at the Ghetto combatants' positions), field guns, anti-tank guns and mortars.

(Files of the Government Delegate's Office, Archives of the Institute for the History of the [Communist] Party, Warsaw, 202/II-21, pp. 29–34.)

[17] It is not possible to ascertain exactly the number of persons who fought in the uprising. According to highly probable data assembled by B. Mark, 750 to 800 combattants fought in the ranks of the Jewish Combat Organization (Z.O.B.). The number of combatants of the Jewish Military

here in detail the course of the fighting with the Germans in April 1943. Separate groups were fighting in the Ghetto, in the bristle workshops in Swietojerska Street, on the terrain of the Schultz and Toebbens workshops, etc. There was fighting on the roofs of blocks where Polish and Zionist (blue-white) flags were fluttering. From the fourth floor of 32 Nalewki Street I was an eye witness of fighting like this at Muranowska Street during the afternoon hours of Monday the 18th of April. In the headquarters of the Order Service the Germans proudly displayed their trophies—captured flags—and gloried in their seizure. The combatants were shooting at passing S.S. and Ukrainian detachments—for example, from the block at 76 Leszno Street, where the K. G. Schultz workshop was situated. Revolvers, machine guns, hand grenades and bombs were thrown at the enemy. General Stroop, who commanded the army operating in the Ghetto, proved to be a second Suvorow, with the difference that the slaughter in the Praga suburb[18] was child's play

---

Union (*Zydowski Zwiazek Wojskowy* — Z.Z.W.), estimated by B. Mark at about 400 persons, is more open to question. If we assume that another few hundred combatants fought in loose groups not affiliated to the above organizations, the total number of persons who fought in the uprising can be estimated at a maximum of 1,500. The combatants' arms were almost exclusively ordinary pistols (with a very small quantity of ammunition), besides a small number of hand grenades and incendiary bottles.

At the very outside—and this maximum estimate is seriously questioned both by historians and by people who took part in the fighting—the combatants disposed of no more than 25 submachine guns and 10 machine guns, besides the small arms mentioned above.

(Bernard Mark, *op. cit.*, pp. 27-36.)

[18] After the capture of Praga (a suburb of Warsaw) on 4 November 1794, the Russians were "in a great fury against the Jews, on account of their setting up a special troop to defend the town" (referring to the Jewish brigade of Berek Joselewicz, numbering 500 men, which took an active part in the defence of Praga, where the greater part of the Polish Army was concentrated), and they maltreated the Jewish population with particular cruelty. An eyewitness, not a Jew, wrote that he was incapable of describing the appaling and barbaric spectacles that were to be seen when the Russians penetrated into Praga after the general attack and set it alight with a fire that quickly swept through the wooden houses of the quarter. The Commissioner of Prussia relates that the

compared to what was done by these Teutons. The Cossacks' "football game" of tossing Jewish children from one to another on pikes in Praga was indeed a game compared to the deeds of German soldiers in the Ghetto in the year of grace 1943.

In order to prepare the ground for their cruelties with proper German orderliness, the German command and press announced that they were suppressing a revolt of the Jews, who had organized partisan detachments to murder German soldiers. The German soldiers were told that bandits living in the Ghetto were hiding in bunkers and preparing to attack the German Army from there. Rumours were spread that besides the combatants in the Ghetto there were Soviet parachutists, Bolshevik prisoners-of-war who had fled from German captivity, and German deserters, all of them well supplied with arms, equipment and food, which was being dropped to them systematically from Soviet planes. It was also announced that the Ghetto was expecting Soviet help in the form of weapons and reinforcements. Belief in this help was so widespread that on Good Friday, according to an eye witness, the whole surviving population of the Ghetto was on the look-out for a white patch in the sky, supposed to be the parachute of a Soviet parachutist. This was the only ray of hope for the *morituri* in the Ghetto and for the remnant of the combatants still fighting in blocks not yet burnt down.

Cossacks cruelly murdered 16 Jews and that he succeeded in redeeming 35 children out of Cossack captivity by giving a zloty per head and thus saved them from the danger of being killed. Shmuel Yakobowitz Zwitkower, a member of the Jewish plutocracy of Warsaw, who had fled immediately on the outbreak of the revolt against the Russians in the capital on 17 and 18 April 1794, now appeared at the time of the bloodshed in Praga and in his suffering and sorrow over the victims of fire and sword he proclaimed that for every inhabitant of Praga, without distinction of religion, that was brought to him alive he would pay a golden dinar and for every one that was brought to him dead a silver dinar. Two casks, one full of gold and the other silver, stood in the middle of the courtyard of Shmuel Zwitkower: both were emptied. (J. Kermish, *Warsaw Jewry in the Kosciuszko Revolt* (Hebrew), in: Israel Klozner (Editor), "Sefer Hayovel mugash lekhvod Dr. Natan Michael Gelber, Tel-Aviv, 1963, p. 228.)

On the Aryan side there was intense interest in what was happening in the Ghetto. It was related that the Germans were afraid to show themselves in the Ghetto, and that they operated on burnt ground only, moving forward by burning down block after block. The Germans were spoken of with contempt because of their atrocities. They were laughed at for not being able to put down a handful of Jews fighting for their honour. The news spread by word of mouth of the losses suffered by the Jews in their fight against the Germans, about tanks drenched with petrol by the Jews and set on fire this way, and about other weapons seized by the Jews. It was said that thousands of Germans and Ukrainians were killed in the fight against the Jews.[19] There were rumours about Jews' reconquering the Pawiak and releasing the prisoners there, who then joined the fighting. A story was spread in town about a handful of Jews who had captured a tank, got into it and left the Ghetto area. Popular fantasy also created a Jewish Joan of Arc. At 28 Swietojerska Street, the bristle workshop, a beautiful 18-year-old girl dressed in white had been seen firing a machine gun at the Germans with extraordinary accuracy, while she herself was invulnerable—she was apparently wearing some sort of armour, said popular rumour. For several weeks the Ghetto reverberated with constant shooting, the glow of fire marked the lines of advancing German handiwork. The Germans utilized every possible means to cut off the struggling, bleeding Ghetto from the Aryan population, so as not to let any news get across from the battlefield and not let anyone leave the Ghetto alive. For this purpose, Aryans

---

[19] The Warsaw Ghetto rising, the greatest feat of arms in occupied Poland up till then, had tremendous repercussions throughout the country. Thus it is understandable that reports tended to exaggerate the losses inflicted on the Germans by the insurgents. For example, the clandestine Polish paper, *Mysl Panstwowa,* No. 37 of 30 April, 1943, in an article called, "The Biggest Crime in the World", wrote that German losses amounted by then to about 1.000 dead and several times more than that wounded. But in reality, the insurgents did not dispose of sufficient arms to enable them to inflict losses of this magnitude. But on the other hand, the losses reported by Stroop—16 killed and 90 wounded—are certainly too low. The fighting went on for several weeks and the German losses must have been higher.

were forbidden to move freely in the streets bordering on the Ghetto, that is, Leszno, Bonifraterska, Swietojerska Streets, etc. Tramway traffic in these streets was eliminated and detoured to peripheral streets. Among the rumours being spread on the Aryan side at that time there was a good deal of fantasy, but there were also authentic facts, if somewhat altered. The legend about the Jewish Maid of Orleans had its origin in the fact that Jewish girls took part in combat alongside the men. I knew these heroic girls from the period preceding the "action". Most of them belonged to the *Hashomer Hatzair* and *Hechalutz* movements. Throughout the war, they had carried on welfare work all the time with great devotion and extraordinary self-sacrifice. Disguised as Aryan women, they had carried illegal literature around the country, managed to get everywhere with instructions from the Jewish National Committee; they bought and transported arms, executed O.B. death sentences, and shot gendarmes and S.S.-men during the January "action". Altogether they completely outdid the men in courage, alertness and daring. I myself saw Jewish women firing a machine gun from a roof. Clearly one of these heroic girls must have distinguished herself in the heavy fighting waged by the O.B. at Swietojerska Street, and that was probably the origin of the story of the Jewish Maid of Orleans.

The April 1943 "action" became known abroad. American and English radios, which learned of the course of the April fighting from a short-wave transmitter, called on the Polish people to help the Jews with material means and to hide them (broadcast of 5 or 6 May, 1943). There was already cooperation with the Polish side during the April "action".[20] Weapons were supplied in the

---

[20] During the Warsaw Ghetto rising, the Polish underground organizations carried out a number of armed actions in order to demonstrate their solidarity with the Ghetto in its fight. The Home Army carried out four such armed operations on a more considerable scale on 19 and 23 April, and some smaller ones on the following days.

On 19 April, the operation was carried out by a detachment of 25 men under the command of Captain Pszenny. On 23 April armed sallies near to the Ghetto walls were executed by: (a) a detachment of seven men from the "Diversion Command", led by Captain Lewinski, and

usual way, that is, across the walls and through sewers. Combatants and others who escaped from the Ghetto were being given a certain amount of aid. The Home Plenipotentiary of the Polish government [-in-Exile] issued an appeal, filled with praise for the Warsaw Jews who were defending their honour with arms in their hands; the appeal called on the Polish population to give aid to those who were trying to escape from the burning Ghetto. The P.P.S. issued an appeal with a similar content.

The Jewish combatants transferred the fight to Aryan territory. The leader of the Swietojerska Street combat group made a speech from the Ghetto wall calling on the Polish population to cooperate. According to an eye-witness report, he ended this fine speech with the cry: "Long live Poland!" At night the combatants broke through the walls, armed with revolvers, killed the Ukrainian guards or Lithuanian *Shaulists* and took cover on the Aryan side. It often came to fighting with Germans and even with the Blue Police in squares neighbouring on the Ghetto. Similar sallies over the walls

---

(b) another detachment of six men led by officer-cadet Stalkowski. Next in importance was the liquidation of an S.S.-post on Zakroczymska Street by an armed Home Army detachment of 8 men under Lieut. Kern-Jedrychowski.

The *Gwardia Ludowa* staged actions near the Ghetto walls three times, on 20, 22 and 23 April. The forces sent in were: (a) on 20 April, a detachment of 5 men from the "Special Group"; (b) on 22 April, some detachments of unknown size; (c) on 23 April, three detachments of four men each. In the *Gwardia Ludowa* operations, some Jewish combatants also took part, such as Jerzy Lerner (Lerski), commander of one of the combat detachments. Several armed diversions were also executed on behalf of the Jewish combatants in the Ghetto by an 18-man detachment of the "Security Corps" (*Korpus Bezpieczentswa*) under the command of Capt. Iwanski, as well as by some smaller detachments: 1) of the "RPPS"—Militia, under the command of Andrzejczak; 2) of the Socialist Combatant Organization under the command of Leszek Raabe; and 3) of the *Szare Szeregi* under the command of Marian Singer. Moreover, members of the Polish Underground helped some groups of Jewish combatants to escape from the Ghetto in order to continue fighting in the ranks of the partisans.

(Wladyslaw Bartoszewski and Zofia Lewin, *The Righteous Among the Nations,* London, 1969, Chapter: *Solidarity Actions at the Warsaw Ghetto Walls,* pp. 555–570.)

or through underground passages by groups of five combatants happened at Zelaznej Bramy Square, Krasinskich Square, Teatralny Square, Muranowski Square, etc. Near Teatralny Square, the Blue Police on one occasion caught a few combatants who had thrown a hand grenade and tried to escape; they caught them and shot them in one of the ruined blocks on Krolewska Street. A larger group of combatants—about a hundred persons—had a fight with the wall guards and escaped to Kampinoska Forest, where they joined the partisan detachments.[21] An escape with the help of a truck was organized by one of the political parties active in the country.[22] Other Ghetto inhabitants besides the Ghetto combatants also escaped to the Aryan side, though those who were unarmed rarely succeeded. I was told as an authentic fact about a group of sixty Jews who made their way over to the Aryan side across the ruins of a block on Grzybowska Street through barbed wire. People living in this block saw the tragic scene and fortunately no one betrayed these Jews escaping from the Ghetto.

---

[21] This statement is not completely accurate. Only one group of 15 people managed to force an escape from the Warsaw Ghetto to the Kampinoska Forest. They found no partisans there and shortly afterwards they got to the other side of the Vistula and made their way to Polesia (formerly Eastern Poland), where they entered the ranks of Soviet partisans in the neighbourhood of Kobryn. Some members of this group later fought in the ranks of the Red Army. Thus for example Eliahu Eisenberg won distinction as an NCO, Reconnaissance, 333rd Infantry Division of the Red Army, receiving the Soviet decoration *Slava*.

[22] Two groups of combatants of the Jewish Combat Organization (Z.O.B.) managed to escape from the Ghetto thanks to the *Gwardia Ludowa*, affiliated to the Polish Workers' Party. The first group, numbering 40 men, left the Ghetto *via* the sewers on 28 April, 1943; Lt. Gaik then took them by truck to the Lomianki wood near Warsaw. Another group of 34 combatants of the Z.O.B. got out of the Ghetto in the same way and was transported to Lomianki on 10 May 1943. Some weeks later, the *Gwardia Ludowa* took both groups to the Wyszkow forest, where they formed a Jewish partisan unit (the "Mordekhai Anielewicz" detachment).

(On the circumstances of the escape of both these groups from the Ghetto, see: Helena Balicka-Kozlowska, *Mur miał dwie strony*, Warsaw, 1958.)

While "good souls" were calling on the Polish population to hide Jews, "bad lots" in the form of hordes of *schmalzowniks,* police agents and uniformed police threw themselves like carrion-eating hyenas on those fleeing from the Ghetto. Within sight of the burning Ghetto, where captured victims were being burnt alive, amid the constant explosions of dynamite blowing up the bunkers, these villainous hoodlums organized Jew-hunts. An eye witness told me the following story: — On the fourth day of the "action", a column of Jewish workers was marching down Leszno Street. They succeeded in bribing the escort, a German, and in getting permission to break away from the column and go across to the Aryan side. A score of people wanted to take advantage of this rare opportunity to escape from the jaws of death, and they separated themselves from the rest of the group at the corner of Karmelicka and Leszno Streets in order to go over to the Aryan side. They were immediately surrounded by the *schmalzowniks* who were preying on the Jewish tragedy and who drove them back into the burning Ghetto. Another similar case occurred in Swietojerska Street when six Jews got to the Aryan side through the sewers. This was seen by a little boy who was playing on his scooter. Having been taught at home that a Jew is a monster one threatens bad children with ("A Jew will come and put you in a sack"), he attracted the attention of a band of *schmalzowniks* stationed near-by. The fugitives bought themselves off for 5,000 zloty, which did not, however, save them from another blackmailer, who handed them over to the authorities. At this time, many Aryans were also stopped in the streets on suspicion of being of Jewish origin, and were taken in droves to Polish Police stations.

The April "action", the German atrocities, the defence of the Ghetto, the burning of houses and people, formed the subject of conversations in the streets, trams, etc. We quote a number of authentic conversations of this kind: — A pious old granny: "In Holy Week, the Jews tormented Christ. In Holy Week, the Germans are tormenting the Jews." A seventy-year-old priest: "A good thing happened, because the Jews had a large military force inside the Ghetto—if they hadn't turned it against the Germans, they'd have turned it against us." Conversation in a tram: "They are burning the little Jews, but the big Jews rule in America and after the war they will rule over us." A middle-class housewife: "It's terrible to see what's happening in the Ghetto, horrible things! But maybe it's a good thing it's happened this way. The Jews suck our blood. They used to say, 'Your streets, our houses.' They said, 'You wanted to have Poland without Jews, now you have Jews without Poland.' " Two businessmen from Grzybowski Square: one of them was sorry, for the fires in the Ghetto meant that future Poland had lost a great deal, much of the country's wealth had gone up in smoke. The other replied, "Don't have regrets. The Ghetto was a stinking district and it's a good thing that it isn't there any longer. We shall rebuild this district and it will be much finer and cleaner without the Jews." A teacher, an old maid: "One pities a cat. A Jew is also a human being, even if he is a Jew." But after she received a letter from a woman relative from Majdanek Camp telling her that Jewish prisoners-of-war were treating the Poles badly,[23] she said, "I used to pity the Jews, but now that their brethren treat our people so badly, let the Germans slaughter them to the last one." An O.N.R. member formulated his credo regarding the April "action" briefly and tersely', "It's still not enough just to burn the Jews." Another cannibal put it even more succinctly: "The bugs are burning."

Comments regarding the aid that the Ghetto requested from the Aryan side: — A captain's wife, a post-office clerk: "Before the war the Jews spied on us on behalf of the enemy, and now these rascals ask us for help. Don't we have anyone to shed our blood for?!" A P.P.S. member: "The Organization is not prepared for armed action. We sympathize with the Jews in their tragic situation. They ought to be supplied with arms, but active cooperation is impossible. For the sake of the higher aim, for the cause of independence, all must suffer. The Party must choose the right moment for the struggle, and not let itself be deflected by sentiment, however noble." Some high-minded individuals did raise their voices

---

[23] There were no Jewish prisoners-of-war in Majdanek concentration camp. Jewish P.O.W.'s were held in a camp on Lipowa Street in Lublin, where there were no Polish prisoners.

in indignation at seeing the indifference that met this great tragedy which was being enacted in full view of the whole population. "We go on living normally as if nothing was happening. We eat a tasty supper and then go out onto the balcony to take a look at the glow of the fires in the Ghetto. We listen to the detonations of the exploding bombs and dynamite that are blowing up the blocks and hide-outs—and we keep silent!"

In these conversations among the Poles about what was happening in the Ghetto, the anti-Semitic note was predominant in general,[24]

---

[24] Ringelblum's observations are confirmed by numerous memoirs and eyewitness reports of these events. Maksymilian Tauchner, for example, in his memoirs in the Polish historical journal, *Zeszyty Historyczne,* published in Paris, writes as follows: "Warsaw's first reactions to the news that a rising had taken place there, in the Jewish Ghetto, were varied ones. You listened to these echoes avidly, with painful tension, longing to hear something fine and warm from the fellow-citizens on the other side of the wall, who talked about the Jews so often at this time. And indeed there were fine, touching, heart-warming words; words of sympathy, assurances that those closed in behind the walls were not alone. Words that gave courage to survive, words of comfort. Words of admiration for the 'little Jew-boys' who were standing their ground so well —'Who would have expected it?'... Words of appreciation when the Jewish combatants also raised a Polish, red-and-white flag on the Ghetto walls as they were battered into rubble. But these words, alas, were few. Most people received the news of the fighting in the Ghetto with a mocking smile, incredulous at Jews' waging an armed struggle. Not everyone understood that it was not a question of fighting for military victory or even for life itself, but for death as men, death with dignity. People were even heard to say that the Jews had decided to burn Warsaw down and that this could only infuriate the Germans and in the end turn them against the whole population of Warsaw. There was the voice of an indignant fireman saying, 'They're not people, they're cattle,' because when he called to a Jew standing on the roof of a burning house with a child in his arms and asked him to give him his valuables before he jumped into the abyss of fire, the Jew only spat... People stood near the Ghetto for hours on end, looking on at this spectacle unique of its kind. People were burning, children were burning. If even the sight of these children could not move hearts hardened with hate, apparently there were no hearts there at all. Little children with their eyes bound by their parents held convulsively to window-frames already being licked by the flames, lacking the courage to step forward

satisfaction that Warsaw had in the end become *judenrein,* that the wildest dreams of Polish anti-Semites about a Warsaw without Jews were coming true. Some loudly and others discreetly expressed their satisfaction at the fact that the Germans had done the dirty work of exterminating the Jews. Sympathy was given expression in the sense that though it was Jews that were being murdered, still they were human beings. The blocks of flats that were burned down aroused more regret than the live human torches. Joy over Warsaw's being cleansed of Jews was spoiled only by fear of the morrow, the fear that after liquidating the Jews, the Germans would take the Poles in hand. This is what the anti-Semites said about the Jewish combatants' hoisting Polish flags: "They just want to suck up to the Poles."[25]

The anti-Semites gaped with astonishment when they saw that Jews knew how to defend themselves and how to shoot and that they put up resistance to the enemy. Polish public opinion was

---

and meet so dreadful a death. Could anything be more horrifying than the sight of a father or mother's pushing their own child into the arms of death? And still there were people whose hearts remained unsoftened then. A little Jewish girl who managed—by what inexplicable miracle?—to get out of this hell in these terrible days was surrounded by a mob near the Three Crosses Square and handed over with hostile cries to the German gendarmes.

[25] There are numerous sources confirming this range of reactions on the part of the Polish community, with the anti-Semitic attitude decidedly predominant. This atmosphere, which could be felt both in Warsaw and the provinces, also pervaded camps run by the Nazis. A characteristic example of the reaction of Polish officers to the news of the Ghetto revolt is reported by Marian Palenkier, a Polish Army Officer in the German P.O.W. camp for Polish officers, *Oflag Nr. II C* in Woldenberg. Palenkier writes: "Fairly detailed information reached us about the rising. The tragic news reduced us, the Jews, to the deepest depression and despair. The whole of Barrack XII A did penitence, symbolically of course. The Poles reacted in different ways to the news of this Jewish act of heroism. I shall never forget the impression made on us by a letter read aloud by a Captain in Barrack XVIII A (I forget his name, he was an engineer-architect). He had received this letter from his sister in Sochaczew. Parts of it have remained in my memory. This Polish woman wrote, amongst other things: 'The Germans are solving two painful problems so beautifully at one go—the Jewish problem and

greatly interested in the heroism of the Ghetto, which was called "Little Stalingrad", and its defence was compared with that of Westerplatte.[26] Undue hopes were roused by the defence of the Ghetto. It was seen as the first link in a general insurrection throughout the whole country, initiated by the Jews. On the 14th of May, the occupiers issued a proclamation to the Polish people announcing triumphantly that "the nest of Bolshevism, Communism and banditry" had been razed to the ground. At the same time the Polish population was called upon to hand over Jews, on pain of death for anyone daring to hide them. The whole Underground Press—*Biuletyn Informacyjny, Polska Zbrojna, Armia i Panstwo, Siew,* and others—extolled the heroism of the Jews to the heights.[27]

---

the Ukrainian... Our hearts rejoice... The Warsaw Ghetto is burning... The reflection of the flames can be seen even in Sochaczew...' Some kept an embarrassed silence, others reacted positively and still others smiled with joy. There were hardly any who expressed compassion." (Report of Marian Palenkier, Yad Vashem Archives, 0-3/1287.)

[26] Westerplatte: a small peninsula on the territory of the City of Gdansk (Danzig). The small Polish garrison—one company, numbering 182 men—was attacked on the first day of the war, 1 September 1939, and held out effectively for a whole week against much stronger German forces attacking from the air, sea and land.

[27] During the uprising, most of the Polish underground press published articles expressing solidarity with the fighting Ghetto, and admiration for the Jewish combatants and stressing the importance of the rising. The following are a few sample passages from these articles:
Gwardzista, 20 May 1943: "The heroic resistance of the Warsaw Ghetto has already lasted for a month. With the exception of Yugoslavia, where resistance has by now taken on the character of a general uprising, this is the biggest and most prolonged act of armed resistance that has yet been staged in the occupied territories."
Dzien Warszawy, 5 May 1943: "This brave and determined armed resistance, which has already gone on for a score of days against an incomparably stronger enemy, is not merely the instinctive act of a victim in his own defence; it is without doubt action consciously decided on and carried out in the name of honour and human dignity."
W.R.N., 7 May 1943: "Their deeds will not remain without effect. They will become part of the legend of Fighting Poland, the common possession of the Polish people, from which will be built the edifice of the Polish Republic."
Polska Walczy, 30 April 1943: "The communiqué from this battlefield

should be read out aloud before the whole of mankind in its struggle, so that every soldier may boast that he is a comrade-in-arms of these comrades who are perishing today, arms in hand, in the streets and houses of the Warsaw Ghetto."

Gwardia Ludowa, 4 May 1943: "What the Jews of Warsaw have secured for us is a truth that may well be the most important of all—the truth of the Germans' weakness. In the future, when we rise in arms everywhere in Polish territory, we shall have learned from the experience of the Warsaw Ghetto fight."

Wolnosc, 14 May 1943: "Their deed will remain engraved on our hearts. One day in the future, when the joyful moment arrives to rise and fight, we shall remember the heroes of the Warsaw Ghetto as comrades-in-arms who fell at this isolated outpost of the struggle for freedom."

Nevertheless a considerable part of the Polish clandestine press kept up its vicious anti-Jewish campaign even during the weeks of the fighting in the Ghetto. Particularly aggressive anti-Jewish articles appeared in the papers, *Wielka Polska, Nurt, Nowa Polska,* and *Walka.* The following quotations are examples:

Walka, 5 May 1943: "Even there, where Poland and everything Polish were denied the respect due to them, there where the name of Poland was so often besmirched—behind the Ghetto walls, Polish banners appeared when the final life-and-death struggle began. Even the Jew fighting for his life understands that he can move the world with the name of Poland, but not by his own fate, merited a hundredfold."

Wielka Polska, 5 May 1943: "Thus, having the choice between death by shooting or gassing and fighting with arms in their hands—they would obviously choose the latter, which offered at least a possibility of saving their lives. There is no heroism in it at all, nor even any risk. Nor has it anything in common with the Polish cause."

Prawda Mlodych, April–May 1943: "The Jews were parasites on the body of the nations of Europe and were therefore universally hated and despised. They opposed everything, but they did so cautiously, never openly, never with arms in their hands. They were the causal factor, the prime mover in three quarters of all the wars fought in Europe by the different nations, but they carefully masked all trace of their influence." And later: "The Jews are fighting. They are fighting not for their lives, because the fight against the Germans is far too unequal and hopeless—but to exact a price for their lives. Not in order to save themselves from death, but to choose what kind of death they will die. In order to perish like human beings, not like vermin. For the first time in seventeen centuries, they have woken from their vile debasement."

Biuletyn Informacyjny wrote: "At last the Jews rose up in arms. Up till now foreign citizens from the Ghetto, they have at last become near and dear to us. They have purified themselves in the eyes of history, they have defended their lives with arms in their hands. Victory will be theirs if they succeed in weakening the German forces even by a hair's breadth; victory will be theirs if even part of them succeed in escaping from the burning Ghetto; victory will be theirs if they die with arms in their hands." (Quotation from memory.)[28] The article ended with a call to extend help to the Jews, to hide them.

A direct outcome of the liquidation of the Warsaw Ghetto was

---

[28] The reference here is to a passage in an article entitled, *Ostatni akt wielkiej tragedii* ("The Last Act in a Great Tragedy"), in the *Biuletyn Informacyjny* of 29 April 1943. Ringelblum's quotation is inexact; the passage cited runs as follows:

"Up to now, the passive death of the Jewish masses has not created any new values, it has been useless. Death with weapons in one's hands can create new values in the life of the Jewish people, crowning martyred Polish Jewry with the halo of an armed fight for the right to live. This is how the population of Warsaw has understood the defence of the Ghetto, as it has listened appreciatively to the shots fired by the defenders and anxiously observed the glow of the fires and the spreading smoke of the incendiary bombs. Fighting citizens of the Polish State from behind the Ghetto walls became closer and more intelligible to the population of the capital than passive victims allowing themselves to be dragged away to their death."

This article provoked much criticism from both Poles and Jews. A prominent member of the Polish resistance movement, the socialist Wacław Zagórski, wrote: "The article of 29 April in the 'Biuletyn Informacyjny' entitled, 'The Last Act in a Great Tragedy' seems dry and lifeless to me. The very title already shocks me. I should like to see in this struggle—so admirable, given the disproportion between the contending forces—not the last act in a tragedy but the first act in a great awakening ... To me they [the Jews] were always just as close and intelligible as the Poles, who also in fact let themselves be picked up in the streets, pushed into Black Marias and deported to annihilation camps. I don't like big words and flattering superlatives, but in face of the pathos of the fight of these young Jews I am shocked by the pallid words of the article: 'Appreciatively'? It should be, 'Admiringly'! 'Anxiously'? It should be, 'Despairingly!'" (Wacław Zagórski, *Wolność w niewoli*, London, 1971, p. 391.)

that Jews living in flats on the Aryan side were given notice *en masse*. It was feared that after the liquidation of the Ghetto by fire and sword, an analogous "action" would take place on the Aryan side. Fear set in lest the rumoured German threats might be carried out that every block of flats where a Jew was found would be razed to the ground. Another aftermath of the April "action" was street round-ups of Jews.[29] This will be treated later.

---

29 A description of a raid of this kind is to be found in the diary of an eye witness, a Polish worker named Kazimierz Szymczak. His entry of 20 April 1943 reads as follows: "When I got back today after seeing Stasia home, I saw the way a Ukrainian delivered his prey—a Jew—to the Germans standing at the corner of Konwiktorska and Zakroczymska. The Jew was about thirty years old, with a beard of several days growth, all black from the smoke [of the Ghetto fires]; he stood, trembling with cold, his face to the wall, his hands up. He really had very bad luck, for after he had succeeded in escaping from the Ghetto through the sewers and getting above ground—it was here that somebody recognized him as a Jew and denounced him. He fell into the hands of the hangmen, but he managed to distract their attention and escape. He fled to the area of the railway bridge near the Citadel and hid there in a fruit-tree nursery. The Germans would not have found him, because they had already stopped looking and had given up and were leaving the place, when a Polish street-sweeper went up to them and told them where the fugitive was crouching, and they soon took him away."
(The diary of Kazimierz Szymczak appeared under the title, *Dni zgrozy i walki o wolnosc*, in the collection, *Pamietniki robotnikow z czasow okupacji*, Vol. I, Warsaw, 1948.)

11

SOCIAL CLASSES, PARTIES, THE GOVERNMENT AND THE JEWS

The Fascist front and the Labour front. — The Germans intensify anti-Semitism. — The illegal press and the "Judas" press on the Jews. — Radio and posters against the Jews. — How the middle class benefited from the annihilation of the Jews. — Workers by hand and brain help the Jews. — Polish railwaymen rescue fugitives from Treblinka. — The Village and the Jews. — The partisans. — The Polish clergy and the West European clergy in the Jewish problem. — Converts. — Government elements and the Jews.

Before the war, two large camps crystallized in Poland, just as in all the rest of Europe—the Fascist camp and the anti-Fascist. The *Endecja* and the *Sanacja* became more and more imbued with Fascist tendencies. The workers' wing of *Sanacja* inclined towards the broad labour front which was formed in Poland before the war. The trump card of Polish Fascism was anti-Semitism, which had been nurtured with sedulous care over the centuries through the writings of Miczynski,[1] Niemojewski,[2] Jeske-Choinski[3] and other

---

[1] Sebastian Miczynski, a 17th-century Polish anti-Semitic agitator, professor of philosophy at Cracow Jagiellonski University. His famous anti-Semitic pamphlet entitled, *Zwierciadlo Korony Polskiej* (Mirror of the Polish Crown), was published in 1618, and was one of the causes of anti-Jewish disorders that broke out in Cracow at that time. In order to quiet the town, King Zygmunt III Waza forbade the dissemination of the pamphlet. The King's order was disregarded, however, and successive editions of Miczynski's pamphlet appeared, contributing to the birth of anti-Semitic literature in Poland.

[2] Andrzej Niemojewski (1864–1921), a Polish journalist and translator, specialising in religious topics. For many years his position was that

anti-Semitic authors, who derived their wisdom from the works of German anti-Semites, Eisenmenger,[4] Rohling,[5] Lueger,[6] Stoecker,[7] and others. In the Polish Fascist camp there were two prevailing tendencies, the moderate and the radical. The former, represented by the old *Endecja*, wanted to solve the Jewish problem according to the letter of the law. The Polish Diet was to pass a special law concerning Jews in the fields of economy, cultural life, etc. The Jews were to be limited in their access to trade, handicrafts, industry, the liberal professions, etc., and thus be forced to seek scope for their labour by emigration abroad. The radical Fascists did not limit themselves to demanding legal restrictions. They took their example from Nazi Germany, sought to destroy the Jews physically,

---

of a free-thinker. He later joined the Polish nationalists and published many anti-Semitic articles.

3   Teodor Jeske-Choinski (1854–1920), Polish journalist and novelist. A liberal in his youth, he became with the passage of time an active proponent of clerical-conservative and anti-Semitic views. His racialist opinions were expressed in his book, *Neofici polscy* (*The Polish Neophytes*), published in 1905.

4   Johann Andreas Eisenmenger (1654–1704), German anti-Semitic writer, professor of oriental studies at Heidelberg University. His famous anti-Semitic work, *Entdecktes Judentum* (*Judaism Revealed*), appeared in Frankfurt-am-Main in 1700 and became a source of inspiration for numberless German anti-Semitic publicists.

5   August Rohling (1839–1931), German Catholic theologian and anti-Semitic writer, professor at the universities of Muenster, Milwaukee (U.S.A.) and Prague. His work, *Der Talmudjude,* published in 1871, was in fact an abbreviated version of Eisenmenger's *Entdecktes Judentum.* Other important anti-Semitic works of Rohling's were, *Katechismus des 19. Jahrhunderts für Juden und Protestanten*, Mainz, 1878 and *Franz Delitzsch und die Judenfrage,* Prague, 1881.

6   Karl Lueger (1844–1910), leader of the anti-Semitic Christian-Social Party in Austria. Elected to the State Council in 1885, Mayor of Vienna 1897 to 1910. His anti-Semitic activities exercised a considerable influence in forming Hitler's racialist views.

7   Adolf Stoecker (1835–1909), German Protestant theologian and anti-Semitic agitator. He founded the anti-Semitic Christian-Social Party in 1878. He was twice elected to the Reichstag at the end of the 19th Century. His work entitled, *"Christlich-Social"*, with his political and anti-Semitic speeches, appeared in 1884.

to create such an inferno for Jews in Poland that the country would be too hot for them and they would have to seek salvation abroad. These Fascists carried out the extermination of the Jews in a variety of ways, not shrinking from utilizing pogroms or any other excesses. Anti-Semitic terror increased in Poland day by day, parallel with the growth of Fascism, and was crowned by the events in Przytyk, Odrzywol, Brzesc-on-the-Bug, and other places.[8]

The anti-Fascist camp, consisting of workers, peasants and intellectuals, understood that the Jewish problem, like social problems in general, could not be solved within the framework of the capitalist regime. The market stall that had formerly belonged to a Jew could not satisfy the land hunger of the millions of workless, and breaking Jewish students' heads and boycotting Jewish businesses could not provide work for the hundreds of thousands of unemployed, could not give jobs in industry to the enormous army of unemployed young people in towns and villages.

We have mentioned elsewhere that a radical change came about in Polish-Jewish relations during the Polish-German campaign in September 1939. Anti-Semitism, Hitler's weapon for the disintegration of Poland, vanished into thin air. However, this awakening lasted a short time only. The Germans saw in anti-Semitism the only means of bridging the abyss opened up by Auschwitz, Dachau, Oranienburg, Majdanek, etc., and they did everything possible to intensify hatred of the Jews. In all the main cities of the General-Government, German press organs came into existence in the Polish language—*Nowy Kurier Warszawski, Glos Lubelski, Goniec Czestochowski, Kurier Krakowski, Glos Radomski,* etc.—whose task it has been to spread the venom of anti-Semitism among the Polish population. Since those papers are the sole source of news, they are read in mass numbers despite the fact that the Polish Underground ordered a boycott of this reptilian press. Not a day passed without some article, paragraph or notice appearing in this press directed against the Jews. This press very closely resembles the prewar anti-Semitic press, drawing liberally on the prewar arsenal of Polish Fascism, from the past of Poland, etc. During the "resettle-

---

8 See: footnote 2 in chapter 2.

ment actions" the anti-Semitic hue and cry in this "Judas" press was stepped up in order to paralyse any humane impulses on the part of the Polish population. When articles are in short supply, so-called "readers' views" are fabricated, the "readers" declaring themselves against the Jews. The main subject of all these articles is the old hobby horse of the anti-Semitic writers, "Judeo-Communism". A frequent guest in the columns of this press is Father Trzeciak,[9] an *habitué* of anti-Semitic congresses (lots of quotations from his writings and articles). Katyn was excellent fodder for this reptilian press, despite the fact that even the biggest fool of an anti-Semite could find hundreds of Jewish names in these lists of the victims.

Since there are no more Jews left in Poland, the "Judas" press publishes various anti-Semitic articles almost daily—news items and information about the life of Jews in France, Italy, Greece, Hungary, Rumania, etc. News is published with great satisfaction of the Italian Government's introducing Star-of-David arm bands for Italian Jews (*Nowy Kurier Warszawski,* October 1943), of the compulsory registration of Jews in Greece and Yugoslavia introduced by the new German occupying authorities. *Nowy Kurier Warszawski* writes a great deal about the anti-Semitism of the French. Though this press comes to curse, it sometimes stays to bless. Thus we read in the *Nowy Kurier Warszawski* (19th September 1943) in an article on, "The Star of Zion in the Paris Ghetto": "Furthermore, those non-Jews who used to wear Stars of Zion as a sign of sympathy with the Jews have given up these absurd demonstrations." In another article (27th September of this year), the writers draw on the history of France in order to declare to the world, "The French were, and continue to be, anti-Semites", which of course contradicts the previous article (of 19th September).

After the press, comes the radio (the so-called "barker") constant-

---

9 Stanislaw Trzeciak (1873–1944), Rector of the St. Hyacinthus Church in Warsaw, active member of the extreme anti-Semitic Fascist Party, *Oboz Narodowo-Radykalny.* Notorious for his anti-Semitic activities in Poland in the period between the two World Wars. At the beginning of the German occupation, he was one of the founders of the pro-Nazi *Narodowa Organizacja Radykalna.*

ly urging persecution of the Jews, expatiating on their harmfulness to the whole of Europe as war mongers, parasites, etc. Anti-Jewish exhibitions are arranged with the aim of strengthening hatred of the Jews. In September of this year, an exhibition was arranged in the Cracow *Sukiennice* [Cloth Halls]; it was called "The Jewish Plague" (*Weltpest*), and its aim was the revelation that the Jews are the enemy of humanity (*Weltfeind*). This exhibition shows eminent personages of the ancient world, the Middle Ages and modern times declaring themselves against the Jews. Its intention is stated to be "to reflect the destructive forces of Jewry" (*"Die zersetzenden Kräfte des Judentums werden in ihren mannigfaltigsten Erscheinungen widergespiegelt"—Warschauer Zeitung*, 27th September this year).

Besides radio, press, exhibitions, etc., the German propaganda machine almost daily issues coloured posters and proclamations directed against the Jews. On the coloured anti-typhoid posters, there appeared a bearded *Stürmer*-type Jew with an enormous louse, and on one of the posters was an enormous caption: "Jews, lice, typhoid". Posters were put up in the trams and in the streets depicting a Jew making mince-meat with a rat in it, pouring water into the milk, putting a louse into pastry or kneading dough with dirty feet. On another poster appeared the caption, "The Jews rule the world". This poster showed a devil grasping the whole world in his claws. The slogan on yet another poster was, "Whoever helps a Jew, helps Satan". A recent propaganda poster depicts Litwinow[10] and other Jews driving exhausted Soviet soldiers and resigned workers to war.

In a colourful pamphlet entitled, "What is this war for?" the author quotes various fabricated utterances supposedly made by Jews in favour of war, beginning from 1884. "The Protocols of

---

[10] Maxim Litwinow (1876–1951). His real name was Meir Wallach. A Jew who became an eminent Soviet statesman. He was "People's Commissar"—the equivalent of Minister of Foreign Affairs—of the U.S.S.R. from 1930 to 1939. He was removed from this post on the signing of the Molotov-Ribbentrop pact, but returned to the diplomatic service on the outbreak of the German-Russian war in 1941. He was Soviet Ambassador in the United States from 1941 to 1943.

the Elders of Zion" are not omitted, of course, and even Ilya Ehrenburg's fantasy, "The D. G. Trust liquidates Europe", is cited as evidence of the bloodthirst instincts of world Jewry. The author sums up as follows: "Jewry has no other aim but to murder the nations of Europe and establish its final rule over the world." Were it not for the Jews, this war would not have come about— is the final conclusion of this manifesto, the full text of which is quoted in the appendix.[11]

While the German press in the Polish language systematically incites the population against the Jews, only to a very slight extent is it counteracted by the Underground press. The press of the labour movements (W.R.N., *Gwardia Ludowa* and others)[12] are doing their duty as they did before the war. They give information constantly on the persecution of the Jews in the different cities, they print special articles discussing the dangers of anti-Semitism, they describe in detail the heroic struggle of the Warsaw Ghetto, etc. The Government press[13] devotes very little space to the Jewish problem. Many of the most important events affecting the Jews are reported by this press only after long delays, whereas the Fascist-O.N.R. press[14]

---

11 This appendix is missing. It has not been found in the Ringelblum Archives.

12 The author is referring to the underground papers published by both fractions of the Polish Socialist Party, which were active during the Nazi occupation — *Wolność-Równość-Niepodległość* and *Polscy Socjalisci,* as well as by the Communist Party, *Polska Partia Robotnicza.* The main organs of the Polish Socialists were: *WRN, Gwardia Ludowa, Robotnik, Wolność, Żołnierz Rewolucjonisca, Robotnik w Walce, Wieś i Miasto, Chłopska Sprawa, Lewa Marsz.* The main organs of the *Polska Partia Robotnicza* were: *Trybuna Wolnosci, Glos Warszawy, Gwardzista, Przeglad Tygodnia, Glos Warszawy, Przelom, Walka Mlodych, Trybuna Chlopska.*

13 The author is referring to the organ of the Central Staff of the Home Army, *Biuletyn Informacyjny,* as well as the papers, *Rzeczpospolita Polska* and *Dzien Warszawy,* which were the organs of the Delegate for the Homeland of the Polish Government-in-Exile.

14 The following were the principal papers of the Fascist *Oboz-Narodowo-Radykalny,* which waged a systematic anti-Jewish campaign in their pages during the years of Nazi occupation: *Szaniec, Placówka, Praca i Walka, Załoga, Walka, Głos Polski, Nowa Polska.*

devotes a large amount of space to Jewish matters and to constant incitement against the Jews, just like the reptilian press, and propounds a programme for future Poland where there will be no room for Jews as citizens with equal rights. And it has to be admitted with shame and sorrow that the "Judas" press, supported by the anti-Semitic illegal press, evokes a lively response from the population. Under the influence of the anti-Semitic hue and cry in the *Nowy Kurier Warszawski* in April and May of this year, the campaign that the Germans initiated against the Jews on the "Aryan" side evoked a response from large masses of the population. Jews employed in the work-posts, when they crossed over to their work on the Aryan side, knew in advance after an anti-Jewish article in the press or even a "reader's comment" that there awaited them an exasperating day of provocations, stone-throwing by the mob, etc.

The awakening from the anti-Semitic psychosis unfortunately encompassed only a very small proportion of the pre-war anti-Semites, mainly people from the educated class. Thus for example at the end of 1939, Advocate Nowodworski,[15] Dean of the Advocates'

---

[15] Leon Nowodworski (1889–1941), Dean of the Warsaw Bar Council from 1936 on. He was one of the pioneers of the Polish Underground movement during the Nazi occupation: one of the organizers and a member of the *Rada Glowna Polityczna*, the main political body in the first Polish clandestine organization *Sluzba Zwyciestwu Polski*. From mid-1940 on he was Director of the Justice Department in the Office of the Homeland Delegate of the Polish Government-in-Exile. He came from a Frankish family that had produced many jurists. He looked like a Jew, but his views were those of "Endek"—the National-Democrats. He was one of the authors of the proposal to limit the number of Jewish barristers admitted to the Bar, but when the German authorities approached him to expel the Jews from the Bar, he answered them fearlessly, "If there is a need to, we shall do it ourselves in free Poland. But when it's a proposal coming from you, the occupiers, not only shall we not accept it but we shall fight against the expulsion of our Jewish colleagues from our Bar." This answer was one of the reasons why he was removed from his position. (Hartglas, The First Months of the Nazi Conquest, *loc. cit.*, pp. 500–501.) *Cf.* Ringelblum's entry for 2 May 1940. "Nowodworski and other anti-Semitic barristers are sitting in prison because of the Jews. They were summoned and

Council, refused to dismiss Jews from the Bar, because the order to do so came from the occupying authorities. Nowodworski, a pre-war anti-Semite and a defender of the "Aryan paragraph" in the legal profession before the war, now understood the fatal conse-quences of anti-Semitism for Poland. He said that the solution of the Jewish problem must wait till after the war. The same phenom-enon is to be observed among a certain sector of the anti-Semites of the educated class, who view with disgust the criminal practices of the native anti-Semites and recoil from the barbarity of the Huns of our time.

The middle-class population *in toto* has continued to adhere to the ideology of anti-Semitism and rejoices at the Nazi solution to the Jewish problem in Poland. Thanks to Hitler, the Polish middle class, in debt to Jewish bankers, tradesmen, etc., immediately got rid of its unwanted creditors. Thanks to the mass slaughter of the Jews, the programme of *numerus nullus* in industry, handicrafts, trade and economic life in general has been carried out to the full. Thanks to the liquidation of the Jews, the Christian "men of straw" (*Strohmänner*) suddenly became the owners of numerous industrial and commercial enterprises, and partners freed themselves of their Jewish co-partners. Thanks to the liquidation of Polish Jews, Aryan depositaries became the owners of belongings and goods left with them by the Jews. Thanks to all this, tens and hundreds of thousands of Aryans were able to obtain objects of everyday use dirt cheap: clothing, machines, tools, etc. Thanks to all this, the Polish middle class was able to obtain market stalls without a struggle and take

---

questioned on their attitude towards the Jews, and they answered that the question was not on the cards at the moment." Ringelblum, Vol. I, p. 125.)

The continued efforts by the Germans to expel the Jews from the Bar ended tragically for many lawyers. As a result of an enquiry carried out by Dr. Gollert, Head of the Justice Department in the Warsaw Governor's Office, 80 Polish barristers were arrested on 10, 11 and 12 July 1940 and imprisoned in the Pawiak prison because they said that Jews should be admitted to the Bar. These arrested barristers were sent to Auschwitz in September 1940.

(Kazimierz Iranek, Osmecki, *Kto ratuje jedno życie ... Polacy i Żydzi 1939–1945*, London, 1968, pp. 119–120.)

over petty trading after the Jews were gone. Thanks to Treblinka, Jewish fortunes worth millions, which had been amassed over the centuries, passed effortlessly into Aryan hands.[16] For the anti-Semitic middle class to hide Jews or rescue Jewish children was out of the question, since it was in their interest to get rid of the Jews. The O.N.R. announced everywhere that hiding Jews was anti-national and threatened the interests of future Poland. The attitude of the great majority of the Polish middle class could not but be influenced by propaganda like this. The most symptomatic indication of the attitude of a large part of the Polish population was given not only by the conversations about the April "action" which have been reported in their context, but also by the sad fact that the slogan, "Catch that Jew!" was used by the occupiers when trying to capture Polish patriots in the streets.

While the younger generation of *Endecja* openly approved of Hitler's programme regarding Poland's Jews, the older generation

---

[16] This problem has not yet been dealt with by the historians of the Jewish Holocaust. The question is touched on in passing by Prof. Czeslaw Madajczyk, historian of the Nazi occupation period in Poland. He writes: "Jewish factories were partly liquidated, as technically backward, and partly handed over to Germans. A few Jewish shops, workshops and farms were given to Poles, mainly persons who had been forced to leave the Wartheland. Some blocks of flats were handed over to Polish custodians."
(Cz. Madajczyk, Polityka III *Rzeszy w okupawanej Polsce,* Vol. I, p. 530.)
In another place, he states: "Sometimes the Poles who had profited materially from the deportation of the Jews—there were not many of them—displayed hostility [towards the Jews]. Some merchants were given Jewish shops that had been closed down. Polish commissions were appointed to value the goods that had been confiscated in Jewish shops, and not all the members of these commissions proved honest. On the other hand, there were Poles who helped Jews to hide their property; they kept the belongings entrusted to them safe, notwithstanding the severe penalties they were threatened with by the occupiers for doing so. Blackmailers indulged in criminal activities in order to live comfortably at the expense of the Jews whom they hunted down and robbed. They sometimes proceeded in the same way with Poles."
(*Op. cit.,* p. 171.)

concealed its satisfaction and instead made some show of feeling of compassion. Yet the Jews needed sympathy but help in the form of asylum. In this respect, however, unanimity prevailed among both the older and the younger generations, both the radical and the moderate wings of Polish Fascism. Even the most decent individuals who befriended Jews did not give them asylum. They had not made enormous fortunes during the war just to get themselves into trouble with the occupying forces, who threatened them with severe punishment for hiding Jews.

A different attitude towards this problem was displayed by the Polish workers and intellectuals. The latter, who were actively involved in underground work, helped the Jews even while they professed an anti-Semitic ideology. Self-sacrificing people who endangered themselves daily for a great cause understood that to hide Jews was not only a humane duty but also a civic one. It means doing something practical to cross the Germans, who exterminate all the Jews. Thus most of the Jews hiding on the Aryan side are living in the homes of people who are involved in underground activity. Another very important factor uniting the Polish educated class with the Jews is their common suffering at the hands of a common oppressor. There is not one family of the Polish educated class that has not lost someone in Auschwitz, Dachau, Majdanek or Oranienburg. Suffering purifies, suffering ennobles, suffering draws people closer together. We know families of the Polish intelligentsia who had not attached importance to the cause of hiding Jews in their homes, but who changed their attitude after going through the experience of suffering, of receiving news of the loss of someone dear to them in Auschwitz or some other Nazi place of torment.

Polish workers had long before the war grasped the class aspect of anti-Semitism, the power-tool of the native bourgeoisie, and during the war they redoubled their efforts to fight anti-Semitism. Rescuing Jews was in line with their ideological position, although even their attitudes were not free of the germs of anti-Semitism, in this land where mothers threaten their naughty children with an ogre in the form of a Jew ("If you don't behave, a Jew will come and put you in his sack"). There were only limited possibilities for workers to hide Jews in their homes. Overcrowding in the flats was the greatest obstacle to taking in Jews. In spite of this, many Jews did find shelter in the flats of workers. In many cases Polish railwaymen helped Jews who were being deported: they opened the wagons heading for Treblinka, supplied tools to open the wagons, helped the Jews who jumped out of the wagons. One track-walker rescued a Jew, an engineer from Czestochowa, who had escaped from a train on its way to Treblinka. The engineer had broken his arm in escaping, and the track-walker got him medical help, gave him some clothes and sent him on his way to Warsaw. An interesting thing happened to a Jewish lawyer who had been employed in the Toebbens workshop and who escaped on his way to Treblinka in January 1943. He jumped out of a railway carriage where, despite the fact that it was January, the temperature was so high from overcrowding (150 people instead of the 40 to 60 who would normally find room in a carriage like this) that people had stripped to the skin. Two people before him had tried to escape but had been killed by the Ukrainians; he was fortunate enough to escape the bullet of the Ukrainian escort but he broke his leg when he jumped from the train. He crawled with difficulty to the nearest track-walker's hut, where he said that he had got drunk in the train and had fallen out of the carriage. The track-walker called in a medical orderly, but also notified the Polish Police station. Luckily, the orderly proved to have been a client of the lawyer's and he promised to help him. They arranged that if the lawyer was unable to convince the policeman of his Aryan origin, he would show him the "self-evident proof", that is he would let down his trousers and the medical orderly would of course interfere to prevent it at the last moment. The plan succeeded. When the policeman did not believe in the lawyer's Aryan origin in spite of all his eloquent explanations, the lawyer asked the women to leave the room so that he could display the "self-evident proof" of his Aryanism. Thanks to the intervention of the medical orderly, the trousers' let-down was abandoned at the last moment and our lawyer was saved.

Unfortunately we also know of other cases. O.N.R. railway workers would capture the Jews who jumped from the death wagons and hand them over to the Germans after robbing them of whatever they possessed. The German authorities, aware of the fact that many Jews escaped from the wagons[17] regardless of the bullets of the Ukrainian escort, offered rewards (1,000 zloty per person) for the capture of fugitive Jews. At the same time the death penalty awaited those who helped or hid the Jews. As a result of these measures, the Warsaw-Treblinka route became a veritable *via dolorosa* strewn with the corpses of hundreds of Jewish victims who preferred

---

[17] Escaping from the trains was extremely difficult. The risks were great and hopes of success very slight. Nevertheless attempts became very common. This is confirmed by numerous reports from Poles living near the railways on the way to the death camps. For example, the Pole, Stanislaw Szefler, who lived in Malkinia, a station on the way to Treblinka, wrote in his memoirs: "Prisoners tried to escape from the endless transports *en route* to Treblinka. Their failure was marked by the corpses lying alongside the rails and round our settlement." (Stanislaw Szefler, *Okupacyjne drogi,* Warsaw, 1967, pp. 207–208.) The Polish diarist, Dr. Zygmunt Klukowski, made similar observations in his entry for 28 May 1943: "For a long time we heard nothing about the Jews in our part of the country. But now long trains with Jews are again passing through Szczebrzeszyn station in the direction of Chelm. The Jews are transported completely naked, in broken-down luggage vans. They jump from the moving trains on the way and the gendarmes fire at them and in most cases kill or wound them. Everywhere there are naked Jewish corpses along the rails. Some days ago a young Jewess with a 7-year-old child jumped from the train, right near the "Alfa" factory. The gendarmes killed her on the spot with rifle fire, but the child was only hurt by the fall. The "Alfa" workers fed him but informed the Szczebrzeszyn Gendarmerie-post. The gendarmes arrived a few hours later and shot the child before the workers' eyes, telling them to bury the body right there." (Zygmunt Klukowski, *Dziennik z lat okupacji Zamojszczyzny,* Lublin, 1959, p. 336.) In the conditions that prevailed in Poland from 1942 to 1944, it was by no means enough to jump successfully from the train and escape the gendarmes' bullets in order to be safe. There were still further and in most cases insuperable difficulties. For most of the fugitives the only way out proved to be a return to what was left of some Ghetto or to a camp, where death awaited them at the next deportation. Mieczyslaw Pokorny writes about this in his diary: "The Jews deported in January 1943 [i.e. after the "action" of 21 January 1943 in the Warsaw Ghetto — Editors] were mindful of the horrifying reports of what the Germans did in the previous deportations, and many of them decided

death from a Ukrainian bullet to suffocation in the "death factory" of Treblinka. Along this blood-stained route, the track-walkers and the anti-Semitic population in general have many Jewish victims on their conscience. We know of a case of a woman, an employee of Toebbens of Prosta Street, who jumped out of a train headed for Treblinka and had dogs set on her by a track-walker when she failed to stop at his challenge. His dog tore her dress, but she managed to get away, and she reached the Ghetto in one shoe and torn dress. She was caught a second time and sent to Treblinka, and she escaped this time too from the train, but this time she came across honest people who helped her to reach Warsaw.

Relations were good between the Polish railwaymen and the Jewish work-post men employed at the so-called *Ostbahn*. Two weeks before the April "action", all the Jewish workers employed there were assembled and put on a train for an "unknown destination" (Treblinka or Lublin). The Polish railwaymen, who had become friendly with the Jews employed in the work-posts, induced people with a little influence to intervene with the authorities and claim that removal of the Jewish workers would make normal functioning of the railway on this route more difficult. In the meantime the departure of the transport had been held up for two days by the non-delivery of a locomotive. The authorities refused, and

to escape from the trains. Some of them got out through the small windows, and some escaped through holes made in the wooden sides of the carriages with sharp tools. Anyone who was fortunate enough to escape being shot by the escort guards when he jumped from the moving train tried to return to Warsaw.

The fugitives judged from the direction of the trains that they were going to Treblinka. The road back to Warsaw was a real Golgotha. Bleeding from injuries received in jumping from the train, the fugitives moved mainly at night, going in the forests without food and water, hiding from anyone who could give them away to the Germans. Not infrequently these poor wretches were victimized by blackmailers on their way and were forced to buy themselves off with their last piece of money or clothing."

Further on in his diary, Pokorny describes how fugitives survived harrowing experiences on the Aryan side and got back to the Ghetto. (Mieczyslaw Pokorny's diary in Yad Vashem Archives, File 0–25/105, p. 120.)

the transport was sent on its way, but some of the Jewish workers managed to escape with the help of the Polish railwaymen. Railwaymen helped Jews travel from one town to another at a time when Jews were strictly prohibited from travelling on the trains. With the help of the railwaymen, thousands of Jews got back from the territories that had previously been under the Soviets and were now occupied by the Germans. The Polish railwaymen acted as liaison between the different towns, giving information about the situation in other towns, about "resettlement actions", about anti-Jewish measures, etc. Warsaw is indebted to the railwaymen for the first news of the fate of the Jews deported to Treblinka. We know of cases where Polish railwaymen enlightened foreign Jews who were travelling to Treblinka in passenger carriages with their luggage, telling them that this was no agricultural colony but a Nazi place of slaughter. The railwaymen bring members of Jewish families scattered in different labour camps into contact with each other, carrying letters, parcels, money, etc.

Jewish children who were fixed up with workers' families were treated like their own children. I was told about a Polish workers' family which took in two Jewish children on the recommendation of a workers' organization. The son of the host family, an active member of the P.P.S., had entered the Ghetto at the risk of his life and personally transported the children to the Aryan side. In order to dispel the children's fear of going over the wall, he first did it twice himself to prove to them that it was safe. These Jewish children became familiar with the workers' surroundings and grew adjusted to them as if they had been born there. They persuaded their hosts to ask their mother to come to the flat to be together with them. It must be stressed that in general Jews dream of getting into the homes of workers, because this guarantees them against blackmail or exploitation by their hosts.

The attitude of the rural population towards the Jews depended on the atmosphere regarding Jews that had prevailed in the given region before the war. Where a Jew-devouring anti-Semitism had prevailed, the attitude of the rural population towards Jews fleeing from the Nazi knife was not a helpful one. Jewish fugitives from the Ghetto would be captured by the rural population in these places and handed over to the Germans for money. The village guards, whose job it was to fight the partisans, also played a regrettable role here, specializing in hunting Jewish fugitives after "resettlement actions". The Jews' only defence against capture by the peasants lies with the armed Jewish groups which are fighting for their right to survive. I have heard detailed reports about such groups in the province of Lublin.[18] They consist of a score or two of members, under the leadership of former Polish Army soldiers who escaped from German captivity in Lublin or of former Russian prisoners. Armed with "longs" (rifles) and "shorts" (pistols) and sometimes with machine guns, they live by making so-called "jumps" —that is, raids on cattle quotas, etc. Some groups buy food from the peasants. In the province of Lublin, hundreds of Jews who have escaped various "actions" are living under the cloak of such groups and under their protection.[19] A peasant who handed a Jew over to

---

[18] This refers to two Jewish partisan units commanded by Samuel Jegier and Samuel Gruber. Both units operated to the north of Lublin in the neighbourhood of Lubartow and Pulawy. They consisted partly of Jewish soldiers from the Polish Army, who had been captured by the Germans and had escaped from the POW camp in Lublin, and partly of refugees from the nearby Ghettos of Markuszow, Michow, Kurow and Kamionka. Altogether there were about 150 Jewish partisans in these two units and about 110 of them fell in the fighting. Several other Jewish partisan units besides these two fought in the Lublin region. The largest were those led by Jechiel Grynszpan in the Parczew forests, Edward Forst in the Solska forest, Abraham Braun in the Janow forest, Heniek Cymerman to the south of Lublin, and Mendel Heller in the neighbourhood of Tomaszow Lubelski. In time certain Jewish partisan units joined the Polish Gwardia Ludowa and later the Armia Ludowa. Some Jews who had escaped from the Ghettos joined up with Red Army soldiers who had escaped from German POW camps to form common Jewish-Russian or Jewish-Russian-Polish partisan units.

[19] Under the protection of Jewish partisans, family camps came into being in the forests in the Lublin region. Jews hid in these camps after escaping from the Ghettos during the liquidation. The largest of these camps were in the forests around Parczew, in the Solska Forest and in the Lipskie Forests. In the smaller forests in the Lublin region, as well as in other parts of Poland where conditions were not propitious for family camps, numbers of Jewish fugitives hid in solitary

the Germans would be punished with a "red cock", that is, by having his hut burnt down. Jewish armed groups like these operate in other regions of the country as well.[20] Individual Jewish families hide in hide-outs contrived by the peasants in barns, cellars, etc. The German authorities combat the hiding of Jews by peasants with

hide-outs dispersed throughout the forest, getting help and protection from Jewish partisans. In certain areas, some of the Jewish fugitives were given shelter by Polish peasants in the villages, in return for rewards from the Jewish partisans, mostly in the form of goods taken as spoils. In these cases, the partisans also protected the Jews in hiding from blackmailers and informers who might try to hand them over to the Germans.

20 Among the larger Jewish partisan units operating in other parts of Poland, outside the Lublin region, the following should be mentioned:
(a) In the Kielce region:
  the "Zygmunt" Detachment (commander: Zalman Fajnsztat), in the environs of Pinczow;
  the "Lwy" Detachment (commander: Julian Ajzenman), in the environs of Opoczno;
  the detachment of Jechiel Brawerman, in the environs of Cmielow;
  the detachment of Ber Akerman, in the environs of Szydlowiec.
(b) In the Cracow region:
  the detachment of Liebeskind, in the environs of Cracow and Bochnia;
  the detachment of Lejb Birman, in the environs of Rzeszow;
  the detachment of Abraham Amsterdam, in the environs of Radomysl Wielki.
(c) In the Mazovian region:
  the groups of Szmuel Oszlak, Antek Zelechowicz, Hersz Rochman and Josef Mlynowski, in the environs of Zelechow;
  the "Anielewicz"-Detachment, in the environs of Wyszkow;
(d) In the Podlasie region:
  the groups of Yzhak Kleinman and the Paczek brothers, in the environs of Radzyn;
  the detachment of Baruch Libesfrajnd, in the environs of Kock.
(e) In the Bialystok region:
  the "'Forwards" Detachment.
A much stronger Jewish partisan movement existed in the former Polish northeastern territories, incorporated in the Soviet Union (Polesie, Nowogrodek and Vilna). Very scanty information reached Ringelblum, however, about partisan activities in these territories.

very severe decrees, which threaten the "red cock" for those who disobey and offer rewards for catching Jews. This campaign against the Jews is linked with the German authorities' struggle against the partisans and generally against strangers' coming to the villages. Fewer and fewer Jews find shelter in the villages. The situation was better in the years 1940 and 1941, when the peasants kept young Jews on as farmhands and treated them humanely.[21] We also know of cases where help was extended to Jewish prisoners in the camps by the local rural population. Nowadays a peasant is afraid to give asylum to Jewish fugitives from the camps or the Ghettos. For fear of denunciation, a peasant will help a fugitive but is afraid to hide him in his home. The peasant is sometimes so afraid that he will give the fugitive food but not in his home nor even in the yard but at the edge of the forest. Despite all these rigours and difficulties, there are still quite a number of Jewish families hiding in huts in the villages or in specially contrived hide-outs.

The Polish clergy has reacted almost with indifference to the tragedy of the slaughter of the whole Jewish people.[22] Before the

---

[21] As a result of the Nazi terror, a sharp change often took place in the attitude of the peasants towards the Jews. Peasants who had formerly helped Jews often began to take an active part in anti-Jewish activity for fear of Nazi repressive measures. The anti-Jewish attitude of part of the Home Army also exercised a considerable influence. Typical instances of this are to be found in the report of Margaret Draenger, who has this to say on the situation in the Cracow district. "The Polish peasants were hiding Jews in all the forested territories in the environs of Bochnia, Niepolomice, Wisnicz Nowy, Lomma and other places. These peasants had had very close relations with the Jews before the outbreak of the second World War. The Jews were their neighbours, they were well acquainted with them and often did business with them. Therefore when the Nazis occupied the country, the peasants often hid the Jews without reward, at the risk of their lives. But as time passed and the war dragged on, many of them changed their attitude. They gave away Jewish hiding places, sold Jews for a kilo of sugar, joined the Home Army and more than once murdered Jews for their money."
(Report of Margaret Draenger, Yad Vashem Archives, File 0–3/1686.)
[22] The attitude of the Catholic Church in Poland had an important effect on the fate of the Jewish fugitives from the Ghettos and camps. Next

war, the Polish clergy was distinguished for its remarkably anti-Semitic attitude. When year after year the blood of Jewish students was shed in institutions of higher learning, when anti-Semitic savages rioted in Przytyk, Brzesc-on-the-Bug and other Polish towns, the clergy either kept silent or approved these deeds of the anti-Semites. The Rabbis, not having an accurate appreciation of the situation, approached Cardinal Kakowski[23] and asked him to take action against the wave of pogroms and give the Jewish population his protection. This high dignitary of the Catholic Church received the delegation in an abusive manner, and instead of giving an answer told the Rabbis to educate Jewish youth properly. According to the

---

to the Government Delegate's Office, the Church was the institution that wielded the greatest authority in Poland at the time of the Nazi occupation: it was the spiritual ruler of the people of Poland. But as yet little is known of the attitude and the actions of the Church hierarchy in this field. The ecclesiastical archives in Poland are still closed and thus it is impossible to analyze this problem. It is a fact that part of the Polish clergy did help Jews who had escaped from Ghettos and camps. It is difficult to say to what extent this behaviour was the result of a particular cleric's personal initiative and to what extent—if at all—there was guidance at a given level in the ecclesiastical hierarchy. On the other hand there is in the archives a great deal of first-hand evidence of anti-Jewish sermons preached by priests and the anti-Semitic activities of some of them under the Nazi occupation. A characteristic report is that of a Jewish partisan, Joseph Cynowiec, who happened to hear a pronouncement by a priest at a meeting of members of the Home Army in Ostrow Lubelski. Cynowiec writes:

"In my hiding-place I heard everything that was said. One of those present asked a priest, who was also taking part as a member of the Home Army, what one's attitude ought to be regarding the Nazi treatment of the Jews. The priest's answer was that as a cleric he had to say that human beings were involved here and that it was wrong to say that human beings were involved here and that it was wrong to exterminate them mercilessly; but on the other hand, from the political point of view, the Germans were doing a good job."
(Joseph Cynowiec's report, Yad Vashem Archives, File 0–3/3009.)

[23] Aleksander Kakowski (1862–1938), a Polish politician and Catholic prelate. During the first World War he was one of three members of the Regency Council for the Kingdom of Poland set up by the German occupying authorities. He was Cardinal of Poland from 1918 on. Politically he was connected with the *Oboz Zjednoczenia Narodowego.*

Cardinal, Jewish youth propagates Communism in the country and infects Polish youth. Before the war, the clergy in Western Europe fought racialism and anti-Semitism as being opposed to Christian teaching, which does not recognize higher and lower races. A significant part of the Catholic clergy in the West also fought Fascism on the grounds that it was against the principles of the Christian religion. The Polish clergy at that time remained neutral on the problem of anti-Semitism, and to some extent this neutrality constituted approval of the steadily rising tide of pogroms and excesses. For example, the Catholic clergy tolerated the capers of a priest like Trzeciak, who collaborated with Nazi anti-Jewish organizations. One could hardly expect any considerable help from a clergy like this in the present war, if it gave no help at a time when it was still possible to do so. It was in line with the Dutch Church prewar attitude towards the Jews that they should behave with the heroism we have heard about in their defence of the Jews during the present war. At the risk of being sent to concentration camps, this clergy had the courage to deliver daring sermons against the introduction of the Nuremberg laws into Holland. A similar stand was taken by the French Catholic clergy. To illustrate French public feeling, the magazine "Jewish Records" (for 1940) reports the following incident, which took place in a town in the south of France. A priest there read from the Book of Esther, and then against this background delivered a sermon which concluded: "We have read the Book of Esther and seen the sad end of Haman, the oppressor of the Jews. The same thing will happen to the modern Hamans who are persecuting the Jews—the same sad end awaits them." In Belgium, money was collected during church services for the benefit of Jews, for the benefit of Jewish children. The attitude of the clergy towards the Jews was, besides, the consequence of the general feeling among the public in favour of the Jews, which was demonstrated when large parts of the French, Belgian and Dutch populations put on Jewish arm bands as a sign of protest and solidarity with the oppressed Jews. In Poland, this West European attitude is found only in exceptional cases among the Polish clergy. One such exception was the province of Vilna, where the Catholic clergy granted shelter to a certain number of young Jews escaping from the notorious Ponary,[24] where tens of thousands of Vilna Jews were shot.

One of these rare acts of nobility occurred in P.K.,[25] where the local parish priest saved Jews imprisoned in a nearby camp in very difficult conditions. When he found out that the *Lagerschutz* starved the prisoners in the camp and shot them for the slightest offence, the priest delivered a number of sermons to his congregation and called on them to aid their fellow-men. As a result of these sermons, the peasants helped the prisoners in the camp considerably. They threw bread over the wires to feed them, etc. Some of the youngest Jewish children were taken into Church orphanages and convents. In the town of Cz[estochowa] some Jewish children under the age of six were placed in the convent; the age restriction shows explicitly that this is a case where the intention was to save "souls" and not to save Jewish children.

---

24 Ponary: a site of mass executions, situated 8 kilometres from Vilna. Between July 1941 and July 1944, the Nazis shot about 100,000 Jews from Vilna and the environs at Ponary, as well as several thousand Soviet prisoners-of-war. At the end of 1943, the Nazis began to destroy the evidence of these murders by levelling the terrain of the mass graves. They forced a group of Jews to do this work, intending to kill them afterwards. Although the Jews were under strict guard, they managed to dig a tunnel 30 metres long; it took them three months to do this heavy work without any tools. The escape took place on the night of 15 April 1944. Most of the fugitives were killed by the Germans who pursued them; only thirteen succeeded in reaching the Jewish partisans in the Rudniki forest.

25 The author is referring to a priest in the village of Kampinos who saved the lives of many Jews who were imprisoned in a labour camp in this village and who suffered torments. This brave priest preached fiery sermons every Sunday on behalf of the Jewish prisoners, many of whom died in the camp. This enlightened man warmly urged the Christian population to stand by the Jews. He sharply attacked the Christians in charge of the camp and in heated terms denounced the wicked camp guards who beat and murdered the hapless Jews. He called them anti-Christ. And the peasants began to bring their produce to where the prisoners worked. "Scores of us have this noble priest to thank for it that we remained alive."
(Testimony of a prisoner from the Kampinos labour camp in: Huberband, *op. cit.*, pp. 111, 206, 230.)

The same applies to converts.[26] In the Ghetto, the Catholic clergy took care of them. They were given the use of the blocks of flats belonging to the parish on Leszno Street and in the Grzybow district. In the Church of All Saints in Grzybow and in the Church of the Holy Virgin Mary on Leszno Street, Catholic services were held with the participation of convert church attendants and a converts' choir. Real believers could be seen in these churches. Women zealots lay prostrate on the floor, praying fervently. The dead were carried off in a church hearse to the Catholic or Evangelical cemetery. The family was allowed to follow the procession only as far as the Ghetto exit gates. The Catholic association, *Caritas*, took very good care of the converts, opened kitchens for them and saw to it that they received a produce ration from the *Judenrat* Supplies Office. Both the Chairman of the *Judenrat*, engineer Adam Czerniakow, and the Director of the Supplies Office, Abraham Gepner, showed favouritism to the converts, giving them large food rations, admitting them to high positions in the [Jewish] Community institutions, etc. The *Judenrat* management overdid things in its concern for the converts, creating various privileges for them. The point was reached where in order to be accepted for some departments of the Jewish Community administration, it was necessary to produce a certificate of baptism. As regards food provisions, the Supplies Office favoured the converts to such an extent that it was giving them large rations at a time when there was no food for the children in the orphanages. The preference shown to converts was justified in some circles by the argument that the *Judenrat*, functioning as the municipal authority for the Ghetto, had to take care of all inhabitants of the Jewish district, and any shortcoming in this field might be regarded as an act of revenge, of war on Polishdom.

The clergy took steps to secure numerous privileges for the con-

---

[26] At the beginning of the German occupation, the number of converts to Christianity increased. In Warsaw, over 200 Jews converted between November 1939 and March 1940, mainly members of the liberal professions who hoped in vain that anti-Semitic laws and restrictions would not apply to them.

verts. The R.G.O.[27] interceded with the authorities to have the converts left on the Aryan side in a separate area. But when the "resettlement action" commenced, the S.S. took no notice of the cross which protected the blocks where the converts lived. All the inhabitants of the parish blocks were taken to the *Umschlagplatz* and from there to Treblinka. A certain number of the converts managed to save themselves on the Aryan side thanks to their Christian relations. Some converts who had lived on the "other" side for many years and who had Polish relatives helped their Jewish relatives to settle outside the Ghetto. I know a woman convert who had severed her connections with her Jewish family for many years or, to put it more accurately, had been repudiated by her Jewish family. And when the "resettlement action" began, this convert was first to make a sign and help her Jewish family; our convert's anti-Semitic family also agreed to extend this help. To sum up what we have said about converts, it should be stressed that the help extended to them was fine work on the part of the Polish clergy, but it was not done to help Jews.

At this stage we should mention the attitude of government to the Jewish problem in Poland. We do not have at hand any government declarations on this problem. It is known that the Sikorski Government has issued several statements on the Jewish problem in Poland, supporting equal rights for the Jews, who are to be compensated in future Poland for their suffering during the war.[28] We

---

[27] *Rada Glowna Opiekuncza* (R.G.O.)—a social welfare organization for Poles only, set up on the territory of the General-Government during World War II. Head of the R.G.O. till 1943 was Adam Ronikier, and after that Konstanty Tchorznicki, R.G.O. maintained contact with the Jewish mutual aid society (*J.U.S.*). During the first years of the occupation, the directorates of the Polish R.G.O., the Jewish *J.U.S.* and the Ukrainian R.G.O. constituted a joint body known as, *Naczelua Rada Opiekuncza dla Okupowanych Ziem Polskich.*

[28] The first official statement on the Jewish question was a Resolution passed by the Polish National Council in London on 27 November 1942, that is about a year after the first mass extermination camp of Jews in Chelmno had begun operating continuously and six months after the Germans had started on the large-scale deportations that

have already stressed elsewhere that the attitude of the government towards the problem of defending the Ghettos was far from helpful. We shall leave aside the question whether defence of the Ghettos should have been left to the Jews, or if help should have come from the Aryan side. In any case, moral support and help in the form of weapons was possible. Moral support was afforded only in April 1943, when the appeal of the Government Plenipotentiary to hide Jews was published. During the fifty days of the "action" in July, August and September 1942, and again during the "action" of January 1943, the Government remained silent. We offer the same protest in connection with arms, which were demanded long before the Warsaw "resettlement action". The inexplicable behaviour of the officials, who refused to supply arms for months and finally supplied them in totally inadequate quantities, led some people to suspect that this was being done for fear of improper use of these arms in the future. The attitude towards saving Jews, and especially valuable individuals, was indifference. A Council for Aid to the Jews was formed, consisting of people of good will, but its activity

---

were to effect the annihilation of nearly the whole of Polish Jewry. This Resolution condemning German crimes against the Jews was drafted by the representative of the Jews of Poland on the Polish National Council, Ignacy Schwarzbart, and was made public only after protracted and obstinate endeavours on his part in the face of constant systematic obstruction. ¦
The Polish Socialists also accused the Polish Government of deliberately delaying the news and reducing the scale of the crimes committed against the Jewish population. For instance, the clandestine paper, *Robotnik*, belonging to the Polish Socialist Workers' Party [*Robotnicza Partia Polskich Socjalistow*] wrote on 1 May 1943: "We recall facts even a hundred times less important that were known in London almost immediately and were telegraphed to every part of the world. In contrast, the world got the news of the earlier liquidation of the Jews in Poland [i.e. of the deportations to the death camps in 1942 — Ed.], during which over a million and a half Jews perished, only when this was completed and it was all over. The rescue activities of so-called governmental circles (ironically enough, under the leadership of *Endeks*) was also the proverbial shutting the stable door after the horse was gone."

was limited by lack of funds and lack of help from the government.[29] We have stressed elsewhere that saving Jews on the Aryan side was the work of individuals in Poland and not the result of a com-

[29] According to data from Polish sources, the Office of the Government Delegate earmarked 37 million zloty from its budget (approximately 200,000 U.S. dollars at the then current rate of exchange) plus 50,000 dollars for help to the Jews. (See Czesław Madajczyk, *Polityka III Rzeszy w okupowanej Polsce*, Warsaw 1970, p. 341.) This means that the Polish Underground allotted less than 1% of the 30 million dollars it had received from abroad for clandestine activities to help for Jews. Moreover further research is needed to clear up the question as to whether the whole amount earmarked for the Jews was in fact transferred to the Council for Aid to Jews, since the Council records show acknowledgement of receipt of the following amounts only: — January 1943 — 150,000 zl.; February 1943 — 300,000 zl.; April to October 1943 — 400,000 zl. every month; November 1943 — 750,000 zl.; December 1943 — 750,000 zl.; January to July 1944 — 1,000,000 zl. every month.

(See Karyna Fiszman-Kaminska, *Zachod, emigracyjny rzad polski oraz Delegatura wobec sprawy zydowskiej podczas II Wojny swiatowej*, "Biuletyn Zydowskiego Instytutu Historycznego" No. 62 — 1967, p. 55.) Furthermore, Home Army parachutists brought in nearly a million dollars collected by Jewish organizations overseas for assistance to Polish Jews (see Madajczyk, *op. cit.*). Of this amount, only 420,000 U.S. dollars were transferred to the Jewish organizations in Poland for which the money was intended. (See Iranek-Osmecki Kazimierz, *Kto ratuje jedno zycie*, London, 1969, p. 239.) Why the remaining 480,000 dollars were not transferred has not yet been explained. Leaders of the Jewish resistance movement demanded the money several times over, without result. Aleksander Kaminski, editor-in-chief of the underground paper, *Biuletyn Informacyjny*, also intervened. On 18 March 1944, he wrote to his superior, Jerzy Makowiecki, head of the Information and Propaganda Department in the Government Delegate's Office: "They [the Jews] have received nothing since January 1944, although they were advised in December that the Jewish funds had been dispatched. In general, the matter of Jewish funds collected by Jews in the U.S.A., Palestine and Britain for the Jews in Poland appears to be alarmingly obscure in every way. According to what one hears, no one has given the Warsaw Jews (their leaders, that is) a clear explanation why these funds have not reached them in full. I am not perfectly at home in these matters. I only know that doubts arise in the hearts of even those Jews who are most loyal to the Polish

213

mon effort. The subsidies granted by the government to politically and culturally active members of Warsaw Jewry were derisory, and nothing was done to provide valuable individuals with flats. As a result, the handful of scientists, writers, actors, political activists etc., who had been saved in earlier "actions", were killed during the last one in April or sent to the S.S. labour camps in Trawniki, Poniatow, Budzyn[30] and others, to the concentration camp in Lublin, etc., where they are in imminent danger at all times from various "selections" or of extermination at the hands of S.S. or Ukrainians. In order to illustrate the tragic situation of the Jewish intellectuals, it is sufficient to note that the Council for Aid to the Jews did not even have enough means to help a distinguished Jewish historian, a former member of the Diet of the Polish Republic, Dr. S.[31] For lack of a few tens of thousands of zloty for a flat on

---

Republic, doubts that may one day produce fatal results. I write this not as a private note to you but as my considered official opinion. I am extremely anxious about it. The only loyal minority element in existence today will lose all confidence in us if this petty bureaucracy in dealing with their affairs is not ended. I cannot believe that it is due to deliberate ill-will—it is probably bureaucracy and sloth in our offices, phenomena which we in the Information and Propaganda Department in particular ought to end for the sake of propaganda in the fullest sense of the word."

(Records of the Government Delegate's Office, Archives of the Institute for the History of the [Communist] Party, Warsaw, File 202/XV-2, p. 148.)

30 The labour camp in Budzyn (Krasnik district, Lublin province) was a branch of Majdanek concentration camp. The well-known German airplane construction firm, "Heinkel", set up workshops in Budzyn camp and employed Jews imprisoned there. In the second half of 1943, there were about 3,000 Jews in this camp, 800 of them captured during the Warsaw Ghetto revolt. In May and June 1944 the camp was evacuated and the prisoners moved to the labour camps in Skarzysko-Kamienna, Starachowice, Radom and Plaszow. Only a few of these Jews survived.

31 Dr. Yizhak (Ignacy) Schiper, eminent Jewish historian, member of the pre-war Diet in Poland, well-known for his political activities and one of the most popular personalities in Jewish life in Poland and abroad. In his works, Schiper founded the "economic school" of Jewish historio-

graphy. His historical research was closely connected with his political activities as leader of Poale-Zion in Galicia. He made the abnormal structure of Jewish economic life, the causes of which were seen to be rooted in the past, the starting point of his Party's programme. His 4-volume work on the economic history of the Jews (*Dzieje gospodarcze Zydow*) was the fruit of his research in this field. By his further researches into the history of Jewish autonomy and the *Va'ad Arba' Ha'Aratzot,* he wanted to create a basis for dealing with the urgent problem of contemporary Jewish life, the question of autonomy. He opposed the interpretations of historians Balaban and Schorr, who saw in the *Va'ad Arba' Ha'Aratzot,* an incarnation of the most glorious elements in the Jewish past. Dr. Schiper argued that the Jewish Diet was created for purely financial reasons—in order to collect the poll-tax levied on the whole Jewish population. The State taxes, for the collection of which the *Va'ad* was responsible, served the ruling clique of the *Kehillah* as a means for oppressing and exploiting the wide masses of the people. It was no wonder, therefore—argued Schiper—that the masses of the Jewish people revolted against this exploitation. Only a very small part of this research has been published. Schiper's main work (a manuscript of some 600 pages) as well as the manuscript of the fifth volume of his history of the Jewish theatre was lost during the great deportation from the Warsaw Ghetto in mid-1942.

Another book that Schiper put a great deal of work into, *Dzieje Kultury Zydow w Polsce podczas sredniowiecza,* gives an interesting picture of Jewish life and culture in the Middle Ages. Shortly before World War II, he wrote a history of Jewish commerce in Polish territories (*Dzieje handlu zydowskiego na ziemiach polskich*). He wrote some treatises on the period of the Reformation and humanism, showing the strength of the links between the radical currents of the Reformation and Jewish society. In a most interesting monograph on Polish-Lithuanian Jewry and Palestine (*Zydzi polsko-litewscy a Palestyna*), Schiper described the role of these Jews in Messianic movements, in activities in aid of Jews in Eretz Israel as well as in Aliyah. Two other big works of Schiper's that appeared in the pre-war years should be mentioned: "Udział Żydów Kongresówki w powsta-nin listopadowym 1831" (The Share of the Jews of Congress-Poland in the November 1931 Insurrection); 'Cmentarze żydowskie w War-szawie" (Jewish Cemeteries in Warsaw).

Schiper was active in public life during World War II. Together with representatives of other political groups he took part in the work of the Social Committee, which tried to find a basis for cooperation with the *Judenrat,* whose attitude and methods the Committee did not agree with. Schiper represented the Social Committee in the Control Department and the Employment Department of the *Judenrat.* When the Comthe Aryan side, he fell into the hands of the S.S. during the April "action". His wife and children were taken to the "kettle" in Lublin. For several months now he has been maltreated in the Lublin concentration camp, where he is forced to perform hard physical work, despite his advanced age.

The government did not do enough to help against blackmail and terrorizing of Jews on the Aryan side. The complete impunity enjoyed by the blackmailers and the *schmalzowniks* led them to continue on an ever-increasing scale until they endangered the existence of the remnant of Warsaw's Jews. Here, too, help when it did come—and that only in March of this year—was inadequate. It took the form of a warning published by some officials to the effect that blackmailing Jews is a crime punishable under the laws of the Polish Republic. One passage in this declaration stated that punishment for blackmail of Jews would in certain cases be imposed immediately but this threat remained on paper. A larger number of death sentences for blackmailers, together with public announcements of these executions, would certainly have some effect. Up till now, however, very little has been done in this matter which is so vital for the survival of the remnant of Warsaw Jewry.[32]

---

mittee broke off relations with the *Judenrat,* Schiper left these Departments.

During the war Schiper wrote a voluminous and comprehensive work on the Khazars, as well as a history of 19th-century Hassidism. Both these works, as well as other valuable material, were lost together with the above-mentioned manuscripts on Jewish autonomy.

Besides his historical research and his writings, Schiper gave lectures and held courses—he was lecturer in Jewish history in the seminars of *Hehalutz, Hashomer Hatzair,* and the people's university, *Ikor.* He also spoke at big mass rallies, ceremonies, party meetings, etc.

During the Warsaw Ghetto rising, Schiper and his family were caught in a hide-out on Kurza Street, and deported to Majdanek Camp. At a "selection", his wife and daughters were sent to the gas chambers, while he was directed to hard labour. He was shot on 5 November, 1943, during the big liquidation of Jewish labour camps in the Lublin region. (See: Ringelblum, Vol. II, *op. cit.,* pp. 150–160; Dr. N. M. Gelber, *Hahistorionim shel Warsha, Dr. Yizḥak Schiper,* in "Enziqlopedia shel Galuyot, Vol. II, op. cit., pp. 335–346.)

[32] The Polish Underground conducted an energetic fight against Polish

The same can be said about the Partisan movement. We have military cadres of trained young men and adults, prepared to undertake the most dangerous missions to damage the enemy and reduce his defensive strength. In all the towns where Jews were liquidated, large groups of young men and soldiers took to the forests with arms in their hands to escape the slaughterers. They could easily have been utilized in guerilla warfare against the enemy;[33] instead war was declared on them.[34] They were con-

traitors who collaborated with the Nazi invaders or worked for them. Thus, for example, just in the period of only a year and a half from January 1943 to June 1944, more than 2,000 death sentences were carried out of informers and agents among the local Polish population. (See: *Polskie Sily Zbrojne w drugiej wojnie swiatowej,* Vol. 3: *Armia Krajowa,* London, 1952, p. 473.) The Polish Underground displayed far less determination in fighting the plague of blackmailers who attacked Jewish fugitives from the Ghettos and the camps, trying to find a way to survive on the so-called Aryan side. The blackmailers extorted ransom from the Jews in hiding, and often enough, after getting the sums demanded, finally gave the Jews away to the Nazis. As a result of energetic and insistent protests made by leaders of the Jewish resistance movement, the Polish *Komitet Walki Cywilnej* (Committee for Civilian Struggle) issued a warning to blackmailers (published in the clandestine journal, *Biuletyn Informacyjny,* of 18 April 1943), and consequently about ten death sentences were carried out for the murder or persecution of Jews in hiding. These steps, though of a positive nature, bore absolutely no proportion to the magnitude of the crimes committed against the Jewish population or to the Polish Underground's capacity to react, and had little effect in reducing the blackmailing plague.

33 The head of the Jewish Department at Home Army Headquarters, Colonel Wolinski, took the initiative in this matter. In his report of 12 February 1943, he informed his superiors as follows:
"The only real possibility of saving any considerable number of people is to set up support points for them in the forests in the form of partisan groups, a problem I have already treated in my report Z/16 or Z/17 ... This problem is now urgent because of the situation in the Warsaw Ghetto and I am under constant siege from the Jewish National Committee asking for a decision in this matter."
(Passage from Report Z/20 of Henryk Wolinski, in Government Delegate records, in the Archives of the Institute for the History of the [Communist] Party, Warsaw, 202/XV–2, p. 207.)
Wolinski's proposal was not accepted by the Home Army General

demned to the life of bandits who have to live by robbery.[35] Instead

---

Staff. Not a single Jewish partisan unit was taken into the ranks of the Polish Home Army.

[34] Detachments of the *"Narodwe Sily Zbroine"* (N.S.Z.—"National Military Forces") began a campaign at the end of 1942 against Jewish partisans and Jewish fugitives in hiding in the forests. The formal basis for these anti-Jewish operations was an Order of the N.S.Z. Commander, Col. Czeslaw Oziewicz, initiating the so-called "Special Action No. 1". This Order read in part as follows:

"The partisan forces can and must act at once and energetically to cleanse the country of the destructive and criminal bands from among *national minority formations* ([our italics—the Eds.] hostile to us, and to launch counter-attacks (within the framework of self-defence) when the punitive operations of the invader are strikingly unjust and repressive."

(Directives on N.S.Z. Special Action. Archives of the Institute for the History of the [Communist] Party, Warsaw. 207/24, pp. 1–4.)

The Polish historian, Bogdan Hillebrandt, explains the expression "minority formations" as follows: "The N.S.Z. were first of all to conduct a fratricidal struggle, to fight the partisan detachments of the *Gwardia Ludowa* (People's Guard), here called 'destructive bands', as well as 'national minority formations', *i.e. forest groups composed of Jews who had escaped from the Ghettos'* [our italics — the Eds.]."

(See, Bogdan Hillebrandt, *Partyzantka na Kielecczyznie, 1939–1945,* Warsaw, 1967, p. 221.)

Jewish partisan groups were also frequently attacked by different units of the *Armia Krajowa* (Home Army). The *Gwardia Ludowa* Commander in the Lublin region, Mikolaj Demko (Mieczyslaw Moczar), in his report of June 1943 to his Headquarters, wrote as follows about Home Army units' attacking the Jews: "Our detachments now have to fight on two fronts. The Command of the underground struggle [i.e. the Home Army Command — the Eds.] is organizing detachments whose task it is to liquidate 'Communist bands, Soviet POW's [i.e. Soviet soldiers who had escaped from German POW camps and become partisans in forests on Polish soil—the Ed.] and Jews.' They openly admit that these are their tasks and these are the basic principles they are ordered to act on. They are excellently equipped with arms and they act half openly. The Germans do not attack them, they do not attack the Germans."

(See: Zygmunt Mańkowski, Jan Naumiak (Editors), *Gwardia Ludowa i Armia Ludowa na Lubelszczyźnie 1942–1944—Źródła,* Lublin, 1960, report No. 15.)

[35] The author is guilty of some overstatement here, under the influence of

the propaganda put out by certain circles of the Government Delegate's Office and the Home Army. Jewish partisan units and armed groups, who fought the Nazis in order to save their own lives and those of Jews in hiding under their protection—but who also carried out missions for the Polish underground, were lumped together by this propaganda with the bands of outright robbers that were very numerous at the time. The Polish underground press wrote hair-raising stories about these bands, which in fact had nothing in common with the Jewish combatants or the Jews in hiding, but which did sometimes join up with Polish underground organizations. Thus the underground paper, *Regionalna Agencja Prasowa-Podlasie,* belonging to the *"Bataliony Chlopskie"* organization, published an article in its issue of 3 April 1944 entitled, *U zródeł zła* (The Root of the Evil), which said the following: "A wave of banditry is flooding the whole country. The peaceful population lives under threat of terror from the men of the night, a terror no less dangerous, cruel or burdensome than the terror of the daytime bandits—the Gestapo and the gendarmes ... We are at present observing a phenomenon a hundred times more imminently dangerous to the whole life of the community than plain, low-down robbery. We have to name this phenomenon, briefly but laying stress strongly on every word. *Within the ranks of the independent organizations, there is spreading demoralization in the form of drunkenness, banditry, license, lawlessness and hooliganism."* [Italics in the original.]

Neither the Jewish armed groups nor the Jewish non-combatants in hiding in the forests had anything in common with these elements. But the problem of feeding their people beyond question existed, as it did for all the partisan units in the forests. The Jews in the forests were not always in possession of money or valuables with which to buy food from the peasants. Their people of necessity became a burden on the villages. But it is also beyond question that the Government Delegate's Office, the *de facto* Polish clandestine government, with its standing and authority among the overwhelming majority of the Polish population and disposing of funds amounting to scores of millions of dollars coming from abroad, could easily have solved the problem of getting peasants to feed the Jews—both partisans and non-combatant fugitives—who still remained alive in the forests after the first large-scale German round-ups. After all they were at most some ten to twenty thousand Jews, as against the millions of peasants. But the Government Delegate's Office and the Home Army Command preferred a different way, a way that led to the extermination of the Jewish survivors in the forests. On 15 September 1943, General Bor-Komorowski, Commander-in-Chief of the Home Army, issued Order No. 116 to the units under his command directing them to take active measures against the Jews in the forests. The Polish historian connected with the Polish

219

of being brought into the struggle against the invaders, they were forced to live as robber bands. What real meaning is there in passing a resolution to arm the Ghettos, when armed fighters are discouraged and not mobilized to fight against the common foe?[36] This government attitude towards armed Jewish groups forces them to fight against everyone and leads to their being mercilessly liquidated by Polish partisan groups and by the rural population, who capture them and hand them over to the Germans.[37] Thousands from the once

---

Government-in-Exile, Wladyslaw Pobog-Malinowski, sees fit to justify this infamous Order. He comments on it thus: "This Order was occasioned by a tormenting plague that was going unchecked in the country —groups of Jews hiding in the forests who had escaped from the Ghetto; bands of Soviet soldiers who had managed to escape from captivity; Soviet partisans; riff-raff of society looking for easy money; criminals who had escaped from prisons." (See Pobog-Malinowski, Wladyslaw, *Najnowsza historia Polski, 1939–1945*, London, 1960, p. 412.) It is no accident that Pobog-Malinowski puts the "groups of Jews hiding in the forests who had escaped from the Ghetto" at the head of his list, because in fact the Order in question was a weapon aimed at the Jews in the first place.

36 The reference is to an Order issued by the Command of the Home Army in February 1943, regarding the assistance to be afforded to people cut off in the Ghettos who wanted to get out to join in the armed struggle. In accordance with the intention of this Order, Polish Army Commands were enjoined to afford all possible aid to the Jewish concentrations under the authority of the "Jewish Combat Organization" and the "Co-ordinating Committee".
The Jewish armed organizations as well as other people who were ready to help the Jews in their armed struggle in the Ghetto invoked this Order more than once, but the local military elements were unwilling to carry it out. In the last analysis, the Order was not obeyed.

37 Many Polish sources also provide abundant evidence that peasants took part in raids organized by the Germans to track down Jews in hiding and Jewish armed groups in the forests. Thus the Polish chronicler, Dr. Zygmunt Klukowski, whose diary has already been quoted, wrote in his entry of 26 November 1942:
"Among the 'bandits' [quotation marks in the original—the author means the partisans — the Eds.] are many Jews. The peasants, for fear of repressive measures, catch Jews in the villages and bring them into the town, or sometimes simply kill them on the spot. Generally, a strange brutalization has taken place regarding the Jews. People have fallen

numerous Jewish communities in the provinces are now dying this way. The Polish population finishes off the remnant of the Jews left from the large Jewish communities. Jews are not admitted to Polish partisan groups for no known reason.[38] How mistaken this policy is, can be proved by the practice of the Polish Left, which has placed no restrictions on Jews. The future will show that the

---

into a kind of psychosis: following the German example, they often do not see in the Jew a human being but instead consider him as a kind of obnoxious animal that must be annihilated with every possible means, like rabid dogs, rats, etc."
(Zygmunt Klukowski, *Dziennik z lat okupacji Zamojszczyzny*, Lublin, 1959, p. 299.)
Ludwik Landau, another chronicler connected with the Home Army, wrote in his entry of 24 February 1943: "Not many of the Jewish population will survive this war. The situation of the surviving remnant still in hiding is difficult and the conditions that prevail bring about recurrent conflicts of various kinds with the Christian population. The Jewish bands active in the various regions [Landau is here using the terminology of the Home Army; he is of course referring to Jewish armed groups and Jewish partisans — the Eds.] are often reproached with murdering and robbing the local population; even taking food—inevitable in the given circumstances—was enough, rumour has it, to bring peasants in the Opoczno district to such a state of agitation that they helped the Germans round up the Jews and even gave away those in hiding in the villages."
(Ludwik Landau, *Kronika z lat wojny i okupacji*, Vol. II, Warsaw, 1962, p. 223.)

38 The Home Army, unlike the People's Guard (*Gwardia Ludowa*), did not take any Jewish partisan detachments into its ranks. All the efforts made by numerous Jewish armed groups to contact the Home Army and come under its command were unsuccessful, and there were even not infrequent instances of Jewish partisans' being treacherously murdered. (There is much evidence on this subject in the Archives of Yad Vashem and in many other collections of archives as well.) However, individual Jews were accepted in the partisan detachments of the Home Army, particularly those detachments connected with the socialist Left. Jews were even to be found in the higher ranks of these detachments. But as a general rule, Jews who wanted to fight the Germans could only get into most of the Home Army detachments as Aryans, concealing their Jewishness from even their closest comrades.

Polish Underground is indebted to its Jewish members, who sacrifice themselves for the Organization.[39]

We have serious reproaches against the government regarding the rescue of Jewish children. The so-called "resettlement action" was directed mainly against women and children, who were the first to be sent to Treblinka. Only a few Jewish children were left. We expected action from the government to save this handful that escaped extermination. Unhappily neither the government nor the Polish population did any thing about it. There was not even an appeal directed to the population.[40]

---

[39] The story of the Jewish share in the Polish resistance movement has not yet been told in full. The list of Jews who performed acts of unforgettable heroism for Underground Poland is too long to be quoted in this brief footnote. We confine ourselves to giving the names of a number of Jews who reached the higher ranks of the Polish partisan movement:

Col. Ignacy Robb-Rosenfarb (alias "Narbutt"), organizer and commander of several partisan units of the *Gwardia Ludowa* and the *Armia Ludowa*;

Col. Robert Satanowski, commander of the partisan brigade *Jeszcze Polska Nie Zginela*;

Col. Henryk Nebrzydowski, commander of the *Bataliony Chlopskie* in the Miechow region;

Lt.-Col. Henryk Torunczyk, commander of a parachute shock battalion;

Major Menasze (Anastazy) Matywiecki, member of the Warsaw Command of the *Armia Ludowa*;

Major Aleksander Skotnicki, commander of the *Holoda* partisan battalion;

Capt. Izchak (Zygmunt) Gutman, commander of the 3rd Battalion of the *Bem* partisan brigade.

Janina Bier, organizer of the Women's Combatant Units of the *Armia Ludowa.*

Maksymilian Boruchowicz (Borwicz), commander of a partisan detachment of the Socialist Combatant Organization in the Miechow region.

[40] The Children's Department of the Council for Aid to the Jews was headed by Irena Sendlerowa, who was at the same time an employee of the Social Welfare Department of the Warsaw Municipality. This Children's Department placed Jewish orphans with Polish families in individual cases, and also placed them in various orphanages, hospitals, convents and other institutions. There was also a Department for Child Protection in the above-mentioned Social Welfare Department, headed by the

Jews are not admitted in government military organizations, except for the few individuals personally known to the leadership of a given group. We know of instances when the Aryan origin of members of certain Government organizations were checked. If it is ascertained that someone is of Jewish origin, he is removed on one pretext or another.

To conclude: at a time when extermination threatens the Jewish people, the Government has done nothing to save at least a remnant of Polish Jewry. The official attitude concerning the surviving handful of Polish Jews has been completely wrong, viewed in relation to the unprecedented tragedy, which the Jewish people is undergoing in Poland.[41]

---

writer, Jan Dobraczynski; he was actively assisted by Irena Schulz, Jadwiga Piotrowska and others, and this Department saved a number of Jewish children by placing them in various religious establishments as Polish orphans. (Irena Sendlerowa—"Jolanta", *Ci, ktorzy pomagali Zydom*, "Biuletyn Zydowskiego Instytutu Historycznego," No. 45–46 — 1963, pp. 238–239; Szymon Datner, *Materialy z dziedziny ratownictwa Zydow w Polsce w okresie okupacji hitlerowskiej*, "Biuletyn Zydowskiego Instytutu Historycznego," No. 73 — 1970, pp. 135–137.) Jewish children were also hidden on the Aryan side in Cracow, but only a few survived. (A. Hochberg-Marianska, *Dzieci, in "W trzecia rocznice zaglady w Krakowie,"* Krakow, 1946, pp. 153–156.)

However, the efforts of the Council for Aid to the Jews to get the Government Delegate to bring about a thousand children out of the Warsaw Ghetto, while there was still time, met with no success. This fact confirms the accuracy of Ringelblum's verdict on the failure of the Polish Government and the Polish community as a whole to take action in order to save Jewish children.

(See Memorandum of the Council for Aid to the Jews, 30 January 1943, in the collection of documents, "Resistance and Revolt in the Warsaw Ghetto", p. 388. Cf. Turkow Jonas, *Azoj iz es gewesen . . . Churban Warshe*, Buenos-Aires 1948, pp. 363–364.)

41 The author uses the terms "Governmental" or "official elements" or "circles" to indicate the Polish Government-in-Exile and its subordinate representation, the Office of the Government Delegate for the Homeland, together with its agencies in the provinces. The attitude of these agencies towards the Jews depended on the political line of the Government Delegate's Office, which itself resulted from the platforms of the individual political organizations which comprised the Delegate's Of-

fice or cooperated with it. These organizations had the support of the overwhelming majority of the Polish community, and most of them had anti-Semitic platforms, even while they afforded symbolic help to a limited number of Jews, with an eye to world opinion. A document marked No. 171/43) drafted at the end of 1943 by the Home Army H.Q. Information and Propaganda Office treats of the political basis of the Polish underground organizations and their respective influence in the Polish population. This document describes the attitude towards the Jews of these particular political organizations connected with the Government Delegate, as well as their influence among the Poles, as follows:

"(a) *Endecja* (code sign—a square). Attitude to the Jewish minority: *Emigration of the Jews.* Influence among various social strata: This is a party of all strata, based on the bourgeoisie, medium-sized industry, land owners and part of the wealthier peasants.

(b) *Konfederacja Narodu* [Confederation of the Nation]. Attitude to the Jewish minority: *Liquidation of the Jews.* Influence among various social strata: among the intelligentsia, land-owners, clergy and young people.

(c) *Stronnictwo Pracy* [Labour Party] (code sign—a rhomb). [This was the party of the Prime Minister, Wladyslaw Sikorski.] Attitude to the Jewish minority: *Removal of the Jews.* Influence among various social strata: among small artisans, bourgeoisie, clergy.

(d) *Oboz Polski Walczacej* [the Camp of Fighting Poland]: a break-away section of the former *Sanacja.* Attitude to the Jewish minority: *Emigration of the Jews.* Influence among various social strata: elite intelligentsia, former State officials, soldiers' organizations.

(e) *Konwent Organizacji Niepodleglosciowych* [Convention of Independence Organizations]—another break-away section of the former *Sanacja.* Attitude to the minorities: *Full and equal rights* for all minorities except the Germans. Influence among various social strata: like the foregoing.

(f) *Stronnictwo Ludowe* [People's Party] (code name—a triangle). Attitude towards the Jewish minority: *Emigration of the Jews.* Influence among various social strata: peasant strata.

(g) Smaller organizations: *Raclawice, Zwiazek Odbudowy Rzeczpospolitej, Polski Zwiazek Wolnosci, Polska Niepodlegla.* Attitude to the Jewish minority: *Emigration of the Jews,* except for those who have taken part in the fight for independence. Influence among various social strata: *Raclawice*—younger peasants; *Zwiazek Odbudowy Rzeczpospolitej*— mixed strata; *Polski Zwiazek Wolnosci*—intelligentsia and part of the workers; *Polska Niepodlegla* — mixed strata.

(h) *Stronnictwo Demokratyczne* [Democratic Party] (code name—a rectangle). Attitude to the minorities: *Equal rights for all citizens* irrespective of religion and nationality. Influence among various social strata: intelligentsia, brain-workers.

(i) The Syndicalists. Attitude to the minorities: *Equal rights for all citizens* irrespective of religion and nationality. Influence among various social strata: intelligentsia, workers.

(j) *Wolnosc-Rownosc-Niepodleglosc* [Freedom-Equality-Indepence] (a break-away section of the former Polish Socialist Party. Code name— a circle). Attitude to the Jewish minority: *Equal rights with Poles.* Influence among various social strata: industrial workers, agricultural workers, intelligentsia, brain-workers."

As can be seen, nine out of these thirteen political organizations of the Polish underground, connected with the Government Delegate for the Homeland, had an anti-Semitic platform of emigration or liquidation of the surviving remnant of Polish Jewry, and only four of them had a democratic platform of Jewish emancipation in liberated Poland.

Among the main Polish organizations in opposition to the Government Delegate, one, the *Grupa Wielkiej Polski* (Greater Poland Group— break-away section of the *Stronnictwo Narodowe*—National Party) had an anti-Semitic platform of removal of Jews from Poland; the other two, the *Robotnicza Polska Partia Socjalistyczna* (Polish Socialist Workers' Party) and the *Polska Partia Robotnicza* (Polish Workers' Party) stood for full emancipation of the Jews.

(The full text of the document summarized above has been published in an article by Jan Rzepecki, *Organizacja i dzialanie Biura Informacji i Propagandy Komendy Glownej Armii Krajowej,* "Wojskowy Przeglad Historyczny," No. 4, 1971, pp. 147–153.)

12

THE IDEALISTS

The difficult life of a Pole who hides Jews. — Twenty-four hours in the life of railwayman Teodor. — Family M. saves thirty-four Jews. — Roses in the garbage. — The Polish scientific world. — A peasant from Grodno–Gawel K. — Polish sectarians maintain the tradition of tolerance. — A Polish physician aids Jewish partisans. — Domestic servants faithful beyond the grave.

The life of a Pole who is hiding Jews is not an easy one. Appalling terror reigns in the country, second only to Yugoslavia. The noblest among the people and the most self-sacrificing individuals are being sent *en masse* to concentration camps or prisons. Informing and denunciation flourish throughout the country, thanks largely to the *Volksdeutsche*. Arrests and round-ups at every step and constant searches for arms and smuggled goods in the trains are common in the city streets. Every day the press, radio, etc. infect the masses of the population with the venom of anti-Semitism. In this atmosphere of trouble and terror, passivity and indifference, it is very difficult to keep Jews in one's home. A Jew living in the flat of an intellectual or a worker or in the hut of a peasant is dynamite liable to explode at any moment and blow the whole place up. Money undoubtedly plays an important role in the hiding of Jews. There are poor families who base their subsistence on the funds paid daily by the Jews to their Aryan landlords. But is there enough money in the world to make up for the constant fear of exposure, fear of the neighbours, the porter and the manager of the block of flats, etc.? Idealists exist who devote their whole lives to their Jewish friends, who cause them a great deal of trouble! A Jew is a little child, incapable of taking a single step by itself! A Jew cannot move around in the streets. His Aryan friend has to visit him frequently and arrange a thousand and one matters for him. The first is to mobilize funds for his very high living expenses. He has to collect money from the Jew's clients here, sell his property there, turn his valuables into cash, and so on. All the time there are constant instructions and requests to be taken care of by the Christian friend. A Jew rarely lives with his family—usually every member of the family lives in a different place. Keeping contact between the different members of the family is also the duty of the Aryan friend. Jewish flats are constantly "burning". There is hardly a Jew who has lived for any length of time on the Aryan side in the same flat. After a short time something always goes wrong. Nobody knows how someone came to notice that something is being hidden in the flat, that visitors are often received in the kitchen and not in the living room, that much more food is being bought than before, that the hosts have changed their way of life, that they are better dressed, and thousands of other trifling instances. There has not yet been a denunciation, but something is in the air, one feels something. Here the porter drops a word that a stranger was asking about this or that, there a neighbour makes a remark about having something to hide—in short, the flat is "burning" and the Jew has to leave quickly. Sometimes the neighbours, for fear of imaginary collective responsibility, simply come and demand the departure of the Jews. And now the Sisyphean labour of the Aryan friend starts again—to find a flat, to persuade someone to accept the Jews, to convince them that it is a humane deed, civic duty, etc. Troubles, always fresh troubles! And what happens if someone starts blackmailing, if the police make an arrest, if there is an illness, etc.? Then there is a considerable increase in the burden of tasks imposed on our friend. Every Jew on the Aryan side needs a friend or rather friends like this to surround him with a sympathetic atmosphere, to take care of him and put their hearts into fixing up his unending, daily troubles.

I know an idealist like this, a Polish railwayman named Teodor.[1]

---

[1] Teodor Pajewski, railwayman, member of the Home Army. He got Ringelblum out of Trawniki labour camp with the help of Shoshana (Emilka) Kosower, liaison officer of the Jewish National Committee, and brought him to Warsaw.

227

I shall relate in few words what I saw during the twenty-four hours I spent with him. He had just returned from a difficult mission in the provinces. He had been to an S.S. camp with funds and instructions, and at the risk of his life he had abducted a certain socially active Jew from the camp. This railwayman has a ground-floor flat in Warsaw. In the cellar connected with the ground floor he has a hide-out where a Jewish family lives. The porter, a fervent anti-Semite, persecutes Teodor to the best of his ability. Suspecting him of hiding Jews, he arranged together with other tenants in the block for a collective search of his flat, which was fruitless. They did not detect the hide-out. The porter continued to persecute Teodor. In summer he would keep his door open and observe everyone who went into the railwayman's flat, smelling a Jew in everybody. Teodor provides everything for his Jewish sub-tenants. He has mobilized funds for them, he supplies them with food, keeps contact with their friends, etc. Our railwayman's family are staying in the country, and they are hiding two Jewish families there, only some of whose members are registered. There is trouble with these families as well, everyday matters which have to be arranged. Our Aryan friend has still other Jewish acquaintances, who are hiding in a suburban locality. The day I was with him, their flat was "burnt". Teodor went there, found a new Aryan family which undertook to hide them, moved their things, etc. And it goes on like that all the time, without a let-up—constant trouble and things to attend to. There are many such nameless heroes, who help Jews despite the terror, despite the passivity or even the hostility of a considerable part of the population.

In this class of idealists we include the M. family.[2] This family is saving the lives of thirty-four Jews who took shelter with them a year ago. They are a family of market-gardeners, living in the suburbs, 14 kilometres from Warsaw. They have known Jews for a long time. Before the war, Jews lived in their two-storey block of flats. Neighbourly relations prevailed. The Jewish vegetable dealer and the Jewish fruiterer used to buy the produce of their garden

---

[2] The reference is to the family of the Polish Communist, Ludomir Marczak, musician and composer.

and orchard. M. senior was known for his liberal attitude towards Jews. He was an honest man, well known for his nobility of character. "Modern" trends had not reached him, he could not understand hatred for Jews, and he brought his children up in the same spirit. He imbued them with principles of just and equal treatment of all, without distinction of religion and nationality. Heroes flaunting the flag of the "Tuppenny Gazette" did not find it to their liking that a serious and well-esteemed person like M. did not belong to their crowd, so they contemptuously nicknamed him, "the Jews' errand-boy". But these attacks by native anti-Semites did not influence Mr. M's conduct in the least. After the death of her husband, Mrs. M. carried on the family tradition. Her kind, wise eyes, her dignified, grey head, her sedate, majestic Roman matron's tread—all bear witness to the fact that the family rule has passed to a worthy, energetic person, who knows what she wants and is able to keep her numerous offspring in hand.

When the "resettlement" of the Warsaw Jews started and asylum was being sought on the Aryan side, a certain social [workers'] group turned to the M. family with the request that they build a hide-out. The group was prompted to take this step not only because of the M. family tradition, but also because of a fresh proof of the nobility and helpfulness of this family. Mr. and Mrs. M. had disinterestedly taken in a poor Jewish seamstress without being paid and treated her like their own child. It was deduced that the M. family could be trusted with the lives of two score people. This trust was not misplaced! Later we learned that a family council was held, at which it was decided to begin building the hide-out; some members of the M. family came out against the plan for fear of detection, but the family tradition of humanitarianism and tolerance won. What turned the scales was the opinion of Mr. W., who was dedicated to the cause of independence, for which he daily risked his life. Mr. W.'s opinion is respected by the M. family, and he declared that it is the duty of every Pole, a civic duty, to hide Jews. "Look after them like the apple of your eye", Mr. W. concluded. This sentence became the maxim of the whole family and especially of one of Mr. M.'s sons, Mr. Wladyslaw. Then began the epic of collaboration which was to go on for many long months.

229

The hide-out is ruled by "the boss", Mr. Wladyslaw,[3] aged 37, gardener by profession. He decided to save over a score of Jews, in order to thwart the occupiers who sentenced them to death. Mr. W. is devoted body and soul to his beloved mistress, "Krysia" —the nickname for the hide-out. He remembers her all day and dreams about her at night. It was a *tour de force* getting the hide-out built, and it was accomplished by Mr. Wladyslaw with the help of his nephew, the genial and likeable Mr. Mariusz. For some weeks, a score of the future inhabitants of "Krysia" hid in a cellar, over which a *Volksdeutscher* was living. It was with their help that Mr. W. built an underground flat with a kitchen and a lavatory. It was cramped and uncomfortable, but it was safe because it was in the middle of a field, far from human eyes. Since then the lives of Mr. W. and his genial collaborator, Mr. Mariusz, have been devoted to looking after "Krysia". Despite the favourable external conditions, there are many moments of danger for "Krysia". Sometimes the children imprisoned in the cramped room, or rather cellar, make too much noise playing; sometimes the adults, cooped up in a space 28 metres square by 1.83 metres high, speak too loud and sometimes even quarrel when afflicted with the so-called *Stacheldrahtkrankheit*.[4] Mr. W. has to keep an eye on everything. Workers employed in the neighbouring field sometimes come too near the hide-out and may overhear loud conversations, a neighbour may notice light showing through the hatch. There are other predicaments, such as the need to provide food for scores of people without arousing anyone's suspicion. The ingenious Mr. M. and his equally resourceful sisters found a solution to this problem. They rented a grocery store, and all the shopping for "Krysia" is done there. Mr. W.'s beloved mistress is jealous, she demands exclusive rights for herself. For her benefit, Mr. W. has been forced to break off numerous friendly and trade relations. He cannot permit too many visitors or customers to come to the garden, because

---

3   Mieczyslaw Wolski, gardener. He was shot by the Germans together with all the Jews who were in hiding with Ringelblum.

4   Barbed-wire illness: a state of mental anxiety triggered by the barbed-wire fence that cut the camp off from the rest of the world.

any visitor may notice something he is not supposed to, something which could not be foreseen even in the best-conceived plan for a hide-out.

The residents in "Krysia" are bound up with the M. family[5] for life and death. They are bound up with the everyday, routine life that is nevertheless rich in events. They are bound together by the death of one of the residents of "Krysia". A fourteen-year-old girl in "Krysia" died because the Germans had taken her beloved mother away a year before, and in April this year she lost her father, who was killed in some Ghetto bunker. Basia heard terrible stories of what was happening in the Ghetto, she saw her father's face in the glow of the burning Ghetto, she heard his sorrowful moaning in the explosions as the blocks were blown up. She saw and heard her father everywhere. This proud-spirited girl could not bear to be kept by strangers. She became mentally ill. She went on hunger strike, did not eat for three weeks and then died. She was burried in the garden. Her death almost caused destruction of the whole hide-out. A strange worker once happened to come to get some clay from the field. As chance would have it, he started digging at the spot where Miriam (who went by the Aryan name of Basia) was buried. Fortunately the look-out who guarded the place all the time noticed, and Mrs. M. was told. She found some pretext to ask the worker to stop digging for the clay. Mr. Wladyslaw is a fellow of excellent fancy, with a liking for liquor and brawling. He has something of the Mazovian in him, is bold and courageous and enjoys taking risks for their own sake. Mr. Wladyslaw got rid of friends and acquaintances because he did not want them coming too often to the garden where his dear "Krysia" was hidden. However, Mr. W. could not deny himself the pleasure of a practical joke which he can now talk about with justified pride. Mr. W. has a faithful prewar customer, Mr. R., a *Volksdeutscher* who was promoted during the war to a high position in the local Gestapo. Mr. R. has a taste for gardening, he enjoys looking at flowers, hothouse plants, etc. One day he came

---

5 The family of Mieczyslaw Wolski (not to be confused with the Marczak family).

to visit our Mr. W. and asked to be shown the garden in all its springtime beauty. Mr. W. could not forgo the pleasure of inviting the German to the grounds of "Krysia". It went off successfully. The residents of "Krysia" kept dead quiet while Mr. W. took his visitor for a walk over their heads. The German, who had till then walked over Jewish corpses, was now walking over the living.

Mr. W.'s courage is extraordinary. When the present residents of "Krysia" were to be rescued from the Ghetto, he himself arrived on his cart at the spot where they were lying low, loaded their suitcases and bundles on the cart, piled the people on top of the packages, and drove off home. Once he took eight people at one go, men, women and children, and drove them safely home through the main streets of the town in full view of the police, the *schmalzowniks* and the neighbours.

Mr. W. is one of those who likes his liquor. Since "Krysia" was established he drinks less, he even says he drinks very seldom. Never mind whether it's "less" or "very seldom", but even when he is drunk he won't say a word about "Krysia". He may cut capers in the garden but he won't go near "Krysia" even when drunk, it's taboo. He not only remembers it consciously when he is sober, but also unconsciously when he is tight.

Mrs. M. is a real mother to "Krysia". She does not sleep at night because of her. In the morning she goes to "Krysia" to check if everything about the place is in order. She watches over "Krysia", is absorbed in its troubles and joys. Morning and evening she boils milk for "Krysia". She takes care of its residents, arranges a thousand and one matters for them and keeps up their contacts. Whenever she comes to the hide-out, she has a good word for everyone, a gentle smile. She takes an interest in the children, brings them fruit from the garden, comforts the adults and cheers them up. In stormy moments when a quarrel breaks out between "Krysia" and a member of the M. family, Mrs. M. becomes the mediator. Her verdict is objective and just and is unquestioningly accepted as final by everyone. Mrs. M. concerns herself with the problems of all the residents of "Krysia", who have as it were become members of the M. family. There is a mother there whose only son is constantly changing his place of residence, and the mother, imprisoned in "Krysia", goes through crises all the time. She constantly thinks that her son is out on the streets, that he is being harmed all the time. Mrs. M. pacifies the mother, communicates with the son, keeps in contact with his protectors as if she were his own mother. There is another woman living in "Krysia", whose husband, also a resident there, went to the Ghetto to arrange some social matters. He was caught in the firing during the April fighting and landed in an S.S. labour camp. It took a great deal of trouble and money to get the husband back to "Krysia"—he was already considered lost. Mrs. M. dedicated herself body and soul to this cause, sending out letters, communicating with the couriers, etc. The joy with which Mrs. M. greeted the husband of this woman teacher on his return to "Krysia" was a sight to see—she could not have greeted a lost son more warmly.

Mrs. M. is the heart of "Krysia", Mr. Wladyslaw is its brain, and its watchful eyes are those of Mrs. M.'s grandson, Mariusz, who is the guardian angel of "Krysia", its inseparable companion. His task is simple, but the lives of thirty-four people depend on it. Mr. Mariusz brings "Krysia" its food, he carries away the buckets, etc., and, more important, he keeps guard over it all day long to prevent anyone from coming near. From early morning till late at night, Mr. Mariusz guards the life and safety of thirty-four persons. When the first lines of the popular song, *Warum?*, are heard, everyone keeps absolutely quiet. That is how Mr. Mariusz makes it known that an "enemy" is approaching. When he sings the second verse, it means that danger is close at hand, that the "Black Maria" (Gendarmerie car) is getting near or that a stranger has to be brought into "Krysia" territory, someone who must not find out that thirty-four live people who want to survive the war are hiding underground. When this signal is given, everybody goes underground, the hatch is closed and everyone holds his breath. Mr. Mariusz often has very difficult tasks to perform. He has to manoeuvre and manage the work in the garden in such a way as not to permit any stranger to approach the hide-out. He has to make sure all the time that no one will notice the "Krysia" residents from neighbouring roofs, he has to solve such problems as finding somewhere to put the garbage, dish-water, faeces, etc. These are everyday problems, but very important for thirty-four living people.

Besides the three protectors—grandmother, son and grandson— Mrs. M.'s daughters are also a great help in dealing with the "Krysia" residents' everyday problems, shopping, selling belongings, keeping up contact with the outside world. This is a very important matter for people altogether cut off from the rest of the world— every family imprisoned in a hide-out is a world to itself—and so the tasks of the sisters as protectors are many and varied and change every day. A former office-worker in a Polish firm receives an allowance from her former fellow-workers through the intermediary of one of the M. sisters. One of the heroines of "Krysia" has a son who is a "flying Jew", who changes his place of residence every so often, as something always goes wrong. One of the M. sisters sees to his accomodation, which causes a great many difficulties. There are an infinity of other problems: money has to be fetched or exchanged, belongings left with friends have to be collected, etc. The M. sisters arrange all these endless matters whole-heartedly, smilingly, efficiently and energetically.

In April this year, when the Ghetto was burning, when the modern adepts of Nero burned living human torches, when red posters cried from all the walls: "Poles! Woe to him who hides Jews. We shall do to you what we are doing to the Jews", black despair reigned in "Krysia". More than one there saw his brother, sister, etc., in the glow of the burning Ghetto. Mrs. M. and Mr. Wladyslaw used to visit "Krysia" often to try and raise the spirits of the residents. While weak-minded people were frightened by the German threats and gave the Jews notice to leave their flats, thus sending them to certain death, the M. family remained firm in its resolve to rescue the Jews. Mrs. M., the calm, sedate Roman matron, and her boisterous son want to save their Jews in defiance of the Germans, and they intend to carry their plan through in spite of everything and everyone.

The M. family and "Krysia" constitute one family, living with one thought only—may the war end as soon as possible. They have their joys and sorrows in common. Every occurrence in the

M. family evokes an immediate response from "Krysia", the joys and sorrows of the hide-out are discussed animatedly in Mr. M.'s home. When the building of "Krysia" was completed, the two families jointly held a grand celebration. When one of the residents of "Krysia" referred to the history of Poland, saying that centuries ago Poland had hospitably received Jews banished from Germany and that now the M. family was following the finest traditions of the Piasts' Poland by rescuing Jews from extermination, tears appeared in the eyes of stout-hearted Mr. M.

There are more such hide-outs on the Aryan side. In them are hidden the deathless friendship and gratitude of those rescued from the jaws of the Fascist monster. The people who do this should be decorated by future Poland with the "Order of Humanitarianism". Their name will remain precious to us forever. They are heroes who have fought against the greatest enemy of mankind and saved thousands from certain death.

*

People who have earned a title of merit by saving Jews are also to be found in the social stratum where you would least expect it. By this I mean the Polish managers of the German workshops in the Ghetto. Before the historians pronounce judgement on them, this class of persons should be dealt with by the future government Prosecutor's office, opportunists, or as the Germans say, *Konjunkturschweine*—Germans, Jews and Poles—organized these workshops to supply the needs of the German Army. These shops were supposed to rescue the Jews employed there from annihilation. They did not achieve this aim, but became instead slave-labour establishments. This is not the place to discuss the workshops' activities, and it suffices to say that big business sharks are nothing compared with these workshop managers and owners. A noble individual was rarely to be found among these gangsters. One of the rare exceptions was Mr. K--icz,[6] bristle supplier for the German Army. Wishing to save Jewish intellectuals from extermination, he undertook to market the products of a new bristle workshop that was being put up on Swietojerska Street. On his initia-

---

[6] Julian Kudasiewicz.

tive, several hundred people were engaged without their having to pay for it—mainly intellectuals, deserving people, employees of [Jewish] Community institutions who had been dismissed, etc.— while in other workshops, thousands or even tens of thousands of zloty had to be paid over to get someone taken on as a worker. A work card issued by a German workshop was a shield against deportation to Treblinka in the first phase of the "resettlement action". Mr. K. did not confine himself to taking on people in the workshop. He cared for them afterwards as well and saw to it that they were not short of food. He granted larger loans to the intellectuals and deserving people working for the community. He secured them larger food rations and in general looked after their subsistence. Together with the main supplier of brushes, the Jew, Emil Weitz, he had a canteen for educated people opened on Gesia Street.

A fine chapter of Mr. K.'s activities was the protection he afforded Jewish children in the Ghetto. He could be seen in the Ghetto every day, surrounded by swarms of "street children", to whom he gave very generous alms. Knowing very well the life these children led beyond the pale of society, he most generously supported the social initiative taken at that time, especially by the "Centos", in opening boarding homes for "street children". One of these boarding homes, called "Goodwill", was situated at 61 Dzielna Street. It was modernly furnished, and was supported by the bristle workshop and by Mr. K., who contributed tens of thousands of zloty. At the festive opening ceremony of "Goodwill", which had as co-founder the well-known children's friend Chairman Abraham Gepner, Mr. K. was able to see for himself what miracles had been done by creating normal, human conditions for these former thieves, beggars and "snatchers" of food parcels. Mr. K. also saw the proof that the "street children" were very skillful individuals, capable of surviving in the terrible struggle for existence in the Ghetto under the German occupation. In the few weeks between the time that they were rounded up by the Jewish Order Service and the festive inauguration [of their home], the "street children" had turned into nice, likeable children with a great sense of humour and, most important of all, extraordinary musical and other artistic talents. The noble protector of these children also experienced the tragic moment when "resettlement" headquarters took all the children and staff from the boarding home to the *Umschlagplatz.* The boarding home building stood deserted, and through its broken window panes the wind howled and raged. One could hear the lament of Mother Rachel weeping for her ravished children in the deserted building.

During the first "selection" carried out among the bristle makers, Mr. K. defended the children, from the age of ten up, employed in the bristle workshops. The S.S.-man swore at him, *"Du verfluchter Lump",* but Mr. K. calmly explained that the accepted procedure in bristle-making was to have the artisans employ their children from the age of six, and therefore, said Mr. K., these children should not be taken to Treblinka as they were needed in the workshop.

Mr. K. also looked after Jewish fugitives and donated considerable sums for this purpose. He opposed those Jewish workshop managers who appropriated the goods of the craftsmen who registered *en masse* with the workshops and brought their own raw materials and machines with them. When the situation of the bristle workshop became very uncertain, Mr. K. had to find a new legal basis for continuing production—the workshop was to be merged with the *Todt* Organization. Mr. K. opposed the Jewish management's attempt to derive considerable profit from concluding this arrangement. He was indignant when he saw the Jewish *Werkschutz* beating the bristle workers mercilessly for the slightest offence. Because of his noble deeds, the workshop people had the greatest admiration for Mr. K., who is reliably estimated to have spent about a million zloty on relief in a year. His activity was closely paralleled by Emil Weitz, mentioned above, and Karol Silberstein.

Another man of noble character among the Polish workshop managers was Ryszard G.,[7] part-owner of a knit-wear workshop

---

7 Gerhard Gadejski. More information on the help he gave Jews can be found in the memoirs of Jonas Turkow, *Azoj is es geven—Ḥurbn Warshe,* Buenos-Aires, 1948, pp. 186, 316, 330, 337–443, 356.

which appeared to the outside world to belong to a German, one Mueller. This Ryszard took many people in his workshop without their having to pay him for it, mainly Jewish painters and artists. The area of the workshop where they lived was a Jewish island among "wild" blocks or Aryan ones; and when it was difficult to obtain food in this area, Mr. Ryszard would bring in provisions every day and distribute them free of charge among the poor and for moderate prices to the rest of the people living in the workshop. In general, thanks to Ryszard G., the entire activity of this workshop was directed to rescuing people from the clutches of the S.S., who were on the rampage in Warsaw at this time. It did not help much. One day during working hours the whole Mueller workshop was taken to the *Umschlagplatz,* and thus almost all the Jewish masters of painting were killed at one stroke—Trebacz, Sliwniak, Rabinowicz and others. This in no way detracts from the credit due to Ryszard for his attempts to rescue Jews. On the whole, saving Jews is a veritable labour of Sisyphus. No sooner has a Pole or Jew rescued someone from the hands of the S.S. than the next "action" that takes place sends the same people back to the *Umschlagplatz,* but this time irretrievably.

In the gallery of idealists who save Jews are many who are known for their outstanding work as scientists and for their activity in public causes, persons who deserve the highest rank in the hierarchy of selflessness and self-sacrifice. The first is Profesor X.,[8] known before the war for his courage and chivalry. From the time Poland was declared independent, he fought for equal rights for the Jews. He fought on this issue in his writings and by word of mouth, and missed no opportunity of declaring his opposition to restricting Jewish rights. When the colleges became the main battle-ground of anti-Semitism, our professor headed the small band of Polish men of learning to whom the good name of Poland was dear, and who opposed the knights of the razor-blade and knuckle-duster. In every forum open to him, this profes-

---

8 Professor Tadeusz Kotarbinski. Born 1886. Eminent Polish philosopher and logician. Author of some 300 scientific and popular works. After World War II became first President of the Polish Academy of Sciences.

sor condemned native Fascism, called on the people to come to their senses and defended the finest and noblest traditions of Poland. The professor recognized no national differences. At his lectures the O.N.R. ruffians were not allowed to divide the lecture-hall seats into Aryan and Jewish sides. Fascist and racialist attacks smashed against his seminars as against granite walls. When the war broke out, the professor was left without means of subsistence and lived by giving private lessons. He remained faithful to his humanitarian principles. He stayed in touch with his Jewish pupils in the Ghetto, and they practically worshipped him. He wrote them letters full of warmth and sympathy, raising their spirits and encouraging them to believe in a better future. When the "resettlement action" began, he extended a helping hand to his students and acquaintances. He set the example of hiding Jewish intellectuals in his flat, and others followed suit. The professor was unable to save Dr. Markin, a promising woman-scientist who was an assistant at the Warsaw University and who went to Treblinka at the beginning of the "action". He did succeed, however, in saving other eminent scientists who are alive today thanks to the help he organized. Others followed the professor's example. Three Jewish professors from Warsaw University, outstanding personalities of Polish science, were rescued from the Ghetto. Some younger scientists were also saved. Professor X. has been imitated by other representatives of science, the arts, etc., whose homes are always open to fugitives from the Ghetto. They devote their time and energy on behalf of their Jewish colleagues and friends, who are thus saved from homelessness, starvation and poverty.

Gawel H.,[9] a peasant from Grodno with a middle-sized farm, belongs with those idealists who served the Jewish cause. In the summer of 1941, there was a Jewish family, husband, wife and baby, staying in his village for their summer vacation. When the Germans entered Grodno, the anti-Semitic local population wanted to hand the Jews over to them. Gawel then defended this family, entirely on his own, arguing that to betray Jews was opposed to the

---

9 Paweł Harmuszko.

principles of religion and morality. He fought against the whole village and succeeded in his aim. That was how his activity in saving Jews began. For a long time he travelled between Grodno and Warsaw, transporting Jews fleeing from extermination. He rescues the wealthy for money, but he transports the poor free and even helps them out of his own earnings. He is known in Warsaw and in Grodno and enjoys infinite trust. He is entrusted with large sums of money and, more important, with human lives. Mr. Gawel is very modest and does what he does from humanitarian feelings and a sense of his duty as a citizen. During a relatively lengthy stay in Warsaw, he helped young Jews get in touch with the partisans in the forests, he brought Jews who had been soldiers into contact with the proper military organizations, and he helped to fix up Jews he knew on the Aryan side. He tried to get them Aryan papers, looked for flats for them, transported their belongings from the Ghetto, and generally helped them on the Aryan side.

In our category of idealists we shall also include Mr. Z., a former Evangelical clergyman, a Pole of exceptional moral worth. He is hiding four Jewish children in his home, two of them free of charge and the other two for 600 zloty a month. He was employed by a German firm in the Ghetto, and crossing Zamenhoff Street one day he found a Jewish baby only a few months' old, whose parents had been taken away in the "action". He took the child under his care, called him Moses because of the Biblical parallel and said, "Perhaps this child will grow up to become a great man, even a second Moses." He gave the child to a Jewess to raise and in its stead took her two children to look after. Our Protestant took very good care of little Moses, bringing milk, semolina and other foods every day. But then Mr. Z. fell ill with typhus. The Jewess, who had no other outside source of subsistence, was forced to send Moses to a boarding home, and he was taken to Treblinka in the first "selection". When Mr. Z. found out after his recovery that Moses was no longer there, he cried like a child. Our saintly Protestant did not confine himself to helping children, he also helped adults to the best of his ability. In his work of charity he encountered difficulties from his own wife, a veritable Xanthippa, from whom he was obliged to conceal his expenditure for the purposes described. Mr. Witold,[10] a Methodist lawyer, could have passed for a *Volksdeutsche* because of his German origin and could have benefited from the privileges which *Volksdeutsche* were entitled to. He did not do so, but remained a Pole, faithful to his humanitarian principles. Notwithstanding the fact that he had been imprisoned in *Pawiak* for nine months as the result of denunciation by a Jewish Gestapo-man, Joske Erlich, Mr. Witold did not stop his charity work. He responded to the Jews' pain and suffering. He could not stand aside, indifferent to the torment and agony of the Jews. Walking along Bonifraterska Street one day, he saw a large crowd. It appeared that a gendarme had caught a fifteen-year-old Jewish smuggler on this side of the wall, and he ordered him to face the wall, intending to shoot him. The Jew was struggling with the gendarme, fighting for his life. At this moment Mr. Witold arrived and came to the smuggler's defence, asking the gendarme to show mercy. The gendarme, furious, pointed the barrel of his rifle at him, but at the last moment he asked, *"Bist du Jude?"* When he received a negative answer, he put down his rifle and took Mr. W. to the guard house, where he was given an appropriate sermon for defending Jews and was released after a few hours. Mr. Witold was employed in an Aryan firm in the Ghetto and he constantly helped Jews, looking for flats for them on the Aryan side, helping them to get across and to transport their belongings and valuables. Mr. Witold's work for the Jews began right away after the bombing of Warsaw, when he collected a very considerable sum of money from his acquaintances and distributed it among the homeless. As long as the Ghetto was in existence, he helped impoverished intellectuals as much as he could, saving them from starving to death. After the "resettlement action" began, Mr. Witold displayed great activity in rescuing all sorts of people, getting them to the Aryan side, finding them flats, transporting their belongings and so on. After the April "action", he rescued fugitives from the Ghetto, searched for them in nearby blocks and fixed

---

10 Witold Benedyktowicz.

them up on the Aryan side. His sister Zosia helps him a lot. She has been hiding Jews for a considerable time and does not take a penny from them. She has been keeping a Jewish child in her flat free of charge for a long time. She is absolutely starving but she does not want to take money for hiding Jews. A Jewess who stayed with her for a longish period said of her: "I'm fifty, but I've never met anyone like her."

Mr. I.,[11] a Methodist clergyman, lives in his own villa near Warsaw. Military authorities occupy it from time to time when they are on leave. This fact does not, however, prevent him from rescuing Jews who have fled to the forests after the "resettlement actions" and are hiding from the Germans. Many Jewish children, particularly, are in hiding in this area and the rural population helps them. Characteristically, even the *Volksdeutsche* living in this locality do not refuse help to Jewish children. This clergyman takes care of adults and children, has them live in his house, feeds and protects them. His wife, who is Latvian by origin, found out about the terrible deeds done by the Latvians, who played the lamentable role of the executioners of Warsaw Jewry. She decided to accuse them openly. She went to the Latvian's barracks and told her fellow-countrymen what she thought of their cruelty. She said she was ashamed to belong to a nation that committed crimes like these, and she ended, "You can shoot me, but what I've told you is absolutely true." Attacked by their compatriot in this way, the Latvians hastened to justify themselves on the grounds that they had been obeying orders, acting under pressure, etc.

There are many such idealists among the Methodists and other sects. This is in line with historical traditions in Poland. Polish Aryans defended Polish peasants centuries back, and also stood up for the Jews of Poland. They were in close touch with Jews and discussed religious themes with them. The tradition of tolerance of Polish sects has come down the ages. The grandchildren of Arian sectaries are today saving Polish Jews, now threatened with extermination.

*

---

[11] Ignacy Kasprzykowski.

Among Polish doctors, individuals can be found who give Jews medical assistance regardless of the consequences. In the Nazi Hottentots' code this is considered a crime. A group of fifteen partisans were operating in a suburban area, M.[12] One day they went to bathe in a nearby river and omitted to take any precautions. They were given away to the local gendarmes, who immediately went to the river. There was a fight with the gendarmes, and some of the partisans were wounded. At midnight, the Jewish partisans knocked at the door of the local Polish doctor, who at once gave them medical assistance and also supplied them with the address of a surgeon. He would not accept a fee, not even to cover the cost of the dressings. When he was told afterwards that he was endangering himself by helping Jews, and Jews who were partisans into the bargain, he replied that he was a doctor, and according to the dictates of his conscience it was his duty to render aid to everyone who turned to him.

Idealists who hide Jews are to be found not only among the tormented, crucified Polish intellectuals, but also among the lower classes, the domestic servants. Before the formation of the Ghetto, the German authorities issued a decree forbidding Jews to employ Christian servants. The *Arbeitsamt* in the Jewish district allowed people to keep on employing their Aryan maidservants in individual cases. The great majority of Polish maidservants parted from their employers in an unfriendly way. They took advantage of the situation where the Jews had no rights and no way of securing a verdict in their favour in any dispute with Aryans. So the servants made inordinate demands on leaving: half-a-year's wages or even more was a standard request; demands for part of the employers' wardrobes, food provisions, fuel, etc. Willy nilly, the Jews had to comply with all these requests, if they did not want to invite inter-

---

[12] The locality referred to is probably that of Marki, in the Wolomin district near Warsaw. A Jewish partisan group of twenty-five people operated in this area under the command of Mosze Zieleniec. The underground paper, *Wiadomosci*, in its issue No. 5 of 1–8 January 1943, gave information on the activities of this group.

(See also, Ringelblum Archives, Part II, 338, in the Archives of the Jewish Historical Institute in Warsaw.)

vention by Gestapo-men or other uniformed policemen who happened to pass by. Some maids, especially those who had been on friendly terms with denunciators, Gestapo-men and their like, very often brought misfortune to their Jewish employers by informing the Germans of hidden goods, valuables, etc. Among domestic servants there were, however, a handful of noble individuals who went against the stream. Treated by their Jewish employers like members of the family for many years, these maids showed great warmth towards them. The devotion and self-sacrifice of these simple people reached a high ethical level that far surpassed ordinary human affection. They became transformed into personages out of fiction, as it were, not from "real life". Many Christian maidservants were sent to Treblinka together with their employers' families by the S.S. and the Ukrainians—explanations that they were Aryans and therefore not liable to "resettlement" were of no help. S.S.-men and their Ukrainian assistants had no time for such trifles as looking through documents which stated that the given person had the right to stay in the Ghetto on the basis of a permit issued by the *Arbeitsamt*. But we know of other cases where the Aryan maids could have extricated themselves from the clutches of the "resettlement" headquarters and could have escaped going to Treblinka by simply showing their Aryan papers and they did not do so, fully aware of what they were doing. This was the outcome of their devotion to the family which they had lived and suffered with for decades. I give as an example the maid of Councillor Rosental, who after twenty years of "faithful service", went voluntarily to Treblinka with her mistress. These maids wanted to share the fate of their employers for better or for worse. They showed deathless devotion, just like the hundreds and thousands of Jewish parents who were released by the Nazi killers during "selections" but who voluntarily followed their children to death.

Maid-servants already employed in new situations by Christians on the Aryan side displayed much kindness of heart and boundless love towards their former Jewish employers. They served as liaison between the Aryan side and the Ghetto. I knew a former servant of lawyer M., who made her way stealthily across the Ghetto walls to bring him the things he had left with her and money she had collected from his debtors, etc. I witnessed her great indignation when the lawyer wanted to remunerate her. Maids helped fix up their former employers on the Aryan side, they arranged the thousand and one things connected with this. We should like to give the example of a maid, Mrs. B., who rented a flat on the Aryan side for her former Jewish employers. Arranging all the formalities connected with renting a flat on the Aryan side usually cost several tens of thousands of zloty, but it cost her only 3,000 zloty, Mrs. B. serves as cover for the flat and arranges everything for her former employers; since their funds have run out she helps them financially by selling her own belongings. She also helps acquaintances of her former employers to find flats on the "other" side. When an acquaintance of mine told her that he had no money left, Mrs. B. answered, "If you had money, I wouldn't help you." I heard very many stories like these about maid-servants.

There are thousands of idealists like these in Warsaw and in the whole country, whether in the educated class or the working class, who help Jews most devotedly at the risk of their lives. Every Jew snatched from the grip of the bloodthirsty Nazi monster had to have an idealist like this watching over him day after day like a guardian angel. The great majority of these people helped the Jews in return for remuneration, but is there in fact money enough in the world to pay for these people's self-sacrifice? People who hid Jews for money only and had no strong moral motivation got rid of their dangerous ballast sooner or later and turned the Jews out of their flats. The ones that kept the Jews in their flats were those who did it not only for Jewish money. This Polish gallery of heroes could provide subjects for wonderful novels about these noblest of idealists, who feared neither the enemy's threats on his red posters nor the ominous obtuseness and stupidity of Polish Fascists and anti-Semites who esteem it an anti-national act to hide Jews.

CONCLUSION

We have come to the end of our remarks and observations on the subject of Polish-Jewish relations. After the war, when archive sources become available and it is possible to draw up the balance sheet of what remains of Poland's three and a half million Jews, the proper time will come for a comprehensive description of Polish-Jewish relations. Our remarks on this subject are an interim report and express the opinion of a handful of Jews who have survived the Nazi slaughter in Poland, but whose fate in the immediate future is not yet known and whose rescue is very problematic. We have pointed out in the appropriate place that the attitude of the Polish population towards the Jews has not been uniform: the Polish Fascist camp had an entirely different attitude from that of the workers. Polish Fascism, incarnated in bestial anti-Semitism, produced conditions that were unconducive to rescuing Jews from massacre by S.S. butchers, Ukrainians, Shaulists and Latvians. The German terror machine, the mass arrests and roundups and the severe penalties for hiding Jews have all combined with the anti-Semitic atmosphere created by the O.N.R. and by German propaganda to constitute unfavourable conditions for hiding Jews in any great number.

In Western Europe, especially in Holland, the Aryan population has hidden Jews on a mass scale, considering this not only a humanitarian act but also the duty of citizens who oppose the German invaders. According to completely reliable information from people who have come from Holland in the past few months, a considerable percentage of Dutch Jews have been able to hide in the homes of the local population, which is sympathetic to the Jews and is encouraged by appeals from independent organizations and the

Church. In Holland even the Fascists are not characterized by O.N.R.-style anti-Semitism. The same thing is happening in Belgium and France, where the Aryan population protested against the yellow patches and wore them *en masse* as a sign of solidarity with the Jews. There the sufferings of the Jewish population meet with great compassion on the part of the Aryans, who render all possible aid. If we take the special conditions in Poland into account, we have to acknowledge that the conduct of those among the Polish educated class, workers and peasants who do hide Jews is exceptionally noble and accords with the tradition of tolerance in Poland's history. These noble individuals face not only the German terror but also the hostility of Polish Fascists, who have not learnt their lesson from the experience of September 1939.

It is difficult to estimate the number of Jews in hiding in Poland. In Warsaw there are said to be about ten to fifteen thousand Jews hidden; some people even estimate twenty-five to thirty thousand, but to my mind this is greatly exaggerated. Probably no more than fifteen thousand Jews are in hiding in the capital, located with approximately two to three thousand Polish families. If we take into account that these two to three thousand families are acting with the knowledge and approval of their nearest relatives we reach the conclusion that at least ten to fifteen thousand Polish families in Warsaw are helping to hide Jews—reckoning four persons to a family, a total of about forty to sixty thousand persons. In the whole country including Warsaw, there are probably no more than 30,000 Jews hiding. Among the Polish families hiding Jews there are doubtless some anti-Semites. It is, however, the anti-Semites as a whole, infected with racialism and Nazism, who created conditions so unfavourable that it has been possible to save only a small percentage of the Polish Jews from the Teuton butchers. Polish Fascism and its ally, anti-Semitism, have conquered the majority of the Polish people. It is they whom we blame for the fact that Poland has not taken an equal place alongside Western European countries in rescuing Jews. The blind folly of Poland's anti-Semites, who have learnt nothing, has been responsible for the death of hundreds of thousands of Jews who could have been saved despite the Germans. The guilt is theirs for not having saved tens of thousands of Jewish children who could have been taken in by Polish families or institutions. The fault is entirely theirs that Poland has given asylum at the most to one per cent of the Jewish victims of Hitler's persecutions.[13]

---

[13] The most reliable estimates are those of Philip Friedman, who puts the number of Jews in Nazi-occupied Poland at from 3,200,000 to 3,250,000. This figure does not include about 250,000 Polish Jews who escaped extermination by fleeing, mainly to the U.S.S.R. Of these three million and more Jews, barely 40 to 50,000 were still alive at the end of the war. Thus not more than 1.3 to 1.6% of Jews survived on Polish soil. (See: Filip Friedman, *Zaglada Zydow polskich w latach 1939–1945*, "Biuletyn Glownej Komisji Badania Zbrodni Niemieckich w Polsce," Vol. I— 1946, pp. 204–205.)

But if we take into account that a certain number of Polish Jews— something between 10 and 20,000—survived in Nazi camps (e.g. 5,600 of them in the "HASAG" labour camp in Czestochowa), we are bound to conclude that Ringelblum was correct in his conclusion that the lives of only one per cent of the Jews were saved in hiding among the Polish population.

APPENDICES

(1)   A Death Sentence for Blackmail

The following is an unfortunately rare announcement by the Court of a death sentence passed on a criminal who blackmailed Jews. We quote the original text only as far as the words, "in addition". The end of the text is based on a report by a third person.

Announcement

In Warsaw, on the 7th of July 1943, Borys or Boguslaw Jan Pilnik, born on the 5th of May 1912, the son of Aleksander and Felicja Szatkowska, residing in Warsaw at 17 Pierackiego Street, was sentenced to death and the loss of public and civil rights by the Special Court, because, during the German occupation of Poland, while collaborating with the German authorities as an informer to the detriment of the Polish population, he handed over Polish citizens of Jewish nationality to the German authorities from whom they were hiding, and, for his own benefit, swindled his victims out of large sums of money under the pretext of needing these sums for the protection of those in hiding; in addition, he swindled families out of valuables and money under the pretext that he would liberate them from Pawiak.

(2)   A German Propaganda Pamphlet

entitled, "What is this war for?" (published by Fuenck); front page in colour with an enormous question mark. "What is the origin of this war? Millions of decent, hard-working people are suffering today under the [the sentence breaks off].

(3) LIST OF PEOPLE SHOT BY ORDER OF THE O.B.

Lejkin, Jakob, head of the Jewish Order Service in Warsaw, which was responsible for the "resettlement action" in Warsaw.

J. Szerynski, Colonel, former functionary of the Polish Police, head of the Jewish Order Service in Warsaw, which was responsible for the "resettlement action". Critically wounded, he recovered, and then committed suicide by taking poison.

Israel First, director of the Economic Section of the Jewish Council. Helped the occupation authorities in the "resettlement action". Maintained close relations with the Germans, showed brutality towards the employees of the Jewish Council.

Arek Weintraub, Gestapo-man, served the Germans and gave away Warsaw hide-outs to them.

Anna Milewicz, Gestapo-woman, one of the Gestapo's most dangerous agents.

Mandel, former co-worker in the Office to Combat Usury and Profiteering in Warsaw, the so-called "Thirteen".

Hirschl, from Gdansk, director of the carpentry workshop B. Hallmann, 58 Nowolipki Street. Helped the occupation authorities in "voluntary" despatching of employees of his workshop to Lublin: he persuaded many to go by pretending that he himself was going there too.

Dr. Alfred Nossig, politically active sculptor, personality on the international level. Collaborated actively with the Germans (Gestapo), giving them information about Jewish life. When he was executed, a report was found in his pocket intended for the Gestapo concerning the January 1943 "action"; in this report the O.B. was termed a "bandit organization".

Ejbeszyc, a dangerous Gestapo agent.

Lolek Skosowski, a very dangerous Gestapo agent. Sentenced by the O.B., he was critically wounded in February 1943; in November of this year he was killed by 18 bullets.

Adas Szejn, Gestapo-man, editor of the illegal provocateur organ, "Zagiew".

Jurek Firstenberg, from Zaglebie Dabrowskie, an officer in the Jewish Order Service, sentenced to death for his leading role in the "resettlement action" in Warsaw, when he acted in the capacity of Director of the *Umschlagplatz*.

Brzezinski, an officer of the Jewish Order Service, "loader" of the death wagons. This monster boasted that he had loaded a quarter of a million Warsaw Jews into the wagons with his own hands.

EDITORIAL APPENDIX

SELECT DOCUMENTS ON THE POLISH ATTITUDE TOWARDS JEWS

1.

Excerpt from Report No. 5/V–1/ of May 22, 1942, of the Internal Affairs Department in the Office of the Government Delegate for the Homeland

THE ATTITUDE OF THE JEWS TO THE POLES

In Jewish intellectual circles, efforts are being made to improve Jewish-Polish relations. These endeavours, while related to the problem as a whole, are however aimed concretely at reducing the friction which has developed during the occupation.

The following assessment of the atmosphere in the Ghetto, coming from intellectual circles there, is offered as a contribution in this direction. The Jews have a feeling of grievance against the Polish community, which ignores the abyss of injury and suffering which the Jewish population is plunged into. Their resentment at this is all the greater for their feeling of solidarity with the Polish community in its misfortune and oppression. As an example of indifference on the part of the Poles, the Jews point to the silence of the Polish press on the situation of the Jews. They reproach Polish official publications on the same grounds.

Among the Jewish masses the opinion prevails that the Polish lower middle class, freed from Jewish economic competition as a result of the situation created by the Germans, feels benevolent neutrality towards the invaders' policy of exterminating the Jewish population.

The general lack of contact with the Polish community is the reason for a deep feeling of bitterness among the Jewish masses, who cannot fail to see as Poles those officials whose attitude was certainly not one of fellow-citizens in their dealings with the Jewish population (tax assessment officials and, first and foremost, the Blue Police).

But enlightened Jewish society realizes that only part of the Polish community can he held responsible for the excesses of individuals (who, like the Blue Policemen, for example, behave in the same way towards their own compatriots), and hence feels solidarity with the rest of Polish society in their common misfortune. Jewish teachers, especially, inculcating love for things Polish, evoke feelings of solidarity, understanding and ties with Polish culture and patriotism.

The above-mentioned intellectual circles put the following desiderata to Polish circles:

1. To declare again publicly the basic stand taken on the Jewish question.

2. To pay more attention to the Jewish situation in publications (and particularly to report systematically on violence done to Jews).

3. To firmly condemn excesses committed by Poles against Jews.

4. To publish statements to instil into the Polish community that Jews are citizens of the Polish Republic in equal standing, and that every violation of the law committed against them falls within the criminal jurisdiction of the laws of the Polish Republic, and particularly that cooperation in any form with the Germans in their extermination policy will be regarded as high treason.

(Files of the Government Delegation, Archives of the Institute for the History of the [Communist] Party, Warsaw, No. 202/II–11, p. 82.)

2.

*Letter of the Jewish underground leader in Bialystok,
Mordekhay Tenenbaum (Tamaroff), to the regional command
of the Polish underground*

To: The Civil Struggle Directorate,
    Bialystok Region
Gentlemen,

In October last year the undersigned, as member of a delegation representing the Jewish National Committee in Warsaw, met the official in charge of the Department for Jewish Affairs in the Office of the Polish Government's Delegate in Warsaw, as well as the press and propaganda chief of the Civil Struggle Directorate in Warsaw and a Polish Army representative, in order to discuss with them conditions, ways and means of active cooperation between citizens of the Polish Republic closed in in the Ghettos by the invader and the Independence Movement in the Homeland. After a number of talks, an identity of attitudes was seen to exist as to methods of fighting the invader, as well as a complete harmony of views on regaining and reinforcing the independence of the Homeland. As a result of the cooperation that developed on this basis, members of the parties and associations which comprise the Jewish National Committee have been enrolled in all sectors of this Movement, from distribution of the Independence press to participation in (or independent execution of) acts of diversion and sabotage within the borders of the so-called General-Government. In the course of our cooperation, comradely relations have developed between us—relations worthy of people serving the same cause.

In December last year I was sent to Bialystok on behalf of the Jewish National Committee. A united organization had been created in the Bialystok Ghetto, encompassing all political views, from the extreme right to the Jewish Socialist Party, the *Bund.* Meanwhile, further evacuation of Jews from Warsaw had taken place and the heroic defence of the Ghetto on January 19–21. In the heroic fighting all members of our Warsaw central committee were killed.

This act of despair would not have been so effective had it not been for the arms deliveries we received from, *inter alia,* the Civil Struggle authorities and the Army Command in Warsaw. We had succeeded in persuading our fellow-Poles that our situation was a specific one; that, constantly facing imminent danger and death, we must be given the possibility—if, at a certain moment in time there is no other, more positive, way out—of dying with dignity, of defending ourselves to the last man, even though we know beforehand that we will be physically defeated. We found understanding in the highest centres of the Movement for the specific problems posed by the Ghetto situation, and for the way of thinking of people under sentence of death, who are prepared to renounce and sacrifice everything for the chance of an effective struggle, of revenge, of a *direct, face-to-face* fight with the invader.

You have turned to us, gentlemen, with the request that we provide you with propaganda material and cooperate with you in distributing publications intended for the Germans. We have provided this material and we are ready to continue providing it. As regards distribution, our reply was that we are prepared to undertake this too, but this cannot be done on a large scale because of the collective responsibility of the Ghetto and for tactical reasons. (It does not make sense for the Germans to get such material from ... Jewish hands.) Then, gentlemen, we put to you a counter-proposal: that you would help arm and transport our men for the purpose of a direct fight with the invader in places and under conditions decided on by Movement authorities.

In this way—indirectly, it is true—contact was established between us. A few days later an answer reached me in my capacity as Head of the Jewish National Committee in Bialystok. This answer read more or less: "We are very sorry, but we ourselves have at our disposal only a limited quantity of arms. And we have many people who are eager to get them. We know that in your attitude to the Germans you take the same uncompromising stand as we do, but after all there is still the unresolved problem of the Soviets..."

At some more suitable moment I could prove to you, gentlemen, that all the organizations, without exception, represented in the Jewish National Committee have been dissolved and persecuted in the Soviet Union. Their leaders have been sent to Siberia and their former members have not enjoyed the authorities' confidence. But this is not relevant. We reached full understanding in Warsaw; why cannot the same thing happen in Bialystok? And as for being "eager" —you can find, gentlemen, nobody more eager, devoted and ready for whatever may be necessary for the sake of *revenge*. A Pole eager to serve the Homeland can do so in other ways; he can afford to wait for the moment when the Government of the Polish Republic will issue its Order of the Day. We cannot wait! Every day is one day nearer to our deportation to the slaughterhouse. *We must act without delay.*

Gentlemen,

This is not the right time for us to carry on political "negotiations" with each other. As citizens of the Polish Republic we turn to you, the representatives of Free Poland. Two hundred grenades and a few score revolvers will not decide the moment of the [national] Rebirth. But they can be decisive for the last day of Poland's second largest Ghetto. And there is still another possibility: take our men out of the Ghetto for active combat service in the countryside.

For these purposes we place at the disposal of the Movement the maximum of what still remains in the Ghetto after its systematic pillage by the Nazi hangmen.

Gentlemen, we await your decision. We hope that at the moment of making it, you will consider, gentlemen, your responsibility before God and History.

M. Tamaroff.
Bialystok, April 2, 1943

(The Mersik-Tenenbaum Ghetto Bialystok Underground files, Yad Vashem Archives, File M–11/10.)

3.

Excerpt from a Memorandum by
Roman Knoll, Head of the Foreign Affairs Commission
in the Office of the Government Delegate for the Homeland

THE JEWISH QUESTION

Among our national problems there is also the Jewish problem. This was only in appearance an internal problem in our country. Actually it has always been connected with international issues and has influenced the conduct of our foreign affairs. We realize that this will be the case to an even greater extent after the end of this war, in which international Jewry officially belongs to one of the warring parties. The mass murder of Jews in Poland by the Germans will reduce the dimensions of the Jewish question in our country; it will not liquidate it entirely. A very considerable number of Jews will certainly survive, and their repatriation after the end of the war may force us to take into account a Jewish population of one or two million. After the terrible persecution suffered by

European Jewry, world public opinion will be much more sensitive to their fate and will devote more care to their interests. At this moment, Christian compassion for the tormented Jews is predominant in the Homeland; at the same time, however, a very strong animus prevails against the Jews in the eastern part of Poland. This is an aftermath of the period of Bolshevik occupation. In the Homeland as a whole—independently of the general psychological situation at any given moment—the position is such that the return of the Jews to their jobs and workshops is completely out of the question, even if the number of Jews were greatly reduced. The non-Jewish population has filled the places of the Jews in the towns and cities; in a large part of Poland this is a fundamental change, final in character. The return of masses of Jews would be experienced by the population not as restitution but as an invasion against which they would defend themselves, even with physical means. Thus it would be a really tragic thing for our policies if, at the moment of settling our frontiers, securing credits, concluding pacts or forming federations, Poland were to be pilloried by world opinion as a country of militant anti-Semitism. Every factor hostile to us would profit by this concatenation of circumstances in order to oppress us and deprive us of the fruits of the victory for which we have paid so dearly. The Government is correct in its assurance to world opinion that anti-Semitism will not exist in Poland; but it will not exist only if the Jews who survive do not endeavour to return *en masse* to Poland's cities and towns. In this difficult situation, the Homeland sees only one way out: the Polish Government must take the initiative—immediately, if possible—with the aim of creating a national centre for the Jews of Eastern Europe. This should be a project drawn up in cooperation with Jewish Zionist circles; this project should focus on an East European territory for the future Jewish State in preference to Palestine, which is too small for the purpose, too exotic and arouses conflicts in the Arab world, and in preference to some tropical colony, to which the Jews will refuse to emigrate. It is perhaps too early to decide precisely what territory should be considered. Our attitude in this matter should not have an anti-Jewish, but a philo-Jewish character. The Jews are a nation, they have a right to possess a territory of their own and to create all [social] classes and strata there. The Diaspora is a curse for Jewry, and the world owes them a recompense for the terrible persecution they are now undergoing. This should be provided, first of all, by those nations which have provided hospitality for the Jews throughout the centuries and which—after a peaceful farewell like this—are willing to participate in economic assistance to and military defence of the new state. We do not know to what extent action of this kind will be feasible, but we consider it necessary to press energetically towards this end by diplomatic as well as propaganda means. This project, it seems to us, will be much easier to realize at a time of general revision of frontiers and creation of new combinations of states than it would be in a period of peace and stability.

(This document, which has no date on it, was sent to the Polish Government in London in August 1943. A copy of it is to be found in the Schwarzbart Records, Yad Vashem Archives, File M-2/262.)

4.

Letter of Dr. Ignacy Schwarzbart, member of the National Council of Poland-in-Exile, to the Polish Government-in-Exile, enclosing a Memorandum from the Representation of Polish Jewry in Tel-Aviv (July–August, 1944)

Dr. Ignacy Schwarzbart
Member of the National Council of Poland

Telephone: Bayswater 0855

Correspondence Register. No:
3035/XIX a/44

45, Queens Court,
Queensway,
London, W.2.

XIX [illegible ms. note]

August 29, 1944

To:
The Prime Minister
Mr. Stanislaw Mikolajczyk,
London.

Dear Mr. Prime Minister,
Acting on instructions from the Representation of Polish Jewry, I beg to submit to you, Mr. Prime Minister, for the kind attention of the Government of the Polish Republic, a Memorandum from the said Representation, dated July 14, 1944, together with a copy of a letter addressed to me on the same date.

The erasures in paragraphs V and VI of the Memorandum have been made by me consequent to a telegraphic instruction from the Representation, which, having already sent the Memorandum, received information from me that convinced it that the thesis expressed in the sentences now erased was a mistaken one. Unfortunately, because of the distance I could only make this alteration in the form of erasures; I apologize for these erasures in the Memorandum, unavoidable in the circumstances.

Three days ago I received a telegram from the Representation, addressed to me and to Engineer Anzelm Reiss, member of the Presidium of the Representation; the text of the telegram was as follows:

"We authorize you to declare in our name that having regard to the situation that has arisen, we agree to abstain from publication of the Memorandum in this situation."

I submit this declaration accordingly.

Dear Mr. Prime Miniser, I should like to make some remarks concerning this Memorandum that I am submitting to you as instructed by the Representation. The Memorandum was drafted and dispatched before you, Mr. Prime Minister, made your journey to Moscow and before the present situation, with all its extremely grave implications for our State, came about. The Memorandum is being presented in circumstances which were not foreseen at the time it was dispatched, and this fact may produce a certain impression of disharmony between the vital interests of our State at the present time and the moment of presentation of the Memorandum. I should therefore like to make the following observations:—

The Representation of Polish Jewry, from the first moment when it was set up in Exile, has identified itself and continues to identify itself with the fundamental issues facing our Government —to fight for and attain independence, full existence and freedom for the Polish Republic. This has found expression in the previous Memoranda of the Representation, dated July 24, 1941, and September 16, 1943, submitted to the Government, as well as in countless declarations by me, presented in the name of the Representation to the National Council of the Polish Republic and to the Government. It has found expression not only in these declarations, but also in the political activities of the Representation. Polish Jewry, by participating as a matter of course in the armed struggle of the Polish Republic, has thus manifested that its fate is completely bound up with the fate of the Polish Republic, its present and its future. Once again, for the third time in this war, the remaining survivors of once great Polish Jewry are today taking part in the heroic defence of Warsaw on the ramparts and barricades. This is more than just a symbol. I voiced this in my last speech in the National Council, in your presence, Mr. Prime Minister, after your exposé of the 25th of this month.

By virtue of this bond it becomes clear why, even at this moment of such gravity for all of us, the Representation is unwilling to postpone submitting its problems and grievances to its own Government; these questions form part of the Polish situation, and at the same time they pose the problem of responsibility for saving at least the last remnant of Polish Jewry.

I should therefore like on this occasion to refer to my letters to you, Mr. Prime Minister, of June 27 and August 18 of this year, and to express my belief that even at this grave moment you, Mr. Prime Minister, as well as the whole Government, will fully and actively concern yourselves also with these problems which are a question of life and death for the remnant of Polish Jewry inside and outside the Homeland. The responsibility in this matter falls on the Representation of Polish Jewry, together with the Government of the Polish Republic. They must answer to their conscience and to history.

Please accept, Mr. Prime Minister, the expression of my high esteem.

[Signed] Ignacy Schwarzbart

COPY

Representation of Polish Jewry
Tel Aviv
July 14, 1944.

Most esteemed Mr. Deputy [Schwarzbart]
Member of the [Polish] Diet.

Enclosed we send you our Memorandum to the Government, together with our Resolution concerning the attitude of the Representation to the Government. We ask you to hand this Memorandum to the Government, together with the Resolution.

With the expression of our high consideration,

[Signed]   Dr. A. Stupp
General Secretary

[Stamp]   I. Lew
Acting Chairman

Representation of Polish Jewry
[This letter-head appears in English, Polish, Hebrew and Yiddish.]
Telephone: 4250
15, Lilienblum Street,
Tel Aviv.
July 14, 1944.

To:
The Government of the Polish Republic.
London.

The Representation of Polish Jewry has dealt in three consecutive plenary sessions with the problem of Polish-Jewish relations during these last years, and after intensive discussion the Representation

261

has passed the Resolutions attached to this Memorandum. The purpose of this Memorandum is to summarize our viewpoint of the said relations.

The tragedy of Polish Jewry in this war, and the war itself, in which the whole civilized world has combined forces to fight against lawlessness and oppression and for the liberty of peoples as well as the restitution of the complete Rights of Man—all this gives the question of Polish-Jewish relations a very different dimension from any that it ever possessed before.

In 1939, Poland joined the ranks of democratic States. It was to be expected that one logical consequence of this decisive step would be the amelioration in the attitude of the Polish community and Government towards the Polish Jews: that this attitude would be purged of the official anti-Semitism of the last pre-war years, when the policies of the Polish Government were under the influence of Nazism, which aimed at disintegrating the States and the peoples of Europe by means of the venom of hate.

Polish Jewry anticipated such a change of attitude. Thus, when the Government made its first declarations proclaiming the full emancipation of the Jews and rejecting slogans of racial hatred, we believed that this could be the beginning of a new era in the existence of Poles and Jews side by side, founded on consciousness of a common fate and on a sense of fairness towards Jewish fellow-citizens.

To our regret we must now observe that these hopes of Polish Jewry have not been fulfilled. This may be caused by the negative attitude of a part of the Polish population that has not yet sufficiently understood that anti-Semitism is one of the various weapons used by the enemy to subjugate Poland, that it is impossible to oppose Hitler and Fascism for Poland's sake and at the same time not oppose Hitler's proposals concerning Jews. Or it may be caused by insufficient influence of the Government and its organs on the population and the lack of any action on the part of the Government which could have proved that the Government wants its own declarations to be taken seriously. Whatever the causes, the actual situation is one in which Polish-Jewish relations are much worse today than at the outbreak of war. The feelings of hurt and disappointment among Polish Jews increase daily with every piece of news that reaches them from the spheres where Poles and Jews interact.

These spheres—taking into account only the most important ones —can be summarized as follows:—

I.

The Homeland and its attitude towards its Jewish population

We do not know all the details of the tragedy of Polish Jewry. From the reports we do have, from the accounts related by eyewitnesses who recently managed to escape from the Homeland, and from *compte-rendus* received from the Government, we have a fair idea of what has happened to the Jews in the Polish territories. On the basis of this material we are bound to observe that the majority of the Polish people have been passive spectators of the mass murder of Jews by the Germans; that they have not been able to bring themselves to take a single step in defence of their fellow-citizens. Some elements of the Polish community have even actively taken measures against the Jews; for example, a delegation of the Polish population of Czestochowa presented a petition to Governor Frank asking to have the Jews there concentrated in a Ghetto.

Here and there, however, individuals can be found, perhaps even small groups, who helped the Jews. We are, of course, grateful for each and every Jewish life that has been saved, for every act that shows genuine compassion. But these have been the exception. On the whole, there has been no collective reaction on the part of the Poles while the common enemy was murdering millions of Jews. And when only tens of thousands remained out of the hundreds of thousands of Warsaw's Jews, and they decided to defend themselves against the Germans and turned to the Poles for material help, the answer they received was: "We understand you —you cannot wait; but for us the time has not yet come." This did not prevent the Home Army from undertaking various armed actions against the Germans at this very time; and even earlier, actions were undertaken which had no connection with the German extermination of the Jews. Government sources have made statements about a number of such actions by the Home Army.

Even in this last year, when only a fraction of Polish Jewry still existed and when, because of this tragic fact and at the approach of victory the atmosphere in the Homeland changed somewhat, even in this recent period the Jews in Poland have not been able to observe any collective action aimed at stopping their extermination. Among numerous attacks by the Home Army directed against various German objectives there has not been a single one against the so-called death camps. There was, however, a strong attack on a concentration camp in Pinczow that helped over 400 non-Jewish internees to escape to freedom. The very fact that the Jews themselves managed to destroy the death camps of Treblinka and Sobibor is proof that such actions were not impossible. The Germans expected an adverse reaction on the part of the Poles. There were Germans who, for fear of this reaction, argued against beginning the extermination. But later, as already stated in our of our reports, the Germans stressed the fact that Poles did not defend the Jews. Because of this failure to react on the part of the Poles, Polish soil has become the execution place and the graveyard for millions of Jews from all of Europe.

During this whole period, the Home Army has either not accepted Jews into its ranks or has done so only in very rare instances.

Furthermore, Jews were left practically without arms and have had to pay large sums of money for weapons that were often in very bad condition.

Thus, receiving practically no help from the surrounding population and having practically no arms at their disposal, the Jews have gone to their death *en masse*. And often on this last road they were accompanied by sneers from the Poles around them at their "letting" themselves be massacred.

This attitude is also apparent in official reports from Government circles acting in the Homeland. Thus, from Homeland Report No. 5 of 1943, page 135, we quote the following passage: "And there is perhaps no other section of the population more repugnant, with more distinctive and repellant specific traits than the Jews." Further, on page 136, the following remarks occur on the massacring of Jews in Poland by the Germans: "[The Jewish population of] entire villages and towns, big and small, has been shot down, sometimes—it is rumoured—murdered in a bestial way. But to hear about this from afar is not the same as to see it. And we have said to ourselves, at least some of us: 'These methods are horrible, the dishonour falls on these ruffians, on the murderers of women and children,' but... in the political perspective, in the perspective of our future internal relations in Poland, this is liable to be of quite positive importance, because we certainly had a disproportionately high number of Jews." Another document states that the Homeland understands that the Government has to have a pro-Jewish policy; the Government must realize, however, that the concerns and the property cannot be returned to their former owners, because the population would forcibly oppose this.

Reference must be made here to a passage in another official report, which mentions the practice of blackmailing and denunciations of the few Jews in hiding, as well as a passage in another report which refers to Jews hiding in the forests as "Jewish bands" which have become a plague for the surrounding population.

All this together gives a fairly exact picture of the relations that prevail while the tragedy of Polish Jewry, the greatest in history, is taking place on Polish soil, on this soil where more than a thousand years ago the Jews cast in their lot—for better or for worse—with the Polish people.

Against this generally gloomy background, a few brighter points are barely discernible: the relatively rare actions by some Poles to defend and to save individual Jews.

It is impossible to free the Government from at least partial responsibility for what is happening in the Homeland since, in spite of numerous appeals from Jewish circles, the Government did not initiate any action to inform and enlighten the Home population; it did not fight anti-Semitism through the weekly talks that are broadcast on radio for the Homeland; the Government sent no instructions; it did not dismiss any subordinate officials who propagated anti-Semitism. What is more, even in Exile the Government employed active O.N.R. members in propaganda work to issue anti-Semitic pamphlets that were distributed among Polish émigrés and dispatched to the Homeland; simultaneously, a second edition was printed—for Jewish circles abroad—in which the anti-Semitic passages were left out. Jewish circles informed the Government of this [propaganda] "work" at the time.

II.

The Army

Not only in the Homeland under enemy rule, but also in places that lie outside the invaders' sphere of influence, relations between Poles and Jews are far from being satisfactory. The most convincing evidence of this is afforded by relations in the Army. It is a characteristic fact that these relations are the same wherever the Army is present. In the Middle East and in England the same phenomena exist, the same atmosphere prevails everywhere as regards Jewish soldiers. And the consequences are much the same. In the Middle East, Jews leave the ranks *en masse.* They are not evading armed service: very often the same men immediatly enter the ranks of other military forces. But they are escaping from hate-filled surroundings. In England, court trials, debates in Parliament and finally amnesty occur.

The very fact that the same phenomenon has occurred in various places, far removed and distant from each other, proves that they are caused by the generally negative attitude towards Jews that prevails in the Army. Over long years the Government has done nothing to counteract this attitude, or at least nothing sufficiently energetic.

This general attitude, and the necessity for combating it by serious educational activity, has been dealt with in a different context, in our first Memorandum to the Government, dispatched as early as 1941. But our suggestions were not adopted. If the committees for research and education had begun to act energetically in 1941, and if already then the Government had called to account all those who were creating this anti-Jewish atmosphere in the Army, the situation would certainly have been different today.

III.

Countries of Emigration

Another sphere where Poles and Jews come into contact, free from the invaders' oppression is formed by the emigration centres. Here, too, the same thing occurs: an anti-Jewish attitude prevails and Polish official and semi-official institutions treat the Jews badly. In Russia, the [Polish] Army places obstacles in the way of Jews who want to enlist; afterwards, those few Jewish soldiers who have been admitted, are discharged and have their uniforms taken away from them on the eve of evacuation [of General Anders' Army from Russia to the Middle East]; during the evacuation itself, infernal scenes: the well-known conference of the Russian General Zhukov, and the Gehenna created for the Jews, about which volumes could be written. Moreover, the men that were not accepted for military service because of their supposed unfitness were actually perfectly fit for service, as is proved by the fact that they subsequently entered military service in Teheran.

In Hungary, where a small number of survivors of Polish Jewry have found shelter, anti-Jewish leaflets have been published by Poles and disturbances have taken place in the schools. The semi-official Delegate of the Government spends no money at all to aid the Jews, who reach Hungary scarcely resembling human beings, exhausted and in rags, after lengthy wanderings over mountains and through forests.

In Mexico: conflicts. In England: complaints and grievances of leaders of local Jewry, because the Poles spread anti-Semitism among the Scottish population; these complaints were voiced during debates in the English Parliament and in the English press.

Here in the Middle East, too, Polish agencies give not too cordial a reception to the few Polish-Jewish émigrés who have recently arrived here from various countries. The difficulties put in the way of their obtaining Polish documents often give these emigrants the impression that the Polish Government representative before whom they appear simply regrets the fact that these individual Polish Jews have escaped.

After a number of *démarches* and as a result of pressure, some

267

of these situations have improved. The general impression, however, in almost all emigration centres is still that a Jew is received there reluctantly and with ill will.

IV.

The Government

Action by the Polish Government relative to the enormity of the Polish-Jewish tragedy has consistently been insufficient and very dilatory. In this field too, as in the whole attitude of the Government towards the Jews, two guidelines are discernible: one intended for the outside world, the other for internal use. For the outside world, declarations of full equality of rights for the Jews. For internal use, these declarations do not commit anyone to anything much.

Where Jews are concerned, the battle to obtain anything has to be fought all over again: in order to get enforcement of any administrative regulation or secure any measure of help, special efforts, interventions and pressures have to be applied. Nothing can be taken for granted on the basis of these Government declarations.

For the outside world, the repeal of the law concerning withdrawal of citizenship; for internal use, old passports are not renewed for fear that the holder might perhaps have had his citizenship withdrawn under this now repealed law. For the outside world, equal rights and duties for all citizens in the armed forces; for internal use, prolonged Government indifference to everything that happens to the Jews in the Army.

The same situation existed later on when, compared to the problem of saving the Jews from complete annihilation, everything else became almost unimportant and virtually outdated. For the outside world, declarations that the Government was doing everything in its power to save Jews; on the inside, no consideration is given to even so modest a request as to delegate a few Jews to the Polish agencies in neutral countries, so that they can get into touch with the Jews in the Homeland as well as initiate and organize rescue activity.

Furthermore, the Note of the Government of the Polish Republic to the Allied Governments of December 1942—for which we are, indeed, grateful to the Government—also came too late. Over a lengthy period the world had been given no information on what was happening to the Jews in Poland. Even some of the Polish parties laid the blame for this on the official element in the Homeland; these reproaches were also echoed in the foreign press.

Later, when Polish soil became one big death camp for millions of Jews, and when strong and decisive reaction on the part of the Polish population could still have turned the scales, it proved for long, very long, impossible to get the Government's broadcasts to call upon the home population to help the Jews. And it was late, very late, when orders arrived—and only semi-official orders at that—directed against those who collaborated with the Germans in annihilating Jews, though the Government knew from its own reports that certain elements in the Polish community were collaborating with the Germans in this field. Even now these broadcasts are too few, and the orders are not firm enough.

As already mentioned, evidence of the attitude of the Government's Delegates in the Homeland is provided by the reports of these Delegates themselves. The spirit of these reports, like the orders of certain Army commanders, cannot possibly be reconciled with the declarations of the Government. Nevertheless, Government Delegates in the Homeland are continued in their posts. Thus the Delegates and all their collaborators cannot but deduce from this the only possible conclusion: that the Government line intended for the outside world and the Government's wishes regarding relations inside the country are two quite different things. This is also, it seems, the opinion of all Government organs about the role, importance and destination of Government declarations regarding the Jews. The Government for its part has done nothing to persuade them [its organs] and the community as a whole that this is not the case.

The financial help given to the Jews in the Homeland remains in no sort of proportion to their needs. The figures mentioned in the report of the Council for Aid to Jews in the Homeland, covering the period of December 1942 to October 1943, prove that the

Government has given next to nothing for aid to Jews (in January 1943, 150,000 zloty; in February 1943, 300,000 zloty; etc.); even the amount budgeted for this purpose for 1944—a million zloty a month—is of symbolic rather than practical importance. These eloquent figures have a significance which hardly accords with Government declarations.

V.

The Council for Matters Concerning the Rescue of the Jewish Population in Poland

Only towards the end of the fifth year of war, when only a small remnant of Polish Jewry was still alive, the Government decided to establish a Council for Matters Concerning the Rescue of the Jewish Population in Poland. For a long time the Representation [of Polish Jewry] had been clamouring for the creation of a special Under-secretaryship of State or Department for Jewish Affairs, endowed with fairly wide powers and an adequate budget, that would be primarily concerned with saving Jews. The Government did not meet this demand. Instead, a small organization was set up that bears no relation to the public renown bestowed upon it. This Council has been equipped with a budget of only £ 200,000, *and the expenditure of even this small amount has been made dependent on world Jewish organizations' giving donations at the same time.* [The passage between the asterisks is crossed out.]

In our opinion, not much can be done in the way of saving Jews with an amount of £ 200,000. *And we must absolutely refuse to accept the principle that where Jews are concerned the Government considers itself bound to help them only insofar as world Jewry also subsidizes these activities at the same time.* [The sentence between asterisks is crossed out.] When the enemy is murdering 10% of the Polish population, large-scale rescue operations are the prime duty of the Polish Government. We are sure that world Jewish organizations will not refuse to help, *but we cannot agree that this should be a condition for the Government's taking action. The whole attitude of the Government in this matter, too, is liable to give the impression that it is prompted by the desire to produce an external effect more than anything else.* [The passage between asterisks is crossed out.]

VI.

The Attitude of the Government towards this Representation
The attitude of the Government to the Representation itself is reflected in its way of meeting our demands. During the four years of our work, we cannot point to a single matter, major or minor, that was settled in accordance with our desiderata.

That, briefly summarized, is what Polish-Jewish relations have been during nearly five years of war. These relations are underlined by the Resolutions we have passed in our capacity as the Representation of Polish Jewry.

Our desiderata are known to the Government from our previous Memoranda, from numerous cables and from the Memoranda of our representative in the National Council. They covered the following points, the majority of which even at this late date are still urgent and can be realized:—

1. Frequent Government broadcasts to the Homeland regarding aid to Jews on the part of the Polish community, in particular hiding Jews, providing them with false papers and facilitating their escape; also broadcasts condemning anti-Semitism.

2. Concrete steps to be taken by the Home Army against the murder of Jews, i.e. destruction of death camps and of roads and other means of communication with these camps.

3. Appropriate financial help for the Jews in the Homeland.

4. A decree announcing the death penalty for all persons collaborating with or helping the Germans in acts of murder or pillage of Jews.

5. Enrollment in units of the Home Army of Jews presenting themselves or presented by Jewish organizations.

6. Earmarking a quantity of arms as adequate as possible for Jewish combatants.

7. Removal from their posts of Government representatives in the Homeland who have displayed anti-Jewish attitudes.

271

8. Educational activities in the Army aimed at removing anti-Semitism; persons who spread anti-Semitic propaganda in the Army should be punished.

9. Aid for Jewish refugees in Russia.

10. Issue of Polish documents to [Jewish] refugees who reach the free countries.

11. Creation of a Department or Undersecretaryship of State for Jewish Affairs in the Prime Minister's Office.

12. Participation of Jews in Polish delegations to international bodies such as UNRRA, etc.

13. Appointment of Jews to Polish agencies in neutral countries.

14. Creation of conditions for effective, large-scale activity by the Council for Matters Concerning the Rescue of the Jewish Population in Poland, through a considerable increase in this Council's budget, *and by making the expenditure of this budget independent of subsidies from Jewish organizations.* [The passage between asterisks is crossed out.]

The implementation of these desiderata depends on the Government alone and in the first place on the readiness of the Government to acknowledge its own declarations concerning the Jews and to put them into effect.

For our part, we can only repeat once more that we shall be glad if the Government enables us by its deeds to change our attitude towards it.

The Representation of Polish Jewry

[Signed:] Izchak Lew   [Signed:]   Dr. Abraham Stupp
Acting Chairman   General Secretary

Resolutions
passed at the Plenary Session of the Representation of Polish Jewry on June 21, 1944

The attitude of the Representation towards the Government

1. The policies of the Polish Government regarding the Jews; the non-implementation of our concrete demands put to the Government repeatedly over the last four years; the failure to take into account our desiderata even in the matter of rescuing and aiding

the Jewish population, which was in the process of being massacred in Poland; the passivity of the Government in combating anti-Semitism in the Homeland, in the Army and in the emigration centres—have undermined the Representation's confidence in the Government.

2. Our desiderata have been concerned with the most vital and elementary needs of the Jewish population in Poland. The failure of the Government to implement even these demands has been in contradiction to the Government's own declarations on equal civil rights for the Jews; the Government itself is therefore to blame for the crisis of confidence in our attitude towards it.

(Schwarzbart Records, Yad Vashem Archives, file M–2/609)

POSTSCRIPT

by JOSEPH KERMISH

The work by Dr. Emmanuel Ringelblum on the Polish-Jewish relations during the Second World War, written in hiding at the time
the war was still going on, has some obvious limitations. This is
why I feel, that some further remarks on this important subject may
be useful.

*

Immediately after the entry of the Germans into Warsaw, anti-
Semitic elements were already to be found, and in considerable numbers, lending a hand to the Germans against the Jews. This anti-
Semitic riff-raff busied itself with pin-pointing Jewish flats and informing against rich Jewish shop-owners, from among it came the
rioters in the frequent pogroms that took place from the beginning
of October until the establishment of the Ghetto in November 1940.
In these disturbances Polish youngsters, including school-children,
armed with sticks and all sorts of destructive implements, would
attack passers-by of all ages, men and women, and beat them up
savagely. They would break the few remaining shop-windows and
steal whatever they could lay their hands on in the shops and houses.
The Polish Police looked on with equanimity. The attackers were
sometimes driven off by Jewish workers. Wherever the Jews dared
to defend themselves, the mob of attackers would disperse and flee.
In photographs published in newspapers in the Reich, the Germans
wanted to show the anger of the Polish people directed at the Jews.
In the disturbances of March 1940, the Germans photographing the
pogrom pretended to be defending the Jews. Apart from this, Polish
hooligans spent their time not only in throwing stones over the
Ghetto walls, but did not even shrink from taking hammers and
smashing the grave-stones in the Jewish cemeteries in Okopowa and

275

Praga (where, e.g., the gravestone of Zwitkower was badly damaged).[1]

It was from among the anti-Semitic riff-raff that squads of labour-camp guards were formed later on *(Lagerschutz)* who maltreated Jewish camp inmates and often tortured them to death. This riff-raff was master of the streets and became the main link between Polish Jew-haters and the Nazis. They were the extortioners and the agents of the Germans. By their doing and "thanks" to the Polish uniformed police tens of thousands of Jews were murdered.

The German occupation authorities spared no efforts to intensify Jew-hatred. In all the main cities, Nazi newspapers in the Polish language began to appear, the main purpose of which was to spread the poison of anti-Semitism among the Polish population, and it must be admitted that this press influenced its readers to a very considerable extent. There was a strong public response, in spite of all the anathema pronounced against this foul press by the Polish underground.

With the attack on the Soviet Union, the German authorities let loose an uninhibited campaign of anti-Semitic provocation over the whole country. Hatred grew ever more intense and more inflamed. The German press was full of news about Jewish desecration of churches, about Jews' murdering Polish intellectuals and other such invented atrocities. Polish-language leaflets were distributed among the Polish riff-raff full of poisonous agitation against the "Jewish Bolsheviks". German agents penetrated even into the villages with this propaganda, which succeeded in arousing the worst instincts and undermining all that was good in the hearts of the people.

As Ringelblum rightly points out, anti-Semitic trends were strengthened when thousands of Poles returned from the areas that had been conquered by the Russians in 1939 and that were later occupied by the Germans. These Poles spread reports of the cruel deeds of the

---

[1] Emmanuel Ringelblum, *Ktovim fun geto,* Vol. I, op. cit., pp. 78–79, 81, 83, 104–105, 133; Adam Czerniakow, *Warsaw Ghetto Diary,* op. cit., entries for above-mentioned dates as well as for 30 June and 9 July 1940; *Sefer hazevaot,* op. cit., pp. 34, 45–47, 49, 53, 55.

Soviet security forces (N.K.V.D.), supposedly carried out by Jews in the service of the Russian secret police.[2] According to Breslaw's record of his conversations with the Polish woman employee of the Warsaw City Council, a believing Christian, of patriotic and democratic convictions, she declared, "If the Poles are to be judged guilty because of their attitude to the Jews, if it is pointed out that actions like theirs in fact assist the conqueror—you can assume beforehand that you will hear the reply that this is in reprisal for what happened on the other side of the Bug. I don't know what happened on the other side of the Bug—it certainly wasn't one per cent of all the things people here say, because otherwise not a single Pole would have got back alive from the provinces in the East. I believe this is a sort of pretext, one of the ways of stilling our consciences. Since the war against the Soviets, this factor has weakened somewhat".[3]

It is worth adding here that in the negative reply of the Polish Home Army authorities to the request for aid to the Jewish Partisan movement, a request made by the Commander of the Jewish Combat Organization after the reppression of the Warsaw Ghetto rising, reference was made to "the hostile impact on the Poles caused by the Jewish attitude at the time of the Soviet conquest".[4]

Mordekhai Tennenbaum-Tamaroff, in his letter of 2 April 1942 to the Bialystok District Commander of Civilian Resistance (the letter in which the Commander of the Jewish Combat Organization requested to be supplied with 200 grenades and a score or so of pistols—a letter published here in full for the first time)[5] gave a trenchant answer to the attacks made on the Jews regarding close collaboration with the Soviets. "If the times and the conditions were other than they are", he wrote, "I could prove to the Poles that all the organizations comprising the Jewish National Council" (he is re-

2 Emmanuel Ringelblum, *Ktovim fun geto*, Vol. II, op. cit., p. 261.
3 J. Kermish, *Relations between Jews and Poles. A hiterto unknown record by Shmuel Breslaw*, "Yalkut Moreshet", No. 11, 1970, p. 105.
4 The Commander of the Jewish Combat Organization (Antek) to the Commander of the Home Army, 26 November 1943. Published in "Resistance and Revolt in the Warsaw Ghetto", op. cit., p. 143.
5 See above, Appendix 2, pp. 253–256.

ferring to the Zionist parties and the *Bund*) "were dissolved, their members suffered torture and their leaders were exiled to Siberia." For obvious reasons this sentence was cut out of the letter when it was published a number of times in Poland. It is worth adding that Tennenbaum called Zionist activity in the underground under Soviet rule "our heroic period" . . .[6]

Not a day went by without anti-Jewish articles, reports and reminders in the official German and Polish daily papers. The illegal anti-Semitic publications expressed themselves in the same terms. The underground *Endek* paper, *Miecz i Plug,* in its issues of 7 and 14 June 1942, wrote frankly, "One of the main points in our ideological programme is expulsion of the Jews from Poland. Immediate and final expulsion . . . We shall not kill the Jews . . . We shall force them to emigrate".

In June and July 1942, *Przebudowa,* the theoretical organ of the Peasants' Party (*Stronnictwo Ludowe*), also complained that there were still too many Jews in Poland, and that was why many problems still remained unsolved in the political, economic and cultural life of the Polish people. "Our latest experiences have proved", declared the writer, "that the Jewish masses are hostile to Poland or in the best of cases indifferent. Although we are far from using the cruel methods of the Germans, our stand is that the decisive majority of the Jews must leave Poland. We know perfectly well that this question cannot be solved in our country alone, that it is a question on a world scale and can only be solved on that level."

What was the attitude of the left-wing and democratic Polish press? *Nowe Drogi* wrote on 5 August 1941: "Let us frankly admit that the left-wing and democratic press of the Polish underground has mainly passed over the problems of anti-Semitism in silence. It has not given it the place it should have, it has not warned the Polish public against its insidious, ideological snares". The underground paper, *WNR* of mid-August 1941 rightly sounded the alarm over the fact that while the Polish underground press faithfully published all the announcements and appeals of the Polish Government in London, it systematically suppressed all the warnings sent from

---

[6] M. Tennenbaum-Tamaroff, *Dapim min hadleyka,* op. cit., p. 42.

there against anti-Semitism and against collaboration with and imitation of Hitlerism in this respect. In an article entitled, "Drops of Poison", the underground paper, *Nowe Drogi* organ of the Democratic Party, wrote on 5 August 1941: "On the Jewish question we are adopting the enemy's methods and becoming infected with his morbid psychosis". The paper explained clearly to its readers, "Anti-Semitism is the channel through which the enemy introduces poison into the Polish organism . . . It serves as a bridge of understanding between part of the Polish population and the Hitlerite invaders, since everyone who is pleased at the eviction of Jews from the economic life of Poland, everyone who makes a living by working with the Germans and who gets rich, builds the pillars of this bridge". Aryanization (de-Judaization, clearing out of Jews) is seen by the Polish writer as "a means to direct the masses into the struggle against the Jews in order to divert them from the struggle against the invader, against Hitlerism . . . For the time being, Poles have been allowed to take the place of the Jews, in order to break up united Polish-Jewish resistance to German domination over the economy of Poland. Jews and Poles did not constitute separate economic groups in Poland. Everything was interlocked, the cogwheels turned each other, the Jewish workshop complemented the Polish. Hitler's system was to drive a wedge between Jews and Poles, to get rid of the Jews first in order to do away with the Poles afterwards. And that it what is happening now: the Germans themselves are taking over the key positions in industry, commerce and banking".

The organ of the Polish Socialists, *Barykada Wolnosci,* also sharply criticized local reactionaries, the Polish ones, for robbing the Jews. In an article of 15 February 1942, it wrote: "Wonderful are the ways the spirit moves a Polish nationalist. He easily combines his new-found hatred for Hitler with complete agreement with his anti-Jewish actions. Auschwitz he severely condemns, but camps for the Jews he greets with satisfaction. Palmiry[7] and Wawer[8] were

---

[7] A place on the Warsaw-Modlin highway where some 1,800 Poles were killed.

[8] A place near Warsaw where 2 German policemen were killed by Polish

a crime, but the killing of tens of thousands of Jews in the east is for him of no consequence if not actually something to be pleased about. For him, the struggle against Hitler is connected with enthusiasm for the idea of the Ghetto. According to the notions of a Polish nationalist, Hitler is the two-faced deity; when he shows his anti-Polish visage the nationalist shakes his fist at him, but when he revolves to show his anti-Jewish countenance—he bows down and worships him".

There is no doubt that part of the Polish people, the class-conscious workers by hand and brain, regarded the campaign against the Jews as despicable and saw it as an instrument of the Germans for undermining the united front of the Polish people and encouraging collaboration with the invaders. But not only did the majority of the Poles not manifest any active resistance to the anti-Jewish campaign—there was no discernible, outward expression of disapproval or disavowal, by word of mouth or in writing, of the gang of collaborators with the Germans, and nothing was done that might have weakened the impression that the entire Polish population at every level supported the shameful actions of the Polish anti-Semites.

Ringelblum criticizes sharply the attitude of the Polish Government in exile towards the Jews. It is worth pausing here on this problem. The Sikorski Government published a series of declarations on this question, according to which Jews were promised equal rights in post-war Poland. After the signature of the Polish-Soviet Friendship Treaty on 30 July 1941, General Sikorski, Prime Minister of the Polish Government-in-Exile, made a public pronouncement promising that Poland would be reconstructed on "foundations of democracy, political, economic and social", and that there would be "equal rights for every Polish citizen without distinction of religion, race or nationality".

In October 1941, the Polish Government in London published a policy declaration laying down the basis on which Poland would be reconstructed in the future. One of the main passages in this declaration promised equal national rights for the Jews in the fol-

criminals. 107 persons (97 Poles and 10 Jews) were then shot by German police.

lowing terms: "Poland will be a democratic country, based on the equality of all its citizens without distinction of race or nationality". It should be recalled that this declaration led to a government crisis. Representatives of the National-Democrats and the *Sanacja* did not want to accept this provision and left the Government. (They returned in January 1942 in unexplained circumstances.) The anti-Semitic agitation in London occasioned by this declaration of policy spread to occupied Poland itself. The illegal publications of the N.D., the *Sanacja* and other reactionary Polish groups—and this under a regime of blood-stained terror—swarmed with articles against giving rights to Jews, and entire programmes were drawn up for after the war about how to complete the process so successfully begun by the invader of wiping out the Jews. Isolation (*sc.* Ghettos) should be retained in the future too, and Jews should not be allowed to return to their previous economic positions. True, the invaders' bloodstained methods of murdering Jews should not be adopted, but the Jews should be considered foreigners and should be obliged to leave the country and go elsewhere.

The Polish underground press that was subject to the influence of the Polish Government and its constituent bodies made absolutely no attempt to preach the Government's declared principles or imbue its readers with the idea that the Poland of the future should be constructed on foundations of national justice and equal rights. It will of course be apparent that this does not apply to the Polish Underground Socialist press. There was for example the controversy in the underground paper, *W.R.N.* The organ of the right-wing of the Socialist Party (P.P.S.), in its number of February 1941, took issue with the reactionary anti-Semitic groups in the underground, declaring that a liberated Europe would be unthinkable if it were not democratic and socialist. "Today when the power of the British Labour Party is steadily increasing, when the socialist proletariat in the occupied countries is organizing for revolt against the invader— today there is some Utopianism, some break-away from the very notion that after the overthrow of Hitler there will arise a new Fascist Poland. Even the English Conservatives have understood that England and the rest of the world as well will not be able to return to the pre-war forms of capitalism." The Polish Government's underground press did not even try to fight the anti-Semitic propaganda so systematically and purposefully spread by the Germans after the invasion of Russia. (At that time the German press was full of "news" about "Jewish criminal activities" against the Church and "Jewish murderers of the Polish intelligentsia" and other fabrications of the kind. They also distributed anonymous pamphlets in Polish filled with poisonous incitement against "Jewish Bolsheviks".)

At the same time, the Sikorski Government continued to made statements in favour of the Jews. The "Poles of the Mosaic persuasion" in the Warsaw Ghetto had absolute faith (expressed in their underground publication, *Zagiew*) that the Poland that would arise after the war would be the motherland of all its citizens without distinction of religion and nationality—"General Sikorski's declarations leave no doubt on the subject". Responsible circles in the Jewish Underground movement, on the other hand, were not over-impressed by General Sikorski's declarations, since "promises are simply the fruit of a certain political climate, of opportunism" (*Proletarischer Gedank*, February 1942).

In a message broadcast to the Homeland on 19 October 1942, General Sikorski stressed that the anti-Semitic campaign was not supported even by right-wing politicians and was absolutely opposed by Catholic circles. General Sikorski voiced the wish that full expression be given to democratic principles in Poland, "because the struggle that is being waged is for democratic aims".

The declaration issued by the Council of National Union in March 1944, entitled, "What Poland is Fighting For—Poland to be a State of Nationalities", was probably based on this broadcast. The periodical, *Wielka Polska Dwutygodnik Mlodziezy*, organ of the *Wielka Polska* ("Great Poland") group in the National Party *(Stronnictwo Narodowe)*, published an article attacking this declaration. The article, published on 27 April 1944, was entitled, "The Curse of Tolerance" *(Przeklenstwo Tolerancji)*. It affirmed, "Only Poles can have (these) various political rights in Poland. In particular, these rights cannot be possessed by Jews, Germans and Ukrainians". The curse of tolerance had brought Poland to the edge of the abyss, and the only way to avoid making the same mistakes, was to transform Poland into a national State (i.e. not a State of nationalities).

In actual fact, the real attitude of the Government-in-Exile regarding the Jews of Poland was expressed in the decision of the National Council of October 1942: "The National Council of the Polish Republic expresses the opinion that the Jewish question—the question of a nation without a country—must be resolved at the Peace Conference. The Jewish people must be afforded conditions for normal development within the framework of its own State with its own government. The Jewish people, which has given proof of its extraordinary vitality during the 2,000 years of its Dispersion since the fall of its own historical State, must no longer be deprived of a territory of its own". Plainly, if we discount the polite restraint with which it is formulated, this position has many points in common with pre-war projects for "settling the Jewish question".

The sad truth is that nothing is known of any organized action by the Government-in-Exile representatives to save the Jews.

This state of affairs was a cause of stupefaction to those Poles who regarded the "final solution" of the Jewish problem in German-occupied Poland with abomination. Evidence of this is furnished by the angry observation in the diary of a woman active in the underground movement, Wyleżyńska: "The Polish Government in London did not stand up for its guets (the Jews) here (in Poland), even if it did start assistance to Jewish refugees who escaped from France to Switzerland". Incidentally, her notes also express astonishment at the absence of any call of Jewish international solidarity.

At the time of the first "action" in the Warsaw Ghetto, in August 1942, an attempt was made to establish links with the Polish underground and with its armed organization in order to get help in organizing effective resistance of the German "action". Even before this, the Jewish underground (representatives of *Hehalutz* and members of the *Bund*) had been in touch with Sikorski's people. "We used to supply them with information," records Mordekhai Tennenbaum-Tamaroff, "about what was going on in our vale of tears, and they used to print it from time to time in their (underground) press and pass it on to London." The Jewish Affairs Section at underground (Home) Army Headquarters also prepared a lecture based on the situation of the Jews, as well as a "Black Book", which reached London early in December and was published there at once.

283

Representatives of the Jewish National Council made contact with the Polish underground authorities in October 1942. A meeting was held by M. Tennenbaum with the head of the Polish Government Delegation's Jewish Affairs Section, the head of the Information and Propaganda Department of the Command in charge of Civilian Struggle, and a representative of the underground (Home) Army, in order to discuss ways and means of effective cooperation between "citizens of Poland imprisoned in Ghettos by the invader" and the liberation movement in the Homeland. After a number of talks, an identity of attitudes was seen to exist as to "methods of fighting the invader, as well as entire harmony of views on regaining and reinforcing the independence of the Homeland . . ." However, official circles of the Polish underground saw their main task as information, education and civilian struggle, chiefly in the economic sphere. Any kind of direct action that involved actually fighting the occupying authorities they considered as provocation, since German reprisals for any act of direct resistance would be on a scale out of all proportion, and, they claimed, "The time has not yet come; we must reserve our strength for the day the Polish Government gives the order to bring out our arms".

M. Tennenbaum had several meetings with representatives of the Polish underground. The latter displayed goodwill, they were prepared to extend aid in individual cases and to promise support by a number of people from outside the Ghetto, but they refused all requests to arm the Ghetto.[9]

The Jewish National Council, which united all the main political trends in the Jewish community (the Zionist Movement, *Poalei-Zion* Zionist-Socialists, Left *Poalei-Zion, Hehalutz, Hashomer Hatzair,* and *Dror*) and which was in communication with all the important Jewish groupings in occupied territory except the *Bund,* was subsequently represented by "Jurek" (Aryeh Wilner) in all contacts with representatives of the Polish underground. The first two state-

---

[9] M. Tennenbaum-Tamaroff, *Dapim min hadleyka,* op. cit., pp. 129, 130, 134. See also: N. Blumental and J. Kermish, *Resistance and Revolt in the Warsaw Ghetto,* op. cit., p. 126; also there, p. 400. Survey of the activities of the Jewish Section in the Home Army's Main staff, by Colonel Henryk Wolinski ("Zakrzewski", "Waclaw").

ments submitted by this Council to the head of the Jewish Affairs Section were directed, one to the Polish military and civilian authorities, requesting that arms be supplied to the Jews for use against the occupiers, and the second to the Government Delegation, requesting recognition on the part of the military and civilian authorities for the Jewish National Council as representing the Jewish population. Thereupon, by order of the High Command, the Jewish Combat Organization received—ten pistols and a not very large quantity of ammunition; these weapons were in extremely poor condition, and in fact only a few could be used at all.

The Jewish National Council and the *Bund* co-ordinated their activities through the Co-ordinating Committee, which served as the political representation of the Jewish Combat Organization. "Jurek" wished to set up, contact with the underground military and civilian authorities in the country in order to co-ordinate activities with them, receive briefings and in general secure Army help for the Jewish Combat Organization. This contact was established by virtue of two identical statements addressed, one to the High Command and the other to the Home Delegation, signed on behalf of the Co-ordinating Committee by "Jurek" and by "Mikolai" (Dr. Leon Feiner, a well-known leftist *Bund* leader). The statement pointed to the need to supply the Jewish Combat Organization *without delay* with large quantities of arms; since the ten pistols received were inadequate for an armed uprising or any other action whatsoever of a collective and not individual nature. The Army Commander-in-Chief, Grot, gave his reply in the form of an Order of the Day dated 11 November 1942. This reply is not on record. All that is known is that it took cognizance of the Jewish representatives' statement; commended the readiness to fight displayed in it; and recommended organizing the Jewish combatants in fighting units of five men. The reply of the Home Delegation was delivered verbally.

In the military sphere, the Jews demanded arms and professional military aid in preparation for the final battle of the Warsaw Ghetto. The Jewish Combat Organization demanded effective help on a scale far and away greater than that received, and it declared itself ready to devote a good part of the funds at its disposal to buying arms. These demands were met only to a derisory extent. In the first half of January 1943, the Organization received another ten pistols, and some instruction material on sabotage, explosives, and army operations ... While feverishly preparing for the fight, the Jewish Combat Organization persistently kept on demanding help from the army, which treated their appeals with distrust and the deepest reserve. It was only when the "action" that was begun on 18 January 1943 for the purpose of liquidating the Ghetto met with a fierce, armed resistance from the Combat Organization which brought it to a halt after four days, it was only then that the Warsaw Region Army Commander, Konar (Chruściel) agreed to give the Ghetto material help and instruction and also spoke of the possibility of help from fighting units from the outside. Work began at once under the direction of the Warsaw Region Chief of Staff, Stanislaw Weber—known as "Chirurg" (the Surgeon), and contact was established between "Jurek" and Polish Army Officers. In December 1942, the Combat Organization received 49 pistols (of which only 36 could be used at all, because of the shortage of ammunition) a fact which Anielewicz regarded as showing "mockery at our fate"), quantities of bullets, about 80 kilograms of material for preparing Molotov cocktails and a certain number of hand-grenades. A bottle factory was got going in the Ghetto. Apart from this, more facilities were given for the arms purchases which the Combat Organization was making independently on its own behalf. A joint plan was also prepared for the Ghetto fighting and it included possible help from Army units. But (Henryk Wolinski-Zakrzewski—"Waclaw"), head of the Army's Jewish Affairs Section, relates that while the Army's attitude to the Jewish organizations was dictated by recognition that it was obliged to cooperate with them for political reasons, at the same time it regarded the Jews with resentment and distrust. The Jewish representatives were keenly aware of this resentment and distrust. Thus, for example, Konar's officers, who worked together with "Jurek", and who liked him and appreciated him, used to declare their dislike and distrust of the Jews openly to his face, much to his pain and sorrow. Once, when some Polish Army personnel with "Jurek" at their head we setting out to transport a fairly effective supply of arms to the Ghetto, the officers in charge of the operation gave vent to their poor opinion of the Jews, in spite of which they then proceeded to carry out the transport itself courageously and to deliver the arms according to plan within the Ghetto walls.

It must once more be pointed out that this was the only effective arms delivery that the Ghetto fighters were privileged to receive from underground Government Army circles. It was to no avail that Mordekhai Anielewicz made his dramatic appeal on 13 March 1943, in his letter to the Co-ordinating Committee representatives on the Aryan side, when he asked them to demand emphatically and at once that Army authorities and Government representatives supply at least 100 hand-grenades, 50 pistols, 10 rifles and several thousand rounds of large-calibre ammunition. Anielewicz wrote in this letter that within two days he could produce exact plans of the combatants' positions, with maps, "so that there could be no doubt whatever about the need for arms to be found". He went on, "Since the 18th of January [1943], the Jewish population of Warsaw has been fighting continuously against the Germans and those who do their bidding. Anyone who denies this or throws doubt on it is nothing but an anti-Semite—saying it out of spite".

Neither was there any response when Mordekhai Tennenbaum-Tamaroff, head of a unified Jewish underground movement (stretching all the way from the extreme right to the Socialist *Bund*), turned to the Bialystok Region Command in charge of Civilian Struggle and in a letter dated 2 April 1943 requested 200 grenades and a few score pistols, which, he said, "could sway the issue regarding the last day for Poland's second-largest Ghetto (Bialystok)"; failing this, he suggested "the alternative: taking our men out for active combat in the field". For these purposes, he said, he was ready "to place at the disposal of the Polish underground movement the maximum of what is still left in the Ghetto after its systematic pillage by the Nazi hangmen".

Some aid the Army did extend to the Jewish Combat Organization in the sphere of communications with abroad. It transmitted a number of cables to the Jewish representatives on the National Council in London, as well as to Jewish organizations in England, America, etc. The Combat Organization also received Home Army help in the matter of legalizations, official forms, properly signed and with instructions for their use. In the matter of security, some of the

Organization's representatives ("Antek"—Y. Zukerman, "Borowski" —Dr. A. Berman) were given cover from the German agents that were on the track of the Organization and endangering its existence. The Army published an underground leaflet on the destruction of the Warsaw Ghetto, which was written by the historian Antoni Szymanowski, a member of the Home Army information section, working for the *Biuletyn Informacyjny,* the main Army paper with the widest circulation.[10]

In the same issue of December 1943, a paper was published entitled, "Before the Eyes of the World",[11] which included a chapter, "In the Footsteps of Bar-Kochba", with documents and reports on the Warsaw Ghetto rising. It must be pointed out that while this compilation, the work of the authoress and public figure, M. Kann made a deep impression on its Polish readers, Jewish underground activists had reservations about it, because of its inaccuracies and also because of its judgement on the past of the Jewish people and its general trend, which they considered incorrect. The Jewish National Council in the underground found it necessary to submit critical notes on the subject (written by Ringelblum, Zukerman, and A. Berman) to the Council for Aid to the Jews and to Government representatives.

Army cooperation with Jewish organizations was not confined to Warsaw alone, but was intended to cover the whole territory of Poland. That this was so could be seen from the High Command Order of February 1943 on help to be afforded to Ghettos seeking to break out in order to join in armed struggle. The Jewish military organizations more than once adverted to the spirit of this Order, and so did Poles who were ready to extend every possible aid to Jewish forces concentrated under the control of the Jewish Combat Organization and the Co-ordinating Committee, but the Order met with unwillingnes to carry it out on the part of local military factors. The fact of the matter is that the Order was not carried out. On the strength of this Order, some contact was made

[10] M.B. *Likwidacja Getta Warszawskiego,* Reportaz.

[11] Maria Kann, *Na oczach swiata* (An underground publication which appeared in Warsaw in 1944. As security precaution, the cover of this leaflet had printed "Zamosc 1932", as the place and date of publication.)

in February 1943 with Jewish work-posts in Czestochowa, and abortive preparations were made for defensive action in the camps at Poniatow and Trawniki. The Jewish Combat unit in Czestochowa, which was in hiding in the Koniecpol area, tried to join up with the Army; contrary to the spirit of the February 1943 Order, it suffered grievously at the hands of Army units, twice having heavy casualties inflicted on by the "Eagle" unit (apparently of the N.S.Z.) in spite of an announcement by the local command that the Jewish unit was to be afforded aid and assistance.[12]

Neither, sad to say, was any real help given to the Ghetto in its fight after the revolt broke out. On the first day of the revolt, 19 April 1943, the representatives of the Co-ordinating Committee at the time, Dr. A. Berman (since the arrest of "Jurek" on 6 March 1943) and Dr. Feiner, called for immediate, armed aid for the fighting Ghetto from the Government Delegate, the Army High Command and the Warsaw District Command. The Warsaw District Commander, Col. Konar (Antoni Chruściel), in his letter of 22 April, requested the Head of the Jewish Affairs Department at his Command Headquarters to tell "Antek", "In this crisis, there is no place for personal contacts: it is time now to act. Warsaw's Armed Forces have confidence in the Jews, commend them on their fighting spirit and wish to assist them". Konar stated that his men would go into action on 19 April at 19.12 hours. This action took the form of clashes between Polish underground Army units and Germans in the vicinity of the Ghetto, in Bonifraterska Street, in the course of which the Poles suffered casualties in dead and wounded. Konar informed the Jews that he was unable to provide money or food, and admitted, "The break-through from the Aryan side of the wall has failed, because the German besieging force holds positions in houses on the Ghetto side". It is not surprising, therefore, that on 27

---

12 Henryk Wolinski, Announcement regarding the creation of the underground Jewish National Council, published in: N. Blumental and J. Kermish, *Resistance and Revolt in the Warsaw Ghetto*, op. cit. 115–120. Also there, p. 125, letter from Mordekhaï Anielewicz to Coordinating Committee representatives on the Aryan side, 13 March 1943; pp. 126–127, letter from M. Tamaroff to Bialystok Region Command of the Civilian Struggle, 2 April 1943.

April Co-ordinating Committee representatives sent a further note to the Government Delegate, observing, "Ostentatious sympathy for the Ghetto in its fight has not so far been given practical expression by military circles", and pointing out that in spite of the reiterated appeals by the Command of the Jewish Combat Organization, "The Ghetto has not been privileged to receive even the least help in the form of ammunition and battle equipment".

That in fact no help was given while the Ghetto fought is finally confirmed in the Memorandum of 26 November 1943 sent by "Antek" (Zuckerman), Commander of the Jewish Combat Organization, to General Tadeusz Bor-Komorowski, C.-in-C. Home Army, briefly surveying the cooperation between the Jewish Combat Organization and the Home Army. The Memorandum also recorded that no assistance at all was given in bringing combatants who survived the suppression of the Ghetto revolt out of the Ghetto through the sewers to the Aryan side, and as a result 90 per cent of the surviving men and officers of the Combat Organization perished there in the poison gas.

Combat Organization representatives, the Memorandum stated, had made repeated efforts to secure arms for the Jews in Będzin and Sosnowiec, Czestochowa and Bialystok, but with no success. They had asked for recognition of Jewish partisans, for help in organizing partisan units from among young Jews rescued from the liquidated Ghettos and in contacting the so-called "wild" groups, so that they should not have to have recourse to pillage: they had received an insulting refusal, which stated that execution of the Order of the Supreme Commander of 4 May 1943 (on enrolling in the Home Army surviving Warsaw Ghetto combatants in the Wyszkow area) was meeting with obstacles which proved impossible to overcome: "the atmosphere regarding armed Jews is so completely hostile that we are unable, within the limited possibilities of underground activity, to accept responsibility for the safety of Jewish units in the field. What carries weight here is the hostility engendered by the Jewish attitude at the time of Soviet occupation and the present conduct of Jewish armed groups, harassing the population by acts of pillage and cruelty, and what carries the greatest weight of all is the power of the official propaganda of the occupying regime".

The leaders of the Jewish underground objected to the issue's being presented in these terms and strongly repudiated the grounds put forward. It is true that the Army's answer had also stated, on the favourable side, "There is no Jewish partisan force but it is necessary to give arms to (Jewish) concentrations (i.e. camps and Ghettos still in existence at that date) and to protect them, as well as to keep Jewish units with their arms standing easy, for the purpose of rescuing concentrations or for such special operations as the High Command may order". Nevertheless, the Jewish Combat Organization's requests for help for Poniatow and Trawniki had met with a flat refusal, the Memorandum recorded.

It should be pointed out that that this Memorandum received only a verbal answer from the representative of General Bor. It was to this effect: "They (the Jews) are like a man who is drowning, and we (the Polish underground) are like people standing on the shore who can't swim. All the same, we shall do the best we can to give them as much help as possible. A written reply will follow".

It was learnt later from someone close to Bor that the Memorandum had greatly angered the General. No written answer ever came, and this was in fact the end of the last vain attempt to arouse those who had access to arms and get them to come to the aid of the Jewish remnant in its desperate struggle.[13]

The great "action" in the Warsaw Ghetto—the mass deportation to Treblinka—lasted for fourty-four days. It evoked no response from the Aryan site. Absolute silence—this was the reaction of the Aryan side to the drama that was being enacted under the eyes of hundreds of thousands of Poles. Among the circles on the Aryan side that supported the Jews, there was angry criticism of the Jews for not defending themselves against their oppressors. Instead of committing suicide—they said—it would have been better to attack the murderers, even with bare hands. In an article that appeared at the beginning of November 1942 in the underground paper, *Wiadomosci Polskie,* published by the *Sluzba Zwycięstwu Polski (*The Service of

[13] Joseph Kermish, *The Sources for the History of the Resistance and Revolt in the Warsaw Ghetto,* published in: *Resistance and Revolt in the Warsaw Ghetto,* op. cit., pp. 14–15; also there, pp.141-145, letter of the Combat Organization Commander to Home Army Commander, 26 November 1943.

Poland's Victory), the writer put the blame on the Jews for obeying
the Germans and submitting to them, for wearing the Jewish badge,
for accepting Jewish autonomy at German hands (the *Judenrat,*
the Jewish police), for not preventing social deterioraton and collapse
—the gap between rich and poor had become the abyss separating
the well-fed from the starving, the living from the dead.[14]

In the heated discussions that took place on the Aryan side, the
leaders of the Jewish underground, who were well aware of the state
of affairs in the Ghetto, were obliged time after time to stress that
under conditions of murderous terror like those prevailing in the
Ghetto, no population not even if well trained for resistance and
revolt, could have manifested resistance on a mass scale. This terror,
combined with the cunning tactics of the Hitlerite deportation command, would have succeeded in breaking the backbone of any population for a time, and not only of a population like this, which
had been kept for years in one immense prison or concentration
camp. In the course of such discussions, the Jewish militants passed
on information on the Jewish underground movement and on the resistance currents which would burst out on the surface at a given
moment when the will to fight of the Jewish masses had had time
to harden.[15]

During all this time, the Government Delegation failed to issue
a single statement calling for defensive action, failed to say a single
encouraging word or proffer any kind of support, even if nothing
more than moral support. At the very least, since the Delegation
people certainly knew full well what had been the fate of the Jews
of Lublin, deported two months before to an "unknown destination", they could have told the Jews of Warsaw what was in store
for them if they were deported to Treblinka, that is, simply to be
killed off *en masse.* "If elements among the Polish authorities had
given moral support and provided assistance in the form of arms",
wrote Ringelblum, "then the Germans would have had to pay dearly
for the seas of blood that they shed in July, August and September

---

14 Aurelia Wylezynska, op. cit., p. 220.
15 Abraham Berman, op. cit., p. 697.

1942." Perhaps he was exaggerating somewhat but he wrote with an aching heart.

All the same, thanks to the Council for Aid to the Jews (*Rada Pomocy Zydom—R.P.Z.—Zegota*), which comprised representatives of Polish parties concerned to extend aid to the Jews, and which carried on fairly systematic and extensive activity, thousands of Jews did succeed in escaping with their lives. This Council, which quickly became one of the most active and dedicated organizations in the Polish underground, devoted a great deal of energy to the struggle against extortionists and continued its activities almost uninterrupted right until the liberation.

It is desirable to expatiate somewhat more fully on the commendable work done by this organization—*Zegota*. Its archives contain a number of the most important documents concerning the pressure brought to bear on the Government Delegation in the attempt to secure assistance for the Warsaw Ghetto. Towards the end, of the first "action" in the Ghetto, some sections of the Polish population gave evidence of a wish to extend help to the Jews. The initiative came from two sides: from Catholic circles and from one of the democratic groupings in the underground. One of the main initiators of the move to aid the Jews was the authoress, "Weronika"—Zofia Kossack-Szczucka, a legendary figure in Catholic circles, known for her right-wing, conservative and clerical outlook. The sore fate that befell the Jews affected her so deeply that she saw it as her Christian duty to come to their aid. She set to with great energy, and it was she who was largely responsible for the creation of the Council for Aid to the Jews. At one stage "Wieronika" fell into the hands of the Gestapo and for a time she was held in Auschwitz. When she was released, she carried on as before, trying to rescue Jewish children by hiding them in convents and institutions run by the clergy (missionary feeling played a recognizable role here).

At the beginning, the Council acted on a limited scale, without a wide public basis. It received a tiny budget from the Government Delegation: 50,000 zloty a month. Dr. A. Berman, who had started on his task of representing the Jewish National Committee on the Aryan side, and who had secured the first, temporary, Aryan documents, was asked by the committee of *Zegota* to represent the Ghetto and cooperate with them, informing them of the needs of the Jewish population. A programme of activity for the Council was worked out on a fresh basis, different from and wider than in the beginning. One of the issues on which there was discussion at the time of the reorganization was the role of Jewish representatives in organizing aid. The Catholics were of the opinion that the Council should have a purely Polish character, while the Jewish representatives thought it necessary that they should act as go-betweens between the Council and the Jews, both in the Ghetto and in hiding on the Aryan side, and represent the interests and demands of the Jewish population. Representatives of the Jewish National Council and the Bund on the Aryan side were of the opinion that the aid organization must represent the entire population, Polish and Jewish. This attitude was endorsed by the Polish underground. In December 1942, a clandestine Council for Aid to the Jews was constituted, known in the underground by the secret name, *Zegota Council.* The top echelons of the Council were as follows: Chairman: "Trojan" (Julian Grobelny), a leading member of the P.P.S.—Polish Socialist Party— from Lodz; deputy Chairmen: "Rozycki" (Adv. Tadeusz Rek), one of the leaders of the Polish Peasants' Popular Party, and "Mikolai" (Adv. Leon Feiner); Secretary-General: "Adam Borowski" (Dr. Adolf Berman); Treasurer: "Marek Łukowski" (Ferdynand Arczynski), member of the Democratic Party from Cracow; Council member: "Barbara" (Engineer Emilia Hiżowa), leading woman Democrat. Apart from these members, a young Catholic leader, Wladyslaw Bartoszewski, took part in the Council's activities at the beginning, but the Catholic Movement only took part in the Council's work for a very short period of time. Later, this Movement displayed doubts and reservations concerning activities to aid the Jews, and in July 1943, the Catholic Front for Polish Re-Birth left the Council. Towards the end of 1943, on the other hand, the leftist wing of the P.S. ("Polish Socialists") by then already known as the P.P.S. ("The Polish Socialist Workers' Party") joined the Council, where it was represented by Piotr Gajewski. Witold Bienkowski (variously known as "Wencki", "Jan", "Kalski"), a Catholic publicist and member of the Catholic Front for Polish Re-Birth was appointed to the Council by special letter to speak in the name of a

member of the Government. As director of the *Zegota* department, Bienkowski was given a direct line to to the Command in
charge of Civilian Struggle, the Treasury Department, the *chef de
cabinet* of the Government Delegate, Army headquarters, and the
clandestine communications network (radio, post, couriers). Thus, for
example, during the Ghetto rising, Bienkowski was able to transmit
news from the fighting zone to London seven times a day, at a time
when Party leaders and officials would often have to wait for weeks
on end to communicate with London.

Apart from this, the Council could count on cooperation in important fields of activity from scores of devoted, faithful workers
in the Polish underground, such as Prof. Stanislaw Ossowski and his
wife Maria, Ewa Wasowicz, Zofia Rudnicka "Alicja"), Dr. Maria
Zebrowska and Irena Chmielewska, women assistants of Prof. Baley,
Janina Modelska, Celina Tyszko, Ola Heptinger, Teresa Nowakie-
wicz; Engineer Julian Miszaczek and his secretary, Kazimierz Mlynarski; the Strauss couple; Dr. Szonert and his wife Maria, the
architect Dziewulski,Irena Staszer, Janina Buchholz, Dr. Jan Zabiń-
ski, Jadwiga Piotrowska and her sister, together with their parents—
the Ponikiewski family, Zofia Wędrychowska and Stanislaw Papu-
zinski from Ochota, Izabela Kuczkowska with her mother Kazimiera
Trzaskalska from Goclawek, the woman journalist Irena Schultz,
Wanda Drozdowska Rogowicz, the midwife S. Busoldd, Maria Ku-
kulska, the families of the janitors of the flats at 8, Widok, the woman worker M. Plinska, Dr. Henryk Pilestr and his wife Maria and
their children, Joanna Wald, the Jędzyrzecki family, and others.

During the period it functioned—from December 1942 up till
January 1945—the Council had 61 plenary meetings, over 100 meetings of the presidium (comprising the Chairman, his deputies, the
Secretary-General and the Treasurer), and over 30 meetings of its
control committee, not to mention the large number of sessions of
the separate departments of the Council and of its various committees. The Council had at its disposal a number of secret flats, where
meetings were frequently held and where office work was done. For
security reasons, the Council would move these offices from time to
time; it also disposed of several secret post-boxes as well as places
for caching secret documents.

The Council functioned throughout as a team, in the most complete harmony, in spite of the wide political and ideological differences between its various components, and in spite of the dangers threatening the activists day after day. In spite of the periodic crises when the cover of the secret rooms of the Council was "blown" and its members and their helpers were arrested, the Council went on giving help to Jews under the most difficult conditions imaginable, and the cooperation between the Poles and the Jews was as harmonious and cordial as could be wished.

In the first months of its existence, the activities of the Council were limited to Warsaw alone, and were concerned purely and simply with Jews living in the Aryan district and in the Warsaw Ghetto. Subsequently, it extended its field of action with regard to the following basic tasks: material aid to Jews in hiding on the Aryan side and aid as regards legalization, that is to say, providing these Jews with Aryan papers. The lives of thousands of Jews depended on these two operations.

The majority of the Jews on the Aryan side were without means—members of the educated class, workers, etc. In addition, repeated acts of extortion brought economic ruin to hundreds of people, who would simply have died of hunger had it not been for the Council's help. Then, too, the Council extended its aid to everyone who asked for it, either directly or through the organizations represented on the Council. This help amounted on the average to 500 zloty per person per month. Even if this was not sufficient for minimal survival, it constituted something to count on. In exceptional cases, in connection with the blackmailing of persons with special claims as public activists or personalities in the world of learning or culture, larger grants were made; but there were also cases when the Council was obliged to reduce the average grant to some 300–400 zloty because of the financial straits it was in as a result of the tremendous increase in the number of persons needing help.

The Council got its funds for aid from the London Government Delegation and from no other source, at the beginning. Thanks to the Council's pressure and its urgent demands, the Delegation increased its monthly grant from 50,000 to 300,000–400,000 zloty. (In January 1943, the Council's monthly budget was 150,000 zloty in all, in February 300,000 zloty, in March 250,000 zloty, and from April to October 1943 300,000 zloty a month; in April 1943, a one-time grant was received of 500,000 zloty.) A budget was provided for help in the provinces: 150,000 zloty a month for the months June to October 1943. The total sum of funds allocated to the Council by the Government Delegation for the months January to October 1943 amounted to 4,750,000 zloty. But even this sum was only a drop in the ocean. The Council was unable to expand its sphere of activity until aid funds began to come through from Jewish organizations abroad for the Jewish National Council and the Bund. It should be pointed out that aid funds from Jewish organizations abroad for the Jewish underground in Poland reached their destination *via* Polish underground channels of the Government-in-Exile in London. The Jewish National Council and the Bund also distributed assistance on a large scale in their respective spheres. Up to the time they received funds from abroad, the Jewish organizations were given grants from the Council for their own aid activities, but after that time it was the Jewish organizations thrat financed the Council from their funds. Unfortunately, however, part of the funds arriving from abroad for the Jewish organizations were held up for some time, and some of them were not passed on to those they were intended for.[16]

After the liquidation of the Ghetto, with the tremendous increase in the numbers dependent on aid, the Council's budget was again greatly expanded, and during the peak period of its activity the Council was assisting about 4,000 Jews. At this same period, the Jewish National Council was extending assistance to some 5,000 to 6,000 Jews by means of some hundred or so "cells", and the Bund to 1,500 to 2,000 Jews, so that the total number of Jews in Warsaw and the environs who received help from the underground movement and remained alive thanks to that help was about 11,000 to 12,000. Apart from this, the Council and the Jewish organizations

---

[16] On this subject see footnote 29 on p. 213, the sharp letter of Aleksander Kaminski to Jerzy Makowiecki of 18 March 1944.

alike (the National Council and the Bund) extended considerable help to the Jews in the provinces.

Very vital help consisted of providing Aryan papers to Jews on the Aryan side, entirely without payment. Within its own field of activity, the Council organized an office for "legalizing" thousands of certificates—birth certificates, certificates of baptism, wedding certificates, pre-war identity cards, *Kennkarte* of the occupation authorities, residence certificates, labour-permits of various kinds, etc. For some of the most important cases, the Council also disposed of Government certificates of German institutions and even of S.S. and Gestapo certificates. Six people worked in this "legalization" office, day and night, at the risk of their lives—producing an average of 100 certificates a day. The monthly budget of the office ranged from 30,000–45,000 loty. The workers kept arms at the ready constantly with them, and more than one of them was killed at his post while carrying out the task assigned him. Thousands of certificates were distributed in Warsaw and environs; thousands were sent to the provinces, to the camps or to Jews in hiding in other towns.

The worst problem of all was that of finding a place to live, because of the fearful German terror threatening the population with the death penalty and because of the numerous cases of denunciation and extortion. Nevertheless, the Council devoted considerable means to paying for housing, even setting up a special department for housing matters; but for all that, help in this field was not very extensive. To buy flats specially cost a lot of money and was not effective, for if the flat was "blown" by blackmailers it could no longer be used, while renting rooms in other people's flats was a matter of appalling difficulty.

An attempt was made to influence the public and persuade it to extend help to the Jews by means of underground publications: the information department of the Council issued four leaflets—3 intended for the Polish population, in 25,000 copies each, and one in German, in 5,000 copies, issued supposedly by a secret German organization. These leaflets were distributed in the blocks of flats and were posted on the walls of buildings in Warsaw and in the provinces and were sent to various offices. In addition, the Council produced surveys of events on the "Jewish front" for the underground press, reporting instances of resistance; these surveys were reproduced in socially progressive organs (such as *Robotnik, Barykada Wolności, Glos Warszawy, Glos Demokracji,* etc.). The Council fought energetically against the plague of extortion, which developed into a public evil endangering every Jew on the Aryan side. The extortioners stripped their victims of their every last possession and forced them to flee for their lives. The Council appealed to the Polish underground authorities over and over again for swift and radical measures to fight the blackmailers, for an official proclamation stating that every blackmailer or accomplice if caught would be sentenced to death. And in fact announcements to this effect were published several times in the underground press. The Council itself also issued several leaflets calling on the public to oppose extortion.

The Council set up a special department for children's affairs to care more particularly for orphaned and abandoned children, to place them in institutions or with private families. This department was entrusted to an excellent underground worker, "Jolanta" (Irena Sendler), from the Social Aid Department of the Municipality. Under her professional and energetic administration, and with the help of a series of other underground workers, the department developed its activities in the face of all the manifold difficulties.

Thanks to the courageous, warm-hearted help of the Catholic writer, Jan Dobraczynski, head of the Care Section of the Social Aid Department of the Warsaw Municipality, and his assistant, Jadwiga Piotrowska, a number of Jewish children were sent as Polish orphans to convents and monasteries such as the Rodzina Maria Convent and the Siostry Służebniczki Monastery which administered children's institutions in Chotomow (near Warsaw).

By the end of 1943 there were some 600 Jewish children in various institutions in Warsaw and environs, 53 of them in municipal institutions, 22 in institutions of the R.G.O. (the Central Council for Social Aid) (Jadwiga Strzelecka, directress of one of the R.G.O. children's institutions, took care of nine Jewish children among the 30 children in her institution) and over 500 in other public and Church institutions. Apart from this, Jewish children were scattered in different institutions throughout the country.

The Council's Medical Department employed a number of trustworthy physicians, who visited Jewish patients in hiding on the Aryan side and gave them assistance. It is worth recording the names of doctors who carried out this task with unlimited devotion: Prof. Trojanowski, Prof. Michajłowitz, Dr. Franio, Dr. "Hanke" from Ochota, Dr. A. Meyer from the old city, Sister Helena Szyszko, Dr. Ignacy Olesinski, Dr. K. Szalbska-Wojtowicz, as well as the surgeons: Dr. Feliks Kanabus, Dr. Tadeusz Bazziak and Dr. Kazimierz Kozłowski, who performed plastic operations in order to disguise signs of circumcision.

The Council met with numerous obstacles in extending its activity to the whole of the General-Government. Only in April 1943 did the central Council suceed in initiating a regional Council for Cracow and its surroundings. A regional Council was also set up in Lwow (among its members were the Wnuk family, and Prof. Tessier, the painter, and his wife). The Council's treasurer, Arczynski, personally organized these two regional councils. The Cracow Council is known to have been allocated a monthly budget of less than 20,000 zloty (about a hundred Jews on the Aryan side here were dependent on this help from the Council). A Council for aid to the Jews was also established in Zamosc, it began by taking care of ten Jews in hiding, and this number eventually increased to about a hundred. At the beginning of 1943 there were 193 Jews in hiding in the Zamosc-Lublin Region and at the end of the year 220 in need of aid. The Council for the Zamosc-Lublin Region cooperated with the Socialist Combat Organization S.O.B. *(Socjalistyczna Organizacja Bojowa),* in whose ranks quite a number of Jews were concealed. The Council also maintained contact with the "Peasant Legions" *(Bataliony Chłopskie).* Among the members of Cracow Council were the Democrats Stanislaw Dobrowolski and his wife as well as Maria Strojna, Feliks Jiranek, Wladzia Chaszkiewicz and Franciszka Bro-żek; this Council sent out emissaries who made contact with a series of ghettos and camps that were still in existence at the time in the Cracow region.

For its work in the provinces, the Council set up a special Department headed by the P.P.S. (Socialist) supporter, Stefan Sendlak. The Council made contact, mainly with Lodz, but also with other towns such as Radom, Kielce, Piotrkow and others, through couriers who succeeded in getting into the labour camps and extending a measure of aid to the Jews there. One of the most active emissaries doing this work was the writer and journalist, Tadeusz Sarnecki, who was connected with the Democratic Party.

In spite of the smallness of the sums of money allocated by the Delegate of the Government-in-Exile, the Council for Aid to the Jews succeeded in organizing extensive and well-planned activities and did a great deal of rescue work in many fields, writing a brilliant chapter in the story of aid for Polish Jewry. Nevertheless, there is no doubt that leading members of the Council have given inflated figures of the numbers of Jews covered by the Council in its various activities. Tadeusz Rek writes that in the whole country (including the camps) at least 40,000 Jews received assistance from the Council. Arczynski is of the opinion that at the date of the Warsaw rising, "there were something over 50,000 Jews on the Aryan side". Certainly nearer the truth is the estimate of Dr. Berman, Yitzhak Zukerman, Yaakov Celemenski and Bartoszewski, who agree that in 1943 and 1944 Jews who were assisted directly by the Council for Aid to the Jews in Warsaw itself numbered something over 4,000, out of a total number of 20,000 Jews in hiding in the capital at that time. The fact is that the Council's practical work was severely limited all the time by one thing, and that was the chronic shortage of funds. Even in Warsaw itself, the number of people who received financial assistance (300–500 'loty') in October 1943 did not exceed a thousand.[17]

Polish public opinion was awakened for the first time to resistance in the Ghetto in January 1943, when whole blocks of buildings were stoutly defended by the Jewish population. The Poles compared January 1943 with June 1942, the passive behaviour of the Jews at

[17] Janina Dunin-Wasowicz, *Wspomnienia o akcji pomocy Zydom podczas okupacji hitlerowskiej w Polsce 1939–1945*, published in "Biuletyn Zydowskiego Instytutu Historycznego", No. 45–46, pp. 248–261; Testimonies of Ferdynand Arczynski, Tadeusz Rek, Witold Bienkowski, Stefan Sendlak, Ewa Wasowicz, Jan Zabinski, Kazimierz Mlynarski, Irena Stasiak, published in "Biuletyn Zydowskiego Instytutu Historycznego" No. 65–66/1968, pp. 173–202; Karyna Fiszman-Kamińska op. cit. pp. 55–56.

the earlier date with their active stand now, a stand taken in the light of their previous experience. But none of this had any effect on the attitude of Government factors towards the Jews as regards the issue of defence. In spite of constant and repeated appeals from the Jewish Combat Organization, arms were supplied only in infinitesimal quantities.

This is the source of the lack of understanding between the Jewish Combat Organization and the official Polish underground (A.K.— Home Army). The latter underground, which acted according to the calculations and the wishes of the Government-in-Exile in London, was well-organized and had tens of thousands of soldiers at its command in the underground. But this underground, apart from small sabotage operations and large-scale information activity among the Polish population, was ready and prepared for one thing only— an uprising at the right moment to be fixed and decided on by the movement itself. What was meant was that the right moment would be when the German Army was suffering blow after blow and the front was being pushed back towards Poland's borders. Only then, according to the Polish Government and underground, would a rising be liable to succeed, and the main thing was to see to it that the Polish people, who had suffered so much during the fighting, should not incur heavy losses prematurely to no purpose and no effect.

They demanded the same approach from the Jewish underground, but the Jewish leaders replied that they could not afford to wait, because the enemy was preparing to wipe them out and as liable to begin carrying out this intention of his at any moment. The Polish underground was unwilling to take these arguments into consideration. It was also influenced by fear lest a Jewish rising lead the Poles to revolt as well, too soon. Holding these views, the Polish underground military command refused to supply arms to the Jewish Combat Organization, or at best supplied them in minimal quantities. The Jewish underground made extremely serious accusations against the Government circles because of this opposition on their part to supplying arms to the Ghetto. "There is no explanation", wrote Ringelblum, "for the opposition of Government elements who for months refused to give arms, and when they finally did give them, gave them in such minute quantities, providing grounds for suspicion that their attitude sprang from fear least arms be made use of for undesirable purposes in the future." That he was right is borne out by Bartoszewski, who recorded: "In some A.K. (Home Army) circles, there was a certain reserve in their attitude towards the need to supply the Ghetto with arms in considerable quantities, and this reserve was not connected with the very real material difficulties involved—it sprang from doubts as to the aim of the operation".

It must nevertheless be remembered that A.K. officers of the Staff for Sabotage and Diversion Operations provided the Ghetto emissaries with set, printed instructions on the handling of arms and explosives, instructed them on methods of fighting in urban areas, gave them practical demonstrations of defence against armour at close quarters, and showed them how to make incendiary bombs, mines and hand-grenades. More important still, the Jewish Combat Organization was helped to acquire arms on the free market by certain A.K. cells acting as intermediaries in these dangerous purchase deals.

The military in the Polish underground were also disinclined to be helpful about the Jewish groups that wanted to take part in partisan fighting. The armed groups of young people and former soldiers who went out into the forests after the liquidation of the ghettos in order not to die at the hands of the hangmen could simply have been absorbed into the partisan units that were fighting against the common enemy. Col. Wolinski, Head of the Jewish Affairs Department at A.K. General Headquarters, tried to bring this about. In a report to his superiors as early as 12 February 1942, he wrote: "The only real possibility of rescuing any considerable number" (*sc.* of Jews) "lies in creating support points for them in the forests in the shape of groups of partisan fighters. Given the situation in the Warsaw Ghetto, this is a matter of the utmost urgency, and the Jewish National Council is constantly pressing me to find a way out". It hardly needs to be stated that Wolinski's proposal was not accepted by the A.K. High Command. Instead, actual war was waged against the Jewish partisans and they were condemned to lead the life of bandits, forced to pillage in order to survive. As a result, they were mercilessly wiped out by partisan formations and by the rural

303

population, which hunted them down systematically and handed them over to the Germans. There is no question that official circles in the Polish underground did not extend the aid that was in their power to extend to Jews who were fighting.

Jews were not accepted in Government military formations except in isolated, individual cases. Certain persons are known to have been entrusted with the task of verifying the Aryan origin of members of a given Government organization, and where Jewish origin was proved the man in question was removed on one pretext or another. The Home Army, unlike the *Gwardia Ludowa,* did not accept a single Jewish partisan group into its ranks—every attempt of armed Jewish groups to make contact with the A.K. and join up with it ended in failure and even in some cases in the treacherous murder of the Jewish partisans. However, Jewish combatants were taken into the A.K. partisan units as isolated individuals, more particularly in the units connected with the Socialist left. In these units, Jews were sometimes to be found in positions of command, while in others Jews were only accepted if they were thought to be Aryans and they were obliged to hide their nationality even from their closest comrades-in-arms. Jewish combatants did receive support from the anti-Fascist left (the P.P.R. and the R.P.P.S.) and from Democratic circles on the right-wing known as the "Lodon camp". Yet for all that, everywhere and in all circumstances the Jews had to put up a desperate struggle for the very right to fight, that is to say, to get arms from the national underground movement and be privileged to die fighting.

It is a fact that everywhere in Poland the Jewish resistance movement was fated to exist in isolation. At the day of destruction, each Ghetto was left to its doom, and every community that was prepared to fight was imbued with the tragic realization that there was no-one to come to its rescue.

Characteristically, in every place where there was the smallest crack in the wall of isolation Jewish revolt sprang up, witness Warsaw, Bialystok, Cracow.

One of the few commanders of the Jewish Combat Organization in the Warsaw Ghetto still alive, Mark Edelman, has put on record that every least contact with comrades in arms on the Aryan side produced a certain feeling of a lessening of isolation. A similar notion is to be found in the book of Tuvia Borzykowski. On the other hand, in places where isolation was complete, the revolt was repressed at its very beginnings, as in Lodz.

In the April 1943 rising, there was already some cooperation with the Polish side. Arms were transferred across the walls and through the sewers, and some aid was afforded the combatants and those who escaped from the Ghetto. The Polish Government Delegate published a communique extolling the Jews of Warsaw who were defending their honour with arms in their hands. It called on the Polish population to aid fugitives who managed to escape from the burning Ghetto. The P.P.S. published an appeal in similar terms. These appeals, alas, had little effect.

Polish public opinion displayed great interest in the courageous stand of the Ghetto, calling it "Little Stalingrad" and comparing it to the defence of the Westerplatte (the Polish fortress near Danzig, whose defenders made a valiant stand in the September 1939 campaign). Some saw the rising as a beginning of a revolt on a national scale, which the Jews were helping to get going.

The Germans made every endeavour to cut off the Ghetto, as it shed its blood in the fight, from the Polish population, so as to stop news from getting out of how the fighting was going and to prevent a single soul from escaping alive from the inferno.

While the "forces of light" were appealing to the Polish population to afford the Jews asylum, the "forces of darkness" in the shape of blackmailers, secret agents and uniformed police fell upon the fugitives from the Ghetto. The Polish Government representative in the underground did indeed publish a decree threatening the Polish population with punishment for handing over Jews to the Germans, and cases are known where special courts of the Polish underground condemned informers and black-mailers to death and the sentences were carried out—the Polish underground press reported every such case.[18] But these measures were on the whole

---

18 Witold Bienkowski, who was as mentioned above the Government Delegate's representative on the Council for Aid to the Jews with special powers, writes that he personally signed 117 death sentences for blackmail,

insufficient to prevent the constant increase in the numbers of black-mailers and extortioners (*szmalcowniks*). The nearer the war got to its end, the more they and the N.S.Z. Fascists worked hand in hand to unearth every last Jew and kill him. The vile informers who made a living out of the desperate situation of the Jews, helping for a price to catch fugitives from the Ghetto, were indeed denounced by certain underground papers (e.g. *Czyn*), which published the sentences passed on them, but there were very few references to the base role played by the Polish "Blue" Police, both uniformed and plain-clothed, which served the occupying authorities both by black-mailing Jewish fugitives on the Aryan side and by handing them over to the Germans. The periodical *Iskra* ("The Spark") spoke of this when it attacked the Polish syndicalists in its number of 1 May 1943, adding, "On Thursday last, on Ujazdowskie Avenue, one of these Polish agents was shot by a Jew, who was caught".

As regards active Polish collaboration in exterminating the Jews when the Ghetto rising was put down, there is not unnaturally little information to be found in the Polish press. It is worth while reproducing here the following quite exceptional report, which was published in the paper *Tydzien* ("The Week"), (No. 11, 3 June 1943), under the heading, "A contemptible deed": "In one of the squares near the Ghetto, a German Police unit (S.D.—*Sicherheitsdienst*) was going along with a group of Jews, 20 men and 10 women. The Germans themselves shot the men, and then asked the 'Blue' policemen who were with them to shoot the women. The 'Blue' police refused. And then a fellow emerged from the crowd of curious onlookers watching the executions, a Pole by nationality, and offered to shoot all the wretched women, if the Germans were agreeable, for a payment of 1,000 zlotys. He was paid on the spot. Did anyone of those present", asked the newspaper, "make a note of the name of this criminal?"

Poles everywhere were talking of nothing else—the Ghetto's defending itself, the German atrocities, the burning of blocks of flats

---

of which 85 were carried out by the head of a special unit "Zmudzin". See: "Biuletyn Zydowskiego Instytutu Historycznego", No. 65–66/1968, p. 89.

with the people in them. The conversations were generally anti-Semitic in tone. The Poles were more upset by the burning down of the buildings than by human beings, being turned into living torches. Pleasure over the "cleansing" of Warsaw of its Jews was overshadowed only by fear of the morrow, lest the Germans start on the Poles when they had finished with the Jews.

Ringelblum's conclusion that there was very considerable satisfaction in Polish anti-Semitic circles over the "solution" of the Jewish question is borne out by Polish historians themselves. Here we find Adam Polewka stating, "The great majority of the Polish population was indifferent to the horrifying facts (the extermination of the Jews) and not a few welcomed them with a satisfaction expressed in phrases such as, "Although we don't approve of the methods, one must admit that Hitler did for us what we were incapable of doing so thoroughly. The mass murder of the Jewish population by the German Fascists was seen by these people as their nation's gain".[19]

The Polish public worker, Aurelia Wylezynska, put it in very similar terms: "Some Poles are glad that Hitler has done their dirty work for them, and to spare their nerves they didn't even have to put cottonwool in their ears so as not to hear the cries of their fellow-men".[20]

S. Zeminski, a Polish teacher with a conscience, also wrote: "Many people condemn the German crimes and are revolted by them. Some are smitten by despair when they see what the Germans are doing, but not a few think that though it's not very nice and even very cruel, the Germans are in fact doing us a great service—solving the Jewish problem".[21]

A teacher in a village near Lublin, an educated man from a family with a well-known name, wrote: "We (Poles) must never forget that we also have something to thank the Germans for. Though their methods of exterminating the Jews are inhuman and revolting—what is going on in Majdanek is horrible—... yet this is the only

[19] Adam Polewka, *To boli...* published in "W trzecia rocznice zaglady getta w Krakowie", Cracow 1946.
[20] Aurelia Wylezynska, op. cit., p. 219.
[21] Zeminski, op. cit.

way to solve the problem. The Jews should have been wiped out long ago. They have done it instead of us, and it's a good thing that they have. The Germans will leave, and Poland will remain for the Poles".[22]

Some noble spirits did raise a cry of protest at the indifference displayed in the face of this great tragedy taking place under the very eyes of the entire Polish community. While some people were absolutely opposed to rescuing Jews or even helping them when the rising was repressed and the Ghetto liquidated, it must be remembered that Poles were to be found, including even people who had been prominent anti-Semites before the war, who risked their lives and those of their families in order to try and save Jews, though they did not always succeed.

The situation was well described as early as 20 June 1942 by the Ghetto underground paper of the *Dror* (Freedom) movement *(Yediot* No. 8): "A certain stratum—and to tell the truth a very thin one— of the Polish public displays sympathy with the tormented Jews of Poland and even extends them active assistance. But the masses, the Polish 'street', is well pleased with all the new repressions. 'At least there's one good thing Hitler is doing for us—getting rid of the Jews for us.' Talk like this is heard in the trains and in the market, in the trams and on the streets. Eye-witnesses tell harrowing stories of the behaviour of Poles during the deportations and the slaughter in the 'residential quarter' (Ghetto). The noble actions of those Poles who have not lost elementary feelings of humanity stand out all the more against this dark background".

Finally, as regards saving individual Jews, especially outstanding Jewish personalities, it must be said that the official attitude was lamentable. On 30 January 1943, the Council for Aid to the Jews appealed to the Government Delegate with a proposal for steps to be taken to save the survivors of the Jewish cultural, intellectual and political elite, but without result. The Council had no possible way of undertaking any large-scale action, for it had no extra funds at its disposal and was given no assistance from the Government side. The Government allocated only miserably small sums

22 Modrzewska, op. cit., p. 26.

for aid to these people, and did nothing at all to secure places for them to live—something many times more important than money. The result was the death of the handful of scientists, writers, actors, political leaders, etc., who had been rescued from previous deportations. Thus, for example, the Council for Aid to the Jews was even without means to help the renowned Jewish historian, Dr. Yitzhak Schiper, who could not find the few thousand zloty needed to rent a flat and to survive on the Aryan side.

Another serious and justified complaint of Jewish underground representatives on the Aryan side was concerned with the rescue of children. They had thought that Government factors would take action to save at least the small handful of Jewish children who had survived after the two "actions". Alas, the Polish Government and people did nothing at all.

Under the German occupation, saving Jews by getting them out of the Ghetto was—as Ringelblum writes—a matter of individuals' acting on their own and not the result of a joint effort by any group. This conclusion of Ringelblum's was fully confirmed in the memoirs of Ferdinand Arczynski on the Council for Aid to the Jews, who wrote that help in rescuing Jews was a humanitarian endeavour by individuals who afforded them shelter and immediate assistance while the Council provided "legalization" and so on.[23]

To sum up: at a time when the Jews were condemned to merciless extinction without exception and only a small handful succeeded in fleeing, Government circles did nothing to save the remnant of Polish Jewry.

*

After Ringelblum's tragic death, there was no improvement in relations between the Poles and the surviving Jews—if anything, they worsened. In fact, with the death of Sikorski the decisive influence in the Government-in-Exile and its underground agencies in Poland passed more and more to the right-wing elements, and relations between representatives of the Jewish underground and the Government Delegation, already getting cooler, became more strained and difficult from day to day.

[23] Arczynski, op. cit., p. 173.

The A.K. armed units in the forests soon passed over from a negative attitude or in most cases one of approval of the persecution and killing of Jews to actively taking part themselves in pursuing and wiping out Jewish armed groups in the forests.

When the Council for Aid to the Jews called on the Polish underground movement to issue a proclamation to the public in honour of the first anniversary of the Ghetto rising, there was no response, and Jewish leaders were understandably bitter.

The approach of the Soviet front, as well as the steadily increasing influence of the Polish left, produced great nervous tension in Government Delegation circles and in the A.K. A rapprochement began between the *Sanacja,* the *Endecja,* and openly Fascist organizations such as the "National-Radicals", who were frankly anti-Semitic. In March 1944, the bands of the N.S.Z. ("Nationalist Armed Forces") were officially taken into the A.K., where they were cordially welcomed by General Bor-Komorowski, much to the anger of the Democratic underground movement and to the alarm of the Jewish leaders. This move was opposed by Democratic circles in the A.K. itself: the "New Roads" group, of which "Waclaw" (Henryk Wolinski) was a member (the A.K. representative for the Jewish underground, with his democratic views and his sympathy for the Jews, who had made great but fruitless efforts to change the prevailing hostile attitude in the A.K. towards the Jewish underground and its activities), as well as the historian, Prof. Marceli Handeslman, the lecturer Ludwik Widerszal, Halina Krahelska, etc.

It may be imagined what were the feelings of Jewish leaders and of the Council for Aid to the Jews when in the spring of 1944 the Director of Foreign Affairs in the Government Delegation, Knoll, formerly Polish Minister in Berlin, published a survey in an official Delegation organ, based on the assumption that after the war there would still be "too many Jews" left and that it would be necessary to set up a "closed area" for them in the east. His survey went on: "The prevailing mood throughout the country is not to leave any opening for the Jews, in however small numbers, to return to their previous businesses and workshops. The non-Jewish population has taken the place of the Jews in the towns, big and small, and their return would be regarded not as restitution but as an invasion to be resisted by physical force". Knoll thought that the Government would do well to ensure that there should be no anti-Semitism in Poland—on condition that the Jews who had survived should not try to return *en masse* to the "towns and villages of Poland". And this was written at the time when the Hitlerites were killing off the last remaining remnant of the Jews of Poland.

This was not the only expression of anti-Semitism in official Delegation publications, merely the most outstanding. The paper, *Nowy Wspolny Dom*, published by the Agriculture Department of the Government Delegation, regularly printed anti-Semitic articles. Anti-Semitic tendencies were also obvious in a booklet called, "The Imperialist War", published by a group supported by the Delegation.

Official circles found a pretext for their anti-Semitic campaign in news about Jewish soldiers' "deserting" from the Polish Army in England and the Near East. It was clear to the Jewish underground organizations that these "desertions" were due to the anti-Semitism prevailing in General Anders' Army. The National Minorities Department of the Government Delegation tried to persuade the Co-ordinating Committee of the Jewish National Council and the *Bund* to issue a declaration condemning cases of desertion, but the proposal was at once rejected by the Co-ordinating Committee. The Committee also turned down a Government Delegation proposal that the Jewish Organizations join the "Council for National Unity", which was a sort of substitute secret Parliament alongside the Government Delegation.

Relations reached a peak of tension when a report was received that a unit of the Jewish Combat Organization in a village near Koniecpol in the Czestochowa province had been attacked by the "Eagle" unit of the N.S.Z. or the A.K. and eleven of its twenty-four members killed. The Jewish Combat Organization learnt that similar bands in the Czestochowa, Radom and Kielce areas had murdered some 200 Jews who had been in hiding. Further facts were also uncovered later concerning the collaboration of N.S.Z. bands with the *Gestapo*, the *Gendarmerie* and the *Wehrmacht* in an "action" to kill "Jews and Communists". N.S.Z. bandits even murdered Democratic personalities connected with the A.K., especially those of Jewish origin. N.S.Z.-men organized a special group at

Jozefow near Warsaw to hunt down Jews and kill them off. The alarmed protests of the Jewish Combat Organization over the murder of a group of 18 Jews in the village of Wygoda and other such murders produced no results.

The Council for Aid to the Jews appealed to the Government Delegation to publish a declaration in the underground press condemning the N.S.Z. murders and stigmatizing displays of anti-Semitism. Had a declaration like this been published, it could certainly have helped to clear the hostile atmosphere. The Government Delegate sent a formal reply (May 1944),[24] in which he promised to take measures against the N.S.Z. murders and against blackmail and extortion. But he stated that he was not in favour of making any public declaration, since "he was not of the opinion that the present time was opportune". As regards the general atmosphere relating to Jews, the document proceeded to give grounds explaining it, if not justifying it: frequent cases of Jews' "giving away" their Polish protectors when captured had, he stated, aroused much resentment. Negative reactions had also occurred among the Polish population as a result of the behaviour of Jewish partisans (who, as explained above, were compelled to confiscate food supplies from the peasants in order to survive). Reports that Jews were "deserting" from the Polish Army (and particularly from the II Corps in the Middle East) had added fuel to the flames, since these supposed desertions were seen as an anti-Polish demonstration. Finally, the Government Delegate intimated that the hostile attitude towards the Jews was also a result of memories of their behaviour in the regions previously held by the Soviets.[24]

*

At the time of the Polish rising in Warsaw in August 1944, the number of Jews in Warsaw was about 20,000. Jews who had succeeded in evading the clutches of the Hitlerian monster as "pure Aryans" and even more so Jews who kept in hiding because of their Jewish looks—lived on in the hope that one day they would be

[24] See: Henryk Wolinski Survey of activities... op. cit. pp. 395–402; Berman, op. cit. pp. 726–730; L. Brener, *Ruch podziemny w czestochowskim getcie*, published in "Biuletyn Zydowskiego Instytutu Historycznego", No. 45–46, pp. 172–173; Modrzewska, op. cit., p. 33.

treated as equal citizens. But they met with open hostility from a large part of the anti-Semitic and reactionary Polish population, mainly from the N.S.Z. people but also on the part of the official A.K. Army. It is a fact that the Polish mob turned Jews out of the queues lining up for water, tried to stop them from coming to the popular soup-kitchens and even prevented them from going into the shelters during air raids. Isolated Jews and Jews in groups were killed in secret, and there were cases when Jews were tried and executed for the crime of collaboration with . . . the Germans! The fact that Jews on the Aryan side were without identity papers or had forged papers declaring them to be Poles or even *Volksdeutsche* was a sufficient pretext for accusing them and bringing them to trial.

It is not surpring that a large part of the Jews who were in hiding because of their Jewish appearance stayed in hiding after the Polish uprising as well: firstly, they were not at all sure that the Germans would not return, and on the other hand they were afraid of their neighbours, anti-Semites, blackmailers or plain scoundrels. There were also cases when Polish landlords would not let the Jews leave their hide-outs on the grounds, "The time hasn't yet arrived", or for fear of being "compromised" in the eyes of their Polish neighbours for having hidden Jews and helped to save them. So these Jews stayed on in hiding, and many were killed in the heavy bombardments of the city while the Poles were safe in the shelters.

And in spite of all this, Jews who were not in hiding responded to every call made on the civilian population, doing their duty with dedication. They were among the first to rush and extinguish the fires that broke out, they helped build the barricades, the passages through the walls of houses and buildings, the underground passages, and so on. Yet the Jews as Jews were practically never taken into the A.K., even if they wanted to serve as volunteers. There were cases where Home Army people did not allow the Jews to take part in the work of building fortifications and barricades. But the Jews were not content with doing their duty as ordinary citizens, they demanded to be allowed to fight the enemy with arms in their hands, and if they could not get into the A.K. as Jews in spite of all their efforts then they did so as Poles. "Camouflaged" Jews were already in the A.K. ranks from earlier on. There was a large number of Jewish women who served as runners and couriers and carried out the most dangerous missions.

The proportion of Jews was higher in other military formations: the *Armia Ludowa* (A.L.) set up by the P.P.R. and the P.A.L. "Hundreds and hundreds of Jews served in these formations under false names, not only as soldiers but also in the command," writes the well-known woman member of the underground, Wladka, contact for the Jewish National Council. According to her account, the Jews preferred the P.P.S. units or those of the Communists because in the A.K. "Jewish freedom-fighters were persecuted by their fellow soldiers, who sent them to the most dangerous places and sometimes finished them off, just killed them, like that . . ."

Jewish combatants in the A.L. fought on the most dangerous sectors of the front, held the barricades on Mostowa Streets in the Old City together with A.L. and A.K. cells.

When the situation deteriorated and it was necessary to shift the fighting from the Old City to Zoliborz, which could only be done by way of underground passages, the combatants were guided by Jews who knew the sewers from the time of the Ghetto rising. In most cases the Jews who were killed fell as non-Jews and were buried together with their Polish comrades and their very names are not known.

When the Poles rose in Warsaw, Jewish courage and determination in the fighting secured recognition—many Jewish combatants were decorated. In the report he made to the Polish Government in London before surrendering to the Germans, the Polish commander spoke of the acts of bravery of the Jewish combatants.

The attitude of the Poles to the Jews when the rising was suppressed was one of hatred and enmity, indifference to their sufferings and to their destruction. Jerzy Pytlakowski, a Polish eye-witness writes, "The Jewish tragedy reached its climax with the surrender. The return of the Germans meant instant and cruel death, and on the eve of the surrender Jews who had taken an active part in the rising were murdered secretly. These things were done by men of the N.S.Z. and the right-wing A.K." J. Turkow, in his book, *In Kempf farn Leben*, tells the story of 14 Jews who were murdered by an A.K. unit under the command of an officer named Okrzeja.

Another Jew was killed when he came to a Home Army unit and reported the case of the fourteen.

In some instances "pure" Poles suffered because they looked like Jews. The Polish educated classes behaved no differently towards the Jews from the masses of common people. The contact Wladka relates instances of discrimination against Jews and of the killing of Jews on the part of A.K. soldiers and the Polish civilian population as well.

Part of the Polish population, on the other hand, was moved to a sense of repentance or retribution as the Germans killed Poles mercilessly and burnt down their city, when they remembered how indifferent they had been to the suffering of the Jews in their hour of destruction—though some Poles had said then, What they are doing to the Jews now they will do to us in the end.[25]

At the same time, it must be pointed out that up to the end of the German occupation of Polish soil—and even afterwards—the killing of Jews went on by individuals and by groups in the Polish underground, even when a democratic Polish Goverment had already been set up in a liberated Poland. All over Poland, there were secret murders of Jews who had been saved, Jews who had come back from the camps and from the partisan units. Women and children were murdered too.

---

[25] N. Blumental, *Hayehudim behitkommut Warsha,* in "Enziqlopediya shel galuyot Warsha", volume I, pp. 802–814.

INDEX

317

Index